MEDIEVAL EASTERN EUROPE (500–1300)

READINGS IN MEDIEVAL CIVILIZATIONS AND CULTURES: XXV
series editor: Paul Edward Dutton

MEDIEVAL EASTERN EUROPE (500–1300)

A READER

edited by

FLORIN CURTA

UNIVERSITY OF TORONTO PRESS
Toronto Buffalo London

Toronto Buffalo London
utorontopress.com

ISBN 978-1-4875-4487-4 (cloth) ISBN 978-1-4875-4491-1 (EPUB)
ISBN 978-1-4875-4490-4 (paper) ISBN 978-1-4875-4492-8 (PDF)

LIBRARY AND ARCHIVES CANADA CATALOGUING IN PUBLICATION

Title: Medieval Eastern Europe (500–1300) / edited by Florin Curta.
Names: Curta, Florin, editor.
Series: Readings in medieval civilizations and cultures.
Description: Series statement: Readings in medieval civilizations and cultures | Includes bibliographical references and index.
Identifiers: Canadiana (print) 20230510035 | Canadiana (ebook) 20230510086 | ISBN 9781487544904 (paper) | ISBN 9781487544874 (cloth) | ISBN 9781487544911 (EPUB) | ISBN 9781487544928 (PDF)
Subjects: LCSH: Europe, Eastern – History – To 1500 – Sources. | LCSH: Civilization, Medieval – Sources.
Classification: LCC DJK46 .M43 2024 | DDC 947.0009/02–dc23

We welcome comments and suggestions regarding any aspect of our publications— please feel free to contact us at news@utorontopress.com or visit us at utorontopress.com.

Every effort has been made to contact copyright holders; in the event of an error or omission, please notify the publisher.

Cover design: EmDash
Cover image: Vekenega Evangelistary of 1096

We wish to acknowledge the land on which the University of Toronto Press operates. This land is the traditional territory of the Wendat, the Anishnaabeg, the Haudenosaunee, the Métis, and the Mississaugas of the Credit First Nation.

University of Toronto Press acknowledges the financial support of the Government of Canada and the Ontario Arts Council, an agency of the Government of Ontario, for its publishing activities.

Conseil des Arts
du Canada

CONTENTS

FIGURES

MAPS

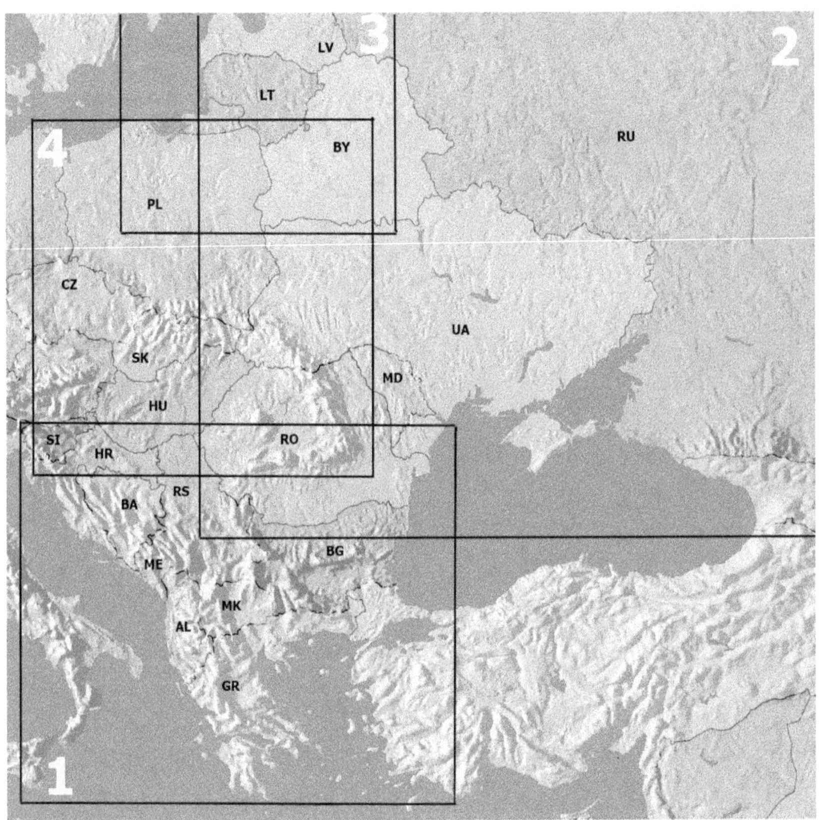

Landscape and political map of eastern Europe
Country abbreviations: AL—Albania; BA—Bosnia and Herzegovina; BG—Bulgaria; BY—Belarus; CZ—Czech Republic; GR—Greece; HR—Croatia; HU—Hungary; LT—Lithuania; LV—Latvia; MD—Moldova; ME—Montenegro; MK—Macedonia; PL—Poland; RO—Romania; RS—Serbia; RU—Russia; SI—Slovenia; SK—Slovakia; UA—Ukraine. The numbers refer to the following detail maps.

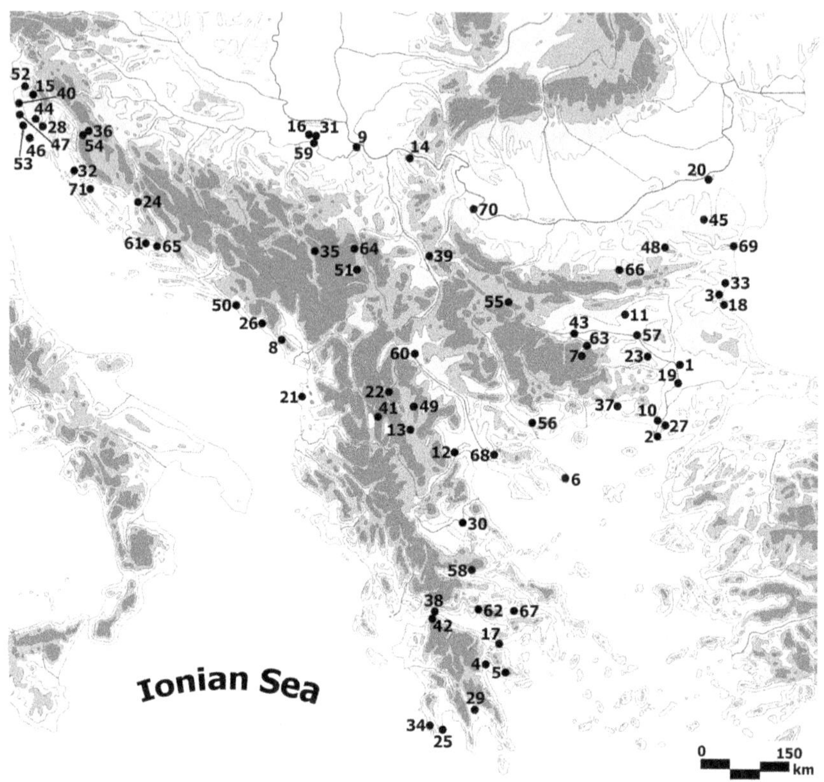

Detail map 1 with place names mentioned in the text (ancient or medieval names in italics and parentheses): 1—*Adrianopolis* (Adrianople); 2—*Ainos*; 3—*Anchialos*; 4—Argos; 5—Athens; 6—Athos, Mount; 7—Bachkovo; 8—Bar; 9—Belgrade; 10—*Bera*; 11—*Beroe* (*Borui*); 12—*Beroia* (Veroia); 13—Bitola; 14—Braničevo; 15—Buzet; 16—Čalma; 17—Corinth; 18—*Deultum*; 19—*Dimotika*; 20—*Dorostolon*; 21—*Dyrrachion* (*Drach*); 22—Kičevo; 23—Klokotnica; 24—Knin; 25—*Korone*; 26—Kotor; 27—*Kypsella*; 28—Labin; 29—*Lakedaimon* (*Sparta*); 30—Larissa; 31—Manđelos; 32—Maun; 33—*Mesembria*; 34—*Methone*; 35—Mileševa; 36—Modruš; 37—*Mosynopolis*; 38—Naupaktos; 39—*Naissus* (Niš); 40—Novigrad; 41—Ohrid; 42—Patras; 43—*Philippopolis*; 44—Pićan; 45—Pliska; 46—*Pola*; 47—Poreč; 48—Preslav; 49—Prilep; 50—*Ragusa*; 51—Ras; 52—Rižana; 53—Rovinj; 54—Senj; 55—*Serdica* (*Sredec, Triadica*); 56—Serres; 57—Simeonovgrad; 58—*Sinon Potamo*; 59—*Sirmium*; 60—Skopje; 61—Split; 62—Steiris; 63—*Stenimachos*; 64—Studenica; 65—Sumpetar; 66—Tărnovo; 67—Thebes; 68—*Thessalonica* (Thessaloniki); 69—Varna; 70—Vidin; 71—Zadar.

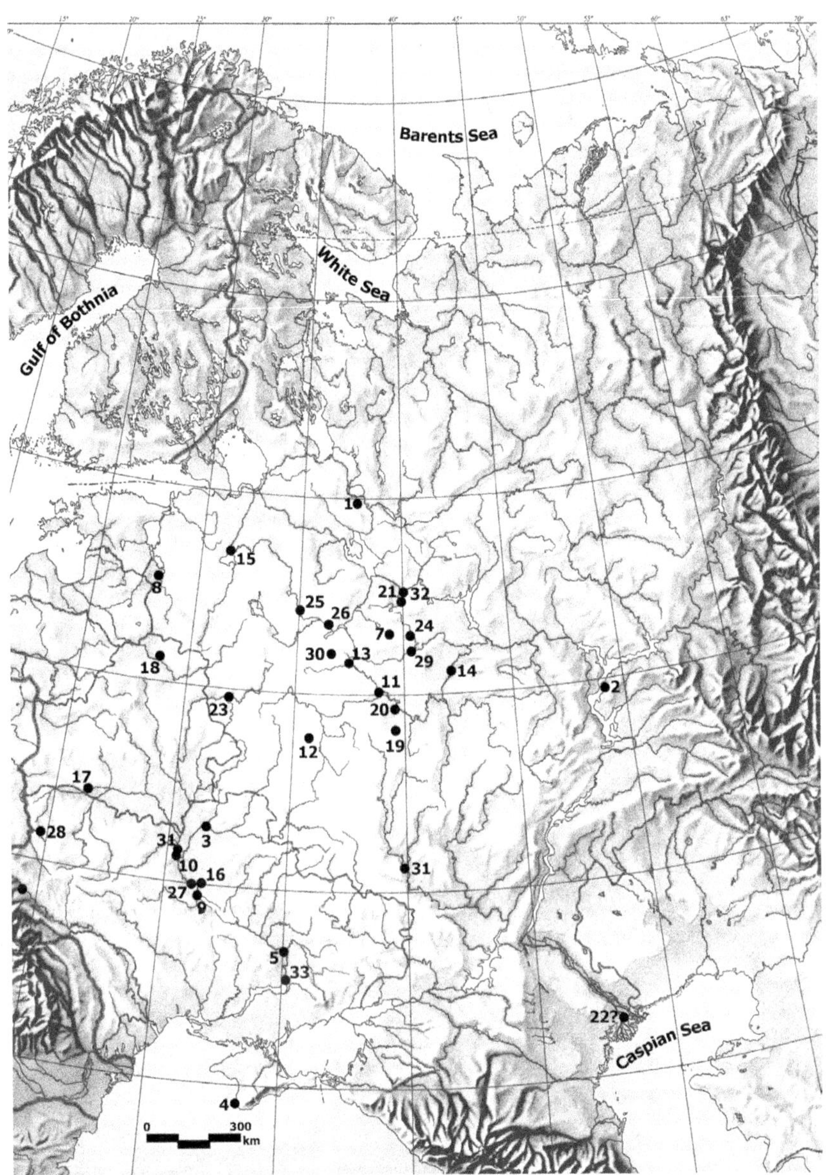

Detail map 2 with place names mentioned in the text: 1—Beloozero; 2—Bolgar; 3—Chernigov; 4—Cherson; 5—Dnipro; 6—Halych; 7—Iur'ev Polski; 8—Izborsk; 9—Kaniv; 10—Kiev; 11—Kolomna; 12—Kozel'sk; 13—Moscow; 14—Murom; 15—Novgorod; 16—Pereiaslavl'; 17—Pinsk; 18—Polotsk; 19—Pronsk; 20—Riazan'; 21—Rostov; 22—Saqsin; 23—Smolensk; 24—Suzdal'; 25—Torzhok; 26—Tver; 27—Vitichev; 28—Vladimir-in-Volhynia; 29—Vladimir-on-Kliazma; 30—Volokolamsk; 31—Voronezh; 32—Vyshhorod; 33—Yaroslavl; 34—Zaporizhzhia.

Detail map 3 with place names mentioned in the text (medieval names in italics and parentheses): 1—*Balga*; 2—*Christburg*; 3—*Dobrin*; 4—*Dorpat* (*Iur'ev*); 5—*Fellin*; 6—Gdańsk; 7—Ikšķile; 8—Koknese; 9—*Kulm*; 10—*Marienwerder*; 11—*Rehden*; 12—*Reval*; 13—Riga; 14—Rubene; 15—Scheidenitz; 16—*Thorn*; 17—*Truso*; 18—Turaida.

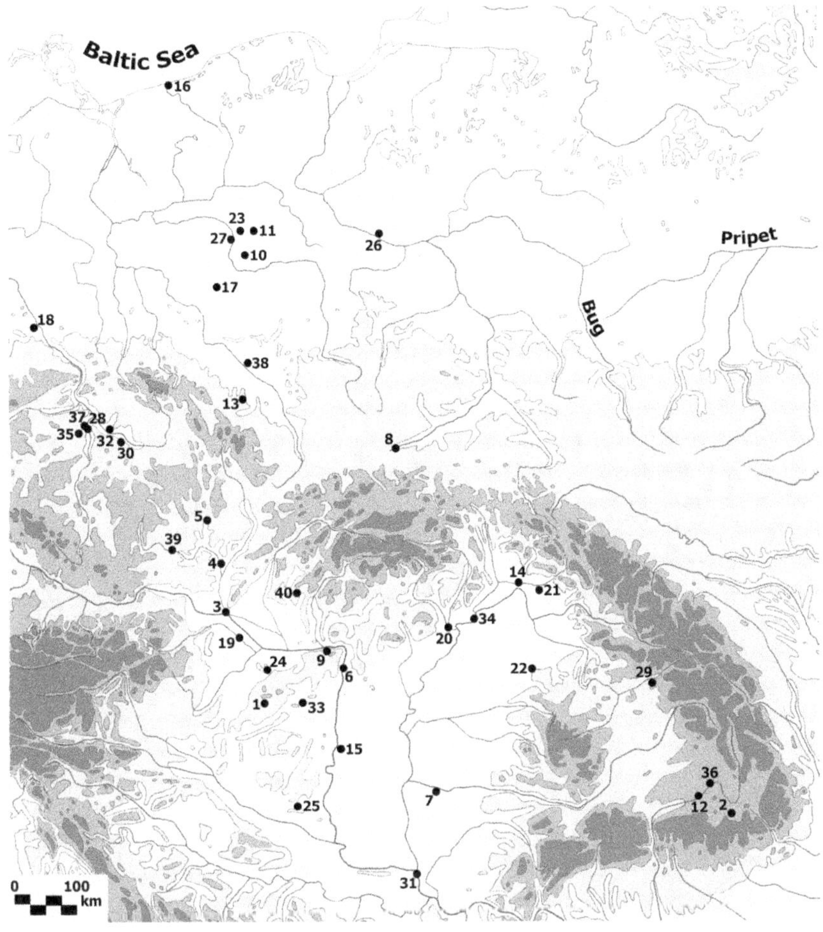

Detail map 4 with place names mentioned in the text (medieval names in italics): 1—Bakonybél; 2—Braşov; 3—Bratislava; 4—Břeclav; 5—Brno; 6—Budapest; 7—Cenad; 8—Cracow; 9—Esztergom; 10—Giecz; 11—Gniezno; 12—Hălmeag; 13—Henryków; 14—*Hung*; 15—Kalocsa; 16—Kołobrzeg; 17—Lubiń; 18—Meißen; 19—Mosonmagyaróvár; 20—Muhi; 21—*Munkács*; 22—Oradea; 23—Ostrów Lednicki; 24—Pannonhalma; 25—Pécs; 26—Płock; 27—Poznań; 28—Prague; 29—Rodna; 30—Sadská; 31—Slankamen; 32—Stará Boleslav; 33—Székesfehérvár; 34—Tarcal; 35—Tetín; 36—Ungra; 37—Vyšehrad; 38—Wrocław; 39—Znojmo; 40—*Zobor*.

INTRODUCTION

Most courses on eastern Europe offered in North American universities focus on the nineteenth and twentieth centuries, the period of nationalism. The medieval history of the area is given comparatively less attention, which often amounts to slightly more than total neglect. The underlying assumption is that the lands in that area "entered" Europe only during the Modern Age, and then only partially. On the other hand, for most students of medieval history, eastern Europe is marginal and eastern European topics somewhat exotic. Textbooks of medieval European history typically contain maps of the continent "cut off" at the River Elbe. When showing the entire continent, the eastern part is typically left blank, except for some physical features and a couple of cities such as Prague or Constantinople. Judging from such textbooks, one is left with the impression that eastern Europe was deserted in the Middle Ages, and if any people lived in the sparse communities in the eastern part of the continent, they did not matter much and left no sources or testimonies of their lives.

This reticence may be explained in part, at least, by means of the relatively recent interest in the study of the medieval history of eastern Europe. The very idea of "eastern Europe" goes back to the intellectual milieu of the Enlightenment, but the serious study of the region's history during the Middle Ages began less than a century ago. Three consecutive international congresses of historical sciences that took place in the interwar period—in Brussels (1923), Oslo (1928), and Warsaw (1933), respectively—first established the topic and its fundamental directions of research. During World War II, Oskar Halecki (1891–1973), a historian specializing in the history of late medieval Poland and a refugee from the lands occupied by the Nazis, transplanted that new scholarly interest to America. For a decade or so at the beginning of the Cold War, the interest in medieval eastern Europe was directly linked to the west-east division of the continent and served as its justification. After c. 1960, however, that interest simply died out, as the ideological and political confrontations of the Cold War moved outside Europe. The interest in the medieval history of eastern Europe was revived only in the late twentieth century, largely, again, as a reaction to the political developments following the demise of the communist regimes. The eastern European Middle Ages have therefore become a remarkably dynamic field of study only during the last three decades or so.

What is eastern Europe, after all? The vast area of the European continent situated between the Czech lands to the west and the Ural Mountains to the east, and from beyond the Arctic Circle to Greece on a north-south axis may be best described as the land mass between latitude 36° and 70° north, and from longitude 12° to 60° east. If dividing that land mass arbitrarily into two slightly unequal slices, east central Europe is the western half, between 12° and

35° east; and eastern Europe the eastern half, between 35° and 60° east. The western half may be further subdivided latitudinally along 45° north to distinguish southeastern Europe, located to the south of that parallel. These internal divisions of the area and their conventional names represent two-thirds of the entire European continent. The vast extent of the area is only matched by its incredible variety, which was directly reflected in the economic and political developments of the Middle Ages. Despite the political meaning commonly attached to "eastern Europe," in this book the phrase is used in a primarily and purely geographic sense.

Historians in eastern European countries have long struggled with periodization, especially when attempting to match the order of events in western Europe and to find a place in the history of the continent for their respective countries. Such problems concern both the beginning and the end of the Middle Ages. To be sure, much of what Oskar Halecki called east central Europe and the whole of eastern Europe never formed a part of the Roman empire. In southeastern Europe, the withdrawal of the Roman armies in the early seventh century provides a convenient marker, but many scholars prefer to begin with the coming of the "barbarians," especially the Slavs, c. 500. With no event to fall in place conveniently like a curtain at the end of Antiquity, some historians have now placed the "dawn of the Dark Ages" in 568, the year in which the Avars defeated the Gepids and the Lombards migrated to Italy. However, the "arrival of the Slavs" marks the beginning of the Middle Ages to such an extent that the adjectives "Slavic" and "medieval" are used interchangeably in many Slavic-speaking countries.

Much more difficult is it to reach some agreement among historians about the end of the Middle Ages. Generations of Hungarian historians, for example, have used the year 1526 (in which the Hungarian army was crushed by the Ottomans at Mohács) as the dividing point between the ages called medieval and modern. It is worth noting that in that interpretation, the modern era begins with a national tragedy, with foreign rule, with misery. Similarly, Bulgarian historians of the late nineteenth and early twentieth centuries unanimously condemned the period of Ottoman rule as one of utter subjugation, national disaster, and misery. "Dark Ages" to Bulgarian historians of an earlier generation was not another name for the Early Middle Ages, but a most appropriate description of the centuries following the fall of Tărnovo in 1393. According to such views, the Ottoman conquest was a turning point in Bulgarian history, for both state and church were abolished, with Bulgaria now being divided between two eyalets (or administrative divisions of the Ottoman empire), and the lands previously under the jurisdiction of the patriarch of Tărnovo taken over by the patriarch of Constantinople, the patriarch of Peć, and the archbishop of Ohrid. The Ottomans allegedly stopped the gradual process of economic convergence between Bulgaria and the rest of the European continent.

The difficulty in finding an appropriate marker for the end of the Middle Ages creates further problems for the assessment of later periods, especially when there are clear signs of continuity from the Late Middle Ages. Were seventeenth-century Hungary under Habsburg rule or eighteenth-century Bulgaria under Ottoman rule still medieval in any sense? Can one speak of the Middle Ages for pre-Petrine Russia? When do the Middle Ages end, and when did modernity begin in eastern Europe? These are complicated questions involving a deeper analysis of multiple factors of development, and no answers have so far been provided. Most historians have in fact rejected the attempt to pigeonhole the history of the region into preconceived chronological boxes. The existence of multiple criteria for periodization makes arbitrary any attempt to "cut" the Middle Ages to size.

For the purposes of this book, however, the cutoff date of 1300 may be a felicitous, if arbitrary, choice. Several economic and political transformations were well underway by 1300: intensive agriculture, nucleated settlements, the arrival of a great number of "guests," particularly from the German-speaking areas of central Europe, increased urbanization, the rise of the money economy, and changes in the structure of the nobility. All of these transformations opened a new chapter in the history of the region. The year 1300 also marks a watershed in the history of southeastern Europe, as it is directly linked to the early Ottoman conquest. Moreover, the native dynasties of Hungary and Bohemia died out around that year. The loss of the Holy Land prompted the Order of St-Mary (the Teutonic Knights) to abandon its headquarters in Venice and to move to Marienburg in Prussia, a move that many historians regard as the pivotal point in the development of the Teutonic Order and of its state in the Baltic region. In neighboring Poland, the year 1300 witnessed the restoration of the kingdom after the coronation in 1295 in Gniezno of Przemyśl II, duke of Greater Poland. Several other developments in the course of the first half of the fourteenth century may evidently be tagged as novel, from the rise of the Serbian empire of Stephen Dušan (1331–55), the dispute between Moscow and Tver over Vladimir's position as grand prince of (1304–27), the rise of the Gediminid dynasty in Lithuania and of the Shishmanid dynasty in Bulgaria, to the Islamicization of the Golden Horde after the conversion of Khan Üzbek (1313–41). The eight centuries between c. 500 and c. 1300 represent therefore a sufficiently long segment to follow the medieval history of eastern Europe.

Much of the renewed interest in that history derives in fact from an attempt to move away from the practice, so prevalent during the Cold War, of using it as a justification for modern divisions. On the other hand, an "add-eastern-Europe-and-stir" approach to the history of the continent proves to be reductionist:

a way to distill the specific history of the region to a simple solution, one that can easily match (and confirm) models created on the basis of western European history. That in turn results from the idea that eastern Europe *had* to imitate the much earlier developments taking place in western Europe, for progress moved from west to east. To the extent that eastern Europe forms an entity worth studying by historians of the Middle Ages, its distinctive feature is therefore identified as a supposed lateness of development, in economic, political, and cultural terms. Some go so far as to deny that the eastern part of the continent became "European" before the tenth century. Others have already noted, however, that in many respects, eastern Europe followed its own path, often in contradiction to that of the western regions of the continent. A chasm has meanwhile been created and continues to grow between the production of outstanding works by talented historians of eastern Europe in the Middle Ages and the reception of that scholarly output, its impact on historiography in general, and its supposed incorporation into "global history." At this juncture, it is therefore necessary to bridge that chasm and to correct, if only partially, the many misperceptions and stereotypes that plague this field of study. This book, the first of its kind on the subject, aspires to provide a solid documentary basis for that scholarly and educational endeavor, and to make a significant contribution to the understanding of the problems raised by the medieval history of eastern Europe.

Writing and literacy came to eastern Europe from the outside as part of the "cultural kit" accompanying the conversion to Christianity between c. 800 and c. 1000. Moreover, new scripts were created at the time of the conversion to Christianity (first Glagolitic, then Cyrillic), and remained characteristic of the medieval culture of the region, for they do not appear elsewhere in Europe. Chanceries began to operate in the tenth century in Croatia and Bulgaria, and in the following century in Hungary, Poland, Bohemia, and Rus'. The earliest surviving charters are those from eleventh-century Hungary, Bohemia, and Poland, followed by Serbia and Rus' in the twelfth century. Some Benedictine monasteries in Croatia have extensive cartularies, containing copies of charters issued by Croatian and Hungarian rulers. The private use of writing, for example in letters, is a later phenomenon. The most extraordinary body of letters providing a unique glimpse into the daily lives of medieval people in eastern Europe is the ever-growing corpus of letters written not on parchment, but on birchbark. The birchbark letters are not preserved in archives but have been found during archaeological excavations since 1930 on several urban sites in Russia, Belarus, and Ukraine. The contemporary evidence of writing from Bulgaria consists of inscriptions. Fewer such documents are known from Bohemia and Poland, but foundation inscriptions in churches appear in Hungary and Croatia.

The medieval history of eastern Europe is not very rich in narrative sources. Very few such sources exist for the period before c. 1000, and most "national" chronicles are of a later date. The earliest is the so-called *Primary Chronicle*, which is in fact the work of several annalists, the last of whom finished writing c. 1113. About the same time, in Poland, an anonymous author of possibly French origin (hence his conventional name, Gallus Anonymus) wrote the *Deeds of the Prince of the Poles*. A decade later, Cosmas of Prague finished his *Chronicle of Czechs*, which was then continued by an anonymous author known as the Canon of Vyšehrad to 1142, when another canon from Prague named Vincent wrote an independent chronicle covering the years 1140–67. His work was then continued by Gerlach, the abbot of the Premonstratensian house of Milevsko. In Hungary, the earliest surviving historical writing is the *Deeds of the Hungarians*, written in the 1220s by the former "notary" (secretary) of a king named Béla, most likely Béla III. Slightly earlier are the annals compiled in the Vydubichi Monastery near Kiev, known as the *Kievan Chronicle*. In the early thirteenth century, Master Vincent Kadłubek, the future bishop of Cracow, finished his *Chronicle of the Kings and Princes of Poland*. In the course of the thirteenth century, several annals were compiled in Cracow, in a number of monasteries in Silesia, in Poznań, as well as in Prague and Bratislava. Both the *Hungarian-Polish Chronicle*, a fantastic version of Hungarian history combined with Polish historical elements, and the *History of the Bishops of Salona and Split* of Archdeacon Thomas of Spalato were written in the mid-thirteenth century or shortly thereafter. The last decades of that century witnessed the appearance of another work entitled the *Deeds of the Hungarians* by Master Simon of Kéza, the *Silesian-Polish Chronicle* and the *Chronicle of the Poles*, written in Greater Poland. Shortly before 1300, the *Chronicle of Halych-Volhynia* was also finalized. Most, if not all, of these narrative sources were written by churchmen who, with few exceptions, had no reliable sources for the earliest periods in the history of their respective countries. For the first centuries of eastern European medieval history, historians have therefore had to rely on foreign sources—Byzantine (in Greek), west European (in Latin), but also Arabic and Hebrew.

Contrary to the common misconception, there is an abundance of written sources on the medieval history of eastern Europe. This book is meant to provide a helpful sample for students and other readers. Far from aspiring to cover eight hundred years of history in just 118 documents, my intention is to offer a glimpse into the variety of the material available and to supply sources that could complement textbooks and monographs used in history courses. The following sections include a few texts that are known to many, such as the "invitation" of the Varangians to Rus'—a story to be found in the *Primary Chronicle*—or Geoffrey of Villehardouin's account of the conquest of Zara at the beginning of the Fourth Crusade. However, most other texts are less well known, even if the reader may be familiar with their authors' names—Wulfstan, Anna Komnena, Bernard of Clairvaux, Benjamin of Tudela, Robert de Clari, or William of Rubruck. In such cases, the sources shed a different light on the range of concerns that those authors had and will help integrate many chapters of eastern European history into a broader discussion of medieval Europe. Many more texts may simply be unknown to the reader, much like their authors—ibn Fadlan, John the Exarch, Kekaumenos, Thomas of Spalato, Cosmas of Prague, Gallus Anonymus, Simon of Kéza, Abu Hamid, Vincent of Prague, John Kaminiates, Henry of Livonia, Vincent Kadłubek, Niketas Choniates, or Roger of Torre Maggiore.

There are also charters, legal and fiscal texts, private letters, inscriptions, and treatises without which an in-depth understanding of the history of eastern Europe during the Middle Ages would not be possible. I have tried to provide a balanced view by selecting sources of many kinds, including such "oddities" as homiletic literature and penitentials. While the presentation of the selections is largely chronological, some sections are purely thematic (economy, society, religion, law), in an attempt to cover as much ground as possible within the given space. It is of course impossible to include everything and I am conscious of omissions, but convinced that the selection is representative at least of the current directions of research on the history of eastern Europe in the Middle Ages. My hope is that readers will be encouraged to delve further into primary texts dealing with eastern Europe in the Middle Ages. The clusters of documents on certain topics, such as law, will benefit particularly those readers who are interested in a comparative approach. I have provided the necessary context in the introduction to each reading, but have kept my interventions to a minimum, in order to allow students to discover on their own the points of view of the medieval authors.

The questions asked at the end of each section are mere suggestions for further discussion of those points of view. The juxtaposition of genres in certain sections (for example, Chapter 6, "New Powers") should prompt readers to note conflicting, complementary, and divergent views and ideas about power, law, and rule. My own editorial interventions within the texts are meant to assist with the clarification of the context. I have kept such interventions to a minimum, as in the introductions. I draw attention to particular themes that have been highlighted by research into eastern Europe or are currently popular study topics, but understanding the medieval history of the region involves the study of many texts and documents from several other parts of Europe and Asia, written in many different languages. My goal with this collection is to highlight the geographic, historical, and linguistic diversity of the primary source materials relating to medieval eastern Europe.

A NOTE ON THE TRANSLATIONS

Unless otherwise noted, all texts are translated for this reader. Editorial insertions appear in square brackets. Most personal names and some place names have been anglicized. For example, Ivan Asen II appears as John II Asen, Václav as Wenceslas, and King István as Stephen, as well as King András as Andrew. By the same token, I have used Prague instead of Praha, Cracow instead of Kraków, and Thebes instead of Thiva. I have also preferred Kiev to Kyiv, and Vladimir to Volodymyr, because of the usage established in the literature on Rus' written in English. With the exception of cases where common English spelling was preferred, the transliteration of personal and place names follows a slightly modified version of the Library of Congress system.

CHAPTER ONE

FROM LATE ANTIQUITY TO THE EARLY MIDDLE AGES

Figure 1.1 Triumphant Avar Warrior on Horseback. Medallion image on one of the golden jugs of the Sânnicolau Mare hoard (c. 800).

1. PROCOPIUS ON THE SLAVS

Procopius of Caesarea is one of the greatest historians of Late Antiquity. He was born around 500 and died c. 560, having thus lived much of his life as a contemporary of Emperor Justinian (527–65). Procopius was an assessor (legal adviser) on the staff of General Belisarius and accompanied him on campaign in Mesopotamia, Africa, and Italy. His longest and most important work consists of a history of the wars of Emperor Justinian, comprising two books on the Persian, two on the Vandal, three on the Ostrogothic wars, and a final book continuing the story on all three fronts. The work covers the period 527–51 and is one of the most important sources for the sixth-century history of the empire and its barbarian neighbors. The excursus (digression) on the Slavs in Book 7 is the longest description of any barbarian group in the work on Justinian's wars, an indication of the special interest Procopius and his audience had in things Slavic. The excursus was most likely written in 550 or 551 on the basis of information that Procopius may have obtained through interviews with Sclavene and Antian mercenaries in Belisarius's army in Italy.

Source: trans. H.B. Dewing and A. Kaldellis, Procopius, *The Wars of Justinian* (Indianapolis: Hackett, 2014), pp. 408–09.

7.14.22–30. For these nations, the Sclavenes and the Antes, are not ruled by one man, but they have lived from of old under a democracy, and consequently everything which involves their welfare, whether for good or for ill, is a matter of common concern. In almost all other matters these two barbarian peoples have had the same institutions and beliefs from ancient times. They believe that one god, the maker of lightning, is alone lord of all things, and they sacrifice to him cattle and all other victims; but as for fate, they neither know it nor do they in any way admit that it has power over men. Whenever they face death, either stricken with sickness or at the start of a war, they promise that, if they escape, they will immediately make a sacrifice to the god in exchange for their life; and if they escape, they sacrifice just what they have promised and consider that their safety has been bought with this same sacrifice. But they also revere rivers and nymphs and some other spirits, and they sacrifice to all these too, and they make their divinations in connection with these sacrifices. They live in pitiful hovels that they prop up far apart from one another, and, as a rule, every man is constantly changing his abode. When they enter battle, the majority of them go against their enemy on foot carrying little shields and javelins in their hands, but they never wear breastplates. Indeed, some of them do not wear even a shirt or a cloak but hitch their trousers up by their private parts and so enter battle with their opponents. Both people have the same language, which is utterly barbarous. Nor do they differ at all from each another in appearance. For they are all exceptionally tall and hardy men, while their bodies and hair are neither very fair nor blonde, nor indeed do they incline entirely to the dark type, but they are all slightly ruddy in color. They live a hard and unrefined life, just like the Massagetae, and like them, they are at all times covered in filth; however, they are not malicious or evildoers, but preserve the Hunnic character in all its simplicity. In fact, the Sclavenes and the Antes had a single name in the remote past; they were both called Sporoi in ancient times, because, I suppose, living apart one man from another, they inhabit their country in a sporadic fashion. In consequence of this fact, they hold a great amount of land, for they alone inhabit the greatest part of the northern bank of the Danube. So much then may be said regarding these peoples.

Questions: How does Procopius present the Sclavenes and the Antes? What elements of their lifestyle does he choose to highlight? How reliable is his description of their religious beliefs? How do the Sclavenes and the Antes fare when compared to the Massagetae?

2. THEOPHYLACT SIMOCATTA ON THE ORIGIN OF THE AVARS

Theophylact Simocatta lived in the early seventh century, most likely in Constantinople. Born in Egypt to the family of a high-ranking civil servant, he was prefect and imperial secretary in Constantinople during the reign of Emperor Heraclius (610–41). He probably witnessed the siege of Constantinople by Avars and Persians in 626, and the desperate defense organized by Patriarch Sergius. He was a protégé of the patriarch, who encouraged him to embark on writing a history of Emperor Maurice, which Theophylact finished in 638. Theophylact's History *deals with developments on the eastern front with Persia, as well as with the wars against the Slavs and Avars in the Balkans. Theophylact's style has been characterized as bombastic, which is often blamed for the many obscurities in his work. But Theophylact wrote his work with a great degree of skill and a feeling of anticipation. Like most Byzantine historians, he was fond of tradition and employed archaic names to describe contemporary peoples and places. Although he called the Avars by their own name, he also believed them to be "Scythians," a label he apparently reserved for steppe nomads. To him, the Danube is the "Ister" and "Europe" is not a continent (a concept totally foreign to him), but the Byzantine province by that name surrounding Constantinople, one of the few parts of the Balkans that was still in Byzantine hands by the time Theophylact wrote his* History.

Source: trans. M. and M. Whitby, *The History of Theophylact Simocatta: An English Translation with Introduction and Notes* (Oxford: Clarendon Press, 1986), pp. 188–90; rev.

7.7.6–8.6. But since we have made reference to the Scythians, both those in the Caucasus and those who face northward, come then, come, let us interrupt our history and present, like an intercalated narrative, the events which attended these very great nations during these times [in the sixth century]. When summer had arrived in this particular year, he who is celebrated by the Turks as khagan [a title, sometimes spelled *chagan* or *qagan*, of both Turks and Avars] in the east, dispatched ambassadors to the emperor Maurice; he composed a letter and inscribed in it victory-praises. The letter's salutation was as follows, word for word: "To the king of the Romans, the khagan, the great lord of seven races and master of seven zones of the world." For this very khagan had in fact outfought the leader of the nation of the Abdeli (I mean, indeed, of the Hephthalites, as they are called [the Hephthalites or White Huns were a nomadic confederation in central Asia that had acquired considerable power in the fifth and sixth centuries before being destroyed by the Turks]), conquered him, and assumed the rule of the nation. Then he was greatly elated at the victory and, making an alliance with Stembischagan, he enslaved the Avar nation. But let no one think that we are distorting the history of these times because he supposed that the Avars are those barbarians neighboring on Europe and Pannonia, and that their arrival was prior to the times of the emperor Maurice. For it is by a misnomer that the barbarians on the Ister have assumed the appellation of Avars; the origin of their race will shortly be revealed. So, when the Avars had been defeated (for we are returning to the account), some of them made their escape to those who inhabit Taugast [a semilegendary city believed to have been established by Alexander the Great after his victory over the Bactrians and the Sogdians; the name is used generically here for the land of China]. Taugast is a famous city, which is a total of one thousand five hundred miles distant from those who are called Turks, and which borders on the Indians. The barbarians whose abode is near Taugast are a very brave and numerous nation, and without rival in size among the nations of the world. Others of the Avars, who declined to humbler fortune because of their defeat, came to those who are called Mucri; this nation is the closest neighbor to the men of Taugast; it has great might in battle both because of its daily practice of drill and because of endurance of spirit in danger. Then the khagan embarked on yet another enterprise, and subdued all the Ogur, which is one of the strongest tribes on account of its large population and its armed training for war. These make their habitations in the east, by the course of the River Til [or Itil, an old name for the Volga River], which Turks are accustomed to call Melas. The earliest leaders of this nation were named Var and Chunni; from them some parts of those nations were also accorded their nomenclature, being called Var and Chunni. Then, while the emperor Justinian was in possession of royal power, a small section of these Var and Chunni fled from that ancestral tribe and settled in Europe. These named themselves Avars and glorified their leader with the appellation of khagan. Let us declare, without departing in the least from the truth how the means of changing their name came to them. When the Barselt, Onogurs, Sabir, and other Hun nations in addition to these, saw that a section of those who were still Var and Chunni had fled to their regions, they plunged into extreme panic, since they suspected that the settlers were Avars. For this reason, they honored the fugitives with splendid gifts and supposed that they received from them security in exchange. Then, after the Var and Chunni saw the well-omened beginning to their flight, they appropriated the ambassadors' error and named themselves Avars: for among the Scythian nations that of the Avars is said to be the most adept tribe. In point of fact, even up to our present times, the Pseudo-Avars (for it is more correct to refer to them thus) are divided in their ancestry, some bearing the time-honored name of Var, while others are called Chunni.

Questions: What kind of barbarians were the Avars according to Theophylact Simocatta? Why did they adopt the name Avars? How did the Turks regard the Avars? How does their attitude compare to that of Procopius of Caesarea toward the Slavs (Doc. 1)?

3. AVARS AND SLAVS

Menander wrote a now lost History *during the reign of Emperor Maurice (582–602). Only fragments survive, which were incorporated into* De Legationibus *and* De Sententiis, *two collections compiled under Emperor Constantine VII Porphyrogenitus in the mid-tenth century. Menander, though trained toward a legal career, never practiced as a lawyer. Instead, as he himself confesses, he became a loafer and a fop. His life took a turn at Emperor Maurice's ascension to the throne. The nickname "the Guardsman" used by modern historians to refer to Menander is the English translation of the title "protector," which in the sixth century referred not to a bodyguard, but to a diplomat. Menander's* History *may have in fact been commissioned by Emperor Maurice through a powerful minister, for it seems that Menander enjoyed ready access to imperial archives. The work probably had ten books covering the period 558–82. The core of the work was built around the careers of the two men who are at the center of the narrative, Tiberius and Maurice. The outlook is Constantinopolitan, and the city's concerns are paramount. Menander relied heavily, if not exclusively, on written sources, especially on material from the archives (minutes of proceedings, supporting documents and correspondence, reports from envoys of embassies and meetings). His views were traditional and his main interest was in Roman relations with foreign peoples, in particular the Persians and the Avars. The Slavs appear therefore only in the context of relations with the Avars. Despite Menander's considerable additions to speeches, which served both to characterize the speakers and to explore the issues at stake, it is likely that they were fairly close to the available records. It is not difficult to visualize the possible source for the speech attributed to Dauritas in the passage below. The whole episode may have been based on a report by John, "the governor of the isles."*

Source: trans. R.C. Blockley, *The History of Menander the Guardsman: Introductory Essay, Text, Translation and Historiographical Notes* (Liverpool: Cairns, 1985; rpt. 2006), pp. 193 and 195.

Greece was being plundered by the Slavs, and a succession of dangers was threatening there on all sides. Since Tiberius [II, emperor between 578 and 582] did not have a force strong enough to resist even a part of the invaders (and certainly not the whole horde of them) and since he was unable to face them in battle because the Roman armies were occupied with the wars in the east [against Sassanian Persia], he sent an embassy to Baian, the chief of the Avars. At the time he was not hostile toward the Romans, and, indeed, from the very beginning of Tiberius's reign had wished to be friendly with our state. Tiberius, therefore, persuaded him to make war on the Slavs, so that all those who were laying waste Roman territory would be drawn back by the troubles at home, choosing rather to defend their own lands. Thus, they would cease to plunder Roman territory, preferring to fight for their own.

The caesar [emperor], then, sent this embassy to him, and Baian agreed to his request. John, who at this time was governor of the isles [*quaestor exercitus*] and in charge of the cities of Illyricum, was sent to assist him. He came to the land of Pannonia and transported Baian himself and the Avar forces to Roman territory, ferrying the multitude of barbarians in the so-called "large transports" [special barges]. It is said that about sixty thousand armored horsemen were brought across to Roman territory. From there Baian crossed Illyricum, reached Scythia [Minor, now Dobrudja in southeastern Romania] and prepared to recross the Danube in the so-called "double-sterned" ships. When he gained the far bank, he immediately fired the villages of the Slavs and laid waste their fields, driving and carrying off everything, since none of the barbarians there dared to face him, but took refuge in the thick undergrowth of the woods.

The Avar attack on the Slavs arose not only out of the embassy from the caesar and the desire of Baian to return a favor to the Romans in exchange for the great generosity which the caesar had shown to him, but also because Baian was hostile to them out of a personal grievance. For the leader of the Avars had sent to Dauritas and the chiefs of his people ordering them to obey the commands of the Avars and to be numbered among their tributaries. Dauritas and his fellow chiefs replied, "What man has been born, what man is warmed by the rays of the sun who shall make our might his subject? Others do not conquer our land, we conquer theirs. And so it shall always be for us, as long as there are wars and weapons." Thus boasted the Slavs, and the Avars replied with a like arrogance. After this came abuse and insults, and because they were barbarians with their haughty and stubborn spirits, a shouting match developed. The Slavs were so unable to restrain their rage that they slew the envoys who had come to them, and Baian received a report of these doings from others. As a result, he nursed his grievance for a long time and kept his hatred concealed, angered that they had not become his subjects not to mention that he had suffered an irreparable wrong at their hands. Moreover, thinking both to win favor with the caesar and that he would find the land full of gold, since the Roman empire had long been plundered by the Slavs, whose own land had never been raided by any other people at all, [he gladly obliged].

Questions: What can the confrontation between Avars and Slavs tell us about the balance of power on the northern frontier of the Roman empire in the 570s? What was the attitude of the Slavs of Dauritas toward the Avars, and how did Baian regard the Slavs? What was the purpose of Emperor Tiberius II in entering an alliance with the Avars against the Slavs?

4. SLAVS, AVARS, AND FRANKS

The Chronicle of Fredegar *is the first source to shed light on Slavs in (east) central Europe. To be sure, Fredegar, a sixteenth-century name for an unknown author writing c. 660 for an Austrasian audience, employed juridical and administrative formulaic language for his account of the Wends, which suggests that he was close to or even involved in the activity of the Frankish chancery. A number of elements in this narrative betray his goals and the identity of his audience. From a Frankish point of view, to say that the "Huns" slept with the wives of the Slavs is to place the Slavs in a position of inferiority, also signaled in the text by their role as* befulci *and the many burdens they had to endure. The explanation that Fredegar gives to that word (cannon fodder for the Avars) suggests a (re)interpretation of a "native," presumably Wendish account, possibly an ethnogenetic myth of sorts. For him, the Slavs had no valor as warriors, and no value other than that of tribute-paying subjects. Being of mixed blood, the sons born from those unions of Avar men and Slavic women were therefore not truly Slavs, but could not suffer the Avar oppression of their mothers and sisters any longer. They, and not the Slavic weaklings, rose in rebellion and under the leadership of Samo—a Frank—managed to defeat the Avars. To mark the difference, Fredegar decided to apply the name "Wends" to those who followed Samo. In doing so, he may have drawn inspiration from Jonas of Bobbio's* Life of Saint Columbanus, *written sometime between 639 and 643. According to Jonas, Columbanus had once thought to go preaching to the Wends, who are also called Slavs, but gave up his mission of evangelization because those people's eyes were not yet open to the light of the scriptures. Where was Samo's "state" located? According to traditional views, the Wends over whom Samo ruled must have lived somewhere in Bohemia, given that after their revolt against the Avars, they are said to have repeatedly raided Thuringia, until Dervan, the duke of the Surbi, decided to leave his Merovingian overlords and join Samo's rebels. Nonetheless, the Slavs among whom the "Huns" wintered every year and with whose wives and daughters they slept lived within the territory under Avar control, if not also within the Avar khaganate (that is, the territory under the direct rule of the khagan). In order for Samo's polity to become independent from the Avars, it must therefore have been effectively separated from the Avar khaganate. Moreover, when deciding to wage war upon Samo, King Dagobert was helped by Lombards who most likely came from the Duchy of Friuli. The territory of the present-day Czech Republic cannot possibly have been the original area from which Samo's state began to develop, and which must therefore be sought farther to the east and southeast, in Lower Austria or in the region of the present-day border between the Czech Republic, Slovakia, and Austria.*

Source: trans. F. Curta from *Quellen zur Geschichte des 7. und 8. Jahrhunders. Die vier Bücher der Chroniken des sogenannten Fredegar*, ed. H. Wolfram, A. Kusternig, and H. Haupt (Darmstadt: Wissenschaftliche Buchgesellschaft, 1982), pp. 206, 208, 210, 234, 236, and 238.

48. In the fortieth year of the reign of Chlothar [II, king of Neustria between 584 and 613, and king of the Franks between 613 and 629], a Frankish man named Samo from the part [of the kingdom of the Franks known as] Senonacus [unknown location] joined some merchants and went to the Slavs called Wends, to trade with them. The Slavs had already begun to rise in rebellion against the Avars called Huns and their king, the khagan. For the Huns, the Wends had been from time immemorial *befulci*: whenever the Huns attacked another army with their troops, whichever army it happened to be, they gathered their troops in front of their [own] camp, and waited there, while only the Wends were fighting. If the Wends managed to have the upper hand, then the Huns would advance to grab the booty; by contrast, if they were beaten, the Huns would provide them with reinforcements. That is why they were called *befulci* by the Huns, because they would advance twice in battle with their military standards and marched ahead of the Huns. The Huns came every year to spend the winter among the Slavs and they took the wives and daughters of the Slavs to their beds [to sleep with them]. In addition to other burdens, the Slavs paid tribute to the Huns. Eventually, the sons of the Huns, born from the wives and daughters of the Slavs, could not tolerate such injustice and exactions anymore. Refusing to obey the Huns, as I said [before], they started to revolt [against them]. As they had attacked the Huns with their army, Samo, who was trading with them, as I have mentioned before, joined them. He distinguished himself by such bravery against the Huns, that they were amazed, and a great number [of Huns] perished by the sword of the Wends. Becoming aware of Samo's valor, the Wends chose him to be their king. He ruled them well for thirty-five years. Under his rule, the Wends engaged in many battles with the Huns and, on the basis of his

advice and valor, they always won against the Huns. Samo had twelve wives from among the Wends, twenty-two sons, and fifteen daughters. . . .

68. In that year, a great multitude of Slavs called Wends killed [a number of] Frankish merchants in the kingdom of Samo and robbed their goods. This was the beginning of a quarrel between Dagobert and Samo, the king of the Sclavenes. Dagobert dispatched to Samo his envoy [named] Sicharius and asked him [Samo] to bring [the perpetrators to] justice and to offer compensation for the merchants whom his people had killed and for the goods which they have illegally taken. As Samo refused to see Sicharius and did not allow him to find [and talk to] him, Sicharius, dressed up like the Sclavenes, managed to appear, together with his people, in front of Samo. He told Samo everything that he had been ordered to say. However, for that is the pagan character and arrogance of bad people, Samo did not offer any compensation for what his people had done but insisted that a *placitum* [public trial] be organized to adjudicate over those and other differences that had [meanwhile] appeared between them [that is, between the Franks and the Wends], so that justice would be done to both sides. Sicharius, like a stupid envoy, uttered inappropriate words [in reply], for which he had no [royal] authority, and began to threaten Samo, saying that he [Samo] and the people of his kingdom were in the service of Dagobert. Taking offense, Samo answered: "The land in which we live is Dagobert's, and the same is true for us. We are his [subjects] as long as he is willing to preserve our friendship." "It is not possible," Sicharius replied, "for Christians and servants of God to be friends with dogs." "If you are the servants of God and we the dogs of God," retorted Samo, "then when you continuously act against him [God], we believe we are permitted to tear you to pieces." Sicharius was therefore thrown out of Samo's presence. After he told Dagobert what happened, the king, moved by pride, summoned an army from the entire kingdom of the Austrasians [to move] against Samo and the Wends. An army of three corps moved against the Wends. In addition, the Lombards [coming from Italy] came to Dagobert's assistance and attacked the Wends. The Slavs, in turn, prepared themselves [to resist] on those and other fronts, when an army of Alamans, led by Duke Chrodobert, won a victory where they had entered [the land of the Wends]. The Lombards were also successful and both Alamans and Lombards took a great number of prisoners from among the Slavs. As for the Austrasians, they surrounded the fort at Wogatisburc [unknown location], where a very large number of valiant Wends had withdrawn. They fought for three days and many men of Dagobert's army died by the [Wendish] sword. Fleeing [the battlefield], they abandoned their tents and the goods that they had, in order to return home [as soon as possible]. Several times after that, the Wends attacked Thuringia and other parts [of the Frankish kingdom], for plunder. Dervan, who was the duke of the Surbi [either Sorbs or Serbs], who were of the nation of the Slavs and had for a long time

belonged to the kingdom of the Franks, willingly joined the kingdom of Samo together with his people. This victory that the Wends obtained over the Franks was not as much because of Slavic valor as it was the result of the demoralization of the Austrasians, who realized that they were the target of Dagobert's hatred and that they were incessantly despoiled [by him].

Questions: What were the personal qualities responsible for Samo's success? What triggered the revolt of the Slavs ("Wends") against the Avars ("Huns")? What attitudes toward the Slavs and Avars emerge from this text? What is the role of religion in the conflict between Dagobert and Samo?

5. THE SERMESIANS AND THESSALONICA

The Miracles of Saint Demetrius *is a collection of homilies offered as a hymn of thanksgiving to God for his gift to the city of Thessalonica (now Thessaloniki, in northern Greece). The homilies refer to events taking place between c. 580 and c. 680. The first fifteen homilies, which deal with miracles that the saint performed for the benefit of his city and its inhabitants, were written by Archbishop John of Thessalonica during the first decade of Heraclius's reign (610–20). Six other miracles form Book 2 of the* Miracles, *which was written by an unknown author at some point during the last two decades of the seventh century. In addition to the coverage of several attacks on the city by Avars and Slavs, the* Miracles *offer glimpses into the changes that took place during the sixth and seventh centuries in one of the most important cities in the empire. In that respect, and despite its preoccupation with miracles and miraculous deeds, the collection is invaluable for its information on the early medieval history of the Balkans. The author of Book 2 used oral sources, especially those of refugees from cities such as Naissus (now Niš, in Serbia) and Serdica (now Sofia, in Bulgaria). Some have argued that he used written sources as well, perhaps the annals or the chronicle of Thessalonica, if any existed. In contrast to Archbishop John, the unknown author of Book 2 has less interest in miracles and miraculous deeds and seems to have relied more heavily on documentary material. Moreover, unlike Archbishop John, who used history to glorify Saint Demetrius and to educate his fellow citizens, the author of Book 2, despite his obvious desire to imitate John's style, took a different approach. He wrote seventy years or so later than John, but shortly after the events narrated. His account is better informed, and his narration approaches the historical genre. Paradoxically, this is what made Book 2 less popular than Book 1, despite the growing influence of the cult of Saint Demetrius in the course of the following centuries. There are numerous manuscripts of the miracles in Book 1, but only one rendering Book 2. In the late ninth century, Anastasius the Librarian translated into Latin ten miracles from Book 1, but only one from Book 2. Unlike Archbishop John, the author of Book 2 was more concerned with facts supporting his arguments and often referred to contemporary events, known from other sources. This is clear from the story of the Sermesians in the fifth homily of Book 2.*

Source: trans. F. Curta from *Les plus anciens recueils des miracles de Saint Démétrius et la pénétration des Slaves dans les Balkans*, ed. P. Lemerle (Paris: Editions du Centre national de la recherche scientifique, 1979), vol. 1, pp. 227–30.

If one summoned all forms of art and expression, it would still not be enough to praise Saint Demetrius. For humans cannot comprehend the things that concern God, and the miracles of Saint Demetrius, which are produced by God, are beyond the [descriptive] skills of poets and writers. Nonetheless, leaving aside the sophisticated compositions of logographers [chroniclers] and philosophers, which are outside our competence, we will describe with small words the big things. For in all truth, one must do that, even if one has forsaken the memory of most instances of assistance in wars and of healings, one must celebrate this miracle of the savior of our city, for it [certainly] was a great miracle.

We have already talked earlier about the Sclavenes, that is of Chatzon [chieftain of the Slavs who besieged Thessalonica in 615], and about the Avars, how they devastated Illyricum almost entirely, namely the provinces of the two Pannonias [Pannonia Prima and Pannonia Secunda], the two Dacias [Dacia Mediterranea and Dacia Ripensis], Dardania, Moesia, Praevalitana, Rhodope, as well as Thrace and the region of the Long Wall next to Byzantium. The khagan [leader of the Avars] ordered the entire population to be moved forcefully to the country next to Pannonia, on the Danube, where the old capital was once Sirmium, and they were all settled there as his subjects. They began to mingle with the Bulgars, the Avars, and others, had children with them, and turned into a numerous people. However, each child received from the father the traditions of his fatherland and the zeal of his nation, according to the Roman customs. And just like the Hebrews have grown in number in Egypt under the pharaoh, this time, again, by the orthodox faith and the holy baptism, the Christian people grew stronger. And each one of them talked to the other about the land of their ancestors, and thus stirred in each other's heart the desire to return. Sixty years or so had passed since the barbarians had taken their parents captive, and now another, new people appeared in those parts. In time, most of them had become free. The khagan of the Avars, who regarded them as a particular ethnic group, followed their custom and appointed a chief for them, named Kuver. Learning through his men that the people wanted to return to the cities of their parents, Kuver gathered and raised all Romans, as well as pagans (as is recorded in the Mosaic book about the exodus of the Jews, that is the proselytes [in the Greek version of Exodus 12:47, the word "proselytes" refers to strangers dwelling among the Hebrews, who wanted "to keep the Lord's Pascha"]), with weapons and luggage. They were all now rebels revolting against the khagan, who pursued them, but was defeated in five or six battles, so that he had to flee with the rest of his army and withdrew to the northern parts. Kuver, having obtained the victory, crossed the Danube with all his people, came to our parts, and occupied the Keramesian plain [probably the region around Bitola, in southern Macedonia]. Once settled there, those who were Orthodox [that is, Christian] demanded that they return to the cities of their parents, some to Thessalonica, others to Constantinople and to the other cities of Thrace.

With his people thus disposed, a number of wicked advisers [of Kuver] had the bad idea of him not letting anyone go to the places to which they wanted to return. Instead, Kuver had to keep them all together, as they were at the beginning of their trek, with him as their chief and khagan. For if he had attempted to look for the emperor, he would have taken those people and dispersed them, thus removing them from Kuver's power. So he sent an embassy to the emperor asking that he be allowed to stay where he was, together with his people. He also asked that the neighboring people of the Drugubites [a neighboring Slavic tribe] be ordered to supply them with everything necessary. That is what was done. So, to get what they needed, the people of Kuver went to the tents of the Slavs, asking about our city, and learning that it was not too far [from them]. So, taking their women and children with them, the Romans began to pour into our parts. Once there, the prefect sent them by sea to Constantinople.

Their chief Kuver, learning about all this, secretly concocted with his advisers a plan to use one of his leaders who was particularly smart, and who knew very well our language, as well as those of the Romans, the Slavs, and the Bulgars. He would pretend to distance himself from Kuver, get into our city together with others, and would proclaim himself a subject of the emperor. He would bring with him to our side as many accomplices as possible, then he would cause a civil war, and in the process take over the city. At that point, Kuver would come [to Thessalonica], establish himself here together with the other chiefs. He would reorganize his people and [from Thessalonica] he would attack all the neighboring peoples, whom he would conquer, then the islands [in the Aegean Sea], Asia [Minor], and finally the emperor himself.

Once the plan was concocted, they sealed it by [taking] oaths. Then one of them, named Mauros, came to Thessalonica supposedly as a refugee and began to persuade the [city] authorities to send to the emperor a favorable report about him. The emperor was convinced [of Mauros's good credentials], and sent a written order bestowing upon Mauros the title of *hypatos* [honorary title of prefect] and a standard [symbol of imperial authority]. He also ordered that all the Sermesian refugees [the people who had lived around Sirmium under Avar rule], who were coming from Kuver, be placed under his [Mauros's] orders. As soon as this imperial ordinance was published and registered in the rolls, all those who were seeking refuge in Thessalonica were given to Mauros, who became their *strategos* [general, military leader]. To be sure, there were people of Roman stock among them who knew about the machinations of Mauros, a man without faith, a perjurer, and a scoundrel. They knew that he could not be trusted. However, those who exposed his secret and terrible machinations were in turn denounced [to him] by his allies, and he immediately put them to death, and sold their wives and children [into slavery]. Thus nobody dared to say what he knew, nor to oppose Mauros, and even the [city] authorities were afraid of him.

Questions: How did the Sermesians travel? What kept them together during the migration? What role did religion play in their mobilization? How did Mauros plan to take over Thessalonica and why?

6. THEOPHANES ON THE BULGAR MIGRATION

Born in Constantinople c. 760, Theophanes was the son of high-ranking and wealthy parents. He became a courtier of Emperor Leo IV (775–80) and married Megalo, the daughter of a patrikios *(high-ranking court official), who was a friend of the emperor. The marriage was most likely formal and quite short, as both Theophanes and Megalo decided to take monastic vows and to live apart from each other. Theophanes founded a monastery near Sigriane on the Asian shore of the Sea of Marmara, where he remained until 815 or 816. At that time, iconoclasm was revived by Emperor Leo V (813–20) and Theophanes, like all other monks, was asked to sanction the destruction of images. He refused and for that reason was imprisoned in Constantinople and then exiled to the island of Samothrace, where he died in 818. His* Chronography *covers the years 285–813 and was written as a continuation of the work of George Synkellos, a fellow monk who had written the history from the Creation to 284. In his* Chronography, *Theophanes presents his account as objective truth, but thinks of himself as no more than a humble narrator. The source that Theophanes used for his account of early Bulgar history is not known, but it may have been a now lost chronicle known as the* Great Chronographer. *If so, then the ultimate source of his information may have been envoys coming to Constantinople from Bulgaria in the Balkans. At any rate, the geographical description at the beginning of the Bulgar account shows Theophanes's use of earlier sources based on ancient geographical concepts about eastern Europe more than genuine Bulgar notions of the "homeland."*

Source: trans. Harry Turtledove, *The Chronicle of Theophanes. An English Translation of* Anni Mundi *6095–6305 (A.D. 602–813)* (Philadelphia: University of Pennsylvania Press, 1982), pp. 55–57.

It is necessary to discuss the ancient history of the Onogondur Bulgars and the Kotrigurs. In the area on the north side of the Black Sea (in the Sea of Azov) there enters a great river called the Atel, which descends from the ocean through the land of the Sarmatians. The Don leads into it; the Don itself springs from the Iberian gates in the Caucasus Mountains. From the mingling of the Don and the Atel (which branches before the Sea of Azov) comes the Kouphis River, which delivers itself up at the end of the Black Sea near Nekropela at the cape known as the Ram's Face. Sea and river are one and the same beyond the Sea of Azov, which leads into the Black Sea through the territory of the Cimmerian Bosporus. The *mourzoulin* and other fish like it are caught in this river. In the area east of the lake lies Phanagouria and Jews live there. The ancient Great Bulgaria stretches from the Sea of Azov along the Kouphis River, where the *xyston*, a Bulgarian fish, is caught. The Kotrigurs, who are related to the Bulgars, also live there.

During the period when Constantine was in the west, Krobatos, the lord of Bulgaria and the Kotrigurs, died. He left behind five sons, not at all imagining they would give up living by each other: for they were the masters of all they surveyed and were slaves to no other people. But a little while after his death these five sons separated from one another, along with the folk subject to each of them. The first son, called Batbaian, kept the injunction of his father and has remained in his ancestral lands until the present day. The second brother, called Kotragos, crossed the Don River and settled across from the first. The fourth and fifth brothers crossed the River Ister (that is, the Danube). One came to the land of the Avars in Pannonia, was subjected by the Avar khagan, and remained there with his forces; the other reached the five cities by Ravenna and came under the control of Christians. Now the third brother, called Asparukh, crossed the Dnieper and the Dniester and reached the Oglos (these rivers are north of the Danube), settling between them and the Danube. He thought the location secure and invincible from all sides, for it was marshy ahead and surrounded by rivers in other directions. It provided his people, who had been weakened by their division, relief from their enemies. After the Bulgars had been divided into five parts and thus diminished, the great Khazar people came from the far interior of Berzilia in first Sarmatia [a generic term for the steppe lands farthest from the Black Sea] and became the masters of the whole northern coast of the Black Sea. They made Batbaian, the first brother and ruler of first Bulgaria [that is, the part of Bulgaria in the steppe lands north of the Black Sea], their subject and have taken tribute from him until the present.

The emperor Constantine [IV, emperor between 668 and 685] was galled to learn that a foul, unclean tribe was living between the Danube and the Oglos, and that it had sallied forth to ravage the land near the Danube (that is, the land which is now ruled by the Bulgars, but then was held by Christians). He ordered all the thematic armies [armies from the *themata*, or provinces, of the empire] to cross over into Thrace, equipped an expeditionary force, and moved against the Bulgars by land and sea, attempting to dislodge them by force. He marshaled his army on the land by the Oglos and the Danube, anchoring his ships at a nearby promontory. When the Bulgars saw his battle line's numbers and density, they despaired of their salvation. They took refuge in the fastness which has been mentioned and, for the first three or four days, did not dare go outside this stronghold of theirs. But when the Romans did not join battle because of the swamp, the disgusting tribe guessed their empty vanity, regained its strength, and grew more courageous. Since the emperor was suffering severely from gout, he had to withdraw to Mesembria for his usual baths with five warships and men friendly to him. He left behind his generals and army, ordering them to use their lances to drag the Bulgars out of their stronghold, and to attack them if they came out. If not, then his men were to besiege them and hold them in their defensive position. However, the cavalry spread it about that the emperor had fled; they were overcome by fear and ran away themselves, though none pursued. When the Bulgars saw this, they did pursue, putting many to the sword and wounding others. They chased them to the Danube, crossed it, and came to Varna near Odyssos and its hinterland. They saw that it was securely located: from behind because of the River Danube and from the front and sides because of the mountain passes and the Black Sea. When the Bulgars became masters of the seven tribes of Sclavenes in the vicinity they resettled the Severeis from the mountain passes before Verigava to the lands to the east, and the remainder of the seven tribes to the south and west up to the land of the Avars. Since the Bulgars were pagan at that time, they bore themselves arrogantly and began to assail and take cities and villages under the control of the Roman empire. The emperor had to make peace with them because of this and agreed to pay them an annual tribute. This was the fault of the Romans' disgrace over their great defeats.

Questions: How concerned were the Romans about the Bulgar threat? What does the story of Krobatos reveal about Roman control over the steppe lands north of the Black Sea? What does it say about conflicts between different steppe peoples? How likely was it that Asparukh and his successors would respect the peace that Emperor Constantine IV made with the Bulgars? What is the attitude of Theophanes toward them?

7. EMPEROR CONSTANTINE VII PORPHYROGENITUS ON THE MIGRATION OF THE CROATS

Although initially attributed to Emperor Constantine VII Porphyrogenitus (913–59), the treatise On the Administration of the Empire *is most likely a compilation of texts written in the mid-tenth century by different authors acting as ghostwriters. The emperor certainly initiated the collection of those texts, and he was involved in its editing, at times even dictating passages inserted into the compilation. The general goal of the treatise was didactic. Emperor Constantine's purpose was to educate his son, as clearly spelled out in the proem. In other words, this was meant to be a kind of manual for the future emperor, who needed to know about all nations and countries surrounding the empire, their traditions, customs, and current affairs. Although generally drawing inspiration from different sources, including perhaps "native" accounts of ethnic history,* On the Administration of the Empire *pays little if any attention to such details as the "ancient" history of the nations described. The ultimate goal of this compilation is more practical, namely, to classify and to explain. The compilation was never finished, in that different constituent texts were left without transition, and the editor(s) clearly neglected internal contradictions. This is the case in the two chapters (30 and 31) dedicated to Dalmatia and the Croats respectively. Since this is the first source mentioning Croats,* On the Administration of the Empire *played (and still plays) a very important role in the writing of the early history of Croatia. However, upon closer examination, the two versions of that history offered in Chapters 30 and 31 raise more problems of interpretation than answers to what happened in the Balkans more than three centuries prior to the compilation of the treatise.*

Source: trans. R.J.H. Jenkins, Constantine VII Porphyrogenitus, *De Administrando imperio* (Washington, DC: Dumbarton Oaks Center for Byzantine Studies, 1967), pp. 143, 145, 147, and 149.

30. But the Croats at that time were dwelling beyond Bavaria, where the Belocroats are now. From them split off a family of five brothers, Kloukas and Lobelos and Kosentzis and Mouchlo and Chrobatos, and two sisters, Touga and Bouga, who came with their folk to Dalmatia and found the Avars in possession of that land. After they had fought one another for some years, the Croats prevailed and killed some of the Avars and the remainder they compelled to be subject to them. And so, from that time this land was possessed by the Croats, and there are still in Croatia some who are of Avar descent and are recognized as Avars. The rest of the Croats stayed over against Francia [that is, remained in those territories that are next to the Franks], and are now called Belocroats, that is white Croats, and have their own prince; they are subject to Otto, the great king of Francia, or Saxony [Otto I, 936–73], and are unbaptized, and intermarry and are friendly with the Turks. From the Croats who came to Dalmatia a part split off and possessed themselves of Illyricum and Pannonia; they too had an independent prince, who used to maintain friendly contact, though through envoys only, with the prince of Croatia. For a number of years, the Croats of Dalmatia also were subject to the Franks, as they had formerly been in their own country; but the Franks treated them with such brutality that they used to murder Croat infants at the breast and cast them to dogs. The Croats, unable to endure such treatment from the Franks, revolted against them, and slew those of them whom they had for princes. On this, a large army from Francia marched

against them, and after they had fought one another for seven years, at last the Croats managed to prevail and destroyed all the Franks with their leader, who was called Kotzilis. From that time they remained independent and autonomous, and they requested the holy baptism from the bishop of Rome, and bishops were sent to baptize them in the time of Porinos their prince.

31. The Croats who now live in the region of Dalmatia are descended from the unbaptized Croats, also called "white," who live beyond Turkey and next to Francia, and have for Slavic neighbors the unbaptized Serbs. "Croats" in the Slavic tongue means "those who occupy much territory." These same Croats arrived to claim the protection of the emperor of the Romans Heraclius before the Serbs claimed the protection of the same emperor Heraclius, at that time when the Avars had fought and expelled from those parts the Romani, whom the emperor Diocletian had brought from Rome and settled there, and who were therefore called "Romani" from their having been translated from Rome to those countries, I mean, to those now called Croatia and Serbia. These same Romani, having been expelled by the Avars in the days of this same emperor of the Romans Heraclius, their countries were made desolate. And so, by command of the emperor Heraclius, these same Croats defeated and expelled the Avars from those parts, and by mandate of Heraclius the emperor, they settled down in that same country of the Avars, where they now dwell. These same Croats had at that time for prince the father of Porgas. The emperor Heraclius sent and brought priests from Rome and made of them an archbishop and a bishop and elders and deacons and baptized the Croats; at that time these Croats had Porgas for their prince.

Questions: How does the story of the migration of the Croats compare to that of the Bulgars (Doc. 6)? What is the role of the Avars in this story? Why do you think Emperor Heraclius is mentioned as instrumental for the conversion of the Croats to Christianity? Why were some Croats called "white"?

CHAPTER TWO

EARLY POLITIES AND CONVERSION

Figure 2.1 Saints Cyril and Methodius. Painting in the church of the Holy Cross in Prague.

8. NOTKER ON THE AVARS

Notker (also called "the Stammerer"; c. 840–912) was a monk in the Benedictine abbey of St-Gall in what is now Switzerland. Born in the region of the River Thur (the modern canton of St-Gall), Notker was raised by a former soldier of Charlemagne named Adalbert, who is mentioned as a veteran of the wars against the Avars and the Slavs under the command of Kerold (the brother of Charlemagne's second wife, Hildegard). Adalbert's son, Werinbert, was in fact a monk at St-Gall. Notker seems to have entered the monastery at an early age. He is mentioned as librarian at St-Gall in 890 and as master of the guests in that same abbey between 892 and 894. The author of a collection of stories about martyrs, he also wrote a vita *of Saint Gall, and a collection of sequences (poems for remembering pitches used during the singing of a single syllable of text when chanting). His two books of didactic anecdotes about Emperor Charlemagne were composed for the emperor's great-grandson, Charles the Fat (881–88), who visited the abbey in 883. According to Notker, who clearly relied on oral sources, Charlemagne attacked the Avars (whom Notker anachronistically calls "Huns") because they had blocked the way to Constantinople. They had amassed extraordinary wealth behind their fortifications, the description of which in the passage cited below has no confirmation in any other sources. However, the idea that the war Charlemagne waged against the Avars was ultimately no challenge at all is illustrated by Notker's story about Eishere, which he had heard in his native region of Thur.*

Source: trans. F. Curta from Notker Balbulus, *Gesta Karoli Magni imperatoris*, ed. H.F. Haefele, *Monumenta Germaniae Historica, Scriptores rerum Germanicarum*, n.s. 12 (Berlin: Weidmann, 1959), pp. 49–51 and 74–75.

Adalbert described [to me] those [hiding] places [of the Huns] in the following manner: "The land of the Huns is surrounded by nine rings." And as I could not fathom anything like that, I asked him: "What was so extraordinary about them, sir?" And he answered: "It was surrounded by nine hedges." And again, because I did not know of any hedges other than those that one [commonly] plants around the cultivated fields, he continued, when I asked another question: "Every single ring was so wide, that it comprised as much room as between the fort in Zürich and Konstanz [about thirty-six miles, as the crow flies]; it[s rampart] was made of oak, beech, spruce, and fir logs in such a way that its width was twenty feet from one end to the other, and just as much in height. The entire space inside it, however, was filled in with hard stones and with solid clay, while, finally, the top of those dikes was completely covered with sod. Small trees were planted between the edges and, as one often sees, they were trimmed so that they would let leaves and branches grow sidewise. Between the dikes, there were villages and manors arranged in such a way that someone's voice could be heard from one place to the other. Opposite those buildings [that is, in the villages], and between them, were modest gates cut into the impregnable walls, through which those from the outside, but also those from the inside could go on plundering expeditions. The inner space of the second ring, which was built [much] like the first one, stretched for twenty German miles, that is forty Italian miles [about 94 US miles, or 151 kilometers] all the way to the third ring, and they continued in that manner up to the ninth ring, although each one of those rings was narrower than the one before it. From one ring to another, the estates and the houses were arranged in such a manner that the sound of the trumpet that would announce any news could reach from one to the other. Inside those fortifications, over a period of two hundred and more years, the Huns stored all the riches of the western nations. . . ."

The magnanimous Charles [Charlemagne] was however upset that he had to go in person against those barbarian peoples, instead of letting any one of his dukes do that job [for him]. I will show how that came about by means of the deeds of one of my fellow countrymen. He hailed from Thurgovia [a region of eastern Switzerland, on the western shore of Lake Constance and along the River Thur, a left-hand tributary of the Rhine River] and his name, Eishere, could be translated as the "greater part of the terrifying army." He was so tall that one could have taken him to be a descendant of the sons of Anakim [Deut. 2:10], if the distance in time and space [between them] would not have been so great. When the River Thur was swollen and overflowing because of the torrents coming down from the Alps, since he could not force his large horse to step into the water, much less into the stream, he would take the reins and would make the horse swim behind him, saying: "By Saint Gallus, you will come after me, whether you want to or not!" So, as this man marched in the army of the emperor, he was mowing down Bohemians, Wiltzi [a Slavic tribe in the Lower Elbe region], and Avars as if they were grass in the meadow, hanging them onto his lance, as if he were a bird-catcher. When returning home victoriously people would ask him how he managed the land of the Wends [Slavs], he responded partly with contempt, partly with anger: "What do you expect me [to have done] with those toads? I carried around with me seven or eight or even nine of them pierced through my lance, as if on a spit, while they were still mumbling something. The Lord King and I have wasted our time fighting those worms."

Questions: What is Eishere's attitude toward the Avars? What do we learn from this text about the Frankish-Avar wars under Charlemagne? Compare this account with that of Theophylact Simocatta (Doc. 2). Which one is better informed? What does Notker reveal about the social organization of the Avars?

9. THE *ANNALS OF FULDA* ON MORAVIA

The Annals of Fulda *is the name given in 1600 to a substantial work of the annalistic genre covering the history of the East Frankish kingdom between 838 and 901. The first part to c. 869 was most likely written by Rudolf, a monk at the Benedictine abbey of Fulda (in central Germany). It has been suggested that the last part of the annals is the product of the East Frankish royal chapel. However, both the part written by Rudolf and the last part of the annals focus more on events in the neighboring Slavic lands, including Moravia, than on those in the East Frankish kingdom. This emphasis makes the* Annals of Fulda *a unique source for the political history of Moravia in the ninth century.*

Source: trans. F. Curta from *Annales Fuldenses*, ed. F. Kurze, *Monumenta Germaniae Historica, Scriptores rerum Germanicarum in usum scholarum* 7 (Hanover: Hahn, 1891), pp. 36, 45–46, 68–69, 73–74, and 110–11.

[846] As nothing came out of that, by mid-August he [Louis the German, king of East Francia, 843–76] moved with an army against the Slavs on the Morava, whose intention was to rise in rebellion. He put things in order there and settled matters according to his wish and placed upon them as duke a nephew of Mojmir [first duke of Moravia, c. 820 to 846] named Rastislav [duke of the Moravians between 846 and 870].

[855] And King Louis had to return without any victory, after taking an army into the land of the Moravian Slavs against their rebellious duke Rastislav and accomplishing little. He would rather leave alone for the time being an enemy who had fortified himself behind strong ramparts than risk [inflicting] losses on his troops in a dangerous battle. Nonetheless, his army plundered and burned a good part of that province and eliminated a not negligible number of enemies, who had tried to storm the king's camp, but received due punishment [for that]. As the king withdrew, Rastislav and his men followed him and plundered many borderlands across the Danube.

[869] In August, King Louis gathered his troops and divided them into three: he ordered . . . the Bavarians to provide assistance to Carloman [Louis's eldest son, future king of Bavaria, 876–79], who wanted to wage war on Svatopluk [duke of Moravia between 870 and 894], a nephew of Rastislav. He kept the Franks and the Alamans for himself in preparation for war against Rastislav. And when the war was about to break out, he fell ill and, putting his trust in the Lord as to the outcome of this affair, he had to leave the command of the army to the youngest of his sons, Charles. As he [Charles] and the army that had been given to him reached a fortification of Rastislav that could not even be described and was unlike any other known from ancient times, with the help of God he managed to burn down all the ramparts in that region. He and his men found

and robbed everything that was hidden in the woods or buried in the fields and he chased or killed all those who stood against him.

[871] Under accusations of perfidy, Svatopluk, the nephew of Rastislav, was arrested by Carloman. However, the Moravian Slavs, who thought that their duke was [now] dead, elected as [their] prince a man named Sclagamar, who was a priest and a relative of the duke. He accepted the office out of necessity, as they threatened to kill him if he refused. He therefore began to wage war against Carloman's commanders Engilschalk and Willihelm, and to drive them out of the towns they had occupied. . . . In the meantime, because nobody had been able to prove the crime of which he had been accused, Svatopluk was released [from prison] and sent back to his realm, after receiving [many] royal gifts. He was accompanied by an army of Carloman, which was supposed to fight against Sclagamar. For indeed he [Svatopluk] had slyly promised that much to Carloman, if he were allowed to go back to this homeland. . . . While the others [that is, the army that had accompanied him] set up camp, Svatopluk went into the old town of Rastislav and immediately broke his promise according to the Slavic manner, forgot his oath, and applied both his power and his efforts not to fighting against Sclagamar, but obtaining revenge for what Carloman had done to him. So, with a great force he attacked the camp of the Bavarians, who did not suspect anything evil and were paying no attention to him. He took many captives and killed almost all the others, except those who had prudently gone outside the camp before those events. . . . Upon receiving the news of the disaster of his army, Carloman was truly dumbfounded. He was therefore forced to gather all hostages in his realm and to send them back to Svatopluk, while he could barely get a single man named Ratbod back from that place, and he was half dead.

[884] The king, the old Louis, had granted to two brothers, Willihelm and Engilschalk, the command over the frontier of the kingdom of Bavaria in the east, against the Moravians, and, as it is said, they had fought hard to defend the fatherland. As they eventually came to the ends of their lives, while still in office, that honor was not bestowed upon their sons, but instead the king appointed Arbo as count [in that place]. . . . Arbo befriended Svatopluk, the duke of the Moravian people, and in order to seal the alliance, he did not hesitate to send his son as hostage [to Moravia]. . . . In the year in which the sons [of Willihelm and Engilschalk] robbed the abovementioned count Arbo of the honors bestowed upon him by the king, Svatopluk, the duke of the Moravians, with a fully deceitful and sly mind, and thinking of the great evil that had been perpetrated upon his people by the ancestors of those young men [that is, the sons of Willihelm and Engilschalk] while they had been in charge of the borderland in Bavaria, and considering also the oath and friendship binding him to Arbo, decided to take revenge on this, and was entirely successful at that. For Werinhar, the middle son

of Engilschalk's three boys, as well as Count Wezzilo, who was his relative, were captured in the lands to the north of the River Danube. Their right hands were cut off, as well as their tongues and—what is more shameful—genitals, so that no trace of them would remain. And upon return, some of their men had either the left or the right hand cut off. At the duke's orders, the army [of the Moravians] destroyed everything by fire. Moreover, archers were sent across the Danube. They set fire to every property or estate of the said sons that they could find.

Questions: How are the actions of Svatopluk described in this text? According to the Frankish annalist, what made Moravians successful so many times against the Franks? What does this text suggest about the relations between Franks and Moravians?

10. THE CONVERSION OF THE CARANTANIANS

The treatise known as the Conversion of the Baiuvars and the Carantanians *was written in 870 or 871 by an unknown Bavarian churchman in the service of the archbishop of Salzburg. His goal was to provide support for that archbishop's claims against Methodius, who had recently been appointed bishop by Pope Hadrian II (867–72) in a territory that was under Salzburg's jurisdiction. The occasion for those claims was the synod in Regensburg (fall 870), where Methodius was tried before being imprisoned in the Reichenau Abbey. Without any mention of Constantine (Cyril), the* Conversion *accuses Methodius, "a certain Greek," of discrediting the Latin language, the Roman teaching, and the time-honored traditions of the Latin script. The preference he showed for Slavonic letters supposedly encouraged the Slavs to criticize church services celebrated in Latin by the Bavarian clergy. In support of the claims made by the archbishopric of Salzburg, the* Conversion *brings historical arguments to prove that the disputed territory had been under jurisdiction of that see from a much earlier date. That is the context in which the story of the Carantanians is brought to the fore, namely as an opportunity to list in detail how much Salzburg had invested in the Christianization of those people, a century before Methodius and his mission to Moravia.*

Source: trans. F. Curta from *Die "Conversio Bagoariorum et Carantanorum" und der Brief des Erzbischofs Theotmar von Salzburg*, ed. F. Lošek (Hanover: Hahnsche Buchhandlung, 1997), pp. 102, 104, 106, and 108.

4. Shortly after that [c. 740], the Huns [Avars] began to inflict serious violence upon the Carantanians. Their duke at that time, named Boruth, told the Baiuvars that the Hunnic army was moving against them, and asked for their assistance. The Baiuvars immediately obliged, expelled the Avars, and secured [the safety of the] Carantanians, while making them subjects of the kings, along with their neighbors. And they took hostages with them to Bavaria. One of

those [hostages] was the son of Boruth named Cacatius, who asked his father to be raised in the Christian way and to become Christian; and so it was done. The same happened to Cheitmar, the son of his brother [Boruth]. When Boruth died after he had already become a Christian, at the order of the Franks, the Bavarians sent Cacatius back, for the Slavs had requested him. [The Carantanians] made him [Cacatius] their duke. However, after three years, he died. Once again with the permission of Lord Pepin, the king [Pepin III, king of the Franks, 751–68], Cheitmar was sent back to those same peoples. In the meantime, he too had become Christian. The priest Lupo, who had been ordained by the see of Salzburg for the island named Auva in the Chiemsee [most likely the Ladies' Island in the middle of Chiemsee, a lake in Bavaria, near Rosenheim; a Benedictine nunnery was established on the island in 782], gave [to Chietmar] his nephew named Maioranus, who had [also] been ordained priest, to accompany him [to Carantania]. And since the same priest Lupo had been his [Chietmar's] sponsor at the baptismal font, he instructed him to place himself under the jurisdiction of the monastery in Salzburg, in humble fulfillment of his Christian duties. Chietmar was welcomed by his people, who chose him to rule the duchy [of Carantania]. He kept by his side the priest Maioranus, who had been ordained in the monastery of Salzburg. Maioranus urged Chietmar always to bow his head to that monastery, in the service of God. And he acted accordingly and promised to serve that see. He kept his promise and was in the service of that place year after year, while receiving from there teaching and advice as to how to fulfill his Christian duties for the remainder of his life.

5. After a short while, the abovementioned duke of the Carantanians asked Bishop Virgil [of Salzburg] to come and visit the Christians among [his] people and to encourage them in their faith. However, [Virgil] could in no way respond at the time to the invitation. Instead, he delegated a bishop named Modestus to instruct those people, and together with him [he also sent] his priests Watto, Reginbertus, Cozharius, and Latinus, as well as a deacon [named] Ekihardus with [many] other churchmen. He [Virgil] granted Modestus the full power to consecrate churches and to ordain priests according to the canons, and without contradicting in any way the writings of the holy fathers. They went to the Carantanians and consecrated there a church dedicated to Saint Mary [today the Maria Saal Cathedral in Carinthia], another in the Liburnia fort [most likely one of the churches in Teurnia, near Spittal an der Drau, in western Carinthia], and a third *ad Undrimas* [probably somewhere in the Upper Mura valley], in addition to others in several other places. And Modestus remained there until the end of his life. After he died, Chietmar again asked Bishop Virgil to come and visit him, whenever possible. Virgil, however, refused, because a rebellion had broken out, which we call a *carmula* [a pagan revolt]. But after a council, he sent the priest Latinus to the Carantanians. However, Latinus quickly left the country and came

back [to Salzburg], as the rebellion was spreading again. Given the outbreak of the *carmula*, Bishop Virgil sent the priest Madalhohus, and then [another] priest [named] Warmannus. Chietmar died [in 769] and another rebellion broke out. For a few years, there was no priest there. Finally, their duke Waltunc dispatched [envoys] to Bishop Virgil and asked him to send priests [to Carantania]. So [the bishop] sent a priest named Heimo and another named Reginbaldus, as well as a deacon named Maioranus together with other churchmen. And a little later, he sent the same Heimo, the priests Dupliterus and Maioranus, as well as other churchmen to accompany them. He also sent to them the priests Gozharius, Maioranus, and Erchanbertus; after them, the priests Reginbaldus and Reginharius; and then the priests Maioranus and Augustinus. A second time, Reginbaldus and Guntharius. And all this was done under Bishop Virgil.

Questions: What accounts for the rise of the polity of the Carantanians? Where did they turn for help against the Avars? What other reasons did the Baiuvars have to intervene militarily in Carantania? What were the conditions under which Christianity began to spread to Carantania? How did Bishop Virgil organize the mission?

11. SAINT CYRIL, OLD CHURCH SLAVONIC, AND THE CREATION OF THE GLAGOLITIC ALPHABET

The Life of Constantine (Vita Constantini) *is the earliest text known to have been written in Old Church Slavonic. The biography was composed sometime between Constantine's death in 862 and December 885 (when we know that the text was in use in Rome), perhaps in 879 or 880 by someone in the entourage of Methodius. The text survives in more than fifty copies, but none of them is earlier than the fifteenth century (the earliest extant copy is from 1469). It has long been noted that although written in Old Church Slavonic, a "new" language in the ninth century, the* Life of Constantine *follows the conventions of the hagiographic genre (biographies of saints) in the Byzantine literature: there is no concern with an accurate or even comprehensive description of the events narrated, and the unknown author's political agenda did not necessarily coincide with the original goals of the Moravian mission, despite the fact that the work was most likely composed during or not long after that mission. The purpose of this text was to justify the canonization of its hero, the would-be Saint Cyril. This explains why the author spends a lot more time on miracles than on facts.*

Source: trans. Marvin Kantor, *Medieval Slavic Lives of Saints and Princes* (Ann Arbor: University of Michigan, Department of Slavic Languages and Literatures, 1983), pp. 25–33 and 65–81.

1. Merciful and compassionate is God, who awaits the repentance of man and will have all to be saved, and to come unto the knowledge of the truth, for

he wishes the sinner not death but repentance and life even if he be given to malice. Neither does he allow mankind to fall away through weakness or be led into temptation by the adversary and perish. Rather, in each age and epoch he has not ceased to grant us his abundant grace, even now just as it was in the beginning: at first through the prophets, patriarchs, and fathers, and after them through the prophets, then through the apostles and martyrs, and righteous men and teachers whom he chooses from amid the tumult of this life. For the Lord knows his own, who are his, as he has said: "My sheep hear my voice, and I know them, and I call them by name and they follow me: And I give unto them eternal life" [John 10:27–28]. He did so also in our generation, having raised up for us this teacher who enlightened our nation, which did not wish to walk in the light of God's commandment, and whose understanding was obscured by weakness and even more by the devil's wiles.

Stated briefly, his *vita* reveals what sort of man he was, so that hearing it, he who wishes—taking courage and rejecting idleness—can follow him. For as the Apostle has said: "Be you followers of me, even as I also am of Christ" [1 Cor. 11:1].

2. There was a certain noble and rich man named Leo in the city of Thessalonica, who held the rank of *drungarios* [high-ranking military officer] under the *strategos* [general and governor of the theme, or province, of Thessalonica]. He was, as Job once was, a pious man, and kept faithfully all God's commandments. He begot seven children of which the youngest, the seventh, was Constantine the Philosopher, our preceptor and teacher. And when his mother bore him, he was given over to a wet-nurse for nursing. However, until the child was weaned, he would not take any other breast but his mother's. This was by God's design so that there be a good offshoot from a good root. And after this the good parents agreed not to lie with each other. They never once transgressed their vow but lived that way in the Lord for fourteen years, parting in death. And when that devout man was wanted on Judgment Day, the mother of this child cried, saying: "I am not worried about anything, except this one child and how he will be nurtured." Then he said: "Believe me, wife, I place my hope in God. He will give him for a father and steward one such as guides all Christians." And so it came to pass.

3. When he was seven the boy had a dream which he recounted to his father and mother, saying: "After the *strategos* had assembled all the girls of our city, he said to me: 'Choose her whom you wish as your wife and helpmate from among them.' Gazing upon them and taking note of each one, I discerned the most beautiful of all, with a radiant face, richly adorned in gold necklaces and pearls, and manner of finery. Her name was Sophia, that is, Wisdom. I chose her."

When the parents heard these words, they said to him: "Son, keep your father's commandment, and forsake not the law of your mother [Prov. 6:20, 23].

For the commandment is a lamp; and the law is light [Prov. 7:4]. Say unto wisdom, you are my sister; and call understanding your kinswoman. For wisdom shines even more than the sun. And if you then take her to yourself as your wife, you will be delivered from much evil through her." When they sent him for instruction, he surpassed all his fellow students in learning, as his memory was very keen. He was then a marvel.

As it was customary among the sons of the wealthy to take sport in the hunt, he one day took his falcon and went out to the fields with his companions. And as he released it, the wind rose by God's design, caught the falcon, and carried it off. The boy became very despondent and dejected by this and would not eat for two days. But in his love for man, merciful God did not wish the youth to become accustomed to things of this world and he lured him easily. Just as he lured Plakidas [Saint Eustathius, who converted to Christianity while hunting] with a deer during a hunt long ago, so now he did Constantine with a falcon. Constantine thought to himself of the vanity of this life and repented, saying: "Is this life such that sorrow takes the place of joy? From this day forth I shall take a different path, a better one than this. But I shall not waste my days in the tumult of this life."

Taking up his studies, he remained at home and committed to memory the writings of Saint Gregory the Theologian [Saint Gregory Nazianzen, one of the Three Holy Hierarchs, a father and major teacher of the Church]. And making the sign of the cross upon the wall, he wrote the following eulogy to Saint Gregory: "O Gregory, you are a man in body but an angel in spirit. You, a man in body, appeared as an angel. For your lips praise God like one of the seraphim and enlighten the universe with the teaching of the true faith. Therefore, accept me who comes to you with love and faith and be my teacher and enlightener." To such things did he pledge himself.

He immersed himself in numerous discourses and in lofty thought but was unable to comprehend their profundity and fell prey to a great sadness. There lived a certain foreigner who knew grammar. Going to him and falling at his feet in humility, Constantine begged him to teach him thoroughly the art of grammar. But burying his talent, the man said to him: "Young man, do not trouble yourself. I have renounced teaching this to anyone for the rest of my life." Again, the youth begged him, saying in tears: "Take all the share due me from my father's house, but teach me." Since the man did not wish to listen further to him, Constantine returned home and prayed that he would gain his heartfelt desire. God soon fulfills the desire of them that fear him. Upon hearing of the keenness, wisdom, and zeal for learning with which he was imbued, the emperor's administrator, called the Logothete [Theoctistus, Logothete of the Swift Course under Empress Theodora, 842–56] sent for Constantine to study together with the emperor [Michael III, at the time only three years old].

Learning of this, the boy joyfully set out. And on the way he knelt in prayer to the Lord, saying: "O God of our fathers, and Lord of mercy, who hast made all things with your word, and ordained man through your wisdom, that he should have dominion over the creatures, which you have made, give me wisdom, that sits by your throne, so that I might understand what is your will and be saved. For I am your servant, and the son of your handmaid." And in addition, he recited the remainder of Solomon's prayer [Wisd. of Sol. 9:5] and, rising, said: "Amen."

4. When he arrived in the imperial city [Constantinople] he was entrusted to teachers to be taught. In three months, he mastered grammar and began other studies. He studied Homer and geometry with Leo [the Mathematician, a great Byzantine scholar, who was archbishop of Thessaloniki between 840 and 843], and dialectics and all philosophical studies with Photius [the future patriarch of Constantinople, 858–67 and 876–86]; and in addition to that, rhetoric and arithmetic, astronomy, and music, and all the other Hellenic arts. He mastered them all just as though he were mastering only one of them. For keenness joined with zeal, the one vying with the other, by which ability studies are perfected. But more than studiousness, a newly serene countenance became him. He conferred with those who were more beneficial and turned from those who turned to malice, for he thought and acted only to acquire heavenly things in place of earthly ones and to quit his body and live with God.

When the Logothete saw that he was so disposed, he gave him control over his entire house and free entry to the royal palace. Sometime after this, he once questioned him, saying: "Philosopher [Constantine], I wish to learn what philosophy is." With his quick mind, he replied immediately: "The knowledge of matters divine and human, to what extent man can approach God and how, through virtue, man is taught to be in the image and likeness of the one who created him." And the Logothete grew to love him even more, as he, this great and venerable man, questioned him about these things. Constantine made known to him the study of philosophy and in a few words showed great keenness of mind. Living in chastity and pleasing God greatly, Constantine became even more loved by all. And many desired and wished to be joined with him through love and, in accordance with their strength, to imitate as fully as possible his virtuous and godly way of life. For all simply loved his keenness of mind greatly. And the Logothete rendered him the highest honors and offered him much gold, but he did not accept. Once, sometime after this, he said to him: "More than anything else your keenness of mind and wisdom compel me to love you. I have a goddaughter whom I took out of the font [that is, for whose baptism I served as sponsor]. She is beautiful, wealthy, and from a good and noble family. If you wish, I shall give her to you as your wife. And from the emperor accept eminence, and a governorship. And expect even more, for soon you will be a *strategos*." Then the philosopher answered him, saying: "This is indeed a great gift for those who have need of it. But for me nothing is greater than learning. Having acquired knowledge, through it I wish to seek the honor and wealth of my ancestors." Upon hearing his reply, the Logothete went to the emperor and said: "This young philosopher does not love this life. Let us not exclude him from the community but tonsure him and give him over to the priesthood and service. Let him be librarian to the patriarch in St-Sophia. At least in this way shall we keep him." And that was what they did with him. After staying with them as such for a short time, Constantine left for the Narrow Sea and hid himself there in a monastery [possibly the Kleidion Monastery on the shore of the Bosporus]. They sought him for six months before they were able to find him. Unable to prevail upon him to accept that position, they convinced him to accept an academic chair and teach philosophy to his countrymen and foreigners with full assistance and aid. And he accepted this. . . .

14. While the philosopher was rejoicing in God, yet another matter arose, and a task no less than the former. For Rastislav, the prince of Moravia [846–70], through God's admonition, took counsel with his Moravian princes and appealed to Emperor Michael, saying: "Though our people have rejected paganism and observe Christian law we do not have a teacher who can explain to us in our language the true Christian faith, so that other countries which look to us might emulate us. Therefore, O lord, send us such a bishop and teacher; for from you good law issues to all countries." And having gathered his council, the emperor [Michael III, 839–67] summoned Constantine the Philosopher and had him listen to this matter. And he said: "Philosopher, I know that you are weary, but it is necessary that you go there. For no one can attend to this matter like you." And the philosopher answered: "Though I am weary and sick in body, I shall go there gladly if they have a script for their language." Then the emperor said to him: "My grandfather [Emperor Michael II] and my father [Emperor Theophilus], and many others have sought this but did not find it. How then can I find it?" And the philosopher answered: "Who can write a language on water and acquire for himself a heretic's name?" And together with his uncle, Bardas, the emperor answered him again: "If you wish, God may give you this as he gives to everyone that asks without doubt and opens to them that knock." The philosopher went and, following his old habit, gave himself up to prayer together with his other associates. Hearing the prayer of his servants, God soon appeared to him. And immediately Constantine composed letters and began to write the language of the Gospel, that is: "In the beginning was the word, and the word was with God, and the word was God" [John 1:1] and so forth.

The emperor rejoiced, and together with his counselors glorified God. And he sent Constantine with many gifts, after writing the following epistle to Rastislav: "God, who will have all men come unto the knowledge of the truth [1 Tim. 2:4] and raise themselves to a greater station, having noted your faith and struggles, arranged now, in our time, to fulfill your request and reveal a script for your language, which did not exist in the beginning but only in later times, so that you may be counted among the great nations that praise God in their own language. Therefore, we have sent you the learned man, a philosopher. Thus, accept this gift which is greater and more valuable than all gold and silver, precious stones, and transient riches. And strive zealously with him to strengthen his work, and with all your heart to seek God. And do not reject universal salvation. Convince all not to be idle, but to take the true path, so that, having led them to divine understanding through your struggles, you too shall receive your reward—both in this age and the next—for the souls of all who wish to believe in Christ our God now and evermore. Thus, shall you leave your memory to future generations like the great emperor Constantine."

15. When Constantine arrived in Moravia, Rastislav received him with great honor. And he gathered students and gave them over to Constantine for instruction. As soon as all the church offices were accepted, he taught them matins and the hours, vespers and the compline, and the liturgy. And according to the word of the prophet [Isa. 35:5], the ears of the deaf were unstopped, the words of the scriptures were heard, and the tongues of stammerers spoke clearly. Because God's word was spreading, the evil envier from the days of creation, the thrice-accursed devil, was unable to bear this good and entered his vessels. And he began to rouse many, saying to them: "God is not glorified by this. For if this were pleasing unto him, could he not have ordained from the beginning that they should glorify him, writing their language in their own script? But only three languages, Hebrew, Greek, and Latin, were chosen as appropriate for rendering glory unto God." These were the cohorts of the Latins speaking, archpriests, priests, and their disciples. And having fought with them like David with the Philistines [1 Sam. 17], Constantine defeated them with words from the scriptures, and called them trilinguists, since Pilate had thus written the word's title [John 19:19–20]. And this was not all they were saying, but they also were teaching other impieties, saying: "Underground live people with huge heads; and all reptiles are the creation of the devil, and if one kills a snake, he will be absolved of nine sins because of this. If one kills a man, let him drink from a wooden cup for three months and not touch one of glass." And they forbade neither the offering of sacrifices according to the ancient custom, nor shameful marriages. Cutting all this down like thorns, Constantine burned them with the fire of the scriptures, saying: "Offer unto God a sacrifice of thanksgiving; and pay your vows unto the Most High. Send not away the wife of your youth. For if having begun to hate her, you send her away, wickedness covers not your lust, says the Lord almighty. And take heed to your spirit, and let none leave the wife of your youth; and that which I hated you have done, because the Lord has

been witness between you and the wife of your youth, whom you have forsaken: Yet is she your companion and the wife of your covenant. And in the Gospel the Lord says: 'You have heard that it was said to them of old time, You shall not commit adultery: But I say unto you, That whosoever looks on a woman to lust after her, has committed adultery with her already in his heart.' And furthermore: 'But I say unto you: That whosoever shall put away his wife, saving for the cause of fornication, causes her to commit adultery: and whosoever shall marry her that is divorced commits adultery.' And the Apostle said: 'What God has joined together, let no man put asunder.'"

Constantine spent forty months in Moravia, and then left to ordain his disciples. On the way, Kocel, prince of Pannonia, received him and took a great liking to the Slavic letters. He learned them himself and gave him about fifty students to learn them. He rendered him great honor and accompanied him. But Constantine took neither gold nor silver nor other things from either Rastislav or Kocel. He set down the word of the Gospel without sustenance, asked only for nine hundred captives, and released them.

16. When he was in Venice, bishops, priests, and monks gathered against him like ravens against a falcon. And they advanced the trilingual heresy, saying: "Tell us, O man, how is it that you now teach, having created letters for the Slavs, which none else have been found before, neither the Apostle, nor the pope of Rome, nor Gregory the Theologian, nor Jerome, nor Augustine? We know of only three languages worthy of praising God in the scriptures, Hebrew, Greek, and Latin." And the philosopher answered them: "Does not God's rain fall upon all equally? And does not the sunshine also fall upon all? And do we not all breathe air in the same way? Are you not ashamed to mention only three tongues, and to command all other nations and tribes to be blind and deaf? Tell me, do you render God powerless, that he is incapable of granting this? Or envious, that he does not desire this? We know of numerous peoples who possess writing and render glory unto God, each in its own language. Surely these are obvious: Armenians, Persians, Abkhazians, Iberians, Sogdians, Goths, Avars, Turks, Khazars, Arabs, Egyptians, and many others. If you do not wish to understand this, at least recognize the judgment of the scriptures. For David cries out, saying: 'O sing unto the Lord, all the earth: sing unto the Lord a new song' [Ps. 96:1]. And again: 'Make a joyful noise unto the Lord, all the earth: make a loud noise, and rejoice, and sing praise' [Ps. 98:4]. And likewise: 'Let all the earth worship you and sing unto you; let it sing to your name, God on high' [Ps. 66:4]. And furthermore: 'O praise the Lord, all the nations: praise him, all the people. Let every thing that has breath praise the Lord' [Ps. 117:1]. And in the Gospel according to John it says: 'But as many as received him, to them gave he power to become the children of God' [John 1:12]. And again, in the same Gospel: 'Neither pray I for these alone, but for them also which shall

believe in me through their word, that they all may be one; as you, Father, are in me, and I in you'" [John 17:20–21]. . . . And with these words and many more, he shamed them and went away, leaving them.

17. Upon learning of Constantine, the pope in Rome sent for him. And when he came to Rome, the apostolic father himself, Hadrian [II, 867–72] and all the townspeople came out to meet him, carrying candles. For he was carrying the relics of Saint Clement the Martyr [the disciple of Saint Peter, who was sent into exile in the Crimea by Emperor Trajan and was martyred there] and pope of Rome. And at once God wrought glorious miracles for his sake: a paralytic was healed, and many others were cured of various maladies. And even captives were at once liberated from the hands of their captors when they invoked Christ and Saint Clement.

Accepting the Slavic scriptures, the pope placed them in the church of St-Mary called Phatne [now the church of Santa Maria Maggiore in Rome]. And the holy liturgy was celebrated over them. Then the pope commanded two bishops, Formosus [bishop of Porto] and Gauderich [bishop of Velletri], to consecrate the Slavic disciples. And when they were consecrated, they at once celebrated the liturgy in the Slavic language in the church of the apostle Peter. And the next day they celebrated in the church of St-Petronilla, and on the following day in the church of St-Andrew. And then they celebrated the entire night, glorifying God in Slavic once again in the church of the apostle Paul [now the church San Paolo Fuori le Mura in Rome], the great universal teacher. And in the morning, they again celebrated the liturgy over his blessed grave with the help of Bishop Arsenius [of Orti], one of the seven bishops, and of Anastasius the librarian. The philosopher and his disciples did not cease to render due praise unto God for this. And the Romans did not cease to come to him and question him. And if someone wished to ask about these things, they received double and triple explanations to their questions from him and would joyfully return to their homes again. Then a certain Jew, who would come and debate with him, said to him once: "Christ has not yet come according to the number of years when the one, of whom the prophets speak, shall be born of a virgin." Calculating for him all the years from Adam by generations, the philosopher told him precisely that he has come, and the number of years from then till now. And having instructed him, he dismissed him.

18. And his many labors overtook him, and he fell ill. Enduring his illness for many days, he once had a divine revelation and began to chant the following: "When they said unto me, Let us go into the house of the Lord, my spirit rejoiced, and my heart was gladdened" [Ps. 122:1]. Having put on his venerable garments, he thus spent that entire day rejoicing and saying: "Henceforth I am neither a servant of the emperor, nor of anyone else on earth, but only of God almighty. I was not, and I came to be, and am forever. Amen." On the following

day, he put on holy monastic dress and, receiving light to light, called himself Cyril. He spent fifty days in that dress. And when the hour to repose and remove to the eternal dwellings approached, he raised his arms to God and, in tears, prayed, saying thus: "O Lord, my God, who has created all the ranks of angels and incorporeal powers, stretched out the heavens and founded the earth, and brought all things into being from nonbeing, who has always heeded those that work your will, fear you, and keep your commandments, heed my prayer and preserve your faithful flock which you appointed to me, your useless and unworthy servant." . . . And thus he reposed in the Lord at forty-two years of age, on the fourteenth day of the month of February, of the second indiction, the 6370th year from the creation of this world [862]. . . . Then Methodius, his brother, entreated the apostolic father saying: "Our mother adjured us that the one of us first to pass away be brought to his brother's monastery to be buried there." . . . Then the apostolic father said: "For the sake of his saintliness and charity I shall transgress Roman custom and bury him in my tomb, in the church of the holy apostle Peter." And his brother said: "Since you do not heed me and do not give him up, let him, if it pleases you, rest in the church of St-Clement, for he came here with him." . . . And thus they put him with the coffin into a tomb to the right of the altar in the church of St- Clement [now the church San Clemente in Rome], where many miracles began to occur.

Questions: What role does education play in the portrait of Constantine (Saint Cyril)? What effects did that education have upon his role in the "mission" to Moravia? Given that that "mission" coincided with the Photian Schism (the conflict between Rome and Constantinople over the appointment of Photius as patriarch), how did Constantine stir up papal enthusiasm and support for his work among the Slavic-speaking people? According to his biographer, what was his main reason for going to Rome? What concerns did he have while traveling there? How did he hope to overcome the institutional obstacles facing his missionary work?

12. KING JOSEPH ON THE CONVERSION OF THE KHAZARS TO JUDAISM

The reply of a Khazar "king" named Joseph to the Jewish vizier of the Umayyad caliph of Córdoba survives in two versions. The long version is a Hebrew text in a thirteenth-century copy, with many errors of transcription, particularly for names and place names. This copy was written in the Crimea or in southern Italy. The text was first found in the 1860s in the Middle East and passed through the hands of Abraham Firkowicz (1787–1874), a Karaite writer and hakham (wise man) from Crimea, later accused of forgery by advocates of Rabbinic Judaism. Because of Firkowicz's reputation for the latter, many have raised doubts about the authenticity of the text. The short version of the reply, which is translated below, is preserved in a sixteenth-century manuscript kept in Oxford. This text is very similar to that discovered by Isaac Aqrish, a Jewish collector of manuscripts, who published it in Istanbul in 1577. The events mentioned in the short version of the reply are partially confirmed by other written sources. For example, the Persian historian al-Tabari (839–923) relates that the Khazars crossed the Caucasus Mountains and invaded Azerbaijan in 730, reaching as far south as Mosul. At Ardabil (mentioned in the short version), they defeated and killed the Arab governor of Armenia and Azerbaijan. Five years later, the new governor of Armenia and Azerbaijan, Marwan ibn Muhammad (the future caliph Marwan II, 744–50), took a large army across the Caucasus Mountains and raided deep into Khazar territory. After several victories, he forced the khagan of the Khazars and his retinue to convert to Islam. As a consequence, some have suggested that the short version is in fact an attempt to rewrite history by describing as Judaization what was in fact a forced Islamicization. In any case, the evidence of the conversion of the Khazars to Judaism cannot be dated before c. 800. In fact, the Khazar dirham imitations (coins struck in Khazaria and copying Muslim silver coins) with the shahadah *(Muslim profession of faith) replaced with "Moses is the apostle (or messenger) of God" in Arabic are precisely dated to 837/38. That the short version of the reply is a tenth-century spin on the political and military events of the eighth century is also evident in the mention of synagogues and study halls that the Khazar kings built after the conversion of Judaism. To this day, archaeologists have not found any synagogue in the entire area of eastern Europe that could be dated between c. 650 and c. 970. Nor is there any reference to Jewish scholars going to Khazaria in the otherwise abundant literature produced in the tenth century in the yeshivot (Jewish religious schools) of Jerusalem and "Babylonia" (Persia) or in the archives of the Cairo Geniza (the storage room of the old synagogue in Cairo). The short version of the reply is written in elegant literary Hebrew, and its author had a very solid knowledge of the geography of the Crimean Peninsula, though not necessarily anchored in the political realities of the mid-tenth century.* Josippon, *a tenth-century chronicle of Jewish history written in southern Italy, mentions Khazar as one of the sons of Togarmah, much like the reply of "king" Joseph. The Oghuz (mentioned as Uauz, the other son of Togarmah) are known to have controlled in the tenth century the lands between the western shore of the Aral Sea and the northeastern shore of the Caspian Sea, where ibn Fadlan encountered them on his way to the Volga Bulghars.*

Source: trans. H. Hirschfeld, *Judah Hallevi's Kitab al Khazari* (London: M.L. Cailingold, 1931), pp. 272–77.

To the lord Hisday [ibn Shaprut, c. 915–c. 970, physician, envoy, and minister of Caliph Abd al Rahman III], the head of the exile, son of Isaac, son of Ezra, the Spaniard, precious and honored by us. I herewith inform you that your honored letter came to us by the hand of R[abbi] Jacob b[en] Eleazar, of Germany. We are delighted with it and are pleased with your sagacity and wisdom. I find written in your description the length and breadth of your land, the descent of its ruler Abd al Rahman, its illustrious eminence, how God helped him to subdue the territory of the east, so that the fame of his powerful rule was heard all over the earth, and all kings fear him. Had not messengers from Constantinople come to us with wares and told you the truth about our kingdom and religion, you would have considered it as untrue and would have disbelieved the matter.

You desire to be informed correctly concerning our kingdom and descent and how our forefathers embraced the religion of Israel, God enlightened our eyes, and crushed our adversaries. You further wish to know the extent of our land, its length and breadth, the peoples around us, those which are at peace and those which are at war with us, if it be possible that our messenger come to you to wait upon your beloved and amiable king who draws men's heart to love him on account of his kindheartedness and the righteousness of his actions, because the Gentiles say that Israel has neither a place of dominion nor kingdom, but that they would benefit if this were so. Their hearts would be lifted up, and they would have a proud answer to those who say that Israel had neither remnant nor a place of dominion. We are answering every point raised in your letter in gladness and admiration of your wisdom. We keep in mind what you mention concerning your land and ruling race. Our forefathers have already exchanged letters of friendly intercourse, as recorded in our books, and known to all elders of our country. I shall now tell you again as between our forefathers and leave it as an inheritance to our children. You ask in your letter to what family, race, or tribe we belong. We are the children of Japheth and Togarmah, his son [according to Gen. 10:3, Togarmah was the grandson, not the son, of Japheth]. We find in our genealogical records that Togarmah had ten sons. The following are their names: Igor [Ujur, possibly Uyghur], Tiros [possibly Tauris, in reference to the Crimea], Avar, Uauz [Oghuz], Bizal, Tarna, Khazar, Zanor [Janur], Bulgar, and Sarir [Sawir or Sabir]. We are descendants of Khazar, the seventh son. He had it on record that our forefathers were few of number, but God gave them strength and they waged war with many mightier nations. With the help of God, they drove them [Bulgars] out and occupied their land. They pursued them even beyond the River Duna [Danube], where they dwell to this day near Constantinople. Their land was taken by the Khazars. Generations passed till a king [*khagan*] stood up whose name was Bulan. He was wise and God-fearing, and trusted him with all his heart. He removed shamans and heathens from the land and relied on God alone. There an angel appeared to him and said: "Bulan, God has sent me to you to say: 'I have heard your prayers, I will bless and multiply you and establish your kingdom to the end of generations. I will deliver all your enemies into your hand. Now rise up in the morning and pray.'" So he did. Then he [the angel] appeared to him a second time and said: "I have seen your ways and am pleased with your actions. I know that you walk after me with all your heart. I wish to give you commandments, law, and judgment. If you will keep my commands, I will bless and multiply you." He answered and said to the angel: "You know, Lord, the thoughts of my heart and you search my kidneys [vital organs in the Hebrew tradition], that I put my trust only in you. Now the people whom I rule are unbelievers, and I do not know whether they will believe me. If I have found favor in your eyes, and your mercy will stand by me, appear to their chief [probably another, subordinate ruler], so that he may assist me." God did as he asked and appeared to the chief in a dream. Next morning, he told the king. The king assembled all his princes and servants and all his people and related all that had happened to them. The matter seemed pleasing in their eyes, they accepted the law and took shelter beneath the wings of God. Then the angel appeared again and said: "Behold the heavens and the heavens of heaven do not contain me [1 Kings 8:27] yet build you a house to my name." The king answered, "O Lord, I am much abashed before you since I have no silver, nor gold, as is proper, and as I should wish." He answered: "Be strong and of good courage [Josh. 1:6, 9]. Take all your hosts with you and go through Daralan [the Daril Pass, also known as the Alanian Gate through the Caucasus Mountains] and Ardavil [Ardabil, in northwestern Iran]. I have put fear and terror in their hearts and will deliver them into your hands. I have kept for you two treasures, one of silver and one of gold. I will be with you and guard you wherever you go. Take the money, return in peace, and build the house for my name." He believed and did as he was bidden, fought, devastated the land, and returned in peace. He consecrated the wealth, and built with it the ark, the menorah, and the table, and the altars, and the holy vessels [2 Chron. 5:5] which are preserved and remain in my hand. Thereupon his fame spread on the earth.

The king of Edom [Rome, Byzantium, and by extension, Christianity] and the ruler of the Ishmaelites [Muslims] sent their envoys with great riches and presents with their wise men to invite him to their religion. The king was shrewd and requested to bring a Jewish sage, and after careful inquiry and searching he put them together [for a disputation,] to let them expound the tenets of their beliefs. Each of them refuted the arguments of the other, without agreeing on one point. When the king saw this, he said to the Christian and Muslim divines [priests, teachers]: "Go to your tents, I will send for you in three days." On the other day, he sent for the Christian priest of the king of Edom and said: "I know that the king of Edom is greater than these kings and his religion is esteemed. I like your faith, but I ask you to tell me truly: is either the Israelite or the Muslim faith the better of the two?" The priest answered: "May our lord the king live forever. Know in truth that in the whole world there is no better religion than the Israelite one, for God chose Israel from all nations, called them his firstborn son, performed great wonders and miracles among them, brought them out of the bondage of Pharaoh, made them pass through the sea dry-shod, drowned their enemies in the sea, made manna come down for them and water from the rock, gave them the Torah out of the midst of fire, made them possess the land of Canaan, and built for them a sanctuary to dwell therein. Then they sinned against him, so that he was wroth with them and cast them from his presence and scattered them to every wind. Were it not for this, there would not be in the world a faith like the religion of Israel." Said the king: "Thus far have you spoken, surely I will honor you." On the second day, he set to the Arab *kadi* [judge] and said to him: "Tell me in truth what is there between the Israelite and Christian religions, which of them is better?" The *kadi* answered: "The Israelite religion is the better, being all truth. They possess the law of the Lord, just statutes, and judgments. Since they sinned and rebelled against him, he was angry with them and gave them into the hand of their enemies. What is the religion of the Christians? They eat all things unclean and worship the work of their hands." Said the king: "You have spoken the truth, and I will surely honor you." The next day, he invited them all together and said to them in the presence of all his magnates and his people: "I ask you to choose the best and truest religion for me." They set to speaking but did not establish their words to the ground. Then the king said to the priest "Is the Israelite, or the Mohammedan [Muslim] religion the best?" And the priest said: "The Israelite belief is the best." Then he asked the *kadi*: "Is the Israelite or the Roman [Christian] faith the best?" The *kadi* answered: "The Israelite is the best." The king answered: "You have now confessed with your own mouth that the Israelite religion is the best and truest. I have chosen it, as it is the religion of Abraham. May the Almighty be my help. The silver and gold which you promised me, he can give without trouble. You go in peace to your country."

Henceforth, Almighty God strengthened him. He and his servants were circumcised. Then he sent for a Jewish sage who explained the Torah to him with all its commandments. Up to this day, we observe this honored and true religion, blessed be the name of God forever. When our forefathers took shelter under the wings of Providence, he humbled all our enemies before us, and subdued all surrounding nations. No one stood up against us to this day, all owing tribute to us by the kings of Rome [Byzantium] and the Mohammedans. Afterward, there arose a king of his descendants of the name of Obadiah. He was just and righteous; he invigorated the kingdom and established religion. He built temples [synagogues] and houses of study, gathered many learned Israelites, and gave them much silver and gold. They interpreted for him the Bible, the Mishnah [a collection of Jewish oral traditions], and Talmud [the book of Jewish law], and the whole prayer book. He was God-fearing and loved the Torah and the commandments. He was followed by his son Hezekiah, then Menasseh, his son, then by Hanuccah, the brother of Obadiah, his son Isaac, his son Zebulun, his son Menasseh, his son Nissi, his son Menahem, his son Benjamin, and Aaron, his son. We all are of royal descent, and no stranger may sit on the throne of our fathers. May it be the will of him who appoints every king that our dynasty may remain steadfast in his Torah and laws.

Questions: How does the account of the conversion of the Khazars compare to the account of the conversion of the Carantanians (Doc. 10)? How does the author explain what happened? What was Bulan's ultimate goal? What can one learn from this account about the relations between different faith groups in the steppe lands north of the Black Sea?

13. THE CONVERSION OF THE VOLGA BULGHARS TO ISLAM

One of the most remarkable sources on the people and the events of eastern Europe in the early tenth century is the account of an Arab man's participation in the deputation sent in 921 by Caliph al-Muqtadir (908–32) to the king of the Volga Bulghars. The Bulghars were an initially nomadic group in the Middle Volga region (present-day Tatarstan and the region of Ulianovsk, in Russia). They played a key role in the international commercial networks of the tenth century, especially after the decline of Khazaria. That is when their conversion to Islam is mentioned in Arab sources. Next to nothing is known about the author of this account, Ahmad ibn Fadlan, except what he says about himself in the text: he was born in Baghdad, was a Sunni Muslim with deep knowledge of law and customs, and appears to have been a confidant of the caliph. As mawla *(client) of Muhammad ibn Sulaiman, a prominent general of the caliphal court, ibn Fadlan worked as his scribe and assistant. To ibn Fadlan, Volga Bulgharia and its ruler were essentially barbarous, and he treats them with a mixture of curiosity, awe, and disgust.*

Source: trans. F. Curta from A.Z.V. Togan, *Ibn Faḍlān's Reisebericht* (Leipzig: Deutsche Morgenländische Gesellschaft, 1939), pp. 1–3, 45–46, and 67–68.

Ahmad ibn Fadlan says: the letter of the Yiltawar [*elteber*, ruler], the king of the Saqaliba [a generic name employed by Arab authors for all inhabitants of eastern Europe], who is the son [of Shalkay], reached the commander of the faithful [that is, the caliph] al-Muqtadir [Abbasid caliph between 908 and 932]. In it, he [the Yiltawar] demanded him [the caliph] to send someone, who could teach him religion, who would have knowledge of the sharia [Islamic law], who could build a mosque for him and a *minbar* [pulpit in the mosque from which the sermon or *hutba* is delivered], so that he [the Yiltawar] could carry the mission of conversion for him [in al-Muqtadir's name] throughout his entire land and in all parts of his realm. Furthermore, he beseeched him [the caliph] to build [for him] a fort, in which he could defend himself against hostile kings. The intermediary [the Yiltawar's representative] was Nadir al-Hurami [probably a eunuch at the caliphal court in Baghdad]. [The caliph] granted him [Yiltawar] everything that he had requested. I [Ahmad ibn Fadlan] was appointed to read to him [the Yiltawar] the letter [from the caliph], to take to him the gifts that he [the caliph] had bestowed upon him [the Yiltawar], and to inspect the jurists and teachers. In order to cover for the costs of the building of that which we have mentioned [the fort] and for the wages of the jurists and teachers, he was granted the revenue from one of the estates of Ibn al-Furat [scribe and vizier of al-Muqtadir], namely Artakhushmitan, which is the land of Khwarazm [a large oasis region in western central Asia now divided between Uzbekistan, Kazakhstan, and Turkmenistan]. . . .

Before our arrival [in Volga Bulgharia], the *hutba* [the Friday or feast sermon] was proclaimed from the *minbar* as following: "God, grant well-being to the king, the Yiltawar and king of the Bulghars!" So I told him [the king] this: "God alone is the king, and nobody else besides him, the mighty and glorious one, should be called by that title from the *minbar*. Your lord, the commander of the faithful, has been satisfied to say about him from *minbar*s in both east and west those words: 'My God, grant well-being to your servant and deputy [caliph], to the imam Ja'far al-Muqtadir bi-llah, the prince of the faithful.' That was done before him by his ancestors, all the previous caliphs. And even the Prophet (may God bless and cherish him!) said, 'Do not exaggerate my status as the Christians have done with Jesus, the son of Mary. Verily, I am only a servant of Allah and his messenger'" [*hadith* in Shahih al-Bukhari 3345]. And he asked me, "What then is the right way for me to do the *hutba*?" I replied, "[Do it] in your name and in the name of your father." "But," he said, "my father was an unbeliever and I do not wish to mention his name next to mine from the *minbar*. [In fact,] I should not even have my own name mentioned, since the one who has given me this name was an unbeliever. But what is the name of my lord, the prince of the faithful?" "Ja'far," I said. And he asked: "Would I be allowed to take his name?" "Yes," I replied. So he said: "Then I will change my name into Ja'far, and that of my father into 'Abdallah." And he turned to the *hatib* [preacher], and it was done as he had wished. The *hutba* was proclaimed for him in this way: "O my God, grant well-being to your servant Ja'far ibn Abdallah, the prince of the Bulghars, and the client of the commander of the faithful." . . .

Among them [the Bulghars], we encountered a clan of five thousand souls, men and women. They had all converted to Islam and are called Baranjar. They [the Bulghars] had a timber mosque built for them [the Baranjar] made so that they could pray. But they did not know how to recite the Quran [while praying], so I taught some of them what they needed [to do] when praying. And through me, a man [in that place] who was called Talut converted to Islam, so I wanted to give him a new name, 'Abdallah. But he said, "I would like you to give me your name, Muhammad" [ibn Fadlan's name, however, was Ahmad]. And I did [as he wished]. His wife, his mother, and his children converted to Islam after that. All his sons took the name Muhammad. And I taught him [Talut] the surahs [Quranic verses] "Praise be to God" [Quran 1, opening of the *Surah al-Fatihah*] and "Say, he is God, One" [Quran 112, *Surah al-Ikhlas*]. And upon learning those two surahs, his joy was greater than if he had become king of the Saqaliba.

Questions: How did ibn Fadlan reconcile his role as caliphal envoy and his expertise in Islamic law? How might the Bulghars have reacted to those two aspects of his personality? Compare ibn Fadlan's description of how conversion proceeded with those sketched by the anonymous author of the Conversion of the Carantanians *and King Joseph (Docs. 10 and 12).*

14. POPE NICHOLAS I ANSWERS THE QUESTIONS OF BORIS OF BULGARIA

Bulgaria in the Balkans was an early medieval power very different from Volga Bulgharia, despite the similar names. The Bulgars had been in conflict with Byzantium for over a century, but under Boris, they eventually adopted Christianity. When the papal mission led by Bishop Formosus of Porto (future Pope Formosus, 891–96) arrived in Bulgaria in November 866, it brought a lengthy response that Pope Nicholas I (858–67) gave to the questions that Boris had addressed to him earlier. The response was in the form of an extensive letter addressed to all Bulgars, not just to their ruler. The 106 chapters of the letter deal with a variety of topics from baptism and marriage to bathing, fasting, and the distinction between sin and crime. Pope Nicholas did not hesitate to compare Boris to Constantine the Great and to encourage him to "convert all things into the battle gear of a spiritual preparation." The general tone of the letter was moderation, for the pope allowed the continuation of some of the old customs and adopted a cautious approach to the conversion of Bulgaria. His insistence upon penitential practices such as were in use at that time in the Roman Church may have had something to do with the Roman attempt to reconcile Boris with those who had risen in rebellion against him.

Source: trans. Stephen Neil Scott, "The Collapse of the Moravian Mission of Saints Cyril and Methodius, the Fate of Their Disciples, and the Christianization of the Southern Slavs: Translations of Five Historical Texts with Notes and Commentary" (PhD diss., University of California, Berkeley, 1989), pp. 222–99.

Numerous replies need not be made to your inquiries, nor have we decided to spend too much time on details, for, at the prompting of God, we have dispatched [in November 866] to your country and to your glorious king, our esteemed [spiritual] son, not only books of divine law, but also our capable legates [led by Bishop Formosus of Porto], who as time and reason dictate, will instruct you in the details; to whom we have also entrusted the book which we deem to be necessary in your land at this time.

1. Therefore, rightly and laudably do you say at the beginning of your questions that your king seeks the Christian law. If one were to attempt to explain this law in any great detail, countless books would have to be written. But to point out briefly on what it chiefly hinges, one ought to know that the law of the Christian consists of faith and good works. . . .

17. Next, you relate how by God's mercy you accepted the Christian religion and had all your people baptized; and how, after they were baptized, they revolted against you with great fury, saying that you had taught them a law that was not good. Moreover, they tried to slay you and set up another king, but with the assistance of God's might you were prepared against them and overpowered them, from the greatest to the least, and took them captive. All their leaders and more distinguished people were put to death by the sword along with all their offspring, but the common and less distinguished suffered no harm. Now you wish to know whether you have sinned with respect to those who were executed. At least one aspect of this affair is tainted with sin, nor could you have done it without being at fault, inasmuch as innocent offspring, who were not in league with their parents and were not convicted of having taken up arms against you, were slaughtered along with the guilty. . . . You acted without weighing this matter more seriously.

25. You say that your country has a custom of posting sentries on your borders to keep watch. And if a slave or a free man somehow manages to flee past one of those watch stations, the sentries are promptly put to death. Therefore, you inquire as to what we feel about this and the laws demand in this case. Heretofore you did not know such a gentle God and Lord, but now, however, let such severe sentencing be far from your mind. Now it is considerably more fitting for you, who have up to the present been putting men to death so readily, to bring those whom you can to life and not to put them to death.

33. You say that you used to carry a horse's tail as a military standard whenever you would enter battle, and you would like to know what you ought to carry now in place of that. What else indeed, except the sign of the holy cross? . . . This is the sign which we carry before us, by which we are defended against all enemies and protected against every assault. This is the sign of faith and the great terror of the devil. Christian rulers always use this in times of distress, and kings who strive after true piety often, by Christ's favor, triumph over their enemies.

42. You say that when your king sits down to eat his meals, it is your custom for no one, not even his wife, to dine with him. Rather you all eat at a distance, seated in chairs on the ground level. Hence you would like to know what we

would admonish you about this. Now, because this custom is not contrary to the faith (although it certainly does contravene good manners), we, not so much admonishing as advising, suggest that you consider the most noble champions of the Christian faith and, pondering the height of their humility, put away from yourselves useless haughtiness.

59. What you seek to learn concerning trousers we consider superfluous. For we do not wish the external fashion of your clothing to be changed, but the morals of the inner man within you. . . . However, because you ask about this sincerely, fearing lest perchance you would be committing a sin by doing something, even in details, contrary to the custom of other Christians, we should tell you, lest we appear to be omitting what you wish to see answered, that in our books trousers are prescribed to be made so that men, and not women, may use them.

62. You say that before your conversion to Christianity, you discovered a certain stone in your land. If someone took this stone for an illness, it would sometimes furnish healing for his body; but sometimes it would have no effect. Now why is it never certain what will happen to those taking this stone daily, so that some receive a remedy for the healing of their affliction, and others languish in their infirmity? Wherefore to your question, so to speak, of whether you ought to use it or do without it, we reply and decree that no one should be allowed to take that stone at all, and that [he] should disavow it in every way and [not] place the hope of all human salvation only in that stone. . . .

72. You ask whether it is possible for a patriarch to be ordained for you. Now concerning this, we cannot give you a definite answer until our legates, whom we are sending over to your country, return and report to us how numerous and united the Christians among you are. But in the meantime, you shall have a bishop; and after Christianity there has expanded through the increase of divine grace, and bishops have been consecrated for individual churches, one of them should then be elected who, if not a patriarch, would at least be called an archbishop.

103. You ask what you ought to do with the profane books which you received from the Saracens [Muslims] and still have among you. Under no circumstances should you keep them, for as it is written: "Bad company corrupts good morals." Instead, you must burn them, as being harmful and blasphemous.

Questions: What kind of concerns did Boris have when asking Pope Nicholas I for clarification? How did the pope answer those concerns? What does his letter tell us about the pre-Christian beliefs of the Bulgars? Why does the pope condemn the books of the Saracens? What does that suggest about the presence of Islam in southeastern Europe? Compare this text with ibn Fadlan's account of the conversion of the Volga Bulghars (Doc. 13).

CHAPTER THREE

MEDIEVAL NOMADS

Figure 3.1 Pechenegs Ambush and Kill Prince Sviatoslav of Kiev (971). Illumination from the *Madrid Skylitzes*, a twelfth-century manuscript of the *Synopsis of Histories* by John Skylitzes.

15. IBN RUSTA ON THE MAGYARS

Next to nothing is known about the author of a tenth-century encyclopedic work known as the Book of Precious Gems, *of which only Part 7 survives in a thirteenth-century manuscript now in the British Library. Ibn Rusta was from the region of Isfahan, in present-day Iran, and he probably lived and wrote in the early tenth century. The description of the Magyars appears between the descriptions of India and Tabaristan (a province of northern Iran, on the southern shore of the Caspian Sea). It has therefore been suggested that either the chapter on the Magyars or those on India and Tabaristan were not in the original work of ibn Rusta, or that they may be from a different author (possibly al-Jayhani, a geographer at the court of the tenth-century Samanids).*

Source: trans. I. Zimonyi, *Muslim Sources on the Magyars in the Second Half of the Ninth Century: The Magyar Chapter of the Jayhānī Tradition* (Leiden: Brill, 2016), p. 39.

Between the country of the Pechenegs and the Äskäl, who belong to the Bulgars, lies the first border from among the borders of the Magyars. The Magyars are a Turkic people. Their chieftain rides at the head of twenty thousand horsemen. The name of their chieftain is *künde.* This name is the title of their king, while the name of the man who practices the royal power of them is *gyula.* Every Magyar does what the chieftain, called *gyula,* commands him to do in making war, repelling invasions, and the like. They are tent-dwelling people. They migrate following the grazing fields and vegetation. Their country is wide. One border of their country reaches the Sea of Rum [Black Sea]. Two rivers flow into this sea. One of them is bigger than the Jayhun [Amu Darya]. The lands of the Magyars lie between these two rivers. When the days of winter come, all of them set up their camps on the river, whichever of the two rivers lies nearer to them. They stay there during the winter catching fish from the river. It is the most appropriate winter quarters for them. The country of the Magyars abounds in trees and waters. Its ground is damp. They have a lot of sown fields. They overcome all the Saqaliba [Slavs] who are their neighbors, imposing harsh provisions upon them, and treat them as their slaves. The Magyars are fire worshippers. They raid the Saqaliba, and they take the captives along the seacoast till they reach a harbor of Rum called Karkh [Cherson, in the Crimea]. It is said that the Khazars entrenched themselves some time ago against the Magyars and other peoples bordering their country. When the Magyars take the captives to Karkh, the Rum [Byzantines] go out to them, and they trade there. They buy Byzantine brocade, woolen carpets, and other Byzantine goods for the slaves.

Questions: What aspects of the Magyar way of life have attracted ibn Rusta's attention? What reasons are given for their involvement in the slave trade? What do we learn from this text about the political organization of the Magyars? How does this description of the "tent-dwelling people" compare to that of Theophylact Simocatta's account of the Avars (Doc. 2)? Why do brocade and carpets figure so prominently among the goods the Magyars desired to obtain from Byzantium?

16. IBN FADLAN ON THE OGHUZ

The Oghuz, whom Ahmad ibn Fadlan encountered on his way to Volga Bulgharia, lived somewhere beyond the Ustiurt plateau between the western shore of the Aral Sea and the northern shore of the Caspian Sea in what is today southwestern Kazakhstan. Historians have treated them as nomads because that is what ibn Fadlan called them. Under that assumption, some believe that the Oghuz moved into the lands between the Amu Darya and the Syr Darya Rivers from western Mongolia. However, the evidence for a migration is very late and problematic. What seems certain is that around 900, a major Oghuz confederacy (or, as some prefer to call it, the "Oghuz Yabghu state") came into being in the lands on both sides of the Aral Sea. Ibn Fadlan's visit happened at this key moment in Oghuz history. To judge from his account, there was no central authority in the Oghuz world, and decisions were taken in assemblies of the most prominent chieftains. This may explain the conflict between different tribes or clans, the most famous of which was that formed from the separation, shortly after the year 1000, of the Qiniq tribe under a chieftain named Seljuk. The Seljuk Turks, as they came to be known, migrated to the south, and their extraordinary history and political success is linked to the lands outside eastern Europe. By the time Seljuk took his Turks to the south, the Oghuz had already moved into the Kalmyk steppe between the Volga, the Don, and the Manych Rivers. Throughout the first half of the eleventh century, the Oghuz, known to Rus' sources as "Torki," were the dominant force in the steppe lands between the Volga and the Dnieper Rivers. They pushed even farther to the west, against the Pechenegs, a conflict that gave the Pecheneg chieftain Kegen a chance to distinguish himself in battle against the Oghuz. An expedition by the combined forces of the Rus' princes of Kiev, Chernigov and Pereiaslavl', destroyed the Oghuz forces, triggering a massive migration into the Balkan provinces of the Byzantine empire. The 1064 invasion of the Oghuz into the Balkans was particularly devastating, but incapable of finding sufficient supplies, the Oghuz were decimated by disease. Some returned to the lands north of the River Danube, others were captured by the Byzantines and settled inside the empire. Oghuz recruits fought (and deserted) at the battle of Manzikert (1071) against the Seljuk Turks. Oghuz auxiliaries are also mentioned as harassing the armies of the First Crusade crossing the Balkans.

Source: trans. F. Curta from A.Z.V. Togan, *Ibn Faḍlān's Reisebericht* (Leipzig: Deutsche Morgenländische Gesellschaft, 1939), pp. 19–22 and 25–28.

After we crossed those [probably the Mugodzhary Mountains in northwestern Kazakhstan, the southernmost extension of the Ural Mountains] and reached a Turkic tribe known as the Oghuz. They are nomads and have houses made of wool [that is, tents]. They stay for a while in one place, and then move on. One can see some of their houses here, and, at the same time, others in a different place, according to the customs and the wandering practices of the nomads. They pitch and strike regularly. Although they have difficult lives, they are like lost [wild] asses [Quran 74:50]. They do not have any religion to see God, are not inclined toward reason, and do not worship anything. Moreover, they call lords their chiefs. When one of them discusses some matter with his chief, he tells him thus: "O my lord, what should I do about this or that?" Their affairs are conducted by mutual consultation [Quran 42:38]. However, when they agree upon something and they are about to put that into practice, someone of the lowliest and commonest rank among them could overturn that upon which they have agreed. I have heard them declare that "there is no god but God, and Muhammad is God's prophet." They say that to get close to those Muslims who come to their land, and not because they believe [in what they say]. When one of them objects to something wrong or [else] something happens to him, to which he does not agree, he raises his head to the heavens and says, "*bir tengri*," which in Turkic means "by one god," for *bir* in Turkic is "one" and *tengri* "God," in the language of the Turks. They do not clean themselves either after defecating or after urinating, and they do not bathe either after *janabah* [impurity caused by contact with semen] or any other [such] circumstances. They do not want to have anything to do with water, especially in the winter.

Their womenfolk do not cover themselves either in the presence of their men, or in that of others [that is, foreigners]. Similarly, a woman does not cover any part of her body in front of anyone. One day we were visiting one of them [the Oghuz] and sat down [in his house]. The man's wife was present, and as we were talking, she uncovered her genitalia and began scratching, and we could see everything. We therefore covered our faces, saying: "God forgive me!" The woman's husband laughed and told the interpreter: "Tell them: we uncover them [the genitalia] in your presence, so that you can see them and control yourselves. But you will not be able to reach them. It is in fact better than when you cover them up, yet they are accessible [to others]." They do not have knowledge of adultery. If they discover someone, who through his behavior turns out to be an adulterer, they tear him into two halves. And they do that by bringing together the branches of two trees, tying him [the culprit] to the branches, and then letting both trees loose. In this way, the man bound to the two trees is torn apart.

Upon hearing my recitation from the Quran, one of them liked it very much, and said to the interpreter, "Tell him: do not stop." One day, that man told me through the interpreter: "Ask this Arab whether our god, who is great and glorious, has a wife." I thought that his question was rude, [so] I began praising God and asking for his mercy. He [the Oghuz man] did likewise—he praised God and asked for his mercy, just like me. So is the custom among the Turks: whenever a Turk hears a Muslim praising God or affirming that he is the only one, he [promptly] imitates him.

Their marriage customs are as follows. In exchange for a certain amount of Khwarazmi garments [garments produced in Khwarazm], [any] of them asks another for a woman of his family, whether a daughter or a sister or any of the others, over whom he has control. When the suitor and the head of family reach an agreement, he [the suitor] brings it [the bride-price] to him [the head of the family]. The bride-price often consists of camels, horses, or other things, and nobody can know any woman before paying the bride-price [in the amount] upon which he and her male guardian have agreed. Once he had paid, he shows up without any warning [that is, unabashedly], gets into the house where she lives, and grabs her in the presence of her father, mother, and siblings. For no one can prevent him from doing that. When a man dies, leaving a wife and sons behind, his eldest son marries her, provided he had not been born of her. . . .

The first of their rulers and chiefs, whom we have met, was the "lesser Yanal." He had converted to Islam but had been told that, "If you embrace Islam, you cannot be our ruler [anymore]." So, he gave up the Muslim faith. When we got to the place where he was, he told us, "I will not let you pass, because this [the Arab embassy going through the land of the Oghuz] is something like we have never heard before and would have therefore not believed that it could take place." We were friendly to him, until he agreed to accept the gift of a Jurjani caftan [that is, a caftan produced in the old capital of Khwarazm at Urgench, near present-day Urganch, in northern Turkmenistan] worth ten dirhams [silver coins], a pair of shoes [probably expensive], some pieces of flat bread, a handful of raisins, and a hundred nuts. When we gave him all this, he bowed [to us]. For that is their custom: when a man honors another, the other bows before him. Then he said, "Were my houses not at a distance from the road, I would have brought to you sheep and [reciprocal] gifts." He let us go through, and we moved on. . . .

He [ibn Fadlan] said: When one of them [the Turks] is ill, and he has slaves—both male and female—they take care of him, without anyone in his family coming in close contact with him. They put up a tent for him, away from the houses, and he remains there until he dies or he recovers. However, when the sick man is a slave or a pauper, they simply abandon him in the desert and leave. When a [prominent] man of theirs dies, they bury him in a large pit in the form of a house and they go to his place, dress him up in his *qurtaq* [tunic] and his belt, and they take his bow. . . . In his hands, they place a wooden cup filled with an inebriating beverage and they [further] place a wooden vessel with an inebriating beverage in front of him. They bring all his wealth and lay it beside him, in the house[-shaped pit]. They then lower his body inside that pit and put a roof above the house, building something like a dome out of clay. Then they take his horses, depending upon how many he had. They slaughter between one hundred and two hundred horses by the grave, down to the last one, then eat their meat, except the head, the hooves, the hide, and the tail, for they hang [all of] those upon wooden posts, saying, "These are his horses, which he rides in paradise." If the man has killed others [in battle] and has been a hero, then they carve wooden statues for each one of those whom he had killed, and place them on his grave, saying, "These are his attendants, who serve him in paradise." Sometimes they postpone for a couple of days the slaughter of horses, before an elder among their prominent men exhorts them, saying: "I have seen so-and-so, that is the deceased, in a dream and he told me, 'Now you see me here. My companions have gone before me, and my feet were too weak for me to go after them. I cannot catch up to them and I have been left here, all by myself.'" At that point, people take his horses, slaughter them, and hang them [that is, the heads and the hides] at his graveside. After one or two days, the same elder comes back to them, and says, "I have seen so-and-so [in a dream] and he said to me, 'Tell my household and my companions that I have caught up to those who have gone before me and I have recovered from my weariness.'"

He [ibn Fadlan] said: All Turks pluck their beards, but not their mustaches. I have once seen an old man [among the Oghuz], who had plucked his beard, but left a little under his chin, and had put on a leather coat. Seen from a distance, he looked like a billy goat. The king of the Oghuz Turks is called *yabghu*; this is the word for ruler, and the one who rules over a tribe has that title. His deputy is called *kudarkin*, and any deputy of a chieftain is called likewise.

Questions: Why is ibn Fadlan shocked by the behavior of the Oghuz women? What can the account of the Oghuz burial tell us about the Oghuz mode of life? Compare the fascination of the Oghuz with "Jurjani caftans" with the Magyar cravings for Byzantine brocade and carpets (Doc. 15): Why were textiles prized by the nomads?

17. JOHN SKYLITZES ON THE PECHENEGS

John Skylitzes was born at some point before 1050 in the Thrakesion theme (province) of western Asia Minor. Little is known about his life and activities, but he is the first in a relatively long list of members of the Skylitzes family to rise very high in the civil service. His name appears in a number of legal documents dated to the early 1090s as "droungarios *of the watch," the principal magistrate of the main judicial tribunal in Constantinople. Skylitzes petitioned Emperor Alexios I Komnenos (1081–1118) to clarify the "new law" concerning betrothals, a confirmation, if any more was needed, that he was a judge. Perhaps because of his merits in that capacity, Skylitzes was appointed eparch of Constantinople, an office similar to that of a modern-day governor, rather than a modern-day mayor. It is unknown whether he outlived Emperor Alexios, but his* Synopsis of Histories *was written during that emperor's reign, most likely in the last decade of the eleventh century. This work is one of the most valuable sources for the long reign of Emperor Basil II, but Skylitzes in fact rewrote the material extracted from previous (but now lost) sources, combining, modifying, and adjusting them to his own goals. It is only in the last part of the* Synopsis, *and especially in the part covering the reign of Emperor Constantine IX (1042–55), that Skylitzes suddenly becomes interested in affairs outside the empire. The digression on the Pechenegs (whom he called "Patzinaks") is one of the finest examples of that shift in emphasis.*

Source: trans. J. Wortley, John Skylitzes, *A Synopsis of Byzantine History, 811–1057* (Cambridge: Cambridge University Press, 2010), pp. 426–27; rev.

The Patzinak people are Scyth[ian]s pertaining to the so-called "Royal Scyth[ian]s." They are numerous and no other people of the Scyth[ian]s is able to withstand them alone. They are divided into thirteen tribes, all of which have the same name in common, but each tribe has its own proper name inherited from its own ancestor and chieftain. They graze their flocks on the plains which extend beyond the Danube from the River Borysthenon [Dnieper] to Pannonia [Hungary], for they are nomads who always prefer to live in tents. At that time, the leader of the people was Tyrach, son of Bilter, highly distinguished by birth but otherwise unremarkable, a man who preferred to live in peace. But there was another person in that people whose name was Kegenes, son of Baltzar, a nobody by birth and practically nameless, but extremely effective in battle and in the waging of war. He had on many occasions routed and repelled the Ouzes [Oghuz] (a Hunnic people) from attacking the Patzinaks, when Tyrach, lacking the courage to go out against them, took refuge in the marshes and lakes along the Danube. The Patzinaks honored Tyrach and his family but they greatly preferred Kegenes for his outstanding bravery and his skill in war. Tyrach was stung to the core when he heard and noticed this; fearing for his position, he sought a way of getting rid of Kegenes. He set several traps for him but always in vain. When his covert schemes repeatedly went astray, he realized that he could delay no longer and must act openly, whereupon he dispatched a company with orders to seize and destroy him. But Kegenes got wind of the plan and fled to the marshes of the Borysthenon, escaping death. From his hiding place there he sent secret messages to his relatives and fellow tribesmen, whereby he was able to divert the affections of his tribe (the Belemarnes) away from the king and also the affections of another tribe, the Pagoumanes. He raised an army and, with two tribes, confronted Tyrach, who had eleven. [Kegenes] held his own for a long time, but, nevertheless, he was eventually overcome by weight of numbers. Wandering in the marshes, he realized that the only way to safety for him and those with him was to take refuge with the emperor of the Romans. So, he came to Dorostolon [now Silistra, in northern Bulgaria] and installed himself with his followers (who number about twenty thousand) on a little island in the river to avoid being taken by surprise. Then he reported to the governor of the region [Paristrion], Michael son of Anastasios, letting him know who he was, what adventures had befallen him before arriving there, and that he wished to transfer his allegiance to the emperor.

Questions: What kind of social organization did the Pechenegs have and why did Kegenes have to flee to escape from Tyrach? What does the outcome of the conflict between Kegenes and Tyrach suggest about the relation between Pechenegs and Ouzes? How and why did Kegenes use the Roman (Byzantine) emperor for political advantage?

18. ROBERT DE CLARI ON THE CUMANS

Robert de Clari's Conquest of Constantinople, *a work written in Old French at some point after 1216, survives in only one manuscript dated c. 1300 that is preserved in the Royal Library in Copenhagen. The work contains a detailed description of the Cumans, complete with all the ancient stereotypes about nomads in general. Some have interpreted this as indicating the interest, largely fed by contemporary romances, that the author's audience of French aristocrats had in exotic peoples. However, as this is in fact the only ethnographic excursus in Clari's chronicle, the description of the Cumans looks odd. Moreover, while in much of the narrative the author employed the simple perfect tense, in the description of the Cumans he suddenly switches to the present or even future tense. Some have also noted that the information in this excursus is remarkably similar to that in the chronicle of Het'um (the Armenian name of Hayton of Corycus),* La Flor des estoire de la terre d'Orient, *which was written in 1307. The description of the Cumans, according to such views, is a much later interpolation. The occasion for that interpolation is Johannitsa Kaloyan being refused and insulted in Constantinople, going to the Cumans, and managing to become their friend and to obtain their military assistance. It is at this point in the narrative that Robert de Clari announces that Johannitsa has become the lord of the Cumans in addition to the Vlachs. Through him, the Cumans became an object of interest for outsiders as well. The participants in the Fourth Crusade had many opportunities to observe the Cumans. Their role in the battle of Adrianople (1205) and the prisoners of war captured in various encounters could have informed many a curious crusader about the enemy from the north. However, Robert de Clari did not participate in the battle of Adrianopole and had no direct knowledge of the Cumans. On the other hand, if the description of the Cumans in the* Conquest of Constantinople *is a later interpolation, it is strikingly similar to contemporary descriptions of the Mongols.*

Source: trans. E.H. McNeal, Robert de Clari, *The Conquest of Constantinople* (New York: Columbia University Press, 1936), pp. 87–88.

Now Cumania is a land bordering on Vlachia, and I will tell you what kind of people the Cumans are. They are a savage people, who neither plow nor sow, and they have neither huts nor houses, but they have tents made of felt in which they shelter themselves, and they live on milk and cheese and flesh. In the summer there are so many flies and gnats that they scarcely dare come out of their tents at all before winter. In winter they come out of their tents and sally forth from their country when they want to make a raid. Now we will tell you what they do. Each one has at least ten or twelve horses, and they have them so well trained that they follow them wherever they want to take them, and they mount first on one and then on another. When they are on a raid, each horse has a bag hung on his nose in which his fodder is put, and he feeds as he follows his master, and they do not stop going by night and day. And they ride so hard that they cover in one day and one night fully six days' journey, or seven or eight. And while they are on the way they will not seize anything or carry it along, before their return, but when they are returning, then they seize plunder and take captives and take anything they can get. Nor do they go armed, except that they wear a garment of sheepskin and carry bows and arrows. They do not worship anything except the first animal encountered in the morning, and the one who encounters it worships all that day, whatever animal it may be.

Questions: What particular features of the nomadic way of life are highlighted in this passage? What was the primary reason for introducing a passage on the Cumans into the Conquest of Constantinople*? How does the attitude in this passage compare with that of ibn Fadlan on the Oghuz (Doc. 16)?*

CHAPTER FOUR

THE IRON CENTURY

Figure 4.1 Saint John of Rila. The saint refuses the gold brought to him by Emperor Peter. Painting in the church of Alexander Nevsky, Sofia, Bulgaria.

19. WULFSTAN TRAVELS TO TRUSO

Nothing is known about Wulfstan, except that he had an Old English name. He may have been a West Saxon in the service of King Alfred the Great (886–89). The account of his journey to the eastern Baltic region was in fact added to the Old English translation of Orosius's Historiae adversum paganos, *a work most likely commissioned by King Alfred. Although it is often assumed that the account below refers to one single journey, it is in fact a mixture of an account of a trip from Hedeby (in Schleswig-Holstein, northern Germany) to Truso (now Janów Pomorski, near Elbląg, in northern Poland) and Estland (Eastern Prussia, now divided between Poland and the Kaliningrad region of Russia), combined with geographical and ethnographic observations on the latter. This combination strongly suggests familiarity with the area, which indirectly points to multiple journeys. If so, Wulfstan may have given an account of his knowledge of the Baltic region, and not of a specific trip to Truso.*

Source: trans. J. Bately, "Wulfstan's Voyage and His Description of Estland," in *Wulfstan's Voyage: The Baltic Sea Region in the Early Viking Age as Seen from Shipboard,* ed. Anton Englert and Athena Trakadas (Roskilde: Viking Ship Museum, 2009), pp. 15–17.

Wulfstan said that he traveled from the Heaths [Hedeby], that he was in Truso in seven days and nights, that the ship was all the way running under sail. Wendland [the southern coast of the Baltic Sea in modern-day Germany and Poland] was on his starboard side, and on his port side were Langeland and Lolland and Falster and Skåne, and these lands all belong to Denmark. . . . Wendland was on our starboard side all the way to the mouth of the Vistula. This Vistula is a very large river, and it separates Witland and Wendland, and the abovementioned Witland belongs to the Ests [umbrella term for all speakers of Baltic languages in modern Lithuania, Latvia, and Estonia]. The Vistula extends out of Wendland and extends into Estlake [most likely the Vistula lagoon], and this Estlake is at least fifteen miles broad. Then the Elbing [now the Elbląg River that connects Lake Drużno with the Vistula Lagoon] comes from the east into the Estlake from the lake on the shore of which stands Truso. And they come out together into Estlake, the Elbing from the east and the Vistula from the south, from Wendland. And then the Elbing makes off with Vistula's name and extends from the lake west and north into the sea; therefore, it is called the mouth of the Vistula.

The abovementioned Estland is very large, and there is very many a stronghold and in each one of them there is a king. And there is a great deal of honey and fishing, and the king and the most powerful men drink mare's milk, while the poor and the slaves drink mead. There is much conflict between them. No ale is brewed amongst the Ests, but there is plenty of mead.

And there is among the Ests a custom that, when a man dies, he lies indoors uncremated with his kinsmen and friends for a month, or sometimes two, and kings and the other high-ranking men as much longer as they have more wealth. Sometimes they lie uncremated for half a year, aboveground in their houses. And all the time that the body is indoors, there has to be drinking and entertainment, until the day that they cremate him. On the day that they intend to carry him to the funeral pyre, they divide up what is left of his property after the drinking and entertainment into five or six parts, and sometimes more, depending on the amount of the property. Then they lay it down, the largest portion about a mile from the *tun* [probably homestead], then the second, then the third, until it is all laid out within that single mile. And the smallest portion must be closest to the *tun* where the dead man is lying. Then all the men with the swiftest horses in the land have to be assembled about five or six miles from the property. Then they all gallop toward the property. The man who has the fastest horse comes to the first and largest portion, and so each after the other, until everything is taken. The smallest portion goes to the man who gallops closest to the *tun* to get it. Each man then rides on his way with the property; they may have it all, and that is why fast horses are excessively expensive there.

And when his wealth is thus dispersed, then the dead man is carried out and cremated with his weapons and clothing. And they use up all his wealth with the long lying of the dead man indoors and with what they lay down by the highways, which the strangers gallop to and take. And that is the custom among the Ests that people of every nationality must be cremated there; and if a single bone is found unburned there, they must atone for it greatly. And there is among the Ests a people, who are able to cause coldness, and that is why the dead men lie there so long without decaying, because they bring about the coldness on him [*sic*]. And although two vessels full of ale or water should be set down, they bring it about that one of them is frozen over, whether it is summer or winter.

Questions: What notions of an afterlife are highlighted in Wulfstan's description of the Ests? In addition to establishing regular trade, what other goals did his visits to Estland have?

20. GEORGE THE BULGARIAN AND THE MAGYARS

The story below is the first of a collection of miracles known as the Narration of the Miracles of the Great and Glorious Martyr Saint George. *The collection was found in manuscripts dated to the fourteenth century, but many details of the text, not least those in the story of George the Bulgarian, indicate a much earlier date, namely the early tenth century. It is likely that some of the miracle stories are translations of texts initially written in Greek (although no such texts have survived), but the story of George the Bulgarian is clearly an original, Bulgarian work. As a matter of fact, tenth-century lead icons have been found on several sites in Bulgaria, particularly in strongholds along the Lower Danube. These small, portable objects show Saint George as a foot soldier and dragon fighter. These were imitations of larger and more expensive icons, but the fact that most, if not all, of them show Saint George strongly suggests that he was the saint to whom many of the soldiers in the garrisons of those forts were praying. Unlike the soldiers, George the Bulgarian was a commoner who was twice drafted for campaigns against the invading Magyars. He narrowly escaped being killed, and the significance of the story is that it shows in detail how, a generation after the conversion to Christianity, saints in Bulgaria came to be perceived as powerful intercessors.*

Source: trans. K. Petkov, *The Voices of Medieval Bulgaria, Seventh-Fifteenth Century: The Records of a Bygone Culture* (Leiden: Brill, 2008), pp. 44–46.

While he [Boris] was still living as a monk and Vladimir, his first son, ruled in his stead, by [Archangel] Michael and God's will Symeon overthrew his brother and sat on the throne [in 893]. Then the Magyars rose against him and captured his people; he fought them, but they won. In that year, I fought in the war. I had no rank, nor did I live where the prince did, but outside, with the people [that is, in the Outer Town of Preslav, in the civilian, satellite settlements serving the court]. When the Magyars gave us the chase, fifty of us took the same road. They followed us, and my horse began to get weary. I called out loud: "O Lord God of the Christians! Help me and deliver me through the prayers of the great martyr George!" Then I turned to Saint George and said: "Saint George, when I took the holy baptism, the priest gave me your name. I am your servant, save me now from the pagans!" Then the right front leg of my horse sunk into the earth and broke, but my comrades kept riding on. There was a small thicket in a gully there. I strung my bow, took the arrows in my hand, and ran toward it and away from my horse. Looking over my shoulder, I saw the Magyars closing on the horse, and I cried aloud: "Lord Jesus Christ, have mercy on me and save me in this hour!" And lo and behold, as soon as I cried these words, all in tears, my horse ran to me, its leg whole. The Magyars ran after it, wanting to catch it, but none of them even came close. I said again: "Glory to you, Lord, for you are never far away from those who call on you from the bottom of their hearts. Great George, be with me!" Then I mounted the horse and through God's power and Saint George's protection the Magyars, although they shot many arrows, did not harm me. Presently I found myself in my village, which is a three-day journey from the place where the Magyars shot at me. Two days later, only two of my comrades came back; the rest have been caught up and killed.

Then Symeon, having heard that the Magyars are threatening us one more time, led us again to war. I was in my house, in bed with my wife, when a clean-shaven man, so bright that I could not look him in the face appeared to me. He told me: "George, you have to go to war, but buy yourself another horse for that one will die suddenly on the third day of the journey. I command you to skin the leg that it broke so that you can see the power of the most holy Trinity and the help of the holy martyr George. But don't use what you will find on that leg for anything but an honorable cross and be silent about it until you see the glory of God." I asked: "Lord, who are you, and why cannot I look you in the face?" "I am," he said, "Christ's servant George, the one whom, when praying, you called on." I arose, as if from a dream, praised God and Saint George, and then, as the saint commanded, purchased another horse. Before I set off to war, I called the priest for a service, slaughtered my most expensive ox, ten sheep, and ten pigs, and gave away the meat to the poor. So, I went to war with two horses. As we rode, on the third day, my horse fell sick, fell down, and breathed its last. We were in a hurry, and my comrades were unwilling to allow me to skin the leg, but after I told them how it broke its leg as we fled, they agreed and waited for me for a while. We skinned the leg and found on it, just under the knee, three iron rings, which held the bone in place, for it had not broken clean off, but had cracked along the bone's length. We tried hard to pull out the rings, but in vain. Then we cut off the bone, laid it down on a rock and shattered it with our axes; thus, we managed to take the irons out. Marveling at the great and unspoken power of the Holy Trinity and the speedy assistance of the holy martyr George, we praised God and set off to war. With God's mercy, none of us died in that war, but we all returned safe and sound.

When I came back home, I found my wife burning with a severe fever. After a couple of weeks, seeing the sufferings of my wife, I took courage and prayed thus: "Lord, through the prayers of the one who gave birth to you, and those of the one that pleases you, Saint George, cure your servant, Maria!" Then I laid the three rings on her and she promptly arose, completely healed, and praised God and the holy martyr George. And I, having realized the Holy Trinity's mercy and love for humanity, called the blacksmith and told him: "Forge me, brother, a cross from these rings." And so he did, just like the saint had told me.

Many other miracles did that cross perform: demons were exorcised with it from the people, and through the prayers of the great and holy martyr George it helped the lame and in wars.

Questions: Why does the document's author mention that the apparition that George saw in his house was "a clean-shaven man"? What does the detail about the blacksmith being available for orders suggest about the social and economic relations in Bulgaria, c. 900? In addition to war, what other things does George do for a living? Why is there so much emphasis on the horse?

21. JOHN THE EXARCH ON SYMEON THE GREAT

John the Exarch was one of the leading scholars in Preslav at the end of the ninth through the first decades of the tenth century. Little is known about his life, except what he says about himself in his work. He was of noble Bulgar origin, a fact to which he often refers with pride. The epithet "Exarch" suggests that he was a member of the high clergy in Preslav. He compiled an exegetical work entitled Heavens, *but his literary reputation rests on a compilation modeled on similar Greek works, entitled* Six Days (Shestodnev, or Hexaemeron). *As the title suggests, in this work John blended the biblical account of the six days of Creation with excerpts from scientific and philosophical works. In addition, John wrote many sermons and eulogies. One of them is* In Praise of Tsar Symeon, *in which John singled out Symeon's education and love for books. All this impressive output shows John to have been well versed in Greek, and most likely educated in Constantinople. He may well have been one of Symeon's classmates. In his* Six Days, *while addressing Symeon, John imagined a visit to the royal court in Preslav.*

Source: trans. K. Petkov, *The Voices of Medieval Bulgaria, Seventh-Fifteenth Century: The Records of a Bygone Culture* (Leiden: Brill, 2008), pp. 90–91.

Sire, let the Creator and Artist without paragon enlighten your heart, O great Christ-lover, Tsar Symeon, and the hearts of all your men and subjects. Let him [God] grant you to learn and understand, to the extent that it is humanly possible, the work of his artful design, and arm you with his commandments, which illuminate the eyes of wisdom. . . . However, if the simple folk who live outside of the capital have a chance to catch a glimpse of the prince artfully painted with colors on the wall—dressed in his gold-woven mantle, wearing a golden necklace, girded with a velvet belt, his shoulders sprinkled with pearls, girded with a golden sword—if they could only see him in such vestments, they will marvel, and as they think about it, they will say: "If his image is so amazing, how much greater should he be in reality!"

If a humble and poor man, or a stranger, catches a glimpse from far away of the towering walls of the princely residence, he is astonished. And as he approaches the gates, he marvels and asks questions. As he enters, he sees towering buildings on both sides, adorned with stone and embellished with wood and other things. But when he comes into the citadel and beholds the tall palaces and the churches, richly decorated with stone, wood, and paint, and on the inside with marble, copper, silver, and gold, he knows not to what he should compare them, for he has seen nothing in his land but straw-covered huts. The poor one is so amazed that he goes out of his mind!

However, if he happens to see the prince—sitting in his mantle covered with pearls, with a golden necklace on his neck, girded with a velvet belt, with bracelets on his arms and a golden sword at his side—and the boyars around him with golden necklaces, belts, and bracelets—and then, when he goes back to his land, if someone asked him: "What did you see there?" he would say: "I don't know how to account for this, because you can only comprehend such beauty and order if you see them with your own eyes. One has to see this with one's own eyes and reflect on it with one's incorporeal mind to be able to truly appreciate it. For one's own eyes do not deceive; they might mislead but still they provide the truest [picture]. . . ."

Questions: According to John the Exarch, what elements of the representation of power are most conspicuous in the eyes of a "humble and poor man"? What are the symbols of power displayed by the prince and the boyars? Compare the representation of power in this document to that in the answers that Boris received from Pope Nicholas I (Doc. 14).

22. A HERMIT MEETS AN EMPEROR

Saint John of Rila is the prime figure of Bulgarian monasticism in the tenth century. He was born in 880 in a village near Sredec (present-day Sofia) and was a shepherd by the time he felt he had been called to remove himself from his village and society. Initially, he chose a tree as his house (a choice indicating that his model of ascetism was that of so-called dendritic saints, such as Saint David of Thessalonica in the late sixth century, who lived in a tree). He then moved to a monastery on Mount Ruen (in the Osogovo Range near the present-day border between Macedonia and Bulgaria), where he took the monastic vows. Soon after that, he left the monastery and went into the wilderness. He lived for three years and six months in a cave in the Rila Mountains. Aspiring to the ascetic values of the early stylites (saints who lived on top of pillars, such as the fifth-century saint Symeon the Stylite), he moved to a rock, on top of which he remained for seven years and four months. From there he moved to another rocky place in the valley of the Upper Struma, then to Mount Vitosha near Sofia, and finally he returned to Rila, where he died in 946. He was immediately recognized as a saint, but despite his enormous popularity, the earliest biography ("life") was written in Old Church Slavonic only in the twelfth century, at some point before 1185, by an unknown author. This text is known as the Folk Life of Saint John of Rila *because another biography was written in Greek in the twelfth century by George Skylitzes, a Byzantine official in Sredec (Sofia). Three other biographies were written later, in the thirteenth and fourteenth centuries, a clear indication of the growing popularity of the saint's cult. The* Folk Life *claims that already during his lifetime, Saint John had become so famous as to attract the attention of Emperor Peter of Bulgaria, who sought an interview with him. This episode is of course a story meant for a monastic audience, to which the unknown author wanted to send a clear message: you should avoid as much as possible royal (or imperial) patronage and entanglement with the secular world, for true hermits reject all of that.*

Source: trans. K. Petkov, *The Voices of Medieval Bulgaria, Seventh-Fifteenth Century: The Records of a Bygone Culture* (Leiden: Brill, 2008), pp. 168–69.

At that time, as the rumor about the saint spread, Emperor Peter happened to be in Sredec. The emperor heard about him, selected nine men, all skillful hunters, and commanded them to go in the mountains of Rila to hunt, telling them: "Do not come back to me until you find the place of the holy father, so that I can go there myself and bow down to him." The men went hunting as they were ordered. They sought the place of the saint but were not able to find it. They spent many days on the mountain, but they neither caught any game, nor found out the saint's whereabouts. They were therefore troubled and did not dare to return to the emperor, for they had accomplished none of the tasks entrusted to them. Moreover, they went hungry for several days. So, they called the name of the saint out loud, and prayed, saying: "Saintly father, reveal yourself to us, so that we do not perish [on the order] of the emperor!" He took mercy on them, for the holy father knew the emperor's decision and thoughts. At that same time, they found a narrow path [in the woods]. They praised God, followed the path, and found [Saint John]. The holy father beheld them and asked: "Children, why have you come [here]? Have you really not eaten anything [until now]?" He had already perceived that they had been fasting for five days, and [indeed] they confessed the entire truth to him. At that moment, an angel from heaven brought food for the saint in the form of rosehip fruits. At God's command, these were transformed into the food of Communion [bread]. [John] called [the hunters] to partake of the food. However, there was a man among them who was used to eating a lot. As he saw the tiny piece of bread, he thought to himself, and said: "What is this minuscule bread to all of us, nine men?" The holy father John learned his thought, sighed, and said in his heart to God: "Lord, as you sated five thousand people with five loaves, work your miracle here and bless this table" [Matt. 14:17–21]. And they all ate their fill and still half of the bread remained. One of those hunters was sick, but after eating the bread, he immediately recovered, as the scripture says: "Man ate the bread of angels" [Ps. 77:25].

After that, the men praised God and left. Rejoicing, they went back to the emperor and told him everything that they had seen when visiting the saint. Emperor Peter listened to their account and praised God. He took along many people and his soldiers and set off to meet the holy father. As he reached the river called Rila, they told him: "Do you see where this river springs? That is where the holy father is and where he lives." [The emperor] followed the river upstream and reached a rocky place called Stog, but could not cross over, for it was steep and narrow. [So] they [took a detour and] went up the mountains called Knishava, and from there [the hunters] pointed out to [the emperor] the forest and the rock on which the holy father dwelt. The emperor wanted very much to go there, but was not able to do so, because of the wilderness. So, he promptly sent out two young men, and told them: "When you get there, tell the holy father: 'Father, I have come to behold your holy face, if possible.'" The holy father replied to them, saying, "Go and tell him: 'Saintly and glorious emperor, what is not possible for man is possible for God. If you see me and I see you, pitch your tent on the peak, and I will make smoke [to signal to you]. You will see the smoke, and I will see the tent, because it has been commanded that we see each other in that way.'" The holy father made smoke [that went up] like a column in the sky. Emperor Peter saw the sign of the holy father, and the holy father looked up at the tent. Both praised God and bowed to each other. Then Emperor Peter filled a cup with gold and sent it to him, saying: "Please accept this from my majesty and use it any way you wish." The holy father John took the cup but sent the gold back telling the two young men that the emperor had sent to him: "Go and tell this to the emperor: 'Your brother says: My brother, man shall not live on bread alone, but on God's word as well, as it is written in the Gospels [Matt. 4:4]. I, brother, have no troops to arm, and no goods to buy. Keep your gold, for you really need it. I will keep the cup as a token to remind me of you, and as a sign of the world.'" And he sent back the gold, keeping the cup, and said to the young men: "Tell this to the emperor: 'Leave this place at once, for it is dangerous, lest you and those with you perish!'" As soon as he heard the words of the saint, the emperor left the place. From that time until this day, that place is called "the Peak of the Emperor." . . .

After many days had passed, Emperor Peter sent [his men] again to find out about the holy father. They searched again but could not find him. [Fearing for their lives,] they returned to the emperor, saying: "We did not find him." The emperor took pity on them, praised God, and said: "Verily, I was not worthy of seeing the saint."

Questions: What does the biographer of Saint John suggest about the relation between Emperor Peter and the Church? What form of monastic life is favored in this text? Why did Emperor Peter insist on seeing Saint John? How did John sustain himself in the wilderness?

23. *SKYLITZES CONTINUATUS* ON THE BULGARIAN-BYZANTINE WAR

Four manuscripts of John Skylitzes's Synopsis of Histories, *all dated to the twelfth century, each contain a supplementary text covering the period between the years 1057 and 1079/80. Some historians claim that this text, conventionally called* Skylitzes Continuatus, *was in fact written by John Skylitzes himself, as an addendum to his* Synopsis. *Others point out that the addition was made by another, unknown, author who, unlike John Skylitzes, was familiar both with the geography and the history of Bulgaria. The unknown author must therefore have written at some point in the early twelfth century, possibly in Constantinople.*

Source: trans. P. Murdzhev from V. Tăpkova-Zaimova, *Bulgarians by Birth: The Comitopuls, Emperor Samuel and Their Successors According to Historical Sources and the Historiographic Tradition* (Leiden: Brill, 2017), pp. 108–09.

When Emperor John [Tzimiskes, 969–76] died and [Bardas] Skleros broke away, and their relative, Emperor Basil [II, 976–1025], set out for the settlements in Thrace, they [Boris and Roman, sons of Boris II, the last emperor of independent Bulgaria] fled from there [Constantinople, where they had been held in captivity by John Tzimiskes] and hurried to reach Bulgaria. However, Boris, while passing through a forest, was hit by an arrow [shot] by some deaf Bulgarian, who did not hear that he was Boris, but because of his clothes decided that he was a Roman, and [Boris] died. Meanwhile, Roman escaped to Vidin [town on the Danube, in northwestern Bulgaria] and after a while, he returned to the capital, as it would be disclosed further. From those four brothers [sons of a certain count named Nikola, hence their collective name of "Comitopuls," that is, "sons of the count," in Greek], David died soon after the rebellion, killed between Kastoria and Prespa next to a place called Beautiful Oaks, by some "traveling" Vlachs. While besieging Serres, Moses was slain by one of the soldiers of Duke Melissinos, as his horse fell. Aaron, who sympathized with the Romans, as it was said, was killed with his entire family on 14 June [probably 977], by his brother Samuel in the place called Ramitsanitsa, as only his son, John Vladislav-Svetoslav was spared by Gabriel Radomir, the son of Samuel.

He [Samuel] carried out the relics of Saint Achilles (who had been the bishop of Larissa during the reign of Constantine the Great and a participant in the Great First Council, together with Riginus of Skopje and Diodorus of Thrace) and moved them to Prespa, where his palaces were located, and built a beautiful and magnificent church, which he dedicated to the saint.

As he [Emperor Basil II] passed through the passes and thickets of Triadica, the former Serdica [now Sofia] (where the council of three hundred western bishops had taken place, under the rule of Constans, emperor of the west, and of Constantius, emperor of the east, both the sons of Constantine the Great), he found out a place called Stiponion, where he built a fortified camp and pondered how to conquer Serdica by siege. . . .

As Samuel and Aaron, along with Roman, took, as it seemed, the disorderly withdrawal [of the Byzantine army] for a rout, they frightened the Romans with war cries and screams, and forced them to flee, and captured their military camp and properties, and the imperial tent, and the banner of the emperor. . . .

The next year, the emperor [Basil II] set off for Bulgaria through Thessaloniki, and Dobromir, the ruler of Beroia [now Veroia, in northern Greece], who was married to Samuel's niece, came and surrendered his town to the emperor, who honored him with the title of *anthypatos* [provincial governor]. The defender of Kolindros, Demetrios Tikhon, who did not surrender his town, was allowed by the emperor to withdraw together with his army, so he left and went to Samuel. . . .

As he [Basil II] approached the town of Skopje, he discovered that Samuel had encamped his army carelessly on the other side of the Axios River (now it is called Bardarios [modern-day Vardar] because of the shifting of its old riverbed through a canal constructed by Bardas Skleros, where it now flows). Then Samuel, who had set ambushes in proper places, captured the patrician John Chaldos, duke of Thessaloniki. . . .

As he was about to drink water, he [Samuel] had a heart attack and died in two days, on the sixth day of October [1014]. His son Gabriel Radomir, who assumed the power over the Bulgarians, surpassed his father in physical strength and power, but in intelligence and alertness, he was very much his inferior.

Questions: What tactics were employed by Samuel to ensure victory against the Byzantines? What was the fate of Dobromir? What does the account in Skylitzes Continuatus *reveal about Byzantine attitudes toward the Bulgarians?*

24. ECHOES OF THE BULGARIAN-BYZANTINE WAR IN FRANCE AND IN SYRIA

Within a couple of decades after the events taking place in the Balkans in the late tenth and early eleventh centuries, the news of the Bulgarian-Byzantine war reached as far west as France and as far east as Syria. To the west, the news probably traveled with pilgrims returning from the Holy Land via Constantinople. Ademar of Chabannes, who at that time was a monk, learned about the events in his abbey of St-Martial of Limoges (Aquitaine), where he was about to finish his History of the Franks *in three books. The last book, which ends with events dated 1028, has the information about the Bulgarian-Byzantine war immediately after the mention of Robert II as sole king of France, following the death of his father, Hugh Capet (997). To the east, details of the conflict in the Balkans reached a Melkite (Christian) physician from Egypt, who had taken refuge from Muslim persecution in Antioch, the great city on the Orontes River that was at that time under Byzantine control. Yahya ibn Said (known to historians as Yahya of Antioch) wrote his chronicle in Arabic to cover the events between the years 934 and 1034.*

Source: trans. F. Curta from Ademar of Chabannes, *Historia*, ed. G. Waitz, *Monumenta Germaniae Historica, Scriptores* 4 (Hanover: Hahn, 1841), p. 131; trans. P. Murdzhev from V. Tăpkova-Zaimova, *Bulgarians by Birth: The Comitopuls, Emperor Samuel and Their Successors According to Historical Sources and the Historiographic Tradition* (Leiden: Brill, 2017), pp. 167–68.

3.32. [Ademar of Chabannes] At that time, the Bulgarians rose in rebellion and laid waste to Greece. Angered by those enemies, Emperor Basil made a vow before God to become a monk, if the Greeks would subdue them. He worked tirelessly to do that for fifteen years, during which he was defeated in two major encounters. At last, after the kings of the Bulgarians, Samuel and Aaron, were killed, not in a battle, but through Greek cunning, he took their entire land, destroyed their strongest towns and forts, ordered Greek troops to move there against [the Bulgarians], and took in captivity the large majority of the Bulgarian people. And as he had promised, he began sporting a Greek monk's robe underneath his imperial attire, [and continued to do so] all the time for the rest of his life, abstaining from pleasures and from eating meat.

[Yahya of Antioch] The two sons of Samuel [in fact, of Boris II], whom John Tzimiskes had captured and who lived as prisoners in the imperial palace, cleverly managed to escape from that place where they were kept [Constantinople] and took off on the horses that they had prepared to have ready in advance. When they reached the gorges leading to Bulgaria, they stopped. They dismounted and went into hiding in the mountains, for they feared being pursued and caught [by the Byzantines]. And they continued their trip by foot. The older brother, who was in disguise, led the way ahead of his younger brother. A party of Bulgarians, who were guarding those mountains against bandits, caught sight of him. One of those guards, who did not recognize him, because he was alone, killed him with an arrow. The younger brother, when finally arriving at that spot, told those people who he was. So, they took him and made him their emperor. He had a slave, known by the name Komitopoulos [Samuel?], who was close to him. The Bulgarians gathered around him and took the country of the Greeks by assault. The emperor [Basil II] marched against them with a great army. He set up camp in front of their town named Abariyah [most likely Triadica, now Sofia] and besieged it. During the night, a rumor started, according to which the pass across the mountains [behind the Greek army] had been blocked. And on Tuesday of the seventeenth of the month of *ab* [August] of the year 1297 [986] . . . the emperor fled with all of his army rushing through the pass. The Bulgarians followed him and plundered all his supplies and treasury, and a great number of his soldiers perished.

Questions: What role does Samuel play in these two accounts of the Byzantine-Bulgarian war? What does Ademar of Chabannes's portrait of Emperor Basil II suggest about the image of the victor? How are the Bulgarian people, in general, depicted in Yahya ibn Said's chronicle?

25. VARANGIANS IN RUS'

The Primary Chronicle *is the name conventionally adopted in English for the first compilation of historical writing in eastern Europe, which is otherwise entitled* The

Tale of Bygone Years. *The text was written in Old Church Slavonic by several authors, most likely monks, the last of whom finished writing in c. 1113. Some argue that the compilation is based on earlier annals, while others believe that the* Tale *is a true chronicle and was written as such from the very beginning. In early twelfth-century Rus', annals and particularly the* Tale *had eschatological significance, for they were a record of human activity intended to be consulted at the Last Judgment or, on the contrary, to offer certain individuals (who are mentioned by name in the annals) the opportunity to repent during their lifetime. The segment in the annals that refers to the history of early Rus' is known only from the* Primary Chronicle, *which is the only source that mentions Rurik, Sineus, Truvor, Askold, and Dir. Nor are any of the sources known on which the author(s) relied for the story of how the Rus' came to Russia. There is therefore a great deal of debate among historians about the veracity of the account of the coming of the Varangians, and about the beginnings of such towns as Novgorod and Kiev. The "calling of the Varangians" in particular is at the center of the "Normannist problem"—whether the medieval state in what is now Russia was established by Scandinavians or by Slavs. The author's insistence that the inhabitants of Novgorod used to be Slavs but were now (during his lifetime) descendants of Varangians has simply compounded the problem, for the political center of Rus' in the twelfth century was in Kiev, not in Novgorod.*

Source: trans. S. Hazzard Cross and O.P. Sherbowitz-Wetzor, *The Russian Primary Chronicle: Laurentian Text* (Cambridge, MA: Medieval Academy of America, 1953), pp. 59–60.

6367 [*anno mundi*, that is, from Creation, which is CE 859]. The Varangians from beyond the sea imposed tribute upon the Chuds [Finns], the Slavs, the Merians, the Ves', and the Krivichians. . . .

6368–70 (860–62). The tributaries of the Varangians drove them back beyond the sea and, refusing them further tribute, set out to govern themselves. There was no law among them, but tribe rose against tribe. Discord thus ensued among them, and they began to war one against another. They said to themselves, "Let us seek a prince who may rule over us and judge us according to the law." They accordingly went overseas to the Varangian Russes: these particular Varangians were known as Russes, just as some are called Swedes, and other Normans, English, and Gotlanders, for they were thus named. The Chuds, the Slavs, the Krivichians and the Ves' then said to the people of Rus', "Our land is great and rich, but there is no order in it. Come to rule and reign over us." They thus selected three brothers, with their kinsfolk, who took with them all the Russes and migrated. The oldest, Rurik, located himself in Novgorod; the second, Sineus, at Beloozero; and the third, Truvor, in Izborsk. On account of these Varangians, the district of Novgorod became known as the land of the Rus'. The present inhabitants of Novgorod are descended from the Varangian race, but aforetime they were Slavs.

After two years, Sineus and his brother Truvor died, and Rurik assumed the sole authority. He assigned cities to his followers, Polotsk to one, Rostov to another, and to another Beloozero. In these cities there are thus Varangian colonists, but the first settlers were, in Novgorod, Slavs; in Polotsk, Krivichians; in Beloozero, Ves', in Rostov, Merians; and in Murom, Muromians. Rurik had dominion over all these districts.

With Rurik there were two men who did not belong to his kin but were boyars [noblemen]. They obtained permission to go to Constantinople with their families. They thus sailed down the Dnieper, and in the course of their journey they saw a small city on a hill. Upon their inquiry as to whose town it was, they were informed that three brothers, Kiy, Shchek, and Khoriv, had once built the city, but that since their deaths, their descendants were living there as tributaries of the Khazars. Askold and Dir remained in the city, and after gathering together many Varangians, they established their dominion over the country of the Polyanians at the same time that Rurik was ruling at Novgorod.

Questions: What is the role attributed to Rurik in the Primary Chronicle*? What dangers did the town of Kiy, Shchek, and Khoriv pose for the Varangian power center in Novgorod? How does the Rus' annalist feel about the Varangian involvement in the affairs of the Churds, Slavs, Krivichians, and Ves'?*

26. EMPEROR CONSTANTINE VII PORPHYROGENITUS ON THE RUS'

There has been much scholarly discussion about the sources of the compilation known as On the Administration of the Empire, *which was commissioned (if not coauthored) by Emperor Constantine VII Porphyrogenitus (913–59). No section or chapter of the text indicates the source of the information, and, with a few exceptions, such cannot be identified. One of the most conspicuous exceptions is Chapter 9, in which a vivid description of the Rus' is given, complete with their movements along the trade route linking Kiev to Constantinople. One of the most interesting aspects of the account in Chapter 9 is a description of the Dnieper rapids, for which the author of the text provides parallel Scandinavian (Rus') and Slavic names. This suggests that the account is based on information obtained from someone who was familiar with the itinerary followed by the Rus' warrior-merchants, with the two languages in which they named the rapids, as well as with the Greek language and some of the monuments in Constantinople, such as the Hippodrome, whose size is compared to the ford at Krarion (now Pavlo-Kichkas, on the northern outskirts of Zaporizhzhia, in Ukraine). Some have ventured to suggest a Rus' merchant who spoke Slavic; others have advanced the idea that the informant must have been a member of the Byzantine embassy sent to Kiev, probably on the occasion of the treaty of 944. Still others have noted that many of the Slavic names in the account display features that are closer to South Slavic (especially Bulgarian), not East Slavic languages (such as Russian). Bulgarians were most likely involved in the negotiations between the Rus' and the Byzantines, and Bulgarian influences have also been identified in the texts of the treaties of 911 and 944, as reproduced (in Old Church Slavonic) in the* Primary Chronicle. *There are seven rapids described in Chapter 9 of* On the Administration of the Empire. *They are now submerged by the water of a very large reservoir between the Ukrainian cities of Dnipro and Zaporizhzhia (the name of which actually means "behind the rapids").*

Source: trans. R.J.H. Jenkins, Constantine VII Porphyrogenitus, *De Administrando imperio* (Washington, DC: Dumbarton Oaks Center for Byzantine Studies, 1967), pp. 57, 59, 61, and 63.

The dugouts which come down from outer Rus' to Constantinople are from Novgorod, where Sviatoslav, son of Igor, prince of Rus', had his seat, and others from the city of Smolensk and from Teliutza [Liubech?] and Chernigov [now Chernihiv, in Ukraine] and from Vyshegrad [now Vyshhorod, on the northern outskirts of Kiev, Ukraine]. All these come down the River Dnieper, and are collected together at the city of Kiev, [and those summons are] also called *Sambatas.* Their Slav tributaries, the so-called Krivichians and the Lenzanenes and the rest of the Slavonic regions, cut the dugouts on their mountains in time of winter, and when they have prepared them, as spring approaches, and the ice melts, they bring them on to the neighboring lakes. And since these lakes debouch into the River Dnieper, they enter thence on to this same river and come down to Kiev and draw the ships along to be finished and sell them to the Rus'. The Rus' buy these bottoms only, furnishing them with oars and oarlocks and other tackle from their old dugouts, which they dismantle; and so they fit them out. And in the month of June they move off down the River Dnieper and come to Vitichev, which is a tributary city of the Rus', and there gather during two or three days; and when all the dugouts are collected together, then they set out, and come down the said Dnieper River. And first they come to the first barrage [one of the rapids on the Lower Dnieper now under a large reservoir], called Essoupi, which means in Rus' and Slavonic "Do not sleep!" . . . Therefore, the Rus' do not venture to pass between them [that is, sail through the rapids], but put in to the bank nearby, disembarking the men on to dry land leaving the rest of the goods on board the dugouts; they then strip and, feeling with their feet to avoid striking on a rock. . . . This they do, some at the prow, some amidships, while others again, in the stern, punt with poles; and with this careful procedure they pass this first barrage, they re-embark the others from the dry land and sail away. . . . It is at this point, therefore, that the Pechenegs come down and attack the Rus'. After traversing this place, they reach the island called Saint Gregory [Khortytsia, near Zaporizhzhia], on which island they perform their sacrifices because a gigantic oak tree stands there; and they sacrifice live cocks.

Arrows, too, they peg in round about, and others bread and meat, or something of whatever each may have, as is their custom. They also throw lots regarding the cocks, whether to slaughter them, or to eat them as well, or to leave them alive. From this island onward the Rus' do not fear the Pechenegs until they reach the River Selinas [Sulina, the middle branch of the Danube delta]. . . . And until they are past the River Selinas, the Pechenegs keep pace with them [on land]. And if it happens that the sea casts a dugout on shore, they all put in to land, in order to present a united opposition to the Pechenegs. But after the Selinas they fear nobody, but entering the territory of Bulgaria, they come to the mouth of the Danube. . . . The severe manner of life of these same Rus' in wintertime is as follows. When the month of November begins, their chiefs together with all the Rus' at once leave Kiev and go off on the "*poliudia*," which means "rounds," that is to the Slavonic regions of the Vervians and Drugovichians and Krivichians and Severians and the rest of the Slavs who are tributaries to the Rus'. There they are maintained throughout the winter, but then once more, starting from the month of April, when the ice of the Dnieper River melts, they come back to Kiev. They then pick up their dugouts, as has been said above, and fit them out, and come down to Romania [that is, Byzantium].

Questions: What was the political situation in Rus' at the moment of Emperor Constantine's account? What role did the tribes in the "Slavonic regions" play in the trade of the Rus' with Byzantium? Judging from the information provided by the later Primary Chronicle, *why was Kiev an important place for summons? What is the attitude of this document's author toward the Rus'?*

27. A TRADE AGREEMENT BETWEEN THE RUS' AND BYZANTIUM

According to the Primary Chronicle, *Igor, prince of Rus', attacked Byzantium in 941. Many historians have interpreted this attack as a raid with political goals, namely to induce terror and to force a revision of the already favorable terms of the commercial treaty of 911 between the Rus' and Byzantium. If that was Igor's intention, the plan did not work. True, a new treaty was established with Byzantium in 944, but this agreement, while repeating the terms of the previous treaty (as well as those of the treaty of 907), introduced a number of changes that shed some light on the realities on the ground that may have prompted Igor to attack Byzantium three years earlier. As the list below clearly shows, there were many more Rus' traders in 944 than in 911. The Rus' were not allowed to spend the winter at the mouth of the Dnieper, an indication that permanent Rus' settlements in the region were regarded as dangerous for the Byzantine territories in the Crimea. The Byzantines put restrictions on the quantity of silk that the Rus' could purchase in Constantinople—no more than the value of fifty gold coins.*

This suggests that the Rus' reexported the silk to the northern parts of Europe in large quantities, as confirmed by archaeological finds in Birka (Sweden) and York (England). The requirement for Rus' merchants to carry seals issued by Igor is another indication of dramatic changes taking place. The seals were meant to guarantee that those men were truly merchants (and not spies), but certificates issued by Igor have a different meaning. The prince in Kiev seems to have been concerned with controlling the volume of trade taking place with Byzantium, no doubt in order to eliminate competitors. As the treaty also mentions that, upon request, the great prince of Rus' could send as many warriors as needed to Byzantium, Igor wanted not only to control the trade with Byzantium, but also to monitor the recruitment of Varangian mercenaries for the imperial army.

Source: trans. S. Hazzard Cross and O.P. Sherbowitz-Wetzor, *The Russian Primary Chronicle: Laurentian Text* (Cambridge, MA: Medieval Academy of America, 1953), pp. 73–75.

Romanus [I Lekapenos, emperor between 919 and 945], Constantine, and Stephen [Romanus's younger sons, co-emperors since 924] sent envoys to Igor to renew the previous treaty, and Igor discussed the matter with them. Igor sent his envoys to Romanus, and the emperor called together his boyars and his dignitaries. The Rus' envoys were introduced and bidden to speak, and it was commanded that the remarks of both parties should be inscribed upon parchment. A copy of the agreement concluded under the most Christian princes Romanus, Constantine, and Stephen follows:

"We are the envoys from the Rus' nation: Ivar, envoy of Igor, great prince of Rus', and the general envoys as follows: Vefast representing Sviatoslav, son of Igor; Isgaut for the Princess Olga; Slothi for Igor, nephew of Igor; Oleif for Vladislav; Kanitzar for Predslava; Sigbjorn for Svanhild, the wife of Oleif; Freystein for Thorth; Leif for Arfast; Grim for Sverki; Freystein for Haakon, nephew of Igor; Kari for Stoething; Karlsefni for Thorth; Hegri for Efling; Voist for Voik; Eistr for Amund; Freystein for Bjorn; Yatving for Gunnar; Sigfrid for Halfdan; Kill for Klakki; Steggi for Jotun; Sverki; Hallvarth for Guthi; Frothi for Throand; Munthor for Ut; the merchants Authun, Authulf, Ingivald, Oleif, Frutaan, Gamal, Kussi, Heming, Thorfrid, Thorstein, Bruni, Hroald, Gunnfast, Freystein, Ingjald, Thorbjorn, Manni, Hroald, Svein, Styr, Halfdan, Tirr, Askbrand, Visleif, Sveinki, Borich: sent by Igor, great prince of Rus', and from each prince and all the people of the land of Rus', by whom is ordained the renewal of the former peace to the confusion of the devil, who hates peace and loves discord, and to the establishment of concord between Greeks and Rus' for many years to come.

Our great prince Igor, and his princes and his boyars, and the whole people of Rus' have sent us to Romanus, Constantine, and Stephen the mighty emperors of Greece, to establish a bond of friendship with the emperors themselves, as well as with all their boyars and the entire Greek nation henceforth and forever, as long as the sun shines and the world stands fixed. If any inhabitant of the land of Rus' thinks to violate this amity, may such of these transgressors as have adopted the Christian faith incur well-deserved punishment from Almighty God in the shape of damnation and destruction forevermore. If any of these transgressors be not baptized, may they receive help neither from God nor from Perun [one of the gods worshipped by the Rus']: may they not be protected by their own shields, but may they rather be slain by their own swords, laid low by their own arrows or by any of their own weapons, and may they be in bondage forever.

The great prince of Rus' and his boyars shall send to Greece to the great Greek emperors as many ships as they desire with their agents and merchants, according to the prevailing usage. The agents hitherto carried gold seals, and the merchants silver ones. But your prince [Igor] has now made known that he will forward a certificate to our government [in Byzantium], and any agents or merchants thus sent by the Rus' shall be provided with such a certificate to the effect that a given number of ships has been dispatched. By this means we shall be assured that they come with peaceful intent.

But if such persons come uncertified and are surrendered to us, we shall detain and hold them until we notify your prince. If they do not surrender, but offer resistance, they shall be killed, and indemnity for their death shall not be exacted by your prince. If, however, they flee to Rus', we shall so inform your prince, and he shall deal with them as he sees fit.

If Rus' come without merchandise, they may not be entitled to receive monthly allowance. Your prince shall moreover prohibit his agents and such other Rus' as come hither from the commission of violence in our villages and territory. Such Rus' as come hither shall dwell by the church of St-Mamas [outside the city of Constantinople]. Our authorities shall take their names, and they shall then receive their monthly allowance, the agents the amount proper to their position, and the merchants the usual amount; first, those from Kiev, then those from Chernigov and Pereiaslavl. They shall enter the city [of Constantinople] through one gate in groups of fifty without weapons, and shall dispose of their merchandise as they require, after which they shall depart. An officer of our government shall guard them, in order that, if any Rus' or Greek does wrong, he may redress it."

Questions: What does the document suggest about the relation between the "great prince of Rus'" and his boyars? Why did Rus' merchants have to carry silver seals when coming to Constantinople? What kind of relations are stipulated between Rus' who were not merchants and the imperial government?

CHAPTER FIVE

THE BALKANS BETWEEN THE NINTH AND THE TWELFTH CENTURIES

Figure 5.1 Inscription of Süleyman Köy (now Sechishte, Bulgaria), with the clauses of the Thirty-Year Peace (816) between Bulgaria and Byzantium.

28. THE RESETTLEMENT OF THE PELOPONNESE

Few are the written sources pertaining to the history of Greece in the Early Middle Ages that have caused more debate than the Chronicle of Monemvasia. *Written in 900 or 901 to support the claims that the metropolitan of Patras made to the suffragan see of Lakedaimon against the metropolitan of Corinth, perhaps in anticipation of a reorganization of diocesan boundaries, this was not a chronicle properly speaking, but a tract with clearly propagandistic purposes. If, as seems likely, the unknown author wrote in Constantinople, his intention may have been to provide a historical basis for the metropolitan of Patras to claim the see of Lakedaimon. Since the bishop of that see had long been a suffragan of Corinth, the only way to justify its subordination to Patras was to claim that the old Lakedaimon in existence during the "thirty-second year of the reign of Justinian the Great" was destroyed by barbarian invasions, which prompted its inhabitants to abandon the city and to move to Sicily. Lakedaimon was then refounded by Emperor Nicephorus I, who repopulated the city with* stratiotai *(peasant-soldiers) from different parts of the empire. When the Justinianic city was abandoned because of the invasion of the barbarians, its bishop, together with that part of his flock that did not go to Sicily, moved to an "inaccessible place by the seashore," where they all built another city named Monemvasia, hence the title of the "chronicle." To give further weight to the argument, the author of the* Chronicle of Monemvasia*—no doubt a learned churchman with access to a number of sixth-, seventh-, and ninth-century sources—introduced the Avars into the narrative, in order to explain that after conquering the Peloponnese, they destroyed and drove out the native "Hellenic nations," and finally settled in the region, which they held for 218 years. However, at the end of that long period of barbarian rule, those whom the* strategos *Skleros defeated under Emperor Nicephorus I were Slavs, not Avars. While ordering the conversion of the defeated barbarians to Christianity, the emperor recalled the old inhabitants from the lands to which their ancestors had initially fled. There is of course no reason to take this story at face value, despite the controversy surrounding the authenticity of the* Chronicle of Monemvasia *ever since the early nineteenth century, when the German journalist Jakob Philipp Fallmerayer (1790–1861) used this source to claim that modern Greeks were descendants not of the ancient Greeks, but of Slavs and Albanians. However, less attention has been paid to the reasons for such an elaborate story, complete with chronological details and geographical references. The unknown author most probably wanted to forestall accusations of infringement of canon law, which clearly prohibited the coexistence of two metropolitans within one and the same province.*

Source: trans. F. Curta from *Cronaca di Monemvasia*, ed. I. Duĭchev (Palermo: Istituto siciliano di studi bizantini e neoellenici, 1976), pp. 18, 20, and 22.

As only the eastern part of the Peloponnese, from Corinth to [Cape] Malea [a peninsula in the southeastern Peloponnese], was free of the Slavic people, because of its rugged and inaccessible nature, the emperor of the Romans sent [to that part] a *strategos* [general and governor] of the Peloponnese. One of those *strategoi* [possibly Leo Skleros, *strategos* of Peloponnesos in 811], a native of Lesser Armenia [the territory of historic Armenia located to the west and northwest of the Euphrates River] and from the family of the so-called Skleroi [prominent family of the Byzantine military aristocracy in the ninth century] came to battle with the Slavic people, bringing them by force under his power and annihilating them completely. After that, he allowed the old inhabitants to recuperate their abodes. Hearing that, the aforementioned emperor Nicephorus [I, 802–11], full of joy, promptly ordered cities to be rebuilt in that region and all the churches that the barbarians had destroyed. He [also ordered] those same barbarians [the Slavs] to be Christianized. Therefore, inquiring about the place where the exiles from Patras lived [at that time] after their migration, he gave an order that they be reestablished in their old homes together with their bishop, whose name was Athanasius. He [the emperor] gave to the city of Patras, which until then had been an archbishopric, the rights of a metropolis.

While our holy father Athanasius was still patriarch [possibly Athanasius, bishop of Methone in the ninth century], he [Emperor Nicephorus I] rebuilt from the ground up both their city and their holy churches of God. He rebuilt from its foundations the city of Lakedaimon [Sparta] and a mixed population [came to] settle [there]—Kapheroi ["apostates," Arab Muslims converted to Christianity], Thrakesians [inhabitants of the theme of Thrakesion in western Asia Minor], Armenians, and others brought together from different places and cities. Moreover, he established [Lakedaimon] as a bishopric, and placed it under the jurisdiction of the metropolis of Patras, to which he gave two other bishoprics—Methone [now Methoni in Messenia, Greece] and Korone [now Koroni in Messenia, Greece]. For that the barbarians, having been catechized with the help and with the grace of God, received the baptism and joined the Christian faith, to the glory and to the grace of the Father, the Son, and the Holy Spirit, now and forever, to the ages of ages, amen.

Questions: How did the Slavs of Greece become Christian, according to the author of this document? What does this suggest about the demographic situation in the ninth century? Why were three bishoprics (a metropolis with two suffragan bishoprics) established in the Peloponnese under Emperor Nicephorus I?

29. THE THIRTY-YEAR PEACE

The peace treaty between the Bulgarian ruler Omurtag (814–31) and Emperor Leo V (813–20) is known primarily from an inscription on half of a massive column, which was found in or near the Satma well next to the village of Süleyman Köy (now Sechishte), a few kilometers to the northeast of Pliska, in Bulgaria. The inscription was most likely brought to Süleyman Köy at an unknown date from Pliska, where it was initially set up. The inscription is damaged and both its beginning and end are illegible. However, much can be reconstructed on the basis of the remaining parts. The first clause of the treaty concerns the delimitation of the frontier along an artificial line drawn across the landscape of northeastern Thrace in the modern Bulgarian districts of Burgas and Haskovo. The landscape was in fact marked with the so-called Great Fence of Thrace (Erkesiya Dike), a thirteen-kilometer-long earthwork stretching from the Black Sea to the Maritsa River. This dike was erected most likely after the Thirty-Year Peace and overlaps the artificial line mentioned in the inscription as the frontier between Byzantium and Bulgaria. Omurtag showed an unusual preoccupation with clear-cut and precisely defined frontiers, both with Byzantium and with the Carolingian empire in the northwest. The Great Fence of Thrace served no military purpose but was a symbol of the power of the Bulgar ruler over his subjects (who toiled to dig the ditches and erect the earthen ramparts) and a demonstration of organizational and mobilizing skills for the Byzantine emperor, with whom Omurtag competed.

Source: trans. K. Petkov, *The Voices of Medieval Bulgaria, Seventh-Fifteenth Century: The Records of a Bygone Culture* (Leiden: Brill, 2008), pp. 7–8.

. . . envoys. And he sent the *kavkhan* [deputy of the Bulgar ruler] Iratais to make peace for thirty years. The first of the eleven chapters agreed upon is about the frontier. Let it be from Deultum [Develt, near Burgas, Bulgaria] to Potamoukastel and between the two Auroleva [most likely two parallel ranges of hills to the southwest of the present-day city of Yambol, Bulgaria] and to the many bridges between Baldazena and Agathoniki [present-day Polski Gradets, near Nova Zagora, Bulgaria] and to Leuka and to Constance [near present-day Simeonovgrad, Bulgaria] and to the Makri Livada [possibly Merichleri, near Simeonovgrad, Bulgaria], and to the River Hebros [modern Maritsa] and the Hemus Mountain [the Stara Planina Range]. We agreed that this will be the frontier. The second chapter is about the Slavs under imperial rule. They should stay where they were when the war began. The third chapter is about the Slavs who live along the [Black Sea] coast and are not ruled by the emperor. He should send them back to their settlements. The fourth chapter is about the Christian prisoners of war and those captured . . . for the *turmarchs* [commanders of military units in the Byzantine army], *spatharii* [imperial bodyguards], and the counts [military officers]. He will give . . . the rank and file will be [exchanged] a man for a man. Two water buffalo will be given for those captured in a fortress, if . . . villages. If a *strategos* [general] defected. . . .

Questions: Why were two chapters of the treaty reserved for the Slavs? What was the basis for the exchange of prisoners? How was the frontier delineated? What do you think the last stipulation, unfortunately damaged, may have been?

30. THE STORY OF DANELIS

The biography of Emperor Basil I (867–86) was written by an unknown author with the approval of (if not a commission from) Emperor Constantine VII Porphyrogenitus (913–59) in the mid-tenth century. The story of the lady Danelis is part of a tradition developed at that time to illustrate the prophecies about Basil's ascent to the imperial throne and to underscore Basil's show of gratitude toward his earlier benefactors. As such, the story was modeled after old narrative patterns, resembling in minute detail that of a widow named Kandaki in the fourth-century Alexander Romance *written by an author known as Pseudo-Kallisthenes. There are also obvious similarities with the biblical story of the queen of Sheba in the first book of Kings (10:1–3). No surprise, therefore, that serious doubts have been raised about the authenticity of the story, especially since it was written down some seventy years after the events described. However, if the account of Danelis befriending Emperor Basil I was exaggerated, there is no reason to doubt that Basil's son Leo (VI) truly became the widow's heir or, at least, the heir of some large property in the Peloponnesos, whether bequeathed by a woman or not. Emperor Constantine VII Porphyrogenitus mentions an imperial bull (charter) issued for Patras by his father, an indication that there truly was an imperial concern with northwestern Peloponnesos under Leo VI, perhaps in connection with the disposition of Danelis's will in favor of the emperor. The detailed description of the gifts Danelis is said to have brought to Constantinople suggests that the unknown author of the biography of Basil I was familiar with high-quality cloths, although no indication of a textile industry exists for ninth-century Peloponnesos. Such evidence, however, is present for the tenth century, during which two industries related to fabrics are known to have flourished in the Peloponnesos—parchment production and murex-shell purple-dye extraction. It is therefore possible that the unknown author of the biography of Basil I projected into the past the realities of his own lifetime.*

Source: trans. I. Ševčenko, *Chronographiae quae Theophanis continuati nomine fertur liber quo Vita Basilii imperatoris amplectitur*, ed. I. Ševčenko (Berlin: de Gruyter, 2011), pp. 45, 253, 255, 257, 259, 261, and 263.

11. The aforementioned lady Danelis summoned him [Basil, the future emperor] and greeted him with many not inconsiderable favors. In an eminently reasonable and wise manner, she dispensed these favors as one casts seeds upon fertile ground, in order to reap a manifold harvest at an opportune time; for she gave him a quantity of gold and thirty slaves to serve him, a considerable wealth of apparel, and a variety of other goods. At first, she made no other request of him, save that he should enter into a bond of spiritual brotherhood with her son John. Basil attempted to reject this appeal as one [directed] to a man above his station, given the lady's distinguished reputation and his own apparent insignificance, but eventually he did as he had been told, yielding to her repeated . . . and entreaties. Only then did she tell him openly, gaining more confidence, as it

were: "God deems you to be a great man and will elevate you to a great honor, and I request, indeed beg, nothing else of you than that you have love and mercy for us." Basil promised that if this were to come to pass, he would proclaim her insofar as possible sovereign over all of that land [Peloponnesos]. . . .

74. As for the son of Danelis the emperor summoned him upon having assumed power, honored him with the dignity of *protospatharios* [court dignity reserved to senior members of imperial administration] and granted him freedom of access to his presence on account of the bond of spiritual brotherhood by which they had been previously united. Although that son's mother was considered almost an old woman by then, she, too, felt a great longing and desire to visit the emperor and, in her declining years, to partake of some outstanding honor as well . . . , on account of her own [earlier] munificence and hospitality. Thus, by order of the emperor, she went to the capital with great honors and with a large retinue and body of attendants. As she was not able either to ride in a vehicle or mount a horse—perhaps also because she was pampering herself on account of her immense and superabundant wealth—she reclined in a litter, having [previously] selected three hundred young and strong men from her household to carry her, and gave them orders to come up [to Constantinople]. In such a manner did she complete the journey from the Peloponnesos to this queen of cities, with teams of men each lifting her couch in turns. A reception was held at the Magnaura Palace, a thing usually done by the emperors of the Romans whenever they receive some great and famous leader of a foreign nation; [and] she too, was brought before the emperor with honors and in splendor. She also brought with her precious gifts, such as almost no foreign ruler had hitherto brought before an emperor of the Romans. Thus, [the gifts] comprised five hundred household servants, including handsome eunuchs one hundred in number, for this powerful and wealthy old woman apparently knew that there is always room for these castrated [men] in the imperial palace, and that they dwell there in numbers exceeding those of flies in a sheepfold in springtime. That is why she had readied them ahead of time, so that she would find them as escorts on account of services of old when she should enter the imperial palace. There were also one hundred female *skiastriai* [serving women], and richly variegated Sidonian fabrics that are now called *sendais* [linen garments dyed in kermes red, a dye obtained from several related species of shield-lice of the Coccidae family, each of which was parasitic to a particular species of evergreen Mediterranean oak], their name seemingly having been corrupted through the ignorance of the many; one hundred *linomalotaria* [cloths made of linen and wool] (for it is best to use common speech in referring to them); two hundred fine linen *amalia* [probably a cloth without nap], and other fabrics more delicate than a spider's web, each of which was inserted into a reed tub, their number being one hundred as well; and many and diverse costly vessels of silver and gold.

75. Danelis was graciously received and treated with a magnificent kindness that matched her devotion and nobility; and she was deemed worthy to be called "mother of the emperor." Having also been granted [other tokens of] imperial hospitality and many honors, she rejoiced and was happy, and asserted that she had obtained full compensation, or rather that she had received much more than she had given. For that reason, she magnanimously added to the aforementioned gifts a large part of the Peloponnesos: as it was property of her own at that time, she made of it a loving gift for her son and emperor. Having sojourned in this great city of ours as long as she . . . of distinctions and rewards, she went back again to her own country as if she were the sovereign empress of those dwelling there, bringing a harvest of honors more numerous and higher than those she had previously enjoyed. She went down to her home in the same fashion as she had come up.

76. At that time construction was proceeding on that most beautiful temple, admired by all, which we had by custom come to call the New Imperial Church; it was being built to bear the names of Jesus Christ our Savior, Michael the very first among the angels, and Elijah the Tishbite. The woman Danelis took the measurements of that temple's interior and had large woolen carpets woven and sent, of the sort that among us are called by a name signifying prayer. They are worthy of marvel on account of both their large size and beauty and were to cover the whole floor whose variety of rare stones, set next to each other like well-fitted mosaic cubes, imitated the beauty and the variegated colors of the peacock. Moreover, so long as the emperor remained alive, Danelis would send yearly gifts, none lesser than those she had brought on the first occasion. As it happened, she lived to a ripe old age, her lifespan having exceeded that of the emperor. . . . She visited the most wise and mild Emperor Leo [VI, 886–912], brought him admirable gifts as well, made him heir of her own property (for by then her son John had departed this life), and asked that an imperial official be dispatched to draw up an inventory of her property and take it over. Then having taken leave of the good emperor, she again departed to her native soil where she had been raised, to place within it the dust of her flesh. She died a short time after her return.

77. When Zenobios the *protospatharios*, who had been appointed and dispatched to carry out all the wishes and dispositions made by the old woman, reached the town of Naupaktos [now Nafpaktos, on the northern coast of the Gulf of Corinth, Greece], he learned from her grandson Daniel that she had departed this life. He arrived at her mansion, provided himself with the copy of her will, and executed everything according to her wish and [the will's] dispositions. He found an exceedingly large quantity of gold in coins, and other property consisting of silver and gold objects, garments, bronze, slaves, and cattle, that surpassed any private fortune imaginable: more than that, it was hardly inferior to a king's

treasure. Her household slaves being a countless multitude, the emperor ordered three thousand of them to be freed and sent as colonists of sorts to the theme of La[n]gobardia [Byzantine province in Calabria, southern Italy]. Her remaining property, assets, and slaves were distributed among those whom she had stipulated in her testamentary dispositions, while her heir, the emperor, too, was left with, among other things, eighty suburban estates as his private legacy.

Questions: What was the source of Danelis's wealth? Why did she insist on making so many gifts to the emperor? What does the technical terminology concerning textiles suggest about the audience of this text?

31. EMPEROR CONSTANTINE VII PORPHYROGENITUS ON THE CONFLICT BETWEEN BULGARS AND SERBS

While the history of ninth-century Bulgaria is well documented in the written sources, next to nothing is known about the Serbs during that same time. Chapter 32 of On the Administration of the Empire, *the work commissioned by (if not attributed to) Emperor Constantine VII Porphyrogenitus (913–59), is the only source for the political history of Serbia in the ninth and tenth centuries. While providing the names of several Serbian rulers, the account in chapter 32 lacks geographic precision. Although mentioning that the Bulgars and Serbs had a common frontier, the author of the account does not describe it, except to say that "Rasi" was on that frontier. Some have argued that the imprecision was the result of the account being based on one source, a native Serbian "chronicle." However, the details of the situation in Serbia seem to indicate archival sources, perhaps reports of imperial envoys to the Serbian rulers. Others have argued that the source of the information on the Serbs and the Croats in* On the Administration of the Empire *was a now lost source in Latin not unlike the* Conversion of the Baiuvarians and the Carantanians. *Still others have noted recently that there were in fact no precise borders between the Serbs and the Bulgars, for power was exercised in the ninth century over people, not territory. Be that as it may, the extent of the territory populated by Serbs in the ninth and tenth centuries cannot be established with any degree of certainty on the basis of chapter 32 of* On the Administration of the Empire.

Source: trans. R.J.H. Jenkins, Constantine VII Porphyrogenitus, *De Administrando imperio* (Washington, DC: Dumbarton Oaks Center for Byzantine Studies, 1967), p. 155.

. . . and up to the time of this Blastimer [Vlastimer], the Bulgars lived at peace with the Serbs, whose neighbors they were and with whom they had a common frontier, and they were friendly one toward another, and were in servitude and submission to the emperors of the Romans and kindly entreated by them. But, during the rule of this same Blastimer, Presiam, prince of Bulgaria [Presian,

Bulgar ruler between 836 and 852] came [to] war against the Serbs, with intent to reduce them to submission; but though he fought them three years he not merely achieved nothing, but also lost very many of his men. After the death of prince Blastimer, his three sons Muntimer and Stroimer and Goinikos succeeded to the rule of Serbia and divided up the country. In their time came up the prince of Bulgaria, Michael Boris [king of Bulgaria, 852–89] wishing to avenge the defeat of his father Presiam, and made war, and the Serbs discomfited him to such an extent that they even held prisoner his son Vladimer [Vladimir, ruler of Bulgaria, 889–93], together with twelve great boyars. Then, out of grief for his son, Boris perforce made peace with the Serbs. But being about to return to Bulgaria and afraid lest the Serbs might ambush him on the way, he begged for his escort the sons of prince Muntimer, Borenas and Stephen, who escorted him safely as far as the frontier at Rasi [Ras, near Novi Pazar, in the southern part of present-day Serbia]. For this favor, Michael Boris gave them handsome presents, and they in return gave him as presents in the way of friendship two slaves, two falcons, two dogs, and eighty furs, which the Bulgarians describe as tribute.

Questions: What is the attitude of the document's author toward the Serbs? How are their rulers portrayed? What can we learn about the power configuration in the Balkans during the ninth century? Why were the gifts from Boris in pairs?

32. SAINT LUKE THE YOUNGER AND BULGARIAN ATTACKS ON GREECE

Born in 896 in the village of Kastorion (now Thisvi), in Boeotia (Greece), Saint Luke the Younger was the son of relatively wealthy parents descended from refugees from the island of Aegina. Luke became a monk in 910, but he lived for only a short while in a monastery in Athens, after running away from home. He began a solitary life on Mount Ioannitza, near Delphi. In 927, he moved to the Peloponnesos, where he remained in the service of a stylite (a hermit living on top of a pillar) in Zemena for ten years. He returned to Mount Ioannitza but moved in 940 to the neighboring village of Kalamion. Three years later, he fled together with the villagers to the island of Ampelon in the Gulf of Corinth, to escape the Magyar raids. He remained on that island until 946. He finally moved to Steiris, where he died in 953 at the age of 57. He was buried inside his cell, which was later turned into an oratory, around which grew the monastery dedicated to Saint Luke the Younger. His biography (vita) *contains precious historical information about the social and political life of early medieval Greece. In 916, Bulgarian troops devastated the territory of the theme (province) of Thessalonike in retaliation for Empress Zoe's annulment of her son's engagement to Symeon's daughter and for her rejection of his imperial title (Zoe Karbonopsina was the fourth wife of the Byzantine emperor Leo VI and the mother of Constantine VII, for whom she ruled as regent between 913 and 919). Following his victory over the Byzantine army at Anchialos (20 August 917), and his campaign against Prince Peter of Serbia, Symeon raided Greece in 918. In 921, he appears to have raided northern Greece again, this time reaching as far south as the Isthmus of Corinth and ravaging northern Peloponnesos. That much follows from the fragment translated below, especially from the prophecy of Saint Luke the Younger. The villagers near Mount Ioannitza, on which Saint Luke lived as a hermit, fled to the various islands in the Gulf of Corinth, but a group of Bulgarians pursued them on a stolen ship. Only a few villagers, together with Saint Luke, escaped the massacre.*

Source: trans. C.L. Connor and W.R. Connor, *The Life and Miracles of Saint Luke of Steiris* (Brookline, MA: Hellenic College Press, 1994), pp. 39, 53, and 55.

24. He foretold many days in advance the coming of the Scythian [generic term employed for barbarians from the steppe lands of eastern Europe] spearhead, which swept across all the mainland and caused almost total destruction; he did not do this explicitly (how could he when the prediction would have given him such glory and glory was precisely what he was avoiding), but through parables and riddles. Some people received different advance indications from his blessed tongue, but others say they heard this: "Hellas will be smitten, and the Peloponnese will see war." . . .

32. This then is the story of the divine Luke before the invasion of the heathens [presumably Bulgarians, who nonetheless were already Christian by that time]—or rather, a small part of his story. The account will now describe the events after he fled and became an exile, for after spending seven years in the wilderness of Iannitze [Mount Ioannitza], he too was forced to flee along with all the others. For Symeon, the ruler of the Scythians [893–927], repudiated the treaty with the Byzantines, and invaded the mainland [in 918]. Our sins gave him the upper hand in battle, as he went about enslaving and ravaging, depriving some of life and others of freedom, forcing them to pay tribute. Some barricaded themselves in cities as if in prisons or garrisons, and others found safety in Euboea and the land of Pelops [that is, Peloponnesos].

33. The villagers who were gathered around the man of God crossed over to the neighboring islands, but envy, preceding them, brought an unexpected danger upon them. For when they thought they were safe, living securely in their righteousness, the Bulgarians suddenly attacked them in a ship which they had stolen and killed almost all of them; only a few of them, including the great man, plunged into the sea and thus were able to escape.

34. After the invaders withdrew, he took a boat and crossed over to Corinth with all his family and acquaintances, just at the age when his cheeks were covered by a beard and the bloom of his virtue was matched by the flower of his youth.

Questions: What role do the Bulgarian attacks on Greece play in the biography of Saint Luke the Younger? How does the author explain their military success against the Byzantines? How did the locals defend themselves against the attacks?

33. KEKAUMENOS ON THE VLACHS

The earliest mention of the Vlachs (the Romance-speaking population of the Balkans, descendants of the Romans) in a narrative source written in Greek is in the prescriptive handbook conventionally known as the Strategikon of Kekaumenos. *Kekaumenos most likely wrote it during the reign of Michael VII Dukas (1071–78), but after the death of Patriarch John Xiphilinos in August 1075. The work survives in only one manuscript copied in or near Trebizond in the fourteenth century. It contains edifying maxims, tips on household management and social relations, as well as counsel about serving as judge in the provinces. The author appears to have been a senior commander in the Byzantine army, and to have been educated in grammar and rhetoric, albeit not at the highest level. The mention of the Vlachs appears in relation to Nikulitzas Delphinas, the author's father-in-law, who, although governor of Larissa (in southern Thessaly, Greece), found himself—apparently unwillingly—at the head of a revolt against a tax surcharge imposed by Emperor Constantine X (1059–67). Nikulitzas belonged to a prominent family in the city. Emperor Basil II had appointed his grandfather as* archon *(leader) of the Vlachs, a local ethnic group that was also at the center of the rebellion of 1066–67. The leaders of that rebellion were all prominent men of Larissa, two of whom are specifically mentioned by Kekaumenos as being Vlachs: Slavota (Sthlavota) Karmalakis and a certain Beriboes (Berivoi), in whose house the conspirators gathered to discuss their plans. While Slavota was later arrested by Nikulitzas, the rebellion drew large numbers of Vlachs living in the hinterland of Larissa, on both sides of the River Enipeas. In anticipation of serious military turbulence, the Vlachs had sent their wives and children to the "mountains of Bulgaria" together with their herds, which suggests that they had more or less permanent settlements there and were possibly involved in transhumant pastoralism. Among the rebels of 1066–67, Kekaumenos also mentions Bulgarians. When Nikulitzas discovered the conspiracy, he promptly warned the emperor about it, but without much success. The governor of Larissa thus found himself in the embarrassing position of being placed at the head of a rebellion that quickly spread to the neighboring Thessalian city of Servia, which controlled the main road from Thessaly to Macedonia. Shortly after the conquest of Servia, the emperor opened negotiations with the rebels and promised to remit the taxes, only to capture Nikulitzas, who was jailed in Amaseia, on the Black Sea coast of Asia Minor. In an effort to defend the political legacy of his relative, Kekaumenos placed the blame entirely on the Vlachs. The description of the Vlachs is modeled on a* psogos *or "invective," the seventh exercise in the* progymnasmata *(rhetorical exercises in Antiquity). Kekaumenos used classical sources (such as the work of Dio Cassius) for the war of Trajan with the Dacians, an indication that his description of the Vlachs was not based on firsthand knowledge of their origin, customs, and history.*

Source: trans. F. Curta, from Kekaumenos, *Raccomandazioni e consigli di un galantuomo: Strate¯gikon*, ed. M.D. Spadaro (Alessandria: Edizioni dell'Orso, 1998), pp. 210, 212, 224, and 226.

4.174. The next day, the conspirators gathered in the house of a Vlach named Beriboes. And after telling the Vlachs, "Even the *protospatharios* Nikulitzas Delphinas is with us" (in fact he was *protospatharios* [title of a court dignitary] at that time), they liked him very much and all wanted to go with him. Suddenly, the conspirators saw him coming toward them, and they all rushed to greet him with a servile attitude. When Nikulitzas dismounted, they welcomed and led him into their midst, saying: "We regard you as a father and a lord, and we do not want to do anything without you. It would certainly be unfair [to do that]. We saw you coming, so tell us what we need to do about this plan." And he answered them: "This is not good. First of all, [it looks like] we are moving against God, stirring his wrath, and then against the emperor, who can move large numbers against us and destroy us. Moreover, it is already June: what are we going to do about the harvest, if there is a rebellion?" He then turned toward the Vlachs: "Where are your flocks and your women?" They answered to him: "In the mountains of Bulgaria" (this is indeed the custom, namely that the herds of the Vlachs and their families stay in the high mountains and in very cool places between the month of April and the month of September). "So," he said, "those who are there, that is those who are on the side of the emperor, will they not tear them to pieces?" And the Vlachs who were there, hearing his objections, agreed with his arguments, but nonetheless replied: "We are not abandoning this plan, and we accept the risks." They then broke off the discussion and sat down for lunch. After their meal and the siesta, at noon, they all returned to Nikulitzas, Vlachs and Bulgarians (sent by the inhabitants of Larissa). As a matter of fact, the inhabitants of Larissa, Nikulitza's fellow townsmen, told the Vlachs and the Bulgarians: "From this moment onward, the plan is not secret anymore, primarily because his [Nikulitza's] two sons, Gregory and Pankratis, are in the city. This is without any doubt an impediment, as the emperor, learning about it, will be able to subdue us." Sharing therefore those things with him, they said: "What you said earlier was correct. But we should not leave the job unfinished." As everybody agreed and they got the better of him, they told him: "From this moment onward, we will regard you as our leader and lord and in the ongoing uprising, we choose you so that you can tell us what is useful for us to do." He, looking for peace, rejected their offer once and twice, and many more times again. After that, some of his friends, coming to see him and swearing in the name of God, told him: "If you do not join their conspiracy, they will kill you." And he (said): "Without wishing it, I became their leader; and wishing to be the hunter, I have become the game." However, since they had all placed their evil hopes in him, they turned him away from God's commandments ("To prevent all their land from being ruined and destroyed, and the people slaughtered and enslaved, I took it upon myself"). And he assumed every burden [of the job]. He got out of his house [from Larissa] in the direction of Pharsala [modern Farsala, in southern Thessaly, Greece] and of Pliris. This Pliris [probably modern Enipeas] is a river which flows on both sides of a large plain and cutting through the [mass of] Vlachs, divides them into two parts. Having camped there, Nikulitzas gathered the Vlachs and the Bulgarians who lived in the environs, so that [in a short while] he put together a mighty army. . . .

4.187. The Vlach people are entirely untrustworthy and perfidious, with no faith in God, the emperor, a relative or a friend, striving to cheat everyone. They lie and they steal. They take oaths every day on the heads of their friends and break them without even thinking twice. They are ready to enter sworn brotherhoods or baptismal alliances, so that, using them, to deceive those who are [sufficiently] credulous [to believe them]. They have not kept faith with anyone, not even with the old Roman emperors (confronted by Emperor Trajan, they were completely destroyed and conquered; their king named Decebalus was killed and his head placed on a pike in the middle of the city of Rome). In fact, those are the people called Dacians and Bessi. They first lived close to the rivers Danube and Saos, which is now called Sava, where the Serbs have recently moved, and [the inhabited] places that were well fortified and difficult to reach. Relying on that [advantage], they feigned being friendly and ready to submit to the old Roman emperors, [but instead] came out of their strongholds, and devastated the Roman territory. So, the Romans, being annoyed with their deeds, destroyed them, as I have already said. Once they left those places, they scattered throughout Epirus and Macedonia, but the majority went to live in Hellas [the Byzantine theme by that name, located in central Greece]. They are very coward: they have chicken hearts, but are impertinent, [a trait] derived from [their] cowardice. Because of that, I recommend that you never put your trust in them. Especially if there is an uprising, and they promise to be friends and loyal [to you] in all seriousness and swear to keep their word on the name of God, do not believe them. It would be better, in fact, not to make them swear to you and you to them. Keep an eye on the evildoers that they are, instead of taking or accepting any oath [from them]. There is actually no need to trust them, unless you feign to be their friend. If there is an uprising in Bulgaria [the Byzantine province by that name, which was located in the central Balkans, to the west of modern Bulgaria], on the grounds of what I have told you earlier, avoid giving them any credit, even if they claim or swear to be your friends.

Questions: What effects did the Vlach revolt in Thessaly have on the Byzantine rule in the region, according to Kekaumenos? What is his attitude toward the Vlachs? Why does he link them to the Dacians and the Bessi of Antiquity? Why does he insist on warning his audience against the Vlachs?

34. KING PETER KREŠIMIR IV DONATES AN ISLAND

King Peter Krešimir IV of Croatia (1058–74) was the son of Stephen, the grandson of King Stephen Držislav (969–97), and of the daughter of the Venetian doge Peter II Orseolo (1008–26). One of the first charters attributed to him is the donation of February 1060 in favor of the abbey of St-John of Rogovo, to which the king gave an island and a manor near Biograd. This document is a record written in Latin of a generous donation made in the presence of the papal legate and of the bishop of Biograd. There is a long list of witnesses, including such important dignitaries as the ban *(provincial governor) Gojzo and all the* župans *(magnates) of the kingdom. One of the court dignitaries listed among these men is Boleslav, who is called both* tepchi *and count palatine, most likely one and the same title. He may well be the man named Boleslav, a court count, who appears nine years later in another charter, a donation to the abbey of St-Chrysogonus in Zadar, to which King Peter Krešimir IV gave the island of Maun (near Pag, in northern Dalmatia). Among the witnesses for that donation is a man named Leo with the title of* katepan *of (the theme) of Dalmatia, an indication that some kind of Byzantine control had been restored to the region. However, in his 1069 charter Peter Krešimir IV emphatically proclaimed himself "king of Croatia and Dalmatia," while listing the Byzantine* katepan *as witness only after his most important court officials. The abbot of the Benedictine monastery of St-Chrysogonus in Zadar is first mentioned in 918, but the monastery had a new beginning in 986, when a monk from Monte Cassino was appointed abbot. During the last decades of the eleventh century, the scriptorium of the abbey of St-Chrysogonus produced many manuscripts, some of them richly illuminated. Two of them are now in the Bodleian Library in Oxford: the Book of Hours of Abbess Cika of the convent of St-Mary in Zadar, written most likely in the 1080s; and the Vekenega Evangelistary (named after the daughter of Abbess Cika), dated to 1095/96. The Benedictine abbey of St-Bartholomew (the abbot of which, Adam, is mentioned as witness in the translation below) was established in the tenth century on the Kapitul Hill near Knin.*

Source: trans. F. Curta from *Diplomatički zbornik kraljevine Hrvatske, Dalmacije i Slavonije*, ed. M. Kostrenčić (Zagreb: Tiskara Izdavačkog Zavoda Jugoslavenske Adakemije Znanosti i Umjetnosti, 1967), vol. 1, pp. 113–14.

The extraordinary sublimity of God divides both the highest and the lowest part of the earth not only by merit, but also on the basis of deep consideration, and by means of finding out [the truth] exalts those who deserve to be exalted, while bending the necks of those [placing themselves] higher [than others] and [acting] arrogantly, so that the ineffable judgment of the ineffable judge be passed, and that the will of the Almighty, coming out of an inexhaustible source, be dispensed by royal authority. Therefore, I, Krešimir, by the grace of God, ruler of Croatia and Dalmatia, the kingdom of my grandfather of sweet memory, King Krešimir [III, 1000–30] and of my father, King Stephen [I, 1030–58], who rests in peace in the

Elysian fields [that is, in paradise], in the year of the Lord from the incarnation of Jesus Christ, our Lord 1069, in the seventh indiction, in the fifth epact [computus concept referring to a phase of the moon], in the third concurrent [computus concept referring to the number of the weekday of 24 March, counted from Sunday], while dining in my inn at Nin, together with our *župans*, counts, and *bans*, and even with chaplains of our royal court, I began to think how to make the Almighty God preserve the government of my hereditary kingdom, that was given to me, and how to give eternal peace to the souls of my predecessors. I found that by means of mercy there is nothing more pleasant to God and nothing worthier of our earthly court than to endow the holy houses of the heavenly citizens and saints [that is, monasteries] with properties and proper gifts. Because God the almighty has spread our kingom by land and by sea, we have decided and are constantly determined to [enrich] the monastery of St-Chrysogonus, whose venerable body rests within the walls of that [same] city [of Zadar]. Also because [we have found] among the deeds of our predecessors that the exalted kings had endowed the aforementioned monastery with many fields and estates, we therefore will not deviate in any way from the path of our ancestors, so for the salvation of our souls and of all our deceased, we offer and firmly give to you, blessed Chrysogonus, the glorious martyr, and after you to lord Peter, the glorious abbot of your holy house, our island in our Dalmatian sea, which is called Maun, on whose eastern side there is an[other] island, which is called in Slavic Vir. Let the said monastery of the holy martyr hold it in perpetuity, and let no mortal touch it [that is, attempt to take it from the monastery]. That is what our good will determined with the consent and at the request of the nobles of our kingdom. And for this gift of ours to be forever established and for it to last forever, we confirm it, and protect it against injury by means of confirmation, as well as the testimony of ourselves and our bishops, and we order that whatever mortal disregarding the judgment of God and overthrowing our royal dignity has the audacity to disturb the monastery of St-Chrysogonus concerning the aforementioned island, which we have given by royal authority, at the same time trampling upon our right, let him incur the wrath of the future Judge and let him be guilty at the Last Judgment. Let him be with Herod, with Judas, and Simon the Sorcerer in the eternal cauldron [of fire], and let him be in the company of Antichrist, and receive from the Almighty God, the holy apostles, and the whole choir of saints, and the blessed Chryosognus an eternal curse, and from our royal court and whoever among my successors will be king, from the *župans*, the counts, or the *bans*, [let him] pay a fine of one hundred pounds of gold and be forever dishonored in our kingdom.

+ I, Krešimir, king of Croatia and Dalmatia.
+ I, Stephen, bishop of Zadar, signed.

And these are the names of the witnesses who were present:

+ Adamčo, *župan* of Nin;
Boleslav, court count, [and] witness;
Viachičo, *župan* of Lučka, witness;
Voleša was witness;
Budeć, chamberlain, *župan* of Bribir, witness;
John, royal chaplain, witness;
Peter, judge of the royal court, witness;
Studeć, royal cupbearer, witness;
Lord Leo, imperial *protospatharios* and *katepan* of all of Dalmatia, witness;
Selislav, judge of Nin, witness;
The monk Adam, abbot of St-Bartholomew, witness;
Peter, *župan* of Sidra, witness;
Dragomir, *župan* of Cetina, witness;
Andrew, head of Biograd, witness

+ I, Anastasius, compiler of this charter, bishop of Croatia and chancellor of the royal court, have written and gladly confirmed [this] at the order and desire of the aforementioned lord, my king, in the town of Nin. Amen.

Questions: Why does the king donate the island to the abbey of St-Chrysogonus? What measures does he take to prevent the deed being rescinded? Who was "Lord Leo" who witnessed the charter? What groups of people were most likely to witness royal deeds in Croatia?

35. THEOPHYLACT OF OHRID ON RECRUITMENT SHORTAGES IN THE BALKANS

Theophylact Hephaistos was born on the island of Euboea (now Evvoia) near Athens at some point between 1050 and 1060. Educated in Constantinople, he became one of the many churchmen serving the great church of Hagia Sophia, while also serving as a professor at the patriarchal school. In that capacity, he was recruited to be the tutor of the son of Emperor Michael VII Dukas (1071–78). He was appointed archbishop of Ohrid in or shortly before 1090 and remained in Bulgaria until his death in 1126 or not long after that. A talented theologian and orator, Theophylact left many homilies, a commentary on the New Testament, and a collection of 135 letters, which have been mined for information about the economic and social situation in the central Balkans during the long reign of Alexios I Komnenos. But when the archbishop complained in a letter about the "bumpkin lifestyle" in Ohrid, that was in fact a quote from Euripides, and so we cannot assume that that is anything like an accurate description of the conditions in Byzantine Bulgaria. Highlighting the literary value of those letters, recent studies have shown that despite his apparent hostility to anything Bulgarian, it is a mistake to take the archbishop's letters as evidence of the

Byzantine administration's systematic effort to eradicate Old Church Slavonic culture and Bulgarian ethnic identity. After all, Theophylact viewed himself as "a Constantinopolitan and, strange to tell, a Bulgarian," and wrote the so-called Long Life of Saint Clement, *in which he did not hesitate to describe his hero as "new Paul to the new Corinthians, the Bulgarians." Nor did he hesitate to criticize even the patriarch for having allowed a certain monk to establish a "house of prayer" in Macedonia, that is within the area under the jurisdiction of the archbishop of Ohrid, to whom Emperor Basil II (976–1025) had granted independence from the patriarch of Constantinople and for which he had established diocesan boundaries as early as 1019/20. In fact, Theophylact may be responsible for the idea that the archbishop of Ohrid was the legitimate successor of the sixth-century archbishopric established by Justinian's novel (new decree) of 535 in Justiniana Prima, an idea of considerable importance for the medieval history of the see of Ohrid. In his letters addressed to prominent members of the Byzantine ecclesiastical and lay elite, Theophylact painted a bleak picture of his life in Ohrid. He protested against the abuses of the tax collectors in the theme of Achrida, called for the assistance of the duke of Dyrrachion (now Durrës, in Albania) against the taxation of monks and of the bishopric of Devol. The letter translated below was sent in 1092 or 1093 to John Komnenos, the duke of Dyrrachion, as a protest against the rounding up of Bulgarian peasants to serve in the army. The letter describes the aftermath of the devastating invasions of the Pechenegs and the Oghuz, as well as the equally destructive wars led against the former by Emperor Alexios I Komnenos.*

Source: trans. F. Curta from Théophylacte d'Achrida, *Lettres*, ed. P. Gautier (Thessaloniki: Association de recherches byzantines, 1986), pp. 209 and 211.

I certainly must appear too bold to those who cannot correctly distinguish reality through the edge of reason, but most likely not to my lord, who is superior to all in intelligence. For anyone blaming an archbishop intervening to defend his flock against abuses must have pitched his tent pretty far from intelligence and reason. Thus, I will speak, and I will write to defend those who were entrusted to me, and I will pray from the bottom of my heart, as the Gospel says, to the one who can have pity. To be sure, most venerable protector, the theme [Byzantine province] of Achrida [now Ohrid, in southern Macedonia], if not spared by your powerful hand, will disappear from the heart of Bulgaria sooner than we think. For it is small, wretched, and barely populated; it is in fact the most pitiful of all themes. May your compassionate and generous power take pity on it in what concerns the recruitment of infantrymen and may the number of recruits be diminished in proportion. Indeed, how could the recruitment of men from this place not trigger a serious weakening of the entire theme? And how could those who were spared [the draft] not despise the soil of their beloved homeland as being hostile [to them] and as bringing disaster, and how could they not fall in love with the bosom of a foreign land?

I beg you, therefore, not just me, but also in the company of two envoys, to consider strict equity, as required by the small size of [our] theme and its position on the side of the road at the same time as [you keep in mind] its role as a haven for those in transit. Unless there is indeed some other reason, it is precisely because, if left intact, [the theme of Achrida] saves those who go across it that [the theme] deserves mercy, particularly from my lord. The infantrymen that we have already sent are a great burden; do not let that draft become even worse for us because of your powerful demands, since our lord lives here to save us. It is true, as I have said, that the drafting of those who were sent [to the army] has seriously depopulated our small theme, for our territory is not Pelagonia [pun based on the name of a region close to Ohrid and the Greek word for ocean, *pelagos*], it is only the small Mykonos [now Mikonos, small island in the Cyclades] of the saying. May the Mother of God, to whom we all belong and to whom you give everything that you give to us, show you as irreproachable in front of God and invincible in front of your enemies, so that you will [indeed] be superior to all, in both divine and human affairs.

Questions: Explain the motives behind Theophylact of Ohrid's plea to the duke of Dyrrachion. What sort of religious leader was Theophylact, judging by this document? How does the archbishop of Ohrid account for the economic and demographic problems of the theme? What does it suggest that he uses a pun when writing to the duke?

36. THE BATTLE OF DYRRACHION

Anna Komnena (1083–1153) was the eldest of seven children born to Emperor Alexios I Komnenos (1081–1118). She received an excellent education in the imperial palace, as indicated by her broad knowledge of astronomy, medicine, history, geography, mathematics, as well as philosophy. Later in her life, she actually taught medicine at a hospital that her father set up in Constantinople. She was married at age fourteen to Nicephorus Bryennios (more than twenty years her senior), who was himself a refined intellectual and historian. Anna bore him six children. Sometime after her husband's death in 1137, she began working on an extensive biography of her father, using oral sources, primarily testimonies from veterans of Alexios's wars, such as her husband, Nicephorus Bryennios, and the general George Pakourianos, who was Anna's uncle. It is quite possible that she relied on memories of her own father, especially for such details as him escaping from attacks by three Normans in the battle of Dyrrachion. Nonetheless, Anna offers extremely detailed descriptions of the Norman army, with names of commanders and details about the origin of the soldiers that would not have been accessible to any of the Byzantine participants in the war. Some have therefore suggested that Anna had access to a copy, possibly in translation, of the Deeds of Robert Guiscard (Gesta Roberti Wiscardi), *which William of Apulia wrote in Latin hexameters at the end of the eleventh century. While the borrowings from the Latin text are quite obvious in certain places, in others Anna used her source quite freely, adapting its content to her own narrative goals. Written in sophisticated Attic Greek, the narrative in the* Alexiad *often imitates the literary style of the ancient historians Thucydides, Xenophon, and Polybius. Anna had disdain for the Norman invaders of 1081, and for their leader, Robert Guiscard, whom she called "most villainous." To her, Robert's wife Sikelgaita was far superior, comparable to the Greek goddess of war, Athena. That Sikelgaita had to stop the Normans from fleeing at a key moment in the battle is a subtle way of saying that the Normans were effeminate and needed a woman to push them along. This may well have been a reply to the Norman anti-Byzantine propaganda at that time, which described Byzantine men in a similar way.*

Source: trans. F. Curta from Anna Komnena, *Alexiade*, ed. B. Leib (Paris: Les Belles Lettres, 1967), vol. 1, pp. 143–44, 150–51, 152, 154, and 159–63.

Robert [Guiscard, Norman duke of Sicily between 1059 and 1085] now occupied the continent, where he set up camp on 17 June of the fourth indiction [1081]. He had with him countless troops of horsemen and foot soldiers, who looked formidable on account of both their appearance and of their manner of waging war. For from that moment onward all his army, which had come from various directions, was now gathered in a single place. His fleet sailed across the sea with its many ships of various kinds, filled with soldiers with long experience in naval combat. The inhabitants of Dyrrachion [now Durrës, in western Albania] were therefore hemmed in on two sides—from land as well as from the sea. Catching a glimpse of Robert's countless troops that were beyond anything one could have imagined, they were terrified. Meanwhile, George Palaiologos [Byzantine general, Emperor Alexios I's brother-in-law, who had just been appointed duke of Dyrrachion], who was a brave man and an expert in the military art, with thousands of battles in the east that he had won, began to fortify the city without panicking. . . . At the same time, he wrote a letter to the emperor to let him know about Robert's invasion and about his goal, namely, to take the city of Dyrrachion. When the inhabitants saw outside [their city] the *helepoleis* [siege engines] and the enormous wooden tower, which was taller than the walls of Dyrrachion and entirely covered in hides [animal skin to protect the structure from fire], with the catapult placed on top [of the tower], and when they saw the entire curtain of walls surrounded by the army, the allies who flocked from all corners to Robert, the neighboring cities [already] devastated by incursions, and the tents [in the camp] that increased in number by the day, they were seized by terror, for they now realized what Duke Robert intended to do. He had not occupied the Illyrian plain [that is, the alluvial plain at the mouths of the Rivers Erzen and Ishëm] in order just to plunder the cities and the hinterland and, once he had gathered much booty, to return to Apulia, as rumors had it. In reality, he coveted the throne of the Roman empire, and he wanted to open his career [as emperor], as they say, with an assault on Dyrrachion. . . .

When he learned about what Robert had done, the emperor [Alexios I Komnenos] immediately wrote to [George] Pakourianos [the commander-in-chief of the imperial forces in the west] to let him know that, in order to stop the irresistible impetuosity [of the Norman,] who had taken Avlona and did not care about the disasters that he had suffered at sea and on land, and even less about the defeat that would open his career, as they say, he [Pakourianos] must without delay gather his troops and join him [the emperor]. Having sent that message to Pakourianos, Alexios departed from Constantinople in the month of August of the fourth indiction, leaving Isaac [Emperor Alexios's elder brother, the first recipient of the title of *sebastokrator*] behind, to maintain order. . . . As for Pakourianos, once he got the [emperor's] letter, he appointed as second in command [under him] a courageous man, Nicholas Branas, who had much experience in war. As for him, at the head of all the heavily armed troops and of the nobility, he left Orestias [the region around Adrianople, now Edirne, in European Turkey] and rushed to join the emperor. Alexios had meanwhile drawn up his entire army in the order of battle and had chosen for the elite troops the best warriors as commanders. He commanded that that order of battle be respected during the march [to Dyrrachion], everywhere that was made possible by nature, so that his men become acquainted with the plan and everyone, knowing his exact position, would not be confused when engaging in battle, but instead would always keep his post regardless of what would happen. . . . After arranging his troops, Alexios moved against Robert in full force. On his way there, a man came from the opposite direction, and he informed him about the situation in Dyrrachion. He thus learned more details about how Robert had brought all the engines necessary for the siege and had moved them next to the walls. George Palaiologos, after resisting day and night the attacks of the *helepoleis* and his [Robert's] schemes, he had given up and eventually [decided to] open the gates. He got out to give the enemy a serious fight. He had been wounded in different parts of his body, especially by an arrow that had hit him next to the temple. After unsuccessfully trying to remove the arrow, he had turned to a professional [that is, most likely a medic or military doctor], who cut the end (the butt of the arrow, with feathers), while leaving the other part in the wound. He [George Palaiologos] bound up his head the best he could under the circumstances and threw himself again against the enemy, fighting until late evening, standing up, tireless. Having learned the news, the emperor understood that Palaiologos needed immediate assistance and sped up his march. When he got to Thessaloniki, the news concerning Robert was confirmed, and in much greater detail. . . .

Since Robert, as reported by the one who told him about those events, was in the process of building a second wooden tower similar to the first one and was readying the *helepoleis* against Dyrrachion, the emperor, convinced by now that the grave situation of those who were defending Dyrrachion required immediate action, arranged his troops and continued his march to the city. Once there, he placed his army in a field with trenches, next to the river called Charzanes [now Erzen, in Albania]. . . . The emperor, planning to attack Robert's camp by surprise during the night and from two different directions, ordered the entire army of allies to advance from the rear, after taking the route passing by the salt pans, and in order that such moves remain unknown to the enemy, he did not hesitate to ask them to take a longer route. As for him, he was to attack Robert from the front as soon as he saw the allies in the positions to which he had sent them. Robert, after leaving his tents empty and crossing the bridge in the middle of the night of 18 October of the fifth indiction [1081], reached with his men a church built a long time ago on the seashore and dedicated to the martyr Theodore. After having tried all night long to assuage God, [the Normans] partook of the pure and divine mysteries. Then [Robert] put his troops in battle order and placed himself at the center. The wing on the side of the sea was commended by Amiketas [Amico di Giovinazzo], who was a distinguished count [of Molfetta between 1068 and 1090], brave of hand and heart, while the other wing was taken by Bohemond [of Taranto, 1088–1111, prince of Antioch, 1098–1111], whose nickname is Saniskos. When the emperor learned about those matters, able as he always was to find the best solution in difficult moments, he adapted to the circumstances and established his troops on the slope by the sea. Since he had divided his army, he did not want to prevent the barbarians [that is, the troops of foreign origin in the Byzantine army], who had already moved, from attacking Robert. Instead, he kept to himself those who carry on their shoulders the two-edged swords [the Varangian Guard], as well as their commander, Nampites. He ordered them to dismount and to march in formation a little in front of the line. Like men of their race, they were carrying shields. After dividing the rest of the army into phalanxes, [the emperor] placed himself at the center. On his right and on his left hand, he appointed as commanders of phalanxes the caesar Nicephorus Melissenos [Emperor Alexios's brother-in-law, who was rewarded with the title of caesar and the city of Thessaloniki for his support in 1080] and the one called Pakourianos, who was the grand domestic. Between him and the barbarians advancing on foot was a strong contingent of warriors skilled at pulling the bow, who were supposed to attack Robert first. . . . Until this point, there had been only skirmishes between one side and the other, but Robert had remained quietly in contact with his men, and the distance between the two armies was growing smaller, when the foot soldiers and the cavalry of Amiketas's phalanx charged and attacked the end of Nampites's line. Meeting a brave resistance from our men, the attackers turned back, for they were not all elite soldiers. . . . At that moment, as it was later revealed, that Gaita [Sikelgaita, daughter of Prince Guaimar IV of Salerno, who married Robert in 1059], Robert's wife, who had accompanied him on this campaign, like another Pallas, even though she was not a second Athena, seeing those men running away, looked at them in anger and told them with a loud voice in her language something that was the equivalent of Homer's verses: "How long are you going to run away? Stop, and be men" [Virgil, *Iliad* 5.529]. As they kept running away, she took a long spear and charged at full gallop after them. Seeing that, they came to their senses and returned to the fight. Meanwhile, those carrying [battle-]axes and their commander, Nampites, due to their lack of experience and their impetuosity, had gone too far and were now at some distance from the Roman lines. . . . When Robert saw that they were both tired and out of breath, and everything [seemed to] confirm his assessment [of the situation]—their rapid advance, the distance that they had covered, the weight of their weapons—he ordered a detachment of infantry to move against them. Already exhausted, they were not as strong as the Kelts [that is, the Normans]. And this corps of barbarians was massacred, and those who escaped ran for safety into the church of the archangel Michael [the basilica of St-Michael in Arapaj, about four miles to the southeast of Dyrrachion]. . . . Meanwhile, the rest of the Roman army was bravely battling the enemy. However, Robert, like a winged horseman, charged the Roman phalanx with his men, pushed it back and cut it to pieces. . . . As for Emperor Alexios, he remained like an unconquerable tower, even though he had lost many of his companions, warriors distinguished by their birth and their military experience. . . . But the battle was still raging on because the emperor could be seen still resisting. At that point, three Latins detached themselves from the rest: one was Amiketas mentioned above, the other Peter, the son of Aliphas, as he described himself, and the third was in no way inferior to them. Charging at full gallop and raising their long lances, they attacked Alexios. Amiketas missed the emperor because his horse swerved a little. With his sword, the emperor deflected the lance of the second man and struck him with all his force on the collar bone, cutting off his arm entirely. When the third took aim at him frontally, [the emperor] with a presence of mind and composure that absolutely nothing could trouble, knew in the blink of an eye what he had to do, for that was how fast his mind worked. At the moment the blow fell, he leaned backward on his horse. The tip of the lance grazed the skin of his body; stopped by the rim of the helmet, it broke the strap that attached it to the chin and cast it on the ground. Meanwhile, the Kelt rode past him, believing that he [Alexios] had been unseated, when the emperor suddenly stood up firmly in the saddle without dropping any of his weapons. But keeping the sword in his right hand, covered in dust colored by his own blood, bareheaded, with his bright red hair flying around his eyes, not without bothering him (for the horse, frightened and impatient of the bit, was jumping about wildly and thus cast his curls onto his face), he recovered his forces the best he could, and continued to resist the enemy. Meanwhile, he observed the Turks [Seljuk Turkish mercenaries in the service of the Byzantines] running away as well, and even [Constantine] Bodin [Serbian ruler of Duklja, 1081–1101] withdrawing with no attempt to fight. Bodin had also taken up arms and, after arranging his troops in battle order, remained the entire day as if he had the intention to come to the rescue of the emperor, if needed, as indicated in the treaty he had concluded with him [Alexios]. He clearly waited to see if the victory was going to the emperor, so that he could also attack the Kelts. If not, he would refrain from entering the battle and would withdraw. That that was indeed his thought [at the time] is apparent from the [subsequent] events. As soon as he realized that the Kelts had the upper hand, he went back without taking any part in the fight. Observing all of this, the emperor, seeing that nobody was coming to his rescue, also turned his back on the enemy. And the Latins began to pursue the [fleeing] Roman army.

Questions: Since Anna was the daughter of Alexios, how might we critically test her text? What considerations might influence someone like Robert Guiscard to attack Byzantium? What role did morale play in this military confrontation? What factors influenced morale? How did each side try to gain advantages during the battle? What kind of military leader was Robert Guiscard? How did Gaita stop the retreat? What does the aftermath of the battle reveal about Emperor Alexios I Komnenos's situation?

37. THE CADASTRE OF THEBES

During the eleventh century, the Byzantine administration kept a systematic record of the tax burdens for each taxpayer. The central land register that formed the basis of the taxation system is known as the cadastre. Excerpts from such land registers kept by the government have survived in monastic archives, especially on Mount Athos. One fragment of a medieval tax register has been known, ever since the 1960s, as the "Cadastre of Thebes," because it deals with the taxation of lands in the suburbs of the city of Thebes (in central Greece). The text is preserved in four sheets of an eleventh-century manuscript written on paper, which were added to a fourteenth-century manuscript containing treatises of geometry and agricultural science. The four sheets may well have been written at some point during the second half of the eleventh century. The tax register contains entries for individuals, each one of them listed by name, with a brief description of the property and the amount of tax due. The section defining the property being taxed often includes the names of other people who had previously owned the property. The oldest possessor is listed first in the taxable matter, followed by all others listed in that part, then by the first person listed as taxpayer, and then by all others in that list. About a quarter of all taxpayers had titles, but those were rather common titles in the eleventh century, and by no means designating the highest echelons of the aristocracy. A few taxpayers (and not those with the most important titles) were assessed for the largest amount of tax, with all the others paying smaller amounts. Some taxpayers had different, often distant pieces of land recorded within one and the same entry, while other taxpayers were recorded several times for different areas.

Source: trans. L.A. Neville, "Local Provincial Elites in Eleventh-Century Hellas and Peloponnese" (PhD diss., Princeton University, 1998), pp. 236–37.

This sown land with the vineyard to the . . . For Peter son of Kosmas Gerasde called Anemosphaktos. On the portion of his grandfather, tax nomisma one twenty-fourth [one *modios* of land of good quality was valued at one *nomisma*—a gold coin; the yearly tax for that land was one twenty-fourth of the fiscal value]; with part of the holding of Leo son of Constantine in this village Terianon, tax nomisma one twenty-fourth one forty-eighth; with holding of Peter son of John in the village Pergion with Kithrid(io?), tax nomisma one forty-eighth; with part of the holding of Maurikios in the village of sown land of the Pasagarikoi, tax nomisma one-sixth one twenty-fourth; with part of the holding of Lampadararios from the village Patronia Ano in the adjacent sown land of the village of Chiomoniou, tax nomisma one forty-eighth; with holding of Rendakios son of Geronta in the village Bathy, tax nomisma one forty-eighth; that is *spatharios* Peter Thymianmare; that is the same Peter. [Tax due] one half nomisma. . . .

For Eudokia wife of *spatharios* Panaretos. On part of the holding of John Gerontas coming from one portion, that is to say, from one-quarter portion; with part of the holding of John son of Eustathios in the sown land of the right side road of the Pasagarikoi; with part of the holding of Marianos son of Leo; the holding in the village Piliana; with part of the holding of Theophilos, John, in the village Brysin; with a quarter part from the half part in Olana; with part of the holding of Heraklios, Theodotos, and Pardos from the village Sisinios, that is Kousounin, and Nicholas son of Gerontas in the village Leotribin near the dry river Eritzon, that is John Melgota with part of the son-in-law Panaretos Athenian. On holding of Panaretos Athenian, tax nomisma one-third one-twelfth Dimitri Thymiakaki, tax nomisma one-eighth. [Tax due] nomisma one-half one twenty-fourth nine [that is, 156 folles].

Questions: What does the document suggest about landholding patterns in central Greece in the eleventh century? According to this document, what kind of people owned land in the suburbs of Thebes? What might this document tell us about names in Middle Byzantium?

38. ARCHDEACON THOMAS ON ARCHBISHOP RAINER OF SPLIT

A notary of the urban commune of Spalato (now Split, in Croatia), canon of the cathedral, archdeacon, and (unsuccessful) candidate for the position of archbishop in that city, Thomas (1200–68) studied canon law in Bologna before returning to his hometown in the early 1220s. Shortly after being elected archdeacon at some point after 1230, he came into conflict with Archbishop Guncel (1220–42). Thomas was instrumental in the election of the first podestà (chief magistrate) of the commune, an Italian from Ancona named Gargano de Arscindis, who held the office between 1239 and 1242. Deeply disappointed in his failure to become archbishop after Guncel's death, Thomas began writing his History of the Bishops of Salona and Split. *However, he did not withdraw from public life, as he served his beloved city as envoy to Béla IV, king of Hungary (1235–70), and to Pope Innocent IV (1254–61). Thomas wanted to write a chronicle of the deeds of the archbishops of Salona and Split, but in the process he managed to produce a work of civic history under the influence of contemporary Italian models. One salient feature of this work is its strong feeling of urban patriotism, as well as a deep admiration for the republican form of government of the city. He had access to numerous sources in the urban archives—all now lost. That makes his coverage of the eleventh- to thirteenth-century history of Dalmatia a unique source for the Adriatic region, particularly for the relations between the Dalmatian cities and Byzantium.*

Source: trans. M. Matijević-Sokol, J.R. Sweeney, and D. Karbić, *History of the Bishops of Salona and Split* (Budapest: Central European University Press, 2006), pp. 123 and 125.

At that time, Manuel [I Komnenos] of glorious memory was emperor at Constantinople [1143–80]. The whole of Dalmatia and nearly all of Croatia were subject to his lordship. However, he was extremely generous to all those subject to him; he did not exact tribute but dispensed his wealth in a most openhanded way. He honored all who came to him, and always reimbursed them from the royal treasury. Once, after receiving a head count of the inhabitants of the city of Split, he sent a gratuity to every single person; he even gave one gold piece each to babies still in their cradles! Moreover, he sent out his dukes with a vast supply of weapons and carrying ample money for their expenses when they came and held the coastal cities and the greater part of Croatia.

And so the people of Split urged Archbishop Rainer [of Split, 1175–80] to proceed to Constantinople and to visit the imperial court. He assented with pleasure and taking with him a number of the important men of Split, he set out for Constantinople. When he had entered into the emperor's presence, he greeted him with deep respect on behalf of his fellow citizens and was received with great honor by the emperor; as long as he remained there, he was lavishly and honorably provided for at the expense of the court. And when he sought permission from the emperor to return, the emperor gave him gifts both many and precious. And so he returned to his church and enriched.

Questions: Why did Archbishop Rainer go to Constantinople? How do you explain the generosity of the emperor? What does this text reveal about relations between the imperial government and the peripheries of the empire? Why was it so remarkable to give a monetary gift to an infant still in the cradle?

CHAPTER SIX

NEW POWERS

Figure 6.1 Assassination of Duke Wenceslas of Bohemia. Illumination from the Gumpold Codex, an eleventh-century manuscript.

39. THE MAGYARS CONQUER HUNGARY

The Deeds of the Hungarians (Gesta Hungarorum) *is the earliest surviving historical work in Hungary, written in Latin by the former notary of a king named Béla, who called himself "Master P." If, as many historians now believe, the king in question was Béla III (1172–96), then Master P. was writing around 1200. The work survives in only one manuscript. Like Gallus Anonymus in Poland, Master P. was initially believed, because of his style, to have received some education in Paris, Orléans, or Italy. However, his Latin is rather simple and his style closer to the urban chroniclers of his time than to university-trained authors. He wrote in a plain style, with a few rhymed sentences, but plenty of legal expressions, with which Master P. may have become familiar in the royal chancery. Master P. used the chronicle of Regino of Prüm (d. 915). A long section in chapter 53 describing the Magyar raid into northern Italy (899–900) is lifted entirely from Regino's work. However, Master P. appears to have altered some of the details in Regino's text. The result is rather ironic, which suggests that the goal of Master P. was to find material for a much more fictionalized narrative, if not a parody. Master P. concocted a story of ancient origin for the Hungarians, imitating the genre of* origo gentis *(the origin of the people) so popular at the time. He therefore turned Scythians into the ancestors of the Magyars, and Magog (a grandson of Noah mentioned in the book of Genesis) into the progenitor of both Attila and Árpád. While crossing "Russia which is called Suzdal," the Hungarians battle both the Rus' and the Cumans, after which they move to the land of Pannonia, which the Romans, after the death of Attila, had turned into pastureland, "because their flocks grazed in the land of Pannonia." Such anachronisms are typical of the kind of myth-making history writing that became popular in the twelfth century, most famously illustrated by the* History of the Kings of Britain *of Geoffrey of Monmouth (c. 1095–1155). The intention of Master P. was most likely not to write a history of (the kingdom of) Hungary, but a "genealogy" of the first chieftains and dukes until the first king, Stephen I. There is conspicuously no mention of the Church, of communes, or of current affairs in the* Deeds of the Hungarians. *Moreover, Master P. pretends to stay away from the "false stories of countryfolk and the gabbling song of minstrels," only to mention them as a source of information. In the absence of any other sources, he also indulged in etymologizing, as is clear from the paragraph below. Given that he derived most place names from, or associated them with, names of noble families in twelfth-century Hungary, Master P. may have written the* Deeds *in order to address (and perhaps criticize) the claims to ancestry made by the recipients of King Andrew II's royal charters. In that case, Master P.'s Hungarians were not a people, but the (warrior) elites who conquered Hungary for themselves.*

Source: trans. Martyn Rady and László Veszprémy, *Anonymus and Master Roger* (Budapest: Central European University Press, 2010), pp. 13, 35, 37, 103, 107, and 109.

2. It now remains to say why the people who set forth from the Scythian land are called Hungarians. The Hungarians are so called from the castle of Hung where the seven leading persons, having subjugated the Slavs, tarried for a time upon entering the land of Pannonia. On account of this, all the nations round about called Álmos, son of Ügek, the prince of Hunguar and they called his warriors Hunguarians. . . .

12. Prince Álmos and his chief men, agreeing to the counsels of the Rus', made a most lasting peace with them. For the princes of the Rus', not to be expelled from their homes, had given, as we said above, their sons as hostages along with countless gifts. Then the prince of Halych ordered two thousand archers and three thousand peasants to go in advance to prepare for them a way through the Havas wood as far as the confines of Ung, and he loaded all their beasts of burden with victuals and other necessities and gave them innumerable flocks for food. . . . And so, coming through the Havas wood, they [the Magyars] came down to the region of Ung. When they arrived there, they called the place that they first occupied Munkács because they had arrived after the greatest toil [pun on the name of the town: *munka* in Hungarian means "work, effort"] at the land that they had chosen for themselves. Then they rested there for forty days from their labors and they loved the land more than can be said [Gen. 27:33]. The inhabitants of the land [Jth. 2:18], the Slavs, hearing of their arrival greatly and of their own accord submitted to Prince Álmos because they had heard that Prince Álmos was descended of the line of King Attila. Although they were Prince Salan's men, they still served Prince Álmos with great honor and dread, offering to their lord, as is fitting, all that was needed to live on. And such fear and dread overtook the inhabitants of the land that they cringed before the prince and his leading men, like servants to their own lords. . . .

47. On the twenty-first day, Prince Árpád, having taken counsel, marched off from Etzelburg [Budapest] to conquer the land of Pannonia as far as the Drava River, and on the first day he encamped beside the Danube toward Százhalom. Then it was decided that the prince should send one part of his army along the Danube to the castle of Baranya, for which he appointed as the chief men and commanders two of the principal persons, namely Etu, father of Öd, and Vajta, from whom the Baracska kindred is descended, to whom for their most faithful service Prince Árpád gave no small gifts, and to Öd son of Etu, he gave land beside the Danube along with innumerable people. There Öd, having conquered the people of that region, built a castle that he called in the vernacular Szekcsö, because he established for himself a seat and station. And to Vajta he gave in the same way a great land toward Sár with innumerable people, which is still called Vajta.

50. Then Prince Árpád and his noblemen leaving Etzelburg with a third of his army encamped beside the field of Sóskút and riding from there they arrived at Bodajk Mountain. On the eastern side, Prince Árpád gave to Előd, father of Szabolcs, a great wood that is now called Vértes on account of the shields of

Germans that were abandoned there [pun on the name of the forest: *vért* means "shield" in Hungarian]. At the bottom of that wood, beside Lake Fertő, a long time later, Csák, nephew of Szabolcs, built a castle. What more? Thus proceeding, Prince Árpád and his warriors encamped beside Saint Martin's Mountain, and they and their beasts drank of the spring of Sabaria. Having ascended the mountain and seen the beauty of the land of Pannonia, they became exceedingly happy. From there, they marched to the Rába and Rábca [Rivers], and laid waste the peoples and realms of the Slavs and Pannonians and occupied their territories. They also stormed the boundaries of the Carinthians on the Mura with frequent assaults, of whom they killed thousands at the point of the sword, threw down their defenses, and took their territories and, with God's help, their posterity keeps it to this present day effectively and peacefully.

Questions: What is the author's understanding of the depth of Hungarian history? In particular, how does he link the events of the past to the present? What does that say about the value of this source for reconstructing early Hungarian history? Who are the main actors of that history?

40. THE ORIGIN OF THE PŘEMYSLID DYNASTY

Cosmas of Prague was born around 1045 and was educated in Prague. At some point in his early life, he went to Liège (now in Belgium) to study grammar in one of the most advanced centers of learning in the late eleventh-century Holy Roman empire. In 1086, he was a witness for an important imperial diploma issued to the benefit of the bishopric of Prague at a synod that took place in Mainz. It is not clear where he lived at that time, but by 1099 he was ordained priest, although he was married and had a son. At some point in the 1110s, he became the dean of the cathedral chapter in Prague, in charge of overseeing the liturgy and the management of the chapter's property and incomes. The first book of his Chronicle of the Czechs *was finished between 1099 and 1122, with Books 2 and 3 following in relatively quick succession until 1125, the year of his death. His story of the origin of the Přemyslid dynasty is entirely fabricated, and some have seen it as a veiled critique of both the authoritarian rule of Vratislav II and of the Czech nobility of Cosmas's own time. Cosmas clearly had in mind an audience of people who could read between the lines, especially at particular points signaled in the text by symbolic elements—the staff that the angry man pounds into the ground in front of Libuše, her own position reclining as if after delivering a baby, or the two oxen of Přemysl's plow. Even if the exact meaning of those allusions is now lost, there can be no doubt that this story has a subtle, perhaps even subversive intention. Although without any direct parallels, Cosmas's story was based on the tenth-century biography of Saint Wenceslas, known as* Legenda Christiani, *which he amplified and modified by means of several bits and pieces culled from ancient literature, both the Bible and Latin authors.*

Source: trans. P. Mutlová and M. Rady, *Cosmas of Prague: The Chronicle of the Czechs*, ed. J.M. Bak (Budapest: Central European University Press, 2019), pp. 21, 23, 27, 29, and 31.

The third [daughter of Krok], by age the younger, but by wisdom the older, was named Libuše. She also built at that time a very powerful citadel next to a forest that stretches toward the village of Zbečno, and called it Libušín after her own name. She was a woman unique among women, prophetic in her thoughts, brisk in her speech, with a chaste body, of virtuous manners, unmatched in deciding people's disputes, and kind to everybody and exceptionally likable, honor and glory of the female sex wisely dispensing male affairs. Yet, as nobody is utterly happy [Horace, *Odes* 2.16.27], even such a praiseworthy woman—what an awful human destiny!—was a seer. Since she foretold the future often and correctly to the people, after her father's death the whole tribe by common consent appointed her their judge. At that time, a major dispute arose between two persons, preeminent by their wealth and birth who seemed to be leaders of the people, concerning a boundary between two adjacent fields. They launched into such a quarrel that they got into each other's thick beards with their nails and, insulting each other with plain swearing, with their fingers shamelessly under the other's nose, they entered the court raving. With a great uproar, they approached the lady and suppliantly asked her to decide the contested case between them according to justice. She, therewithal, as is the wanton indulgence of women who have no man to fear, leaning on her elbow, lay delicately upon decorated cushions as if just delivered of a boy. Proceeding on the path of justice [Prov. 2:20] and disregarding the rank of the men, she brought the matter of the whole controversy that had arisen between them to a state of rightness. Thereupon the one who had lost the case, filled with unjust indignation, three or four times shook his head [Ovid, *Metamorphoses* 2.49 and 1.179], and three times thumped the earth with his staff, as was his habit, openmouthed spattered his beard with spit and exclaimed: "What injustice, hardly tolerable to men! A loose-tongued woman with her wily mind passes judgments that belong to men! Sure enough, we know that a woman even standing or sitting on a throne comprehends little—how much less if she lies on a bed! Is it not then more suitable for her to receive a husband than to speak laws to warriors? Sure, all have long hair but women have a short mind. It is better for men to die than to suffer such things. We alone are set by nature to the shame of all nations and people, we, who lack a male ruler and manly judgment and who suffer under woman's law." The lady ignored this insult to her and, hiding the pain of her heart beneath female modesty, smiled and said: "It is so as you say: I am a woman and live as a woman. However, the reason why you think I am unreasonable is because I do not judge with rod of iron [Ps. 2:9], and since you live without fear, you justly despise me. For where fear is, there is honor [Rom. 13:7]. Now is the time for you to have a ruler harsher than a woman. Thus the doves once also despised a little white kite that they had elected king, as you despise me, and installed a much crueler hawk as their duke. With false charges, the hawk started to kill both guilty and innocent and from then until now the hawk feeds on the doves [Seneca, *Phaedra* 1:31]. Go home now and whomever you will elect as ruler for yourselves tomorrow, I shall take as a husband." . . .

On the next day, as was commanded, they immediately convoked an assembly, and summoned the people. Once all are assembled, the woman sitting on a high throne addresses the boorish men. . . . To this, the base folk rejoice with inarticulate shouting and all as one mouth require a duke to be given to them. Libuše said to them: "There, there behind those mountains—and she pointed a finger to the mountains—is a stream not very big by the name of Bílina, on the banks of which can be found a village by the name of Stadice. In its ambit, there is a piece of fallow ground twelve paces long and wide that strangely enough does not belong to any field, although it lies in the middle of so many others. There your duke plows with two different [colored] oxen, one of which has a white girdle and a white head, the other of which is white from front to back and his hind legs are white. Now, if you please, take my *thalitarium* [perhaps a horse], a change of clothes appropriate for a duke; and go and announce the orders of the people and mine to the man, and bring yourself a duke and me a husband. His name is Přemysl and he will contrive many laws upon your necks and heads, because in Latin this name means 'he who considers or contrives.' His progeny will rule over all this land forever and ever" [Exod. 15:18].

In the meantime, envoys were chosen to announce the lady's and the people's brief to the man. . . . They crossed the mountains and were already approaching the village that they were to reach when a boy ran on the road, whom they asked: "Hey, good, isn't this village called Stadice, and if so, is there a man named Přemysl in it?" "Indeed," he replied, "it is the village you seek and behold, not far from here, Přemysl prods the oxen in a field in order to finish his work soon." To him the envoys come up and say: "You fortunate man, who was given to us as a duke produced by the gods!" As is the habit for the peasants that it is not sufficient to say something once, they repeat with full mouths: "Hail, O duke, hail, with most reverend praise! Dismiss the oxen, change clothes, and mount the horse!" And they showed him the clothes and the neighing horse. "Our lady Libuše and all the people command you to come at once and accept the realm destined for you and your offspring. All that we have and we ourselves are in your hands [Josh. 9:25]. We choose you as our duke, our judge, our governor, you protector, and our only lord." To this, the wise man paused, as if unaware of the future, and thrust the prod he was holding in his hand into the ground and, dismissing the oxen, said: "Go to where you came from!"

Questions: What concerns did the envoys have as they set out to find Přemysl? How might such concerns be different from those the "leaders of the people" had before or after the assembly? What is the role of Libuše in the story? What can the story tell us about the dynastic traditions in medieval Bohemia?

41. THE ORIGIN OF THE PIAST DYNASTY

The Deeds of the Princes of the Poles *was written by an anonymous author known as Gallus Anonymus. Some believe that he was from southern France, others tie him either to Flanders or to Venice. Still others have noticed a great resemblance between the rhythmical prose in the chronicle and the style of the works produced in the late eleventh and early twelfth centuries in central France, in the region of Tours and Orléans, which may indicate that Gallus studied there before coming to Poland. He finished his chronicle at some point between 1113 and 1117, most likely at the Cracow court of Prince Bolesław III Wrymouth (1102–38). Gallus incorporated poems into this narrative, one of the very few examples of Latin poetry from east central Europe dated before 1300, other than hymns. Despite claims to the contrary, Gallus may himself have composed the material supposedly collected from oral sources. This is certainly the case of the legend of Pazt the plowman and his wife Rzepka (a name derived from the Polish word for "turnip"). Some have assumed that the story in the* Deeds *reflects genuine folk (oral) traditions and so it cannot be the learned construction of Gallus Anonymus. More recently, however, that assumption has been questioned and exposed to much criticism. Judging from the dedication of this work, Gallus wrote the chronicle for an audience of friends and supporters at the court of Bolesław Wrymouth. Some have suggested that Gallus was in fact commissioned to write the work at a moment of particular crisis for Bolesław. This may explain the preoccupation with the spatial construction of power and with the struggle against pagans. More recently, scholars have highlighted the sophisticated narrative technique, with its multitude of voices, as well as rhetorical use of age categories (particularly children, as in the story of Pazt). Given that earlier annals in Poland have not survived, the question of whether Gallus used them for his chronicle remains unanswered. It is therefore not clear where he got the idea of the origins of the medieval dynasty of Poland. According to Gallus Anonymus, Mieszko, the first duke of Poland mentioned in the written sources, was a descendant of the family of Pazt, the poor, but kind man. His name was then given in the seventeenth century to the family that ruled Poland from the tenth to the fourteenth centuries.*

Source: trans. P.W. Knoll and F. Schaer, *Gesta Principum Polonorum: The Deeds of the Princes of the Poles* (Budapest: Central European University Press, 2003), pp. 17, 19, 21, and 23.

1. In the city of Gniezno (the name of which means "nest" in Slavic) lived a duke named Popiel, who had two sons. Now when the time came for the cutting of their hair—a custom among the pagans—he prepared a great banquet

and invited large numbers of his nobles and friends. But by God's secret plan it happened that two strangers arrived there. However, not only were they not invited to join the banquet, but they were treated injuriously and driven away from the entrance of the city. Disgusted by the rudeness of the townsmen, they made their way forthwith down into the suburb, where by chance and by fortune they found themselves before a little cottage belonging to a plowman of the aforesaid duke, who was about to make a banquet for his sons. Although just a poor man, he was kind. He invited the strangers into his cottage and most warmly offered them his modest means. They accepted the poor man's invitation with pleasure, and as they entered the hut, they said: "May you truly be glad we have come, and may our arrival bring you abundance of good things, and honor and glory in your offspring!"

2. There were domestics in the house, by name Pazt [Piast] the son of Chośicisko and Rzepka his wife, who with heartfelt goodwill ministered to the needs of their guests, as best they might. When they saw how wise they were, they thought to bring about something secret, if such there was, with their advice. So when they were seated and were talking about this and that as usually happens, the strangers asked if there was any drink to be had; then their good host the plowman said, "I have a jar of fermented ale, which I brewed for the cutting of my only son's hair. But what use is such a small amount? Drink it if you will." For this poor peasant had earlier decided to make ready a few dishes to celebrate his own boy's haircutting at the same time as his lord the duke was preparing a banquet in honor of his sons (for he could not do so at any other time because he was so poor). He had been planning to invite some of his friends and poor people to dinner, or rather to share a breakfast. He had also been fattening a piglet and keeping it for the same occasion. What I am going to say will amaze you—but whose thoughts can encompass the marvelous works of God, or who would venture to question his goodness. For at times he exalts the poor and the humble [Luke 1:52] in this world and does not disdain to reward even pagans for their hospitality. Well, the guests had no qualms in ordering the ale to be served, for they well knew that the ale would not run out but go on increasing the more they sampled it. And indeed, we are told, the ale kept on increasing

> Till the cups that passed among them were all brimful every round
> Even those the duke's companions earlier had empty found.

They ordered the piglet to be slaughtered too, whereupon—marvelous to relate—ten buckets (in Slavic, *cebri*) are reported to have been filled from it. When Pazt and Rzepka saw these miraculous things happening, they realized something of great significance was being foretold for the boy.

So, the duke and all his fellows they were minded to invite, yet they did not dare to do so until they had asked the strangers' advice first. Well, to put it briefly, the two guests counseled and urged to do so, and Pazt the farmer invited their lord the duke and all his guests, nor did the duke disdain to accept the invitation from his peasant. For the duchy of Poland had not yet grown so mighty, nor was the prince of the city so haughty and swollen with pride, strutting in pomp amid crowds of retainers. So, the feasting began as a feast should, with everything laid on in abundance, and the [two] guests cut the boy's hair, and as a presage of the future they gave him the name Siemowit [probably meaning "head of the family" or "prosperity of the family"].

Questions: Compare this story to that of the origin of the Přemyslid dynasty (Doc. 40). What is the role of miracles in those stories? What can the story about Pazt tell us about dynastic traditions in Poland? How reliable is the story from a historical point of view? Where can you identify the interventions of the author to modify the story according to his narrative goals? What concerns did the author have when introducing the story?

42. *DAGOME IUDEX*

One of the most debated sources pertaining to the early history of Poland is a note in a legal collection put together between 1084 and 1087 by the canon lawyer Deusdedit of San Pietro in Vincoli. According to Deusdedit, the note in question was a summary of a document that he had found in "another volume" under an entry dated to the time of Pope John XV (985–96). Both the chronological indication and the content of the summary have encouraged historians to identify "Dagome iudex" with Mieszko I, the first ruler of the Piast dynasty known to history, and "Ote senatrix" with his second wife Oda of Haldensleben, the daughter of the margrave of the Northern March. The other two personal names in the summary are of two of Mieszko and Oda's three children, Mieszko and Lambert, both of whom died at some point in the 990s. Some have assumed that Mieszko and Oda were simply trying to protect their young sons and their inheritance from Bolesław (later known as Chrobry, the first king of Poland), who was Mieszko's son from a previous marriage. To accomplish that, Mieszko and Oda placed the inheritance under the protection of the pope. However, the text clearly mentions Misica and Labertus as donors, along with their parents Dagome and Ote. In other words, the donation in question was made by an entire family. This may therefore have been an attempt to shield the city "called Schinesghe" from those sons of Mieszko who were excluded, primarily from Bolesław. This then is likely a byproduct of the political situation in the Polish lands c. 990, shortly before Bolesław came to power after his father's death. At a much later time, around 1200, another scribe, while copying Deusdedit's Collection of Canons, *inserted a remark concerning the ethnicity of the people whose names are mentioned at the beginning. He (wrongly) assumed that they were Sardinians because*

Dagome appears as a judge. On the other hand, he did not find it necessary to explain the meaning of the "city called Schinesghe." The reason is that he most likely understood that to have been the religious center of the polity, whose boundaries are described in the donation. Schinesghe, in other words, was the main or only see in that polity. This must have been Gniezno, which was indeed the see of the archbishop of Poland by the time Deusdedit compiled his collection.

Source: trans. F. Curta from *Die Kanonessammlung des Kardinals Deusdedit*, ed. V. Wolf von Glanvell (Paderborn: F. Schöningh, 1905), vol. 1, p. 359.

Likewise, within another volume, under Pope John XV [985–96]: *Dagome iudex* ["Judge Dagome," possibly a corruption of "Ego Mesco dux," "I, Duke Mieszko"] and *Ote senatrix* [female senator], as well as their sons Misica [Mieszko] and Labertus [Lambert]—of what nation [those] people are I do not know, but supposedly Sardinians, because they are ruled by four judges—are said to have donated to Saint Peter an entire city called Schinesghe, with all that belongs to it inside the following boundaries: on the first side it begins along the sea [that goes to] Bruzze [Prussia], until the place that is called Rus', and [along] the borders of Rus' extending to Cracow, and from that [city of] Cracow [all the way] to the River Oder, straight to the place called Alemure, and from that Alemure to the land of Milze [Upper Lusatia, "Milsko" in Polish, the region of eastern Germany next to the present-day border with Poland and the Czech Republic], and from the border of Milze directly to the Oder, and from there along the River Oder back to the abovementioned city of Schinesghe.

Questions: What landscape features are used to mark the borders of the polity of "Dagome iudex"? What does Cardinal Deusdedit's confusion tell us about knowledge of the dynastic traditions of Poland outside that country? What ethnic groups are mentioned in this document? What can that tell us about Cardinal Deusdedit's knowledge of the geography of Europe?

43. THE ASSASSINATION OF DUKE WENCESLAS

The efforts to convert the inhabitants of Bohemia to Christianity took a decisive turn under Duke Vratislav (c. 915–21), who built a church dedicated to Saint George in Prague. He married Princess Drahomira of a Slavic tribe in the Baltic region of present-day Saxony. She was the mother of Wenceslas, born in 907, and of Boleslav. Shortly after her husband's death, Drahomira ordered the execution of her mother-in-law, Ludmila, to whom the young Wenceslas had been entrusted. Ludmila was canonized after her remains were moved from Tetín (near Beroun, to the southwest of Prague), the place where she had apparently been murdered, to the church of St-George in Prague. Wenceslas ascended to the ducal throne in

925, and immediately shifted the political allegiance of Bohemia from Bavaria to Saxony. He in fact built a new church in Prague dedicated to the patron saint of the Saxon ducal family, Saint Vitus. However, he was assassinated on 28 September 935, at the orders of his younger brother Boleslav. The dynastic struggle between the older and the younger Přemyslids took a dramatic turn when Boleslav buried Wenceslas in the church of St-Vitus and immediately began promoting his cult as a saint. The cult soon conferred a sacred aura to the family (and the dynasty), which subsequent generation of dukes managed to enhance to their own advantage. From the victim of a dynastic conflict, Wenceslas turned into a martyr by the late tenth century, a warrior and a saintly knight by the twelfth century. Around 1200, he was the "perpetual ruler," his crown becoming a symbol of transpersonal corporation, the "state" of his Přemyslid successors. The political performance of a ruler was measured in the thirteenth century by the degree to which he embodied "the body of Saint Wenceslas." Wenceslas was certainly not the only royal saint of east central or eastern Europe venerated as a patron of a group of people or a country, but no other cult was as strongly associated with the representation and ideology of political power. Over a dozen hagiographic texts about Saint Wenceslas are known, several of which may clearly be dated to the tenth century, which attests to the existence of his cult at that early date. Bishop Gumpold of Mantua wrote his Passion of Saint Wenceslas *at the request of Otto II (967–83) in or around 980. The basis for his text was an earlier* vita *(known as* Crescente fide*), which was written less than a decade earlier by an unknown author. There are also texts in Old Church Slavonic about both Saint Wenceslas and Saint Ludmila. No other text, however, has caused as much controversy since the late nineteenth century as the* vita *attributed to a Czech author named Christian (hence the conventional title of the work,* Legenda Christiani*). Because the text is preserved only in a fourteenth-century manuscript, the dating and authenticity of this* vita *have been the object of much debate in Czech historiography. The balance is currently tilted toward an early date of the text, perhaps in the last two decades of the tenth century.*

Source: trans. M. Kantor, *The Origins of Christianity in Bohemia: Sources and Commentary* (Evanston, IL: Northwestern University Press, 1990), pp. 178–80, 183–84, 186–88, 189–90, and 192.

In the meantime, blessed Wenceslas, who had been elected as ruler [in 921] through the inspiration of Christ, outgrew his adolescence, and was radiant with the bloom of most graceful youth. . . . He warded all this [enmity of his mother] with the weapon of faith and protected himself with the shield of patience. For these wicked men [working for Drahomira] even tried to kill his priests and some monks, with whose instructions he strengthened himself. Constantly plotting against them, they sought to frighten them with grave threats so that none of them would have the courage to go to him. But he knew about all this. And together with men who were loyal to him, he forced an opening in the rear, and when the sun set, he secretly sent for some priests. After he learned all that was useful to him during the night, at the break of dawn he let the teacher or priest dear to him depart in secret. And he carried a booklet hidden beneath his clothes and read it diligently whenever he found a quiet place. Deeply lamenting inwardly, he grieved over the callousness of his people and over their blindness and disbelief. Finally, having girded himself with virtue, and strengthened by God, he sent for his mother and all the magnates. And, as was fitting, he rebuked them, as the Book of Wisdom says: "The words of the wise are like pointed sticks, like nails firmly fastened" [Eccles. 12:11]. Then blessed Wenceslas spoke thus: "O sons of criminals, seed of lies and unjust men, why were you opposed to my studying of the law of our Lord Jesus Christ and heeding his command? If you do not wish to serve Christ, why do you not at least allow others to do so? However, if until now I have lived under your guardianship and control, henceforth I will reject it. I wish to serve Almighty God wholeheartedly."

For this reason and for various others, great differences arose then between the magnates who remained on the side of the pious ruler, and the ones who supported the contemptible side of the wicked regent. And the counselors and foremost men of the land were divided, and the thorns of discord grew between them and led to bloodshed. Although very small, the side of the righteous nevertheless gained the upper hand over the side of the unrighteous which, as always, was disunited. For Prince Wenceslas, who has been mentioned repeatedly, was inspired by the Holy Spirit, and while striving to obtain peace, he planned to banish his mother, the cause of all the malice, from the country. By driving her out, and all her wicked followers, the fury of the rebellion would abate, and peace would thrive in Christ's church, and all would become thoroughly familiar with the true teaching of Christ, having one and the same ruler. And he would call his mother back again to the country with honor after banishing and driving out the sons of discord, and when everything that appeared to serve harmony and the principality was arranged and peace was established. And he in fact accomplished all this with the help of God the Creator, for he exiled his mother in utmost disgrace from the land. . . .

Thus, after blessed Prince Wenceslas pacified and consolidated his princedom with the help of Christ, how he proved himself before Christ, and what a vessel, a chosen one he became! Neither my spirit, nor language and speech, nor a book would be sufficient to describe this. And because I am burdened by a multitude of sins, I would be unable to explain how much harm he caused the devil, fighting for the Lord as a warrior of Christ, and how many sheaves he gathered into Christ's barn as faithful servant. But I can at least tell a little about many things. Even as a boy he did not deviate from divine teachings. He was truthful in speech, just in judgment, honorable and worthy of trust, and merciful beyond the usual measure of human nature. For whenever someone stood accused before an assembly of judges and was condemned to death in his presence by a judge, he withdrew under some pretext and hid, as best he could, mindful of Christ's threat in the Gospel: "Judge not, and you shall not be judged. Condemn not, and you shall not be condemned" [Luke 6:37]. He razed prisons and gallows built during earlier times that still remained. Untiringly he comforted orphans, widows, the poor, the sorrowing, and the wounded. He sated the hungry, gave drink to the thirsty, clothed the naked, visited the sick, buried the dead, and received strangers and wayfarers like his closest relatives. He honored priests, clerics, and monks like the Lord. He showed the way of truth to those who had gone astray, and he practiced humility, patience, moderation, and charity, which stands out above all. He did not deprive anyone of anything by force or deceit. And he provided his retinue not only with the best arms, but also with apparel. . . .

However, since the enemy of mankind, who from the very beginning of the world has attacked multitudes of faithful, could not conquer, even with all his might, the unconquerable servant of Christ, he resorted to an old weapon and strove to destroy the Christian faith. For his younger brother, whom we compared to Cain in the previous narrative, and for whose benefit he intended to give up everything, as we mentioned before, and to lay aside all worldly splendor, was deceived by much advice from evil people, who resented having to forsake their customs and not being allowed to do forbidden things. And they incited him against his most holy brother with the fatal weapon of hatred. . . . This Boleslav [I, duke between 935 and 972], who had his own home or court at the castle which bears his name [Stará Boleslav, on the Elbe, to the northeast of Prague], was now being prodded on all sides by the devil's arrows and aroused by his longing to rule. Considering that the feast of the blessed martyrs Cosmas and Damian was coming [28 September]—the one celebrated before the feast of the blessed archangel Michael [29 September]—they presumed this was now a suitable occasion to invite cunningly his aforementioned, blessed brother as though to a banquet, for a church was there consecrated in honor of these saints, but actually, as the deed demonstrated, to his death. However, although all this was well known to him, nevertheless he maintained a gallant spirit and took leave of all his friends and relatives with a kiss. Having said his last farewells, he set off, protected by the weapons of faith.

When he arrived there, he saw that everything was doubly prepared for him, that is, a banquet had been arranged with great splendor, as well as a powerful band of secretly armed enemies. He then betook himself to the church. After he had properly participated in the divine service, he commended himself to God and Saints Cosmas and Damian, whose anniversary commemoration was being observed that day, and cheerfully entered the banquet hall. And when the hearts of the banqueting villains, which had long been saturated with the venom of murder, were warmed by food and drink, gradually they began to show their hidden weapons. Thinking constantly about the attack, they rose three times, and three times that sat down again, for God through his power prevented them from carrying out that deed, perhaps because he wished to sanctify the following day, since hitherto no feast day fell upon it. Thus, when the saint observed how wild they had become, he indeed maintained his fearless composure, but nevertheless hastened to rise from the table as soon as he could. And as he was leaving, one of his friends approached him from a place near the banquet and said, "Look here, I have secretly prepared a horse for you; mount it, my lord, and be sure to ride away from here as quickly as possible, for death threatens you." However, not paying attention to his words, he returned again to the banquet hall, seized a goblet, and pronouncing a toast in the presence of all, exclaimed in a raised voice: "In the name of the blessed archangel Michael, let us drink with the supplication of prayer that he might now deign to lead our souls to the peace of eternal joy." And when some of those faithful to him answered "Amen," he drained his cup, kissed them all, and returned to his guest dwellings. Allowing his most extraordinary limbs some rest after he prayed to God for a long time and sang psalms, tired, he finally fell asleep.

And the hour to celebrate vigils approached. . . . For as the dear martyr hastened to church before morning devotion, yearning to pray to God the Father as solitarily as possible in the chamber of his most holy heart and undisturbed by the hum of the crowd, a plot was being arranged against him by his brother's faction, and the sword was being sharpened so that an offering would be prepared for Christ. . . . For as soon as he saw the man of God coming, the priest of that church, one of those from whom the iniquity of Babylon proceeds, shut the doors of the church, as commanded by the criminals. The assassins, that is his brother with his entire armed band, stood ready. Seeing his brother, God's chosen warrior wished to thank him. And he embraced him with both arms around the neck, kissed him, and greeted him with the words, "May you always be healthy, my brother, may you have an abundance of the goods of earthly life, as well as of the future one, and may Christ receive you at his eternal banquet with the same generosity you extended to me and my retinue yesterday."

But with a malicious look, he unsheathed the sword, which he had hidden beneath his cloak and replied arrogantly to this: "Indeed I feasted you yesterday, as the moment demanded, but now this is how a brother serves a brother!" And swinging the sword, he struck him on the head. However, since the power of the Lord was shielding him, he scarcely drew blood. For that wretch was so paralyzed by dread over the cruelty of his deed that even when he struck a second time, he saw to his amazement that he was unable to do anything worthy of a strong man. Now, upon seizing the bared sword with his hand, blessed Wenceslas said, "How badly you behave hurts me!" But when he perceived that his brother would in no wise dispense with the deed he had begun, he finally took hold of him, as some say, knocked him to his feet and said: "Do you see how you destroyed yourself by your own decision? I could crush you in my hand like a little whelp, but far be it from the hand of a servant of God to be stained with a brother's blood." And to his brother he returned the sword which he had taken from him, his hands already smeared with blood from it, and he quickly hurried toward the church. However, that wretch ran after him and cried out in a loud voice: "Comrades, my comrades, where are you? You are helping your lord very badly and backing him up poorly though he is in such distress!" And then a whole crowd of villains ran out from their hiding places. Pouncing on him [Wenceslas] with many swords and spears, they mangled him with severe blows and destroyed him before the doors of the church. And then, on the twenty-eighth day of September in the nine hundred twenty-ninth year from God's incarnation [in fact, 935], while heaven rejoiced and the earth wept, his holy soul departed victoriously to the Lord, liberated on this battleground from the prison of this world and glorified in blood.

Questions: Which aspects of rulership are emphasized here? What message is this text communicating to churchmen? What effect was the story of this murder intended to have? What effects was it likely to have on the dynastic traditions in Bohemia?

44. THE GNIEZNO SUMMIT

Bolesław Chrobry's acquisition of the relics of such martyrs as Adalbert of Prague and Bruno of Querfurt attracted the attention of Emperor Otto III, who in 1000 visited Gniezno as a pilgrim to his friend's (Adalbert's) shrine. The significance of this extraordinary visit has been the object of much debate. Although known from other sources as well (such as Thietmar of Merseburg), Gallus Anonymus's account of the Gniezno Summit (as the event is now known among historians) is by far the most detailed. There is little if any doubt that on that occasion Gniezno was elevated to the rank of archbishopric, with Adalbert's half brother Radim (Gaudentius) as the first archbishop, and three suffragan sees were established in Cracow, Wrocław, and Kołobrzeg. On the other hand, it is hard to take the evidence of the chronicle at face value. The reference to a "golden age" in which gold and silver were worthless was lifted directly from Lucretius (De rerum naturae), *whose work Gallus knew well, much like other pieces of classical literature. The reference to princes who went from being friendly to being closest friends is a quote from Sallust's* War against Jugurtha. *However, there is no reason to doubt that, as far as Bolesław's generosity is concerned, things did indeed take place very much like Gallus described them. The fact that Bolesław insisted on giving Otto all the gold and silverware used at the feast together with robes of various colors seems to indicate that he wanted the emperor to remember the way in which he was treated in Poland. Those "gifts" may have been charity, most appropriate for a pilgrim, albeit one of imperial status.*

Source: trans. P.W. Knoll and F. Schaer, *Gesta Principum Polonorum: The Deeds of the Princes of the Poles* (Budapest: Central European University Press, 2003), pp. 33, 35, 37, 39, and 41.

Moreover, when Saint Adalbert came to him on his long wanderings after suffering many indignities through his rebellious Czech people, Bolesław [Chrobry, duke of Poland between 992 and 1025, king in 1025] received him with great veneration and paid faithful attention to his instructions and his sermons. Then, once he saw that the faith had begun to blossom in Poland and the holy church was growing, the holy martyr, alight with the fire of love and zeal for preaching, fearlessly entered Prussia; and there he met with martyrdom and brought his holy struggle to an end [23 April 997]. Afterward, Bolesław obtained his body from the Prussians for a weight of gold and laid him to rest in the metropolitan see of Gniezno with all the honor befitting him. One further matter seems to me worthy of record. In his time, the emperor Otto Rufus [Otto III, Holy Roman emperor between 996 and 1002] went to visit Saint Adalbert to pray and seek reconciliation, and at the same time to learn more of what was reported of the glorious Bolesław (the story can be read at greater length in the book of his [Adalbert's] martyrdom), and Bolesław received him with the honor and ceremony with which such a distinguished guest, a king and a Roman emperor, should fittingly be received. Marvelous and wonderful sights Bolesław set before the emperor when he arrived: the ranks first of the knights in all their variety, and then of the princes, lined up on a spacious plain like choirs, each separate unit set apart by the distinct and varied colors of its apparel, and no garment there was of inferior quality, but of the most precious stuff that might anywhere be found. For in Bolesław's time every knight and every lady of the court wore robes instead of garments of linen or wool, nor did they wear in his court any precious furs, however new, without robes and orphrey. For gold in his days was held by all to be as common as silver, and silver deemed as little worth as straw. So when the Roman emperor beheld his glory and power and richness, he exclaimed in admiration, "By the crown of my empire, the things I behold are greater than I had been led to believe," and after taking counsel with his magnates he added before the whole company, "Such a great man does not deserve to be styled a duke or a count like any of the princes, but to be raised to a royal throne and adorned with a diadem in glory." And with these words he took the imperial diadem from his own head and laid it upon the head of Bolesław in pledge of friendship. And as a triumphal banner he gave him as a gift one of the nails from the cross of our Lord with the lance of Saint Maurice [the lance was believed to have been the one that a Roman soldier used to stab Jesus in the side (John 19:34); Saint Maurice, the leader of the Theban Legion in the Roman army, took the holy lance in battle] and in return Bolesław gave to him an arm of Saint Adalbert. And in such love were they united that day that the emperor declared him his brother and partner in the empire, and called him a friend and ally of the Roman people. And what is more, he granted him and his successors authority over whatever ecclesiastical honors belonged to the empire in any part of the kingdom of Poland or other territories he had conquered or might conquer among the barbarians, and a decree about this arrangement was confirmed by Pope Sylvester [II, 999–1003] in a privilege of the holy Church of Rome. So, Bolesław was thus gloriously raised to kingship by the emperor, and he gave an example of the liberality innate in him when for the three days following his coronation, he celebrated a feast in style fit for a king or emperor. Every day the plate and the tableware were new, and many different ones were given out, ever richer again. For at the end of the feast, he ordered the waiters and the cupbearers to gather the gold and silver vessels—for there was nothing made of wood there—from all three days' courses, that is, the cups and goblets, the bowls and plates, and the drinking horns, and he presented them to the emperor as a token of honor, and not as a princely tribute. His servants were likewise told to collect the wall hangings and the coverlets, the carpets and tablecloths and napkins, and everything that had been provided for their needs and take them to the emperor's quarters. In addition, he presented many other vessels, of gold and silver and of diverse workmanship, and robes of various hues and ornaments never seen before, precious stones and so many other marvelous things, that the emperor regarded such presents as a miracle. Each of his princes was given presents of such magnificence that from being friendly they now became closest friends. But who could count what and how many presents he gave to all the lords, so that not a single servant out of all the multitude went away without a gift? The emperor returned home, delighted with the lavish gifts. Bolesław for his part returned to the business of the kingdom and summoned up again his old anger against his foes.

Questions: What is the relation between Otto III and Bolesław Chrobry in this account of the Gniezno Summit? What is the author's view of (ideal) rulership, as reflected in this document? What types of gifts did the emperor receive? What is the significance of relics in the story?

45. A KING'S MIRROR: THE *ADMONITIONS*

The work known in English as Admonitions *is a king's mirror written for King Stephen I's son, Emeric, by an unknown cleric, probably of Lotharingian origin, shortly before 1031 (perhaps in 1024 or 1025). Despite belonging to a literary genre of* instructio morum, *"educating behavior," associated in the Middle Ages with classical and patristic antecedents, some believe that the Latin text entitled* Libellus de institutione morum *may have been of Byzantine inspiration. Historians have traditionally used the text to gauge the political and cultural changes taking place in Hungary during the first half of the eleventh century. Hungary, for example, is regarded as a thoroughly Christian kingdom, and historians have noted parallels between this text and the first laws issued before the middle of the eleventh century, which insist on the Christian observance of Sundays, fasting days, Lent, and confession before death. The* Admonitions *make the king responsible for the observance of such rules, and in fact for the functioning of the Christian society. The text survives in very late manuscripts, one of the most important, written in 1544, comprising laws as well. On the other hand, the* Admonitions *encouraged the immigration of foreign knights and clerics because they brought with them various teachings and tools that could benefit the kingdom. While taking religious conformity for granted, the author of the* Admonitions *outlined the ideal of a multilingual and multicultural society.*

Source: trans. F. Curta from *Scriptores rerum Hungaricarum tempore ducum regumque stirpis Arpadianae gestarum*, ed. I. Szentpétery (Budapest: Academia litter. hungarica atque Societate histor. hungarica, 1938), vol. 2, pp. 619–20 and 623–25.

3. As I understand and deeply feel that whatever the will of God has created and his most evident predestination has disposed both on the vast sky and on the contiguous lands of the earth is sustained and maintained by law, and as I see all that the grace of God has abundantly brought to the profit of one's life and dignity, know, [my son,] protect, divide, and unite kingdoms, consuls, dukes, counts, high priests, and other dignitaries, partly divine commandments and decrees, partly secular, and the councils and proposals of the noble and the elderly, and as I know for sure that they may all be in order in all parts of the earth, to bear all dignity, not only to command, counsel, and recommend, but also for their sons, their faithful, their servants, so I cannot rest, my son, to give you lessons, orders, advice, suggestions in my life in order to adorn the way of life both for you and for your subjects, if with God's will you will rule after me. And it is proper for you to listen with devotional attention to your father's commandments, according to the admonition of the divine wisdom, which comes from the mouth of Solomon: "Hear, my son, the instruction of your father, and do not reject the laws of your mother" [Prov. 1:8], so that you will increase the number of your life's years. So, you will be reminded by this saying that if you despise what I command with paternal gentleness—let that never happen—you will no longer be a friend of either God or people. But hear the case and loss of the disobedient commanders. For Adam, who was formed in the likeness of the divine Creator by him, who created all beings, was made the heir of all dignity, but broke the chains of the commandments and immediately lost both the high dignities and his dwelling in paradise. The ancient chosen and beloved people of God broke the bonds of commandments established by the finger of God and was destroyed in different ways: in part by being swallowed by the earth, in part by fire, and in part by each other. Solomon's son [Rehoboam], misrepresenting his father's conciliatory words, puffing with pride, threatened the people with the sword instead of lashes of his

father's whips. He therefore endured many evils in his country, and he was in the end expelled from there. That that may not be done to you, take heed, my son; you are a child, my little servant born in wealth, a resident of soft pillows, cherished and nurtured in all his beauty. You have not experienced the toils of the campaigns and the incursions of various people which occupied almost my entire life. It is time for you not to eat soft porridge anymore, for it makes you soft and fussy, and that is a waste of virtues and a dispersion of vices, and a contempt for the laws. But be drunken with wine that is sometimes bitter. . . .

4. The fourth ornament of [good] rule is the loyalty, the strength, the modesty, the favor, and the trust of princes, counts, and knights. For they are the defensive walls of your country, the protectors of the weak, the destroyers of the enemy, and those who increase the size of the borderlands. May they be, my son, your fathers and your brethren. Indeed, never push any of them into bondage, and do not call any of them a bondman. Let them be your soldiers, not servants, and rule over them without anger, arrogance, or hatred, but peacefully, humbly, and meekly. Keep in mind always that all men are born alike, and that nothing elevates but humility, nothing repulses but pride and hatred. If you will love peace, they will call you a king and a son of a king, and many a knight will love you. If you will raise your head above counts and princes in anger, haughtiness, hatred, and strife, the power of the knights will certainly obscure the royal dignity and your kingdom will pass onto others. Beware of this and control the life of the counts with the rule of virtues, so that, assured of your affection, they may always cling undisturbed to the royal dignity, in order for your reign to be peaceful in all respects.

5. The practice of patience and judgment is the fifth ornament in the royal crown. David, the king and prophet, says: "O God, give your judgment to the king" [Ps. 71:1]. And the same elsewhere: "The king's honor loves judgment" [Ps. 98:4]. The apostle Paul speaks of patience: "be patient with all" [1 Thess. 5:14]. And the Lord in the Gospel: "By your patience possess your souls" [Luke 21:19]. To do this, hold fast, my son: if you want to gain honor for your kingdom, love the righteous judgment; if you want to keep your soul in power, be patient. Whenever, my dear son, a case worthy of judgment comes before you or someone who is accused of a major crime, do not act impatiently, do not swear by oath to punish him, because that looks shaky and fleeting, for the foolish vows can be [easily] broken. And you shall not judge yourself, lest your royal dignity be tainted in that vile affair, but rather direct such a matter to judges, for it is their commission to decide according to the law. Beware of being a judge but rejoice being a king and being called that. The patient kings reign truly, while impatient ones are simply tyrants. And when something is brought to you that is compatible with your dignity to judge, judge with mercy, with swearing, so that your crown will be commendable and ornate.

6. Guests and newcomers are such a great benefit that they can rightly stand in the sixth place for royal dignity. For initially, the Roman empire grew, so that the Roman kings were exalted and glorified, and many nobles and wise men came to them from different parts [of the world]. Indeed, Rome would now be a servant, if the descendants of Aeneas had not set her free. For guests come from different parts and provinces, and they bring with them different languages and customs, different testimonies and weapons, all of which adorn the country, glorify the [royal] court, and deter foreigners from puffing. A country with [only] one language and [only] one custom is weak and fallible. Therefore, I command you, my son, to protect and show respect to the newcomers in good faith, so that they may prefer to stay with you rather than live elsewhere. And if you want to destroy what I have built, or scatter what I have gathered, your country will bring a great deal of damage to your kingdom. To avoid that, enlarge your country daily, so that people will regard your crown with even greater respect.

Questions: What are the main traits of an ideal ruler? How much does the king need to imitate Christ? Which virtues may be directly applied to politics? What models does the author propose for the king? What can the emphasis on "guests" and "newcomers" tell us about demographic realities in early eleventh-century Hungary? What clues about specific problems in that kingdom does the text offer?

46. THIETMAR OF MERSEBURG ON BOLESŁAW CHROBRY

A member of one of the most prominent families of eastern Saxony, Thietmar was born on 25 July 975 and received his education in the monastery of Berge before moving to Magdeburg. The cathedral school in Magdeburg was at that time one of the greatest centers of education in north(eastern) Germany, under the leadership of Master Ochtrich and his pupils. Thietmar was appointed bishop of Merseburg, a see founded in 968 when Magdeburg was raised to the rank of archbishopric. However, less than two decades later, Emperor Otto I decided to suppress the diocese, which was restored only in 1004 by King Henry II. Thietmar was thus the second bishop of the restored diocese of Merseburg (1009–18). He witnessed many assemblies, accompanied Henry II on military campaigns, and in all other respects acted as a frontier bishop, which involved intensive work toward the conversion of the local population to Christianity. Three years after becoming bishop, Thietmar began writing his chronicle. His perspective was imperial, especially in matters concerning relations with the new powers to the east, Bohemia and Poland. Although he clearly disliked Bolesław Chrobry, whom he called a "venomous serpent," a "cunning fox," and an "old lecher," Thietmar's portrait of the Polish duke (who became king seven years after Thietmar's death) is not stereotyped and contains many details about relations with the German rulers, especially with Otto III and Henry II. The source of these details must have been firsthand accounts, including those of Emperor Henry II, but also of friends and acquaintances.

Source: trans. F. Curta from Thietmar of Merseburg, *Chronicon*, ed. R. Holtzmann and W. Trillmich (Darmstadt: Wissenschaftliche Buchgesellschaft, 1985), pp. 160, 162, 202, and 204.

4.45. Upon reaching Zeitz [near Leipzig, in Germany], Hugh II [bishop of Zeitz, c. 990–1003], the third one to have that see, came out to meet the caesar [Emperor Otto III, 996–1002] with imperial honors. Then he went straight to the stronghold of Meißen, where he was very well received by Eid, the venerable bishop of that see [992–1015], by Markgrave Ekkehard [985–1002], whom the emperor kept in high regard. Then he traveled across the land of the Milzeni [Upper Lusatia, at the present-day border between Germany, Poland, and the Czech Republic]. At the border of the Diedesi district [the area around Szprotawa, in western Poland, on the River Bóbr], he met with Bolesław, whose name has of old and unjustly been translated as "greater fame" [in most Slavic languages, "Boleslav" means "great glory"]. Bolesław happily honored him with great hospitality in Ilua [unknown location on the right bank of the Bóbr, somewhere near Szprotawa]. Any attempt to describe his magnificent reception of the caesar and of his entourage as they traveled through his country to Gniezno would be truly futile. When he caught sight of the desired city, he [the emperor] continued barefoot. He was received with great honor by the local bishop Unger [of Poznań, c. 983–1012] and led into the church. With tears in his eyes, he prayed to the martyr of Christ [Saint Adalbert] to use his intercessory powers and obtain [for Emperor Otto III] the grace of Christ. He then immediately established there an archbishopric. Let us hope that that was a legitimate decision, for he had not obtained the consent of the bishop, who had under his jurisdiction the entire country [Giselmar, archbishop of Magdeburg, 981–1004]. He entrusted the [newly created] see to Radim, the martyr's brother, and placed him above Reinbern, the bishop of Kolberg [Kołobrzeg, 1000–07], Poppo, bishop of Cracow [1000–18] and John of Wrocław [1000–?]. The only one left out of that was Unger of Poznań. And he erected an altar in that place underneath which he solemnly placed holy relics.

4.46. After taking care of all the issues, the duke [Bolesław Chrobry] honored the emperor with rich gifts, as well three hundred warriors in armor, a present which he liked more than any other. [Moreover,] Bolesław accompanied the emperor with a magnificent retinue up to Magdeburg, where Palm Sunday was celebrated with great solemnity. . . .

5.9. Meanwhile, Bolesław, a son of Mieszko standing so much lower than his father, was gladdened by the news of Markgrave Ekkehard's death [in 1002]. He quickly assembled an army and occupied the entire march of Count Gero [II, margrave of the Eastern March between 993 and 1015] up to the River Elbe. He then sent assault troops ahead [of his army] and took the stronghold of Bautzen [the main town in Upper Lusatia] together with everything that was in it. He then attacked the stronghold of Strehla [on the left bank of the Elbe near Riesa, to the northwest of Meißen] and secretly tried to bribe the inhabitants of Meißen. Those fickle people barely realized one day that that many soldiers in the garrison had gone out to procure fodder [for themselves], that led by Gunzelin of Kuckenburg [brother of Ekkehard of Meißen and brother-in-law of Bolesław, margrave of Meißen between 1002 and 1009], they [the Poles] stormed the eastern gate, where those servants [of the town] live, who are called in Slavic *Vethenici* [Withasen]. Then they killed Bezeko, one of the servants of Count Herrmann [margrave of Meißen, 1009–32], and each carrying his weapons, gathered in the count's chamber, threw large stones at the window, and loudly demanded that Ozer, the commander of the stronghold, be executed. However, the knight Thietmar, who had no other shield [against them] but the room [itself], asked them: "What is this? What [kind of] madness drove you to forget all the favors of Count Ekkehard, upon whom you have yourself called, so that you have now risen up to eliminate his son? Name therefore either in the open or [just] to one of us the reason of your shameful behavior, and I promise you in the name of my lord and of us all, whatever suits you, to put a stop to the abuses that you complain about, as well as assurance against any worries you may have for the future. As long as we live, however, you will not get the man whom you so cruelly want to be delivered to you in order to be put to death. We are just a few but mark my words: either we all die together, or [you let us] leave this stronghold unharmed." Hearing him speak that way, they discussed the matter among themselves and decided to give them a free pass. After that, they invited Duke Bolesław [Chrobry] through intermediaries, and opened the gates for him. And thus was the word of the scripture fulfilled: they "delight in evils and rejoice in evil perversion" [Prov. 2:14]; and again, first they are like honey, but in the end like gall [Prov. 5:3–4].

5.10. This lucky turn of events made Bolesław arrogant; he then occupied the entire territory up to the [White] Elster [river in eastern Germany, a tributary of the Saale that flows through Leipzig] and secured it with garrisons [placed in strongholds]. As our men all came together to prevent him from doing that, the cunning Bolesław sent an embassy to assure them that he had done all of that with the will and approval of Duke Henry [II of Bavaria, who in 1002 became king and then in 1014 emperor]. He told them that he would not touch a hair on any inhabitant's head and that he would always do things according to Henry's will, should he first take [royal] power in his hands. If things went a different way, he was ready to submit to their decision. Upon hearing those nice words [Terence, *Phormio* 3.2.15], our men believed them and shamelessly went to his side as if he was their lord. They thus exchanged their innate honor for subservience and wrongful servitude. How little can our contemporaries measure up to our ancestors! During the lifetime of Hodo [margrave of the Eastern March between 965 and 993], Mieszko, the father of this man, did not even dare to enter dressed up in fur into a house where he [Hodo] knew him, nor to remain seated when he [Hodo] stood up. May God forgive the emperor [Otto III] that he has turned a tributary into a lord and has raised him so high that he has forgotten the manners of his father and continuously and gradually dared to force those of a higher standing into submission, to entice them with the cheap bait of ephemeral wealth, and thus to bring prejudice both to servants and to free men.

Questions: What concerns shaped Thietmar's attitude toward Bolesław Chrobry? What aspects of his personality were deemed particularly important in this portrait of the Polish ruler? Why is Mieszko mentioned as clad in furs? Compare the description of the Gniezno Summit in this text and in the Deeds of the Princes of the Poles *(Doc. 44).*

47. THE DECREES OF BŘETISLAV

Cosmas of Prague finished his Chronicle of the Czechs *shortly before his death in 1125. The chronicle survives in twelve manuscripts dated to the twelfth and thirteenth centuries. Cosmas started work on the chronicle at some point between 1119 and 1122, when he was dean of the cathedral of St-Vitus in Prague. He probably wrote at the request of or on commission from the Bohemian duke Vladislav I (1110–17 and 1120–25) as a plea for a strong rule in the years following the death of Vratislav II (1061–92), who is otherwise the chronicler's main villain. By contrast, the great star of Cosmas's gallery of good princes is Břetislav I (1034–55). The greatest memories of the "golden age" are connected with his rule, for during his reign everything appears to have been in the right place, with peace and justice everywhere in Bohemia. Cosmas looks back to this reign with nostalgia. Having acquired the basics of his education in Prague, Cosmas studied grammar at the cathedral school in Liège, where he became familiar with ancient authors, particularly Ovid, Virgil, and Sallust. Cosmas wrote in elegant Latin and reflected upon the Trojan War, which he often associated with the events in Bohemia. For example, he compares Břetislav to Achilles and Diomedes. Besides classical authors, Cosmas frequently cited the Bible. He also relied on oral sources, which he adapted to his narrative. Skillfully using emotions (especially anger) to highlight episodes or traits of individuals, he created dramatic effects and added color. In the following paragraphs, he may have well used a written source, perhaps from the archive of the cathedral in Prague, for the details of the decrees attributed to Břetislav. However, he embedded that source within the story of how the relics of Saint Adalbert were removed from Gniezno and brought to Prague. In the process, Cosmas made the legislation appear to be sanctioned by the saint.*

Source: trans. P. Mutlová and M. Rady, *Cosmas of Prague: The Chronicle of the Czechs*, ed. J.M. Bak (Budapest: Central European University Press, 2019), pp. 155, 157, 159, 161, 163, and 165.

At that time, Casimir [in fact, Mieszko II Lambert, Casimir's father], the most excellent Polish duke, was taken away from this world, and his sons Bolesław and Władysław were still suckling. Thus for the Poles, the only hope of saving themselves lay in pitiful flight to various places in Poland. Duke Břetislav [I of Bohemia, 1034–55] turned his mind to this in the fourth year of his dukedom and thought it best not to miss the chance of punishing his enemies and repaying the injustice that had been done to the Czechs by Duke Mieszko [this is in reference to the blinding of Duke Boleslav III by Bolesław Chrobry, Mieszko II's father]. Having consulted his men, he decided to attack the enemy as quickly as possible. . . .

When they had in a moment, in the twinkling of an eye [1 Cor. 15:52], assembled the last man, he advanced on Poland, widowed of its ruler, and just as a great tempest furiously rages and destroys everything, he invaded it in force, devastated the villages with slaughter, plundering, and arson, and seized the fortresses by force. When he took Cracow, their metropolis, he totally demolished it and took hold of its spoils; moreover, he unearthed the old treasures hidden by the ancient dukes in the treasury, namely an enormous quantity of gold and silver; and he similarly set fire to other towns and razed them to the ground. . . .

Not far from the aforementioned castle [Giecz], they arrived at the metropolis Gniezno, strong on account of its location and defense but easily conquered by foes because few people lived there. At that time, there reposed in the basilica of St-Mary, Mother of God and Eternal Virgin, a most precious treasure, namely the body of the most blessed Adalbert the martyr. The Czechs take the city swiftly without a fight and entered the threshold of the holy church with great joy. Disregarding all other booty, they asked for themselves only the precious remains of the sacred body that had suffered for Christ. . . . And since the body was buried by the wall behind the altar and could not be reached without destroying the altar, impious hands carried out profane deeds with savage mind. Yet God's punishment was not lacking, for at the moment that they set about their impudent work they stopped, stupefied, without voice or sense or eyesight, for almost three hours until by God's grace they regained their former senses. Moved by remorse [Matt. 27:3], albeit belatedly, they immediately followed the bishop's orders and—as much as they had been punished by God's will, so the more devotedly and indefatigably they persisted in prayers—they fasted and prayed for mercy for three days.

On the third night, the holy bishop Adalbert [Saint Adalbert was bishop of Prague between 982 and 988] appeared in a vision to Bishop Severus [of Gniezno], who was just resting after matins, and told him: "Tell this to the duke [of Bohemia] and to his *comites* [counts]: the heavenly Father will give you what you ask for [Matt. 7:11], provided that you do not relapse into the sins you renounced at the baptismal font." When the bishop announced this to the duke and his *comites* in the morning, they at once entered the church of St-Mary in joy and long prayed together. Then the duke rose and, standing on the ambo [pulpit], broke the silence with these words: "Do you want to repair your transgressions and turn your minds from your evil deeds?" With tears welling up, they shout: "We are ready to repair the sins of ourselves and of our fathers against the saint of God and entirely to cease all wrongdoing." Then the duke stretched out his hand over the sacred tomb and addressed the crowd of people thus: "Raise your right hands together to God, brothers, and pay attention to my speech which I want you to confirm by swearing an oath on your faith. Here is my first and principal commandment: that your marriages, that you have hitherto had as if in brothels and [in] common, like among brute animals, be in accordance with the canons of the church, lawful, singular, and indissoluble, so that a husband lives content with one wife and a wife with one husband. If however a wife rejects a husband or a husband a wife, and a quarrel between them flares into a separation, I do not want the one of them, who refuses to return to the previous, legally concluded marriage, to be pushed into servitude as a violator of wedlock according to the rules of our country, but rather by the force of our irrevocable decree, they should be, regardless of person, banished to Hungary; and they may not buy their way out by any payment or come back to this country lest the pollution of one sheep spread to the whole flock of Christ." Bishop Severus said: "Whoever shall do differently shall be anathema. This punishment shall also apply to girls, widows, and adulteresses, who are recognized as having lost their good name, sullied their reputation, and conceived through fornication. For if they had a free choice to marry, why do they commit adultery and abort their unborn children, which is the worst sin of all sins?" Then the duke added: "If, however, a woman proclaims that she is not loved in the same way she loves but is instead unmercifully put upon and harassed by her husband, let there be God's judgment between them and whoever is guilty, must pay for the offense. Similarly, for those who are accused of homicide: let the archpriest [head of the church organization in a castle district] write down their names for the *comes* [count] of the place and the *comes* shall summon them. And if they resist, he should cast them in prison until they duly repent or, if they refuse, they should be tried by hot iron or blessed water to see whether they are guilty. Fratricides and parricides or murderers of priests and those caught in other capital crimes should be handed over by the archpriest to a *comes* or the duke or expelled from the country, chained on their hands and body so that they wander around in the world as fugitives and vagabonds like Cain" [Gen. 4:12]. Bishop Severus said: "Let this just provision of the duke be confirmed by anathema. For a sword hangs by the thigh of you dukes, so that you may the more often wash your hands in the blood of the sinner" [Ps. 57:11]. Then the duke again: "Let him who opens a tavern or takes one over, which is the source of all evil and wherefrom thefts, killings, fornications, and other errors stem. . . ." Bishop Severus added: "Be anathema." And the duke: "The tavern-keeper who is found to be a transgressor of this decree shall be tied to a stake in the middle of the market, shaved, and beaten for as long as the bailiff is able. His belongings shall not be confiscated, but only the drink poured out onto the ground so that no one may be defiled by the execrable drink. Drinkers, however, if they are caught, shall not leave the prison until each pays three hundred coins to the duke's treasury." Bishop Severus said: "What the duke has decided our authority sanctions." Then the duke continued: "We altogether forbid that markets take place on Sundays as has been generally practiced in our region so as to allow people to work on other days. He who is found doing servile work on a Sunday or on feast days that have been designated for public celebration in the church, the fruits of his labor and the team of beasts found working shall be taken away by the archpriest and three hundred coins paid to the duke's treasury. Similarly, those who dare to bury their dead in the fields or in the woods shall pay to the archdeacon an ox, and three hundred pennies to the duke's treasury. The dead nevertheless shall be buried again in the graveyard of the faithful [that is, church graveyard]. These are the things God hates; these had disgusted Saint Adalbert so that he left us, his flock, preferring to go and instruct foreign peoples. We confirm by our and your own oath that we shall not commit such things anymore." Thus said the duke.

Questions: What kind of social problems did the decrees of Břetislav address? How were those problems to be solved in legal terms? Would this be sufficient to curb the apparent ills of Bohemian society? How reliable is the information provided by Cosmas? What might his contemporaries think about this account of Duke Břetislav's speech in Gniezno?

48. THE COLLAPSE OF THE PIAST STATE

Following Mieszko's death in 1034, a widespread rebellion, combined with a devastating invasion of the Bohemian armies, led to a quick collapse of the state in Poland. Largely because of Gallus's account below, historians continue to treat these events as a "pagan reaction," which supposedly led to the annihilation of ecclesiastical infrastructure in Silesia, Greater Poland, and northern parts of Lesser Poland. To be sure, the archaeological evidence confirms destruction at such central places as Gniezno and Ostrów Lednicki, which may explain why the center of power in the subsequent centuries shifted from Greater to Lesser Poland (from Gniezno to Cracow). However, a careful study of the account in the Deeds of the Princes of the Poles *shows that the emphasis on paganism was Gallus's strategy to enhance the merits of Casimir the Restorer in spreading Christianity after these events.*

Source: trans. P.W. Knoll and F. Schaer, *Gesta Principum Polonorum: The Deeds of the Princes of the Poles* (Budapest: Central European University Press, 2003), pp. 79 and 81.

In the meantime, the neighboring kings and dukes had been riding roughshod over the portion of Poland nearest each of them, adding the cities and castles near the borders to their dominions or capturing them and leveling them to the ground. Yet at the same time as Poland was suffering this devastation and ruin at the hands of foreigners, her own inhabitants were doing even more senseless and ghastly thing to her. For serfs rose against their masters, and freedmen against nobles, seizing power for themselves, reducing some in turn to servitude, killing others, and raping their wives and appropriating their offices in most wicked fashion. Furthermore—and I can barely say it without tears in my voice—they turned aside from the Catholic faith and rose up against their bishops and the priests of God; some they deemed worthy to be put to death by the sword, some by the baser death of stoning. In the end foreigners and her own people had between them reduced Poland to such desolation that she was stripped of almost all her wealth and population. At the same time the Czechs sacked Gniezno and Poznań [in 1038 or 1039] and made off with the body of Saint Adalbert. Such as were able to escape the clutches of the foe or their rebellious fellow-countrymen fled over the River Vistula into Mazovia. The cities aforementioned remained so long deserted and wasted that wild beasts set their beds in the church of St-Adalbert the Holy Martyr and St-Peter the Apostle. It is believed that this disaster struck the whole land in common because Gaudentius, Saint Adalbert's brother and successor, is said—for reasons unknown to me—to have placed the whole land under anathema. But let this suffice on the subject of Poland's ruin, and may it serve in connection of those who failed to keep faith with their natural masters.

Questions: Given the mention of attacks against churchmen, was this a pagan rebellion or a social upheaval? How was domestic turbulence combined with foreign invasion, and to what effect? How does the author explain the collapse of the Piast state?

49. SIMON OF KÉZA ON THE PAGAN REVOLT

Hostility toward the Germans is evident in the Deeds of the Hungarians *written between 1282 and 1285 by Simon of Kéza, a court clerk under King Ladislas IV (1272–90). Simon knew the work of "Master P.," but he augmented it with heavy borrowings from Jordanes, Paul the Deacon, Isidore of Seville, and Godfrey of Viterbo. What he writes about King Samuel Aba (1041–44) demanding that Emperor Henry III return the Hungarian refugees, and about Henry restoring Peter Orseolo to the Hungarian throne in 1044, is in fact based on the* Annals of Niederaltaich. *Simon of Kéza's understanding of history is not very different from that of Master P. He regarded the Huns as Hungarians, who constituted a* natio *on which God bestowed his favors. The account of the events of 1046 that led to the demise of Peter Orseolo is based, however, on "tradition," most likely oral histories of families such as the Tátony mentioned below. The focus in the* Deeds *is in fact on noble clans, a direct reflection of the rise of the nobility as a political body in the kingdom of Hungary during the last quarter of the thirteenth century.*

Source: trans. F. Schaer, Simon of Kéza, *The Deeds of the Hungarians* (Budapest: Central European University, 1999), pp. 123, 125, and 127.

Meanwhile, King Peter [Orseolo, 1038–41, 1044–46] had begun to oppress the Hungarians as harshly as before [that is, during his first reign]. So a general gathering took place in Csanád [now Cenad, near Arad, Romania], where they took counsel and sent a message in common calling for the sons of Ladislas the Bald [duke of Nitra between c. 977 and 995; grandson of Taksony and the brother of Vazul, King Stephen I's cousin and rival] to return to Hungary. The three brothers came as secretly as they could, and as soon as they arrived in Pest, they sent messengers at night to ride swiftly, enter Peter's court, and issue a proclamation that any Germans or Latins found anywhere were to be put to death and paganism restored. So when Peter woke in the morning and demanded to know what was going on he discovered that the brothers were back in Hungary. Peter was deeply unhappy but put on a cheerful front. He sent messengers in secret to Székesfehérvár to secure the town. However, his ploy came out in the open and the Hungarians everywhere rose in revolt, slaughtering Germans and Latins together and sparing neither women, infants, nor priests. Unable to enter Székesfehérvár, Peter fled in the direction of Moson [now Mosonmagyaróvár in northwestern Hungary, at the border with Austria and Slovakia]. There it was rumored that an army was marching against him, so he turned aside from Moson and rode back in haste to Székesfehérvár, the citizens sending word that he should return and that they would surrender the town to him. But when he reached a village near Székesfehérvár, he was suddenly surrounded by the army; he was taken prisoner and his eyes were put out. He survived this, but ended his life sick at heart. He is buried at Pécs, at his own foundation, as it is held.

The three brothers then entered Székesfehérvár where they were received with paeans of praise by the whole populace, bishops, nobles, and people alike, and Andrew, as the oldest of the three, ascended the throne [as Andrew I, 1046–60]. It is sometimes claimed that the brothers were sons of Duke Vazul by a girl [that is, concubine] from the Tátony clan and not his sons by true wedlock, and that the Tátony family derive their noble status from this connection. This tradition is certainly baseless and a quite mischievous invention. The fact is that, being from Scythia, the family were of noble origin in any case, irrespective of the fact that the brothers were the sons of Ladislas the Bald.

During these revolts, Bishop Gerard of Csanád won the crown of martyrdom in Pest when he was pushed off the hill in a cart by Hungarians. He had earlier been a monk in the abbey of Rosazzo in the territory of Aquileia, and later, after coming to Pannonia, spent considerable time as a hermit at Bakonybél [the Bakony Hills near Veszprém, where Stephen I established a Benedictine abbey].

Questions: Can one determine the religious beliefs of the rebels in this account? What were their demands? Compare this account of a pagan revolt to that in the Deeds of the Princes of the Poles *(Doc. 48). Why were hierarchs like Bishop Gerard attacked?*

50. ABU HAMID ON HUNGARY

Born in Granada in 1080 or 1081, Abu Hamid left al-Andalus at a relatively young age (before he was thirty years old) and moved first to northern Africa, and from there to Egypt, where he arrived in 1117/18. Three years later he was in Damascus and in 1123/24 he arrived in Baghdad. He was in Persia in 1130 and, one year later, at Saqsin, a commercial center somewhere in the delta of the River Volga. From there he moved to Volga Bulgharia, where he remained for fifteen years. He came to Hungary in 1150/51, and remained there for three years, as mentioned in the fragment translated below. He returned to Volga Bulgharia through Kiev. By 1154, he was again on the road, this time for the pilgrimage to Mecca, via Khwarazm, Merv, and Isfahan. Upon his return in 1155, he began working on his travelogue, Tuhfat al-Albab *(the "gift of hearts"), most likely in Baghdad. He finished writing in 1165 and died at age ninety in Damascus. In addition to his travelogue, Abu Hamid wrote a description of the wonders of north Africa, the* al-Mu'rib 'an ba'd 'aja'ib al-Maghreb. *A preoccupation with wonders and the exotic is also apparent in the travelogue. To judge from the text, he viewed himself not just as a traveler, but as someone with a mission to spread Islam to the corners of the world. This may explain the human touch of the narrative, as in the description of the skills and diligence of his female slave purifying the honey. Because of his empathy, Abu Hamid's ethnological remarks are often quite detailed. The audience of this text was Abu Hamid's patron Awn al-Din, the vizier of the Abbasid caliph al-Muqtafi (1136–60).*

Source: trans. I. Zimonyi from C.E. Dubler, *Abū Ḥāmid el Granadino y su relación de viaje por tierras eurasiáticas* (Madrid: Imprenta y Editorial Maestre, 1953), pp. 27–29.

27. Later I arrived in the country of the Hungarians, where people lived who are called Bashgird [Bashkirs, the name sometimes given to the Magyars in Arab sources]. They are the first who came from the lands of Atrak [Turks, a

common word used in Arab sources for nomads in central Asia] who entered the country of the Afranj [Franks, the umbrella term used in Arab sources for western Europeans]. They are courageous and uncountable in number.

Their country, which is called Hungary, consists of 108 cities, each of which has many strongholds, villages, farmhouses, mountains, forests, and gardens. In that country live innumerable thousands of descendants of Maghribians [Muslims of north African origin] and equally countless thousands of descendants of Khwarazmians [Muslims from central Asia]. The descendants of Khwarazmians serve the kings [of Hungary] and pretend to be Christians, although they practice Islam in secret. By contrast, the descendants of the Maghribians do not do any service to Christians, except in war [military service], and practice Islam in the open.

28. I met descendants of Maghribians, who honored me greatly. I taught them some things pertaining to science, got them to try Arabic, and did my best to repeat and practice assiduously with them what is needed for the ritual prayer and the other prescriptions of religious service. I also summarized [for them] the teachings about the *hajj* [pilgrimage to Mecca] and inheritance rules. Learning the rules, they began to put them in practice. One of them told me: "I would like to copy those books and learn from them." As he spoke Arabic well, I told him: "Make an effort to learn [those] things by heart, and to understand them well, and do not talk about what books say, without the *isnad* [list of authorities who have transmitted a report of a statement or action of the Prophet Muhammad]. If you are going to do that, you will achieve what you wish for." He replied: "But did you not say that the Prophet—may God bless and save him—said that one needs to combine knowledge with writing?" "There is no knowledge," I retorted, "in the book. There is nothing [there] but writing that leads to knowledge, which exists only when it is retained by memory, because knowledge is nothing but the quality of the wise man." And I recited to him those verses of mine:

> Knowledge rests in the heart, not in the books.
> Do not fall for levity and ramblings.

And the other ones, which are also mine:

> If you write the knowledge, like you would throw it in a tray,
> and you do not learn it by heart, you will never succeed.
> The only way to succeed is to learn it
> after understanding it and protecting it against error.

And I continued: "When you learn something by heart, you write it from memory, because that will be knowledge that you must record in a book, so that it does not go away. But if you write taking it from a book, you will only be a copy, and no knowledge at all. Be aware of that!"

They did not know [about] the public *jummah* [the central weekly prayer for Muslims], and they learned [about] it [from me], as well as [about] the required *hutba* [the sermon held on *jummah*]. I explained to them: "The Prophet—may God bless and save him—has said: 'The Friday *jummah* is the *hajj* [pilgrimage to Mecca] of the poor—those who cannot go on the *hajj*, but attend the Friday prayer, will receive the award of the *hajj*.'" Today, the Friday sermon is preached among them, either publicly or secretly, in more than ten thousand places, for their land is very large.

29. I stayed among them for three years but could only enter into four cities. Their country goes from *Rūmiyya al-'uzama* ["the great land of the Romans," most likely the Holy Roman empire] to the border of Constantinople. There are mountains in that country, from which gold and silver are mined.

This country is more prosperous and comfortable than other countries. Twenty sheep are worth a dinar [golden coin], and thirty lambs and kids cost a dinar. Five hundred *ratl* [unit of uncertain value, between fourteen and thirty-five ounces] of honey are worth also a dinar. A beautiful slave can be bought for ten dinars and, during raids [into enemy territories], one can buy a good female slave or a *rūmi* [Roman, Byzantine] boy for three dinars.

I bought a captive-born slave girl, whose parents and brothers still lived, from her master for ten dinars. She was fifteen years old and was more beautiful than the moon, with black eyes and hair, the skin whiter than camphor. She knew how to cook, how to sew, and how to embroider. I also bought another eight-year-old *rūmi* slave girl for five dinars. One day, I bought for half a dinar two jars filled with honeycomb, with its wax, and I told her: "You have to purify this honey and get rid of the wax." I went to a bench by the door of the house, where people used to gather. After staying with them for a while, I went back into the house, and saw five discs of pure wax like gold and a jar full of liquid honey that looked like rosewater. The honey had been purified and returned to the two jars, all in [just] one hour. I had a son from her, but he died. I gave her freedom and called her Maryam. I even thought of taking her with me to Saqsin [a trade center located somewhere in the Volga Delta, location unknown], but I feared the reaction that the Turkish concubines with children that I had in Saqsin would have to her.

Questions: How does Abu Hamid describe the status and role of Muslims in Hungary? According to the evidence presented in this document, why was Islam tolerated in a Christian country? What does this document suggest about the slave trade in Christian Hungary?

51. VINCENT OF PRAGUE ON KING VLADISLAV II

A canon of the cathedral in Prague named Vincent, who died in 1170, wrote an independent chronicle covering the years 1140–67. Because of his position in the Prague chapter, Vincent traveled often with Bishop Daniel (1148–67) and was therefore well informed about affairs in Bohemia and in the empire. Duke Vladislav II (1140–72, king in 1158) was the hero of Vincent of Prague. Vincent's Vladislav had Samson's strength and David's bravery, and he threw himself into battle to give an example to his soldiers of courage and stamina. This is true both for his battle against his political enemies at home and for his Italian campaign on behalf of Emperor Frederick Barbarossa. He was handsomely rewarded for that: in 1158, in recognition for his military service, Vladislav obtained the title of king. He felt obligated to prove his unconditional support for the efforts of the emperor in Italy and promised he would put Milan under siege. Obtaining the support of his magnates and people for the fulfillment of that promise proved, however, more difficult. At this point, Vincent's narrative encapsulates one of the rare moments of direct speech in his chronicle. Vincent's work, left unfinished, was continued between 1214 and 1222 by Gerlach, the abbot of the Premonstratensian abbey of Milevsko.

Souce: trans. F. Curta from Vincent of Prague, *Annals*, ed. W. Wattenbach, *Monumenta Germaniae Historica, Scriptores rerum Germanicarum in usum scholarum* 17 (Hanover: Hahn, 1861), pp. 668–69.

King Vladislav, therefore, seeing that he had received so many honors [the promise of the crown of Bohemia], and how much that [could] match the honors, promised to go in person, together with his princes and with [his] mighty forces, and put under siege Milan, that most ancient royal city of Lombardy, which was [otherwise] excellently armed and very strong because of wonderful troops. He also promised that he would go against those who refuse to bend their necks before the emperor, and wage war with his weapons. Hearing about that assistance, the imperial forces rejoiced and prepared in their hearts to battle their enemies in various ways. All the youth of Bohemia roared their assistance to the new king of Bohemia. When his business [at the imperial court in Würzburg] was finished, King Vladislav, covered in honors and rejoicing, returned to the royal city of Prague together with his men in order [to announce his intention] to move against Milan. He wanted to proclaim to all in the general court at Prague, in front of the barons of Bohemia, that it was God's will that he would go in person to put Milan under siege. The elders among the nobles of Bohemia, upon learning [about it], said that it was not good that such a decision had been taken without their counsel, and that what had been decided [in the past] with their counsel in reality concerned the cross [that is, the crusade, after Duke Vladislav publicly took the cross in 1147]. And they accused lord Bishop Daniel of Prague of having concocted almost the entire thing, and they treated him with cruelty. The king, seeing that they were against their lord, the bishop, told them this: "I did not promise that [the expedition against Milan] to [my] lord, the emperor, without proper consideration, but out of my own will and in answer to the honors bestowed upon me by him. To whomever intends to help me in this matter, I will be grateful, and I will furnish [to him] money and everything else that is necessary. Whoever disregards [my request], let that man sit at home, safe because of the peace that I have [provided], and content with [silly] games for women and other leisurely activities." When the Bohemians heard that from the king, they rushed to [go] in arms [against] Milan, and the young noblemen roared [in approval] with great vigor. The blockade of Milan [now] resounded in their songs and in their speeches, as on all sides they were getting their weapons ready and fixing [their] weapons, not only the young among the nobles, but also many folks in the countryside, who put aside tilling the fields, laying their hands not on mattocks and plows, but on shields, lances, and the other instruments of war. And the news reached the ears of the wives, who had been delighted by the tender love of their husbands. The news troubled their hearts, and they were waiting with great grief and in wailing the day of the expected departure [for Italy]. The Bohemian court in Prague proclaimed the draft for the army going against Milan and began to recruit soldiers most suitable for the job. The first to move were [the troops under] the pink standard of the lord Vladislav, the king, then the merry corps of the roaring youth in arms. Lord Gervasius, the provost of Vyšehrad and chancellor, whose advice the lord king trusted the most, rushed to join that expedition and that effort on the side of his lord, the king, choosing deeds and exile [that is, being away from his country] over pastimes and pleasures.

Questions: Why did Vladislav II decide to participate with Czech troops at the siege of Milan? How was his initiative received in his own country? What did those who followed the king hope to accomplish by their loyalty? How did Vladislav's decision strengthen his popularity among his subjects? How could an expedition to a foreign land be justified to the "elders among the nobles of Bohemia"?

52. THE GOLDEN BULL OF 1222

Upon returning from the Fifth Crusade, King Andrew II of Hungary faced growing social unrest, which involved especially royal soldiers ("servants of the king") and the garrisons of county strongholds ("castle warriors"). Both social categories were unhappy with the extensive grants of castle lands that the king had made to his barons. These grants had deprived garrisons of strongholds of their source of income, in the process leading to a rapid deterioration of the social status of both royal soldiers and castle warriors. The tensions between a group of noblemen and the king forced Andrew II to issue in 1222 a privilege known as the Golden Bull, because of the golden seal allegedly attached to the original document. Under the guise of restoring liber-

ties granted by King Stephen, the document granted members of the nobility the right to resist should the king fail to keep his promises. More importantly, the bull protected the servants of the king against royal interference and judgment and limited the promotion of foreigners to royal office. The stipulations of the bull reveal that the lesser nobles—servants of the king and castle warriors—felt threatened simultaneously by magnates (barons) and the king's favors to the magnates. None of the seven original documents mentioned below has survived. This is the translation of a text collated from several medieval confirmations, specifically the charter issued by Hungarian churchmen in 1318 and presented to King Charles I (1308–42) for his confirmation, as well as the decree issued in 1351 by his son, King Louis I (1342–82). The division into articles is taken from later transcriptions of the document.

Source: trans. J.M. Bak, György Bónis, and J.R. Sweeney, *The Laws of the Medieval Kingdom of Hungary, 1000–1301* (Bakersfield, CA: Charles Schlacks, 1989), pp. 161–69.

In the name of the Holy Trinity and indivisible unity. Andrew, by the grace of God, king of Hungary, Dalmatia, Croatia, Rama, Serbia, Galicia, and Lodomeria [Vladimir-in-Volhynia, that is, Volhynia] in perpetuity. Since the liberties established by Saint Stephen the king in favor of the nobles [that is, magnates] of our realm as well as of other persons have been diminished in many respects by the authority of certain kings, some of whom in personal anger took vengeance, others of whom paid heed to the false counsel of wicked and self-seeking men, those same nobles have repeatedly importuned our serenity and that of their kings, our predecessors, with numerous petitions and entreaties for the reform of our kingdom. We therefore desire to fulfill their requests in all respects, as we are obliged to do, especially because between them and us this circumstance has often led to no inconsiderable bitterness, which ought rightly to be avoided for the better preservation of the royal dignity which can be done better by no other than by them. We grant both to them and to other men of our kingdom the liberty given by the holy king, and we salubriously ordain what further pertains to the reformation of the state of our kingdom in this manner:

1. That we are bound to celebrate the feast of Saint Stephen annually in Székesfehérvár unless we should be beset by some urgent matter or prevented by illness. And if we cannot be present, the [count] palatine will definitely be there for us, and shall hear cases in our place, and all the servants [of the king, the lesser nobles, who were expected to provide military service] who wish shall freely assemble there.
2. It is further our wish that neither we nor our successors should at any time seize or cause the ruin of any servant [of the king] for the benefit of some magnate, unless they first be summoned and duly sentenced to judicial process.

3. Similarly, we shall levy neither the *collecta* [a royal tax levied in money or in kind] nor the freemen's pennies [a direct tax introduced by King Coloman on all freemen, who were obliged to pay the king eight denars] on the estates of the servants [of the king] and shall not exact hospitality in their houses or villages unless we have been called [there]. We shall not collect any taxes at all from people attached to their churches.
4. If a servant of the king should die without a son, his daughter shall receive a quarter of his possessions, but he shall not dispose of the rest as he wishes. And if, prevented by death, he shall not have been able to make disposition, those relatives closer to him shall obtain [the possessions]. If he shall have no relatives at all, the king shall obtain them.
5. The counts in the counties shall not render judicial sentences concerning the estates of the servants [of the king] except in cases pertaining to coinage and tithes. The counts in the [royal] castles shall render judicial sentences to no one except those attached to their castles. Thieves and robbers shall be judged by royal judges, but only in the presence of the count.
6. Similarly, people united in sworn association shall not be able to accuse thieves, as they have been accustomed to do.
7. If the king, however, wishes to lead an army outside the kingdom, the servants [of the king] shall not be obligated to accompany him, unless it be at his expense and, after his return, he shall not permit judgment against them concerning the campaign. If, however, the army of an enemy should advance upon the kingdom, everyone without exception is obligated to go. Also, if we lead an army beyond the realm, all those who hold counties or receive money from us are bound to accompany us.
11. If foreigners, indeed honorable men, come to the kingdom, they shall not be raised to dignities without the consent of the kingdom [that is, the magnates of the kingdom].
16. We [that is, the king] shall not bestow whole counties or any other dignities as estates or possessions in perpetuity.
19. Castle warriors [dependent freemen who had to provide military service under the command of the count of a royal castle] shall be preserved in the liberties established by the holy king [Saint Stephen]. Similarly, foreign guests of whatever nation shall be preserved in the liberties originally granted to them.
23. Our new coins shall be valid for a year from Easter to Easter, and pennies shall be the same as they were under King Béla [in terms of silver content].
24. Ishmaelites [Muslims] and Jews shall not be allowed to become counts of the chamber of the mint, of salt, and of tolls, [or] nobles of the realm.
27. The *marturina* [a tax levied in Slavonia and Croatia, initially in the form

of one marten pelt annually] shall be rendered in the manner established by King Coloman.

30. Similarly, no one other than these four baronial retainers [of the king]—the [count] palatine, the *ban* [that is, governor of Croatia], the judge royal, and the judge of the queen's court—shall hold two offices [at the same time].

And in order that this grant and ordinance of ours shall be valid in our time as well as in that of our successors in perpetuity, we ordered seven exact copies to be drawn up and authenticated with our golden seal, so that one copy shall be sent to the lord pope and he shall have it copied into his register, the second copy shall be kept in the custody of the Hospital [Order of St-John, or Knights Hospitalers], the third in the custody of the Temple [Knights Templar], the fourth with the king, the fifth at the cathedral chapter of Esztergom, the sixth at that of Kalocsa, and the seventh with the incumbent palatine, so that he, having this document always in his sight, should not deviate from the foregoing terms in any respect, nor permit the king, the nobles, or anyone else to deviate from it, so that they should not only enjoy their liberty but also because of this remain ever faithful to us and our successors and not refuse the obligations rightly due to the royal crown.

We have also decreed that if we or any of our successors at any time should seek to oppose the terms of this settlement, both the bishops and other baronial retainers as well as the nobles of the realm, singularly or in common, both present and future generations, shall by this authority have the right in perpetuity to resist and speak against us and our successors without the charge of high treason.

Questions: What does this text suggest about the relations between king and aristocracy in early thirteenth-century Hungary? Compare the way the nobility and foreigners are treated in this text and in the Admonitions *of King Stephen (Doc. 45). How were the powers of the Hungarian king limited and what means were available to reinforce the terms of the Golden Bull? Compare the stipulation regarding raising an army for an expedition outside the kingdom to the evidence of the document about King Vladislav II of Bohemia (Doc. 51). What is the status of "servants" in the political arrangements of the early thirteenth century?*

CHAPTER SEVEN

ECONOMY AND SOCIETY

Figure 7.1 Saint Adalbert Pleads with Boleslav II, Duke of Bohemia. The saint pleads for the release of Christian slaves by Jewish slave traders. Detail of the main bronze door into the cathedral of Gniezno (c. 1170).

53. THE DIET OF RIŽANA

In 804, an assembly took place at Rižana, not far from present-day Koper (in northwestern Istria), in the presence of the three missi dominici *(imperial inspectors) dispatched for the occasion by Charlemagne. The occasion was a number of complaints lodged by local notables against the provincial governor, a certain duke named John. The plaintiffs accused the duke of depriving them of a range of rights and institutions dating back to the Byzantine era. The complaints derived from a military reorganization of the Istrian peninsula now under Frankish rule. While the highly decentralized system of the Byzantine era was based on urban self-management, the new regime concentrated power in the hands of the duke, replacing the lower offices of* domestici, *vicars, and* locoservatores, *with centarchs (officers of a rank lower than the tribune), who were appointed rather than elected to their offices. Moreover, Duke John appears to have extended the general conscription in Istria to include freed slaves and exempted subjects of the tribunes in each city. It is quite possible that the foreign people whom the duke settled on communal property, and over whom the Istrians had no authority, were also obligated to military service. To meet the increased costs of the new military needs, Duke John introduced new taxes and levies. The resulting* placitum *(diet, or formal deliberative assembly) was a compromise, which preserved the appearance of the customs and institutions in existence in Istria under Byzantine rule, while replacing the customary law with the written conclusions of the investigative process. For all practical purposes, the framework of new military organization of this border province of the Carolingian empire remained intact. In fact, the decisions of Rižana are specifically mentioned a decade later in a charter issued, shortly after he began to rule, by Louis the Pious for Patriarch Fortunatus of Grado and the bishops, abbots, tribunes, and other imperial subjects in the province of Istria. The protocol of the diet of Rižana translated below survives in only one manuscript dated to the sixteenth century.*

Source: trans. F. Curta from A. Petranović and A. Margetić, "Il Placito del Risano," *Atti del Centro di ricerche storiche Rovigno* 14 (1983), pp. 56, 58, 60, 62, 64, 66, and 68.

In the name of the Father, of the Son, and of the Holy Spirit, amen. When at the summons of the most pious and excellent lord Charlemagne the emperor and of his son, King Pepin, we, their servants, were sent, namely the priest Izzo and the counts Cadolah and Aio [duke of Friuli, c. 799–817], [to inquire into] the questions regarding the holy churches of God, our lords, and the violence against the people, the poor, the orphans and the widows. We came first to the district of Capri [present-day Koper in southwestern Slovenia], at a place called Riziano [Rižana, just outside Koper], where the venerable patriarch Fortunatus [of Grado, 802–20], [came together with] the bishops Theodore, Leo, Stauratius, Stephen, Lawrence, and the other magnates and people of the province of Istria.

We then elected from the sole cities and castles [of the province] 172 men to serve as captains and we had them take the oath on the four Gospels of God and on the relics of saints that they would tell the truth when interrogated by us, first about the holy churches of God, then about the justice of our lords, as well as about the violence and the customs of the people of this land, about orphans and widows. Those men have to tell the truth without fear of anything. And they brought documents concerning the individual cities and castles, which were made by the *magistri militum* [top-level military commanders in the Late Roman empire] under Emperor Constantine [the Great? 306–37], asserting that churches had neither the assistance, nor their customary rights [that they used to have]. Patriarch Fortunatus replied: "I do not know if you want to say something against me. However, all of you know that you have liberated me from the customary rights, which my church had in your region since ancient times until now, because where I could, I was helping you, and even now I want to do it. You otherwise know that [I have paid] many tributes [for you] and I have sent messengers for you to the service of the emperor. But now let it be as you like it." All people [present] unanimously replied that in the future it should be as in the past and for many years [to come] for our [their] benefit, "because we have from you [the Franks] many benefits and we hope to have them in the future [as well], provided, when the messengers of your lords will arrive, that your family abides by the ancient custom." Then Patriarch Fortunatus said [the following]: "I beg you, my sons, tell the truth, what customary rights did my holy metropolitan church have among you in the district of Istria?" The leader of Pola [now Pula, in Croatia] spoke first: "When the patriarch comes to our city, if needed because of *missi* [*dominici* sent] by our lords or [because of] some *placitum* [general assembly] with the Greek [Byzantine] *magister militum*, the bishop of our city comes out [together] with the priests and the clergy, all wearing chasubles, with the [processional] cross, the candleholders and incense, chanting psalms as for the supreme pontiff, while the judges come out with the people carrying standards, and [all] welcome him with great honor. When the pontiff [the patriarch] enters the [episcopal] palace of our holy church, the bishop immediately takes the keys of his palace and places them at the patriarch's feet. The patriarch in turn gives them to his mayor and he distributes justice and is master of the palace for three days. Then he spends the fourth day in his own quarters." When we interrogated the judges from the other cities and castles whether that was true, they all said that it was and that they wanted it to remain the same. [And they added:] "We cannot say anything else against the patriarch. Your lord's flocks could graze in the same fields as ours, without any tax; we wish to keep things the way they are for the days to come. However, we have many things to say against the bishops. First, for the legates of the empire and for whatever other contribution or levy, the church [must] give half, and the people [the other] half. Second, when the legates of the empire come to us, they are accommodated by the bishops, and for as long as they do not return to their lord, they [have to] stay there. Third, emphyteutic [lease] contracts, [perpetual] leasehold interests [in land, with fixed and certain fines payable on each transfer], or non-malicious trade-ins of land have never been changed since ancient times as [much] as they are changed today. Fourth, nobody [should] use violence because of the right to hay or acorns on land left fallow, but [should] follow the custom of our ancestors. Fifth, one should not pay from the vineyards a third, as done today, but only a quarter. Sixth, [in the past] the *familia* of the church did not commit any offenses against a free man, nor did they beat him with sticks; in fact, they did not even dare to sit in his presence. Now they beat [people] with sticks and they persecute us with swords. As for us, fearing our Lord, we did not dare to resist, lest it get worse. Seventh, [in the past] the one renting church land until the third rebuke [by others, contesting the right to that land], was never thrown out [of the property]. Eighth, in the public sea [waters], where all people had the right to fish, one cannot fish any more, for fear of being beaten with sticks and having one's fishing nets cut. Ninth, as for the information you ask regarding the rights of our lords, which had been exercised by Greeks until the day we came under the power of our lords, we'll tell you the truth, as we know it: the city of Pola [had to pay] sixty-six *mancosi* [gold coins]; Ruvingium [now Rovinj, in western Istria, Croatia] forty *mancosi*; Parentium [now Poreč, in western Istria, Croatia] sixty-six *mancosi*; the *numerus Tergestinus* [the military district of Trieste, in northeastern Italy] sixty *mancosi*; Albona [now Labin, in eastern Istria, Croatia], thirty *mancosi*; Pedena [now Pićan, in central Istria, Croatia], twenty *mancosi*; Montavuna [now Motovun, in northern Istria, Croatia], thirty *mancosi*; Pinguente [now Buzet, in northern Istria, Croatia], twenty *mancosi*; and the chancellor of Civitas Nova [now Novigrad, in western Istria, Croatia], twelve *mancosi*; which is a total of 344 *mancosi*. At the command of the Greeks, those gold coins were delivered to the palace [that is, to the imperial fisc]. After John became duke [of Istria], he appropriated those coins for himself and did not admit that they were in fact fiscal dues. In addition, he confiscated the estate of Orcione with many olive trees, as well as a part of the estate of Petriolo with vineyards, land, and olive trees, and a house with a mill, then the large estate of Arbe with land, vineyards, olive trees, and a house, the estate of Stephen, the *magister militum*, the Zerontiaca house with all its appurtenances, then the estate of Maurice the consul and of Basil, the *magister militum*, and of Theodore the consul; then the estate which is in Priatello, with lands, vineyards, and olive trees, and many other places. In Civitas Nova, he takes advantage of the public domain, on which, both inside and outside the city, are more than two hundred *coloni*, who, in a good season, could produce more than one hundred *modii* [about nine hundred liters] of [olive] oil, more than two hundred amphorae of wine, grain and chestnuts in abundance. He also usurped rights on fishing, which produce more than fifty *mancosi* yearly, in addition to a sufficient quantity for his own table. The duke has all of this besides the 344 gold coins, which, as mentioned above, are due to the [imperial] palace. As for the force that Duke John used against us, and about which you have asked us, we will tell the truth, as we know it. First, he took away our forests, from which our ancestors had the right to collect hay and acorns. He also took away isolated farms from which, as mentioned above, our ancestors had the right to collect [revenue]. Now, [Duke] John denies that. In addition, he settled on our lands Slavs, who plow our lands and our wastelands, mow our meadows, graze their animals in our fields, and from those lands of ours, they pay rent to John. Moreover, we were left with no cattle and no horses, [for] if we say anything, they order us to kill them. He removed our boundary [markers], which our ancestors had placed [there] according to the ancient custom. Second, in ancient times, when we were under the power of the Greek empire, our ancestors had the right to have tribunes, to be nominated as *domestici* [companions (of the emperor), counts] and vicars as well as *locoservatores* [lieutenants], and on the basis of those charges, they participated in the [provincial] assembly, and sat during the session, each according to his own rank. Whoever desired to be treated better by the tribune, went to the emperor, who appointed him consul. He who had [the title of] imperial consul was ranked immediately after the *magister militum*. Now, our duke John has placed centarchs [commanders of one hundred men] above us, dividing the people between his sons and daughters, as well as his son-in-law, and those poor people [were told to] build his palaces. He abolished the office of tribune, and forbade us from having free men, asking that we go to war only with our serfs. He took away our *liberti* [freed slaves]; we do not have any power, not even over the aliens whom we had to accommodate in our homes and in the pertaining lands. During the rule of the Greeks, each tribune had five exempt [*coloni*] or more, and he [Duke John] abolished that as well. [Back then,] we were not supposed to pay *fodrum* [horse feed, a military tax], to work in the villa [estates of Duke John], nor to cultivate somebody else's vineyard, to make mortar or build houses, to make bricks, to feed the dogs, to make the collections, as we do now. For each animal [brought to the pasture for grazing], we now have to give a *modius* [of grain]. We never had to pay in sheep as we do now—sheep and lambs every year. We never had to go by ship to Venice, Ravenna, or Dalmatia, and on rivers [in order to fulfill transport obligations], but we now have to do that not only for John, but also for his sons, daughters, and son-in-law. When he is called for his duty to the emperor or has to send his men, he takes away our horses by force and our sons with him, charging them to drag loads . . . thirty thousand and more, and then he takes everything that they have and makes them return home by foot, while sending our horses to Francia [as royal gifts] or distributes them among his own men. He tells the people: 'Let us get some gifts for the emperor, as we used to do at the time of the Greeks and let an envoy of the people come with me to present those gifts to the emperor.' We gladly gather the gifts, and when he is about to leave, he says: 'You do not need to come [anymore], I will be your intercessor with the emperor.' He then takes our gifts, goes to the emperor, and obtains from him honors [favors] for him and his sons, while we are left behind in great oppression and distress. At the time of the Greeks, we used to make a yearly collection, if any was needed, for the imperial legates—one of every one hundred sheep, if one had that [many]. But today, whoever today has [only] three [sheep], must give one away, and we cannot complain, for his administrators take it every year. Duke John took into his hands that which in the past the *magister militum* of the Greeks never had, since the tribune always took care of the incoming and outgoing messengers and legates of the emperor. And those collections we have to do annually and every day, whether we like or not. For three years we gave to the pagan Slavs the tithes due to the holy church, when, in his sin, and to our perdition, [Duke John] installed them on the lands of the church and of the people. We comply with all those levies and extra dues under duress, something that our ancestors never had to do. And we have fallen into poverty and have become the mockery of our ancestors and neighbors in Venice and Dalmatia, as well of the Greeks, under whose rule we used to be. If Emperor Charles can help us, we will be saved; if not, it will be better for us to die than to live." Then Duke John said: "Those forests and pastures that you mentioned, I think that for the emperor's sake should be public [state] property; now, if you say otherwise under oath, I deny [it]. No collection of sheep will be done beyond what was in use in ancient times. The same is true for the gifts for the emperor. As for the labor obligations and ship transportation, as well as other dues, if they are burdensome to you, let them be no more. I will give back your *liberti*, according to the law of your ancestors. I will allow you to have free men under your power, as is the case for all those who are under [the power of] our lords. The foreign people residing on your lands, let them be under your power. As for the Slavs that you mentioned, let us go to the lands where they reside and see [what the situation truly is]. If they can reside there without causing any trouble to you, let them stay there. If they cause you any trouble in the woods, in the pastures, in the wastelands, or wherever it may be, we will throw them out [of those lands]. And if you agree, we will send them to deserted places where they cannot be of any trouble to you, [but] where they can be useful to the state, just like everybody else."

Therefore, we, the legates of the emperor, arranged for Duke John to give warranties that he would redress all the abovementioned [grievances regarding] the extra-dues, the right to acorns and hay, the labor dues and the collections, the Slavs, the levies, and the shipping by sea. And the warranties were taken by Damian, Honoratus, and Gregory. And the same people withdrew the charges [against Duke John], provided that such things would not happen anymore. And if he, his heirs, or his administrators continue with those oppressions, let them pay as we have established.

As for the other issues, Fortunatus, the venerable patriarch, the abovementioned bishops, Duke John, the other noblemen and the people agreed that everything must be fulfilled that they remembered under oath and said according to their oath and (in addition, that which is written) in the documents. Whoever does not want to comply, must pay nine pounds of gold in *mancosi* to the imperial palace. This judgment and compromise have been made in the presence of the legates of the lord emperor, the priest Izzo, Cadolah, and Aio, and they signed it with their own hands, in the presence of Fortunatus, patriarch through the grace of God, in this promissory document made by me, and signed by my hand

+ Duke John, signing with my own hand in this promissory document
+ Bishop Stauratius, etc. as above
+ Bishop Theodore
+ Bishop Stephen
+ Bishop Leo
+ Bishop Lawrence

Peter, sinful deacon of the holy metropolitan church of Aquileia wrote this document of promise at the order of my lord Fortunatus, the holiest patriarch, of Duke John, and of the abovementioned bishops and noblemen, and of the people of the province of Istria, and had revised the document after the corroboration of witnesses.

Questions: What were the comparatively larger and smaller taxes paid by communities in Istria? How can you explain the differences? What new dues did the Franks introduce? Which specific sources of income seem to have been targeted by the new regime? What political arrangements existed in the pre-Frankish era? How was the defense of Istria organized? What clues about the social organization in the peninsula does this text offer?

54. JOHN KAMINIATES ON THESSALONIKI BEFORE THE SACK OF 904

Nothing is known about John Kaminiates except what he tells about himself in his account of the sack of Thessaloniki by Muslim pirates in 904, a work entitled The Capture of Thessaloniki. *Together with other members of his family, John was taken prisoner and transported to Tripoli, in Cilicia, to be sold as a slave. Upon arrival, he met a certain Gregory of Cappadocia, who, like him, was a member of a group of prisoners who were on the way to Antioch to be sold on the slave market. The two men consoled each other with stories about their homelands. Prompted by a letter later sent to him by Gregory, John drafted a response during his confinement in Tarsos (now Tarsus, in southeastern Turkey), where he had been taken together with others for an exchange of prisoners with the Byzantines. The letter of response was written shortly after the death of John's father (905). He had already received the news of one of his three children dying at sea and had witnessed in Crete the sale into slavery of his sister-in-law. Before the sack of his hometown, John had been a churchman in Thessaloniki in the service of the local archbishop. His writing shows him to be an educated man, skilled in rhetorical techniques commonly employed in historical narratives. This is especially clear from the description of Thessaloniki at the beginning of the* Capture. *Kaminiates employed in that description standard techniques such as ekphrasis (a description of a work of visual art) and draws inspiration from a long tradition of panegyrics for significant cities of the empire. Curiously, while some have raised doubt about the authenticity of the* Capture *as a whole, the description of the Thessaloniki and its hinterland is often cited as a snapshot of the early tenth-century historical reality in the Balkan provinces of the empire, including relations with Bulgaria under King Symeon.*

Source: trans. D. Frendo and A. Fotiou, *John Kaminiates: The Capture of Thessaloniki* (Leiden: Brill, 2017), pp. 5, 7, 9, 11, 13, 15, 17, and 19.

3. We, dear friend, are natives of Thessaloniki. So, I shall acquaint you with her through whom first I came to know many things which I did not yet know. Quite recently, since I made your acquaintance, I have been collecting information about her. She is a great city and the foremost city of the Macedonians [of the historical province of Macedonia]. . . .

4. The city is, as has been mentioned, of ample proportions, with extensive walls and fortifications affording the inhabitants the full security associated with such defensive structures. It has its slanting coastline washed by the waters of the gulf which extends southward to meet it, so that it offers easy access to shipping sailing in from every quarter of the globe. A magnificent deepwater harbor adjoins the city, allowing mariners to bring in their ships in safety and berth them in an anchorage undisturbed by wind or wave, which its designer cut off from the rest of the sea. For while holding in by means of a wall the volume of sea that had been let in, he contrived to hold off at the same time the stormy waters heaving in from the seaward side. Whenever, in fact, the sea swells up from its depths and spews out a mass of water in the direction of the shore, it is held in check by the wall at this point and finding nothing at which to direct its threatened onslaught, advances toward the opposite ends of the wall until its heaving mass of water

unaccountably subsides, leaving any anchorage thus situated well out of the reach of every storm. At the same time the gulf itself is cut off from the open sea by a sort of isthmus thrust forward like an elbow and reaching very far out to sea, which the locals call the "Jetty" on account of its jutting out so far into the water. Narrowing, therefore, because of the intrusion of this neck of land, so as to form a strait with its opposite shore, the gulf becomes a second harbor. From this elbow of land, right up to the city wall, the water sweeps in a magnificent curving shape, which is bounded longitudinally by a long stretch of facing shores and contracts slightly in width as it approaches the city. And the gulf looks out due south upon the high seas, the harbor looks out upon the gulf and the city on the harbor. But whereas the harbor is enclosed by four corners, the gulf is rounded, with a very deep seabed, and with outer ends restricting and confining the flow of its waters ever at a great distance from the mainland.

5. So much for the south side of the city. The terrain on the northern side is rugged and inaccessible in the extreme. A mountain range stoops over it with overhanging ridges and causes a considerable part of the city itself to be situated on high ground, so that whereas one part of it is level and suited to the needs of its inhabitants, the other stretches right up into the hill country and the mountain peaks. But the mountain range does not extend in such a way as to impair the city's defenses: it does not allow an enemy to come down from its heights in safety and attack the walls of the city. The structure of the mountain, in fact, makes effective surveillance a relatively easy matter at that point owing to the virtually impassable nature of the intervening terrain. For it soars aloft in an easterly direction in a ragged formation of ridges and ravines. Yet the more it races on due east, the more it removes itself from the low-lying areas forming its flanking slopes on each side. On two sides of the mountain, in fact, namely the southern and the northern, there stretches an expanse of low-lying plain land, which is both easily reached and easily exploited and provides the citizens with all the necessary means of subsistence.

The plain which is situated to the south of the mountain and to the east of the city is extraordinarily beautiful and attractive. It is singularly blessed with huge shady trees, multicolored gardens, and an abundant supply of water from both springs and rivers which the mountain thickets bountifully bestow upon the plain and which extend a hand in welcome to the sea herself. Vines planted side by side wreathe the fields in dense array and urge the beauty-loving eye to gladness with the multifarious clusters of their fruit. Large numbers of monasteries, perched on tablelands, nestling in valleys, or ensconced in especially delightful locations, add a novel touch for wayfarer and citizen alike. On the left-hand side of the mountain lies another plain. It too runs to a very great length and stretches back as far as another group of mountains. In the middle stand two wide lakes [now Koronia and Volvi], which take up most of the plain, but also contribute greatly to the necessaries of life, by supporting huge numbers of fish, both large and small and of many different species. These keep the tables of the neighboring villages and indeed of the city itself abundantly supplied. It is almost as though the lakes were competing with the sea in this kind of benefaction and were vying also with each other to see which would produce the greater quantity. But it is a competition from which no clear winner emerges to taunt the loser with defeat. The rest of the plain is given up to agriculture and to animal husbandry, providing a habitat for the obedient animals of the field and for the freely roaming creatures of the mountain. Deer, in fact, come down from the mountains, rejoicing at the sight of water in the lakes, where they drink their fill and mingle with the herds of cattle for a common meal.

6. We have given an adequate description of the eastern and northern parts of the city and also of the southern part. Now let us try to depict as best as we can the general layout of the western part. There is another plain which starts at the Jetty Wall, follows the contour of the mountain on the right, borders the sea on the left, and presents the beholder with a spectacle of untold beauty. For that part which can claim some proximity to both the city and the sea is plentifully irrigated, decked out with vineyards, copses, and gardens and adorned with innumerable dwellings and chapels, most of which have been divided up and held in common by companies of monks, who practice every kind of virtue and live for God alone, toward whom they strive and on account of whom they left the turmoil of civic life and undertook to follow the path that leads to him alone.

After that, the plain extends inland for a great distance with mostly treeless vegetation, but with good agricultural land. It continues to stretch in a westerly direction until it reaches another range of lofty mountains, at which point is situated a city called Beroia [now Veroia, in Imathia, Greece]. It is a famous city in its own right both with regard to its inhabitants and to all other qualities on which a city pins its faith.

In its central portion, this plain also contains a mixture of villages, some of whose inhabitants, the Drugubites and the Sagudates [two Slavic tribes], as they are called, pay their taxes to the city, while others pay tribute to the Scythians [Bulgarians] who live not far from the border. Yet the villages and their inhabitants live very close to one another, and the close commercial relations that are maintained with the Scythians are a considerable asset to the citizens of Thessaloniki as well, especially when both parties stay on friendly terms with each other and refrain from any violent measures that lead to confrontation and armed conflict. They share a common lifestyle and exchange commodities in perfect peace and harmony, and this has been their policy for some not inconsiderable time past. Mighty rivers rising from the land of the Scythians [Vardar and Aliakmon] divide among themselves the aforesaid plain, and they lavish much abundance on the city through supplying it with fish and through being navigable upstream by seagoing vessels, as a result of which a cunningly contrived assortment of profits from commodities flows down those waters. . . .

8. I pointed out she is a city of considerable dimensions and encompasses an ample territory. The parts of the wall that face land are extremely well fortified and of massively thick construction, with a complete system of outworks maintaining an additional safe area, and are everywhere reinforced by a series of wall towers and battlements, so as to leave the inhabitants no occasion for fear. But the part that faces the south is low, and totally unequipped to deal with a military threat. I think that through his not even remotely suspecting the possibility of a serious seaborne assault, the designer of the fortifications long ago neglected to do his job here. . . .

9. . . . And in fact, ever since the sacrament of baptism had brought the Scythian people into the Christian fold and had made them share in the milk of true piety, the tumult of war died down, the murderous blade abandoned its work of butchery, and the predictions of that mightiest voice of prophecy, Isaiah, were in our own times clearly fulfilled: for "our swords were transformed into pruning hooks, and our spears into plowshares" [Isa. 2:4], and war was in no place, and peace governed all the neighboring territory, and there was no material resource of which we did not enjoy a superfluity—on the one hand the abundance of agriculture, on the other the affluence of commerce. Land and sea were appointed to serve us from old and rendered sterling service in every particular and at no cost. Whatever the land was deficient in or was not suited to the production of, the sea contrived to procure and convey in merchant ships, making good the deficiency and supplying what was lacking to those who needed it. What particular thing associated with those who flocked from every land to reside amongst us shall I mention first, which in particular of the benefits which they conferred upon us citizens by giving to us what they had to offer them in exchange? Thanks to the fact that a public highway running eastward from the west [Via Egnatia] passes straight through this city and provides travelers with a very strong inducement for stopping off with us and supplying themselves with everything they need, we made incalculable profits. In consequence, a motley crowd of foreigners and townspeople thronged the streets, so that it was easier to count the sands on the seashore than to count the numbers of those passing through the marketplace and carrying out their various transactions. From this trade, a great many private fortunes were made in gold, silver, and precious stones, and silk garments were as common an item of manufacture as woolens were elsewhere. Not to mention, of course, the other materials, such as bronze, iron, tin, lead, and glass, whereby the crafts that use fire make their livelihood, all of which were in such plentiful supply that another city could have been built and furnished with them.

Questions: Why was Thessaloniki so prosperous, according to John Kaminiates? What is the relation between the description of the landscape and the insistence upon the economic growth in the city? Who are the Scythians mentioned in the text? What is the role that the author ascribes to trade?

55. SLAVES FOR THE BENEDICTINE ABBEY OF ST-PETER IN THE VILLAGE

*A cartulary is a manuscript register containing copies of charters, titles of deeds, privileges, and legal rights. The manuscript of the cartulary of the Benedictine abbey of St-Peter in the Village, written on parchment in Caroline minuscule, but also in Beneventan and Gothic script, is now in the archives of the cathedral of St-Domnius in Split (Croatia). The collection of documents for that cartulary began in 1080, in direct association with the personal history of a nobleman from the town of Split. At an unknown age (but certainly in his adult years) Peter Crni, who was a wealthy man, decided to build a church, together with his wife Anna, for a small community of Benedictine monks in a place called Selo ("the Village," in what is now Sumpetar, near Omiš, in southern Croatia). Nothing else is known about Anna, but years later, after falling seriously ill, Peter took monastic vows and joined the same monastery, after having his nephew George appointed abbot. He also arranged for the building of living quarters for the monks and provided the monastery with land and a labor force. Those deeds, as well as a great number of purchases and donations, are scrupulously recorded in the cartulary. Peter acquired for the monastery of St-Peter a total of some fifty farm workers, men and women, called "serfs" in the cartulary (*servi*). However, as they had often been bought for cash or given as payment of a debt, those people were not serfs in the medieval sense of the word. They were, for all practical purposes, slaves, even though some of them were allowed to have their own property (such as a vineyard) or to pursue some independent trade.*

Source: trans. F. Curta from J. Marušić, *Sumpetarski kartular i Poljička seljačka republika* (Split: Knijževni krug, 1992), pp. 20, 24, 32, 34, 36, and 42.

[1] In the name of Christ and in the one thousand eightieth year of his incarnation, the eighth indiction; at the time of the lord Lawrence, archbishop of the revered see of Split [1060–99], of the king of the Croats Suinimir [Zvonimir, king of Croatia between 1075 and 1089], and of Prior Valizza [Valica, the head of the city government in Split]. Peter Zerni [Crni, "the Black"], son of Gumay, together with the lady Anna my wife, the daughter of Maja Fave, encouraged by the divine clemency and supported by the advice of many servants of God, thought to offer some part of our inheritance to the Almighty God, as much as it is in our means, and according to the custom of the faithful for the salvation of our dead and of course for the redemption of our sins. We decided to do that with God's help. In a place which is called Selle [*selo* in Croatian means "village"], near the church of St-Stephen, which is under the authority of our lord, namely the most blessed

Domnius [the patron saint of the archdiocese of Split], we have begun the building of a church in honor of the prince of all the apostles, Peter the apostle, and we have managed to finish this church with God's permission and the hard work of the master builders. Finally, after the job was completed, on 11 October, we asked the said archbishop and other ministers of the holy orders to consecrate the church. Many men from Split and from Croatia came to this ceremony to receive forgiveness and the remission [of their sins]. Then, guided by divine authority, the said archbishop with the other ministers around him, began asking about the endowment of that church. And we, within the limits of our powers, offered there and then all that was necessary, following the instructions of the servants of God.

First of all, the things needed for the service of the mass: one missal, a silver chalice with its paten, and all the apparel [that is, altar cloths] for [celebrating] the mass; one book about the passions of the saints, one night antiphonary [a liturgical book containing antiphons, short sentences sung or recited before or after a psalm], [and] one psalter.

We have given all the lands in the vicinity of that church, from the boundary of the land of the aforesaid church under the authority of Saint Domnius to the place called Saline, all that is below it, hill or valley, from the shore of the [Adriatic] sea to the vineyard of Tustokosin [Tusta Cosa, perhaps Mutogras near Jesenice, between Split and Omiš, in modern Croatia]. We had acquired all this land at our own expense, so we gave it to the house of God. . . .

[6] But after many years I [Peter] became so ill that there was no hope of coming out of it. That is why, in that illness, I made a vow that if I recover from my illness, in the aforesaid church of the apostle Peter, I will take the tonsure and receive the habit of the most blessed Benedict [that is, become a Benedictine monk]. So, I got out of bed by the grace of God, and with the advice and help of Archbishop Lawrence and of the other clerics, we had the lord Gregory our nephew ordained abbot in the said church [which thus became an abbey church]; and what vowed, I accomplished with God's help. And then we began to build houses for the brothers [cells and other buildings for the monastery], and completed the task with the help of God. . . .

[41] Finally, I purchased half of the abovementioned place from an old priest singing Mass in St-John's at Cremen for two solidi [gold coins] and one gallon of wine to complete the deal, in the presence of the following witnesses: Prodan, the nephew of Matana, the priest Mark, the deacon Dabro, and Duymo de Tule.

[42] In addition, I purchased from Nycola, for a final amount of fifteen solidi, a serf named Cyprian, with his sons and daughters, and his vineyards which are above the road below the church of St-Maximus; in the presence of Peter Cegayta, John de Porta, Dabro Laudula, and Fusco Pucipani.

[43] To the same church we gave a serf named Nycola with his wife Dabrina and with their sons and daughters and the vineyards which are beside Cyprian's

vineyard, having bought them from his brother George. Let it be said that Nycola belongs to the same church. . . .

[44] From Duymo, son of Stresina, I purchased a serf named Negozai for a finite sum of six solidi; in the presence of Fusco Tiberi and Drago Muti.

[45] Similarly, I purchased a serf named Dragaza from the priest of Orechoa for five solidi in the presence of Basil Stasucco and Lampredio Cybriulo, to whom we gave one hundred sheep, two cows, and pair of oxen for the needs of the church in question. Let them all remain there.

[46] From his father, we bought a little boy called Slobba, whom we had educated, and whom we set free and raised to the honor of priesthood for service in the same church, and whom we wish to remain there forever.

[47] In addition, we gave Peter Dracculus whom I bought from the men of Catarum [Kotor, now in Montenegro] for three solidi.

[48] From Bartul the constable, I purchased Zorgi Dracculus for seven solidi, in the presence of the archbishop and of chaplain John.

[49] I purchased a serf named Andriulus, for I had lent his father forty solidi for the work [that he had to do], and as his father could not repay me, I took his aforementioned son for one solidus and one measure of grain to complete the deal, with the condition that if he gives me a serf like him, I will let him go free, but if not, he should be forever the serf of the church. And this was confirmed in the presence of all his brothers and his sisters. . . .

[63] I purchased a serf named Perinna for a total of two solidi.

[64] Then Zacharia gave over his son named Chudali to be a serf of St-Peter's in exchange for the total sum of three solidi.

[65] In a similar way, Raccana gave his son Belotiza to be in the said church forever.

[66] Then Dabressa gave his son Strosti to the said church to be a serf there forever. . . .

[69] The swineherd also went to the church, for the abbot had cured him, at great expense, of the ulcer he had on his head. . . .

[89] I purchased the daughter of Scarana and his son Nadeia for one solidus and two measures of grain to complete the deal; the headman Pradan and his brother were witnesses.

[90] Next I bought the wife of Nevada with her daughter for one solidus and one pound of flax to complete the deal, in the presence of the headman Pradan and his brother, and of Boledrug of Nacle, and of Kerna of Tugare and his brother Belata and of Girdana. . . .

[91] Next, I purchased the mother of Striani from Cirnecha, the prior's son, for three solidi, and I purchased her son from the Lombards [Italian merchants] for ten solidi, with the agreement that all his brothers and sisters should be serfs as well. Duymo the prior and his son were witnesses.

Questions: What were some of the reasons for enslavement, according to the Sumpetar Cartulary? What can the text tell us about the relative value of slaves in medieval Dalmatia? Compare the slaves in this text to those that Abu Hamid bought in Hungary (Doc. 50).

56. THE *TYPIKON* OF ISAAC KOMNENOS FOR HIS MONASTERY NEAR BERA

The monastery of the Mother of God Kosmosoteira near Bera (now Ferres near Alexandroupoli, on the Greek-Turkish border) was founded by Isaac Komnenos, the brother of Emperor John II (1118–43). He had already sponsored the reconstruction of the Chora Monastery in Constantinople. He paid for the construction of an aqueduct for the benefit of a monastery dedicated to Saint John the Baptist near the River Jordan, in the Holy Land. Having plotted against his brother, Isaac was exiled to Herakleia, on the southern shore of the Black Sea. However, when his nephew Manuel became emperor (1143–80), he withdrew to his patrimonial estate in Thrace, at Bera. He began writing his typikon *(a book of directives including rules of life for the monastic community and the rule of prayer) in 1152, as indicated in its preamble, but made several additions later, as he intended to donate his entire property to the monastery. The exact date of Isaac's death is not known, but he was buried in the monastery church, which his son Andronicus visited shortly after becoming emperor in 1183. For his* typikon, *Isaac drew inspiration from the* typikon *of the monastery of the Mother of God Evergetis in Constantinople, established a century earlier. Isaac owned many estates in the region, which he listed in the foundation charter for his monastery. In good rhetorical tradition, the region in which he placed the monastery is said to have been deserted and inhabited only by snakes and scorpions, but elsewhere in the* typikon *Isaac described the hinterland of the monastery in southern Thrace as fertile, cultivated, and quite prosperous. Most of the estates enumerated were Isaac's "immovable properties" that had come to him through inheritance; others had been bought at various points in time.*

Source: trans. N. Patterson Ševčenko, "*Typikon* of the Sebastokrator Isaac Komnenos for the Monastery of the Mother of God *Kosmosoteira* near Bera," in *Byzantine Monastic Foundation Documents: A Complete Translation of the Surviving Founders'* Typika *and Testaments*, ed. J.P. Thomas and A. Constantinides Hero (Washington, DC: Dumbarton Oaks Research Library and Collection, 2000), vol. 2, pp. 798–99, 828–29, 833, 846–47.

[This is the] *typikon* which I, Isaac [the *sebastokrator*], son of the great emperor lord Alexios Komnenos, have composed for the monastery which I restored and newly established in the fifteenth indiction of the year 6660 [1152]. Herein is placed the mosaic image of the Kosmosoteira and Mother of God, in many a thing a benefactress. The region in which this monastery lies was altogether devoid of men and houses, [the haunt] only of snakes and scorpions . . . wild in every way and encircled by wide-spreading branches. This *typikon* of mine here sets forth in detail my decrees for the administration with the aid of God of this monastery, and commands (these decrees which I now set forth in it being in fact [contained] in my last and secret testament as well, if not in their entirety) that my orders remain immutable and undisturbed throughout all time.

This preface and full text of the *typikon* have been issued by me while in a condition of grave illness. This is the preface to the full text of this present work which I, the restorer of the holy monastery, as has been said, have set forth in burning faith for my benefactress, the Mother of God and Kosmosoteira. A flawless ally in every way, I now invoked you, since it is with your aid, O all-seeing universal queen, that I would express the wishes nourished in this at present so wretched mind of mine. . . .

69. Those of my immovable properties that came to me from family inheritance through imperial decrees and commands, and those that I have assigned to the monastery for its use and ownership from now on, so that it may have them entirely inalienable till the end of time, with all their territory, safeguard and tenure, and with all rights and privileges over them, just as I declared above, are as follows: Neokastron with its dependent peasants settled both inside and outside, and its houses, mine and those of others; also the rights over the fairs taking place there annually, and over the catch from the Rivers Samia and Maritsa for a good supply of fish. Also the estates Tou Kanikleiou, Lykochorion, and Tou Drachou, and the promontory Banianous. The following estates: the village Sykea and the estate before it that is called Tou Triphylliou are to be counted, by imperial ordinance, as belonging to Neokastron after the death—and from then on—of Aspeiotes, who at present holds it for his own use. I wish also for it to be relocated close to the monastery, where I also put Lykochorion and Tou Drachou—unless some difficulty arises, due to the length of the road between, for the inhabitants living in the village, in harvesting in summertime of the fruits of the farms, and the transportation of them to their relocated houses.

In addition, all those immovable [properties] belonging to me as their owner both inside and outside of Ainos [now Enez, near Keşan, in the southwestern part of European Turkey], which have been disintegrating for such a long time—these I wish to be restored. The estate Neochorin, the estate Kourianis, the estate Tou Choirosphaktou, the village Batzinea, the village Tou Chousderi, the estate Tou Sinale, the newly built estate Beros, Soter ton Blachon, the estate Hagios Nikolaos, the two military villages Tou Dilianou and Dragabasta, the fort Aetos with the village Tzechoba, the estate Sukaragi, the village Braniste, the estate Neboselous, the estate Delbotzianous, the estate Tzampe, the estate Raunianous, the village Sophous—if it is not sold in my lifetime—the market Sagoudaous, with the dependent peasants and residents settled in it, with its ships and the right *tou basilikatou* [a tax] and its warehouse [state warehouse for grain and other foodstuffs]. These things [the monastery will gain possession of] after my decease. . . .

Also the twelve ships that were granted to me with exemption through the imperial decree of the late lord my father, and which have a capacity of four thousand *modioi* [over 9,200 gallons]. . . . Moreover, in addition to these I present and assign to the monastery those farms that I own outside Traianoupolis [now Traianoupoli, northeastern Greece]. I pray therefore to all-seeing God to prolong the remainder of my life for the sure fulfillment of these orders, and for the erection [and reclamation] of those dwellings and cultivated areas in Ainos, which, through time and indifference of superintendents, have already collapsed and gone to seed. . . .

74. And so I think that the charms of the monastery and the site will draw many men to them. There is the spot itself—even if previously it was the dwelling of snakes and scorpions—the River Ainos [Maritsa], the sea with its surf and its calm waters, the pasturage and grazing land of evergreen meadows to nourish horses and cattle. There is the site on the crest of the hill with its easy access. There is the fine temperateness of the currents of air and the power of strong breezes with the everlasting reeds rustling in tune with them about the mouth of the river. There is the immense plain, and the panoramic view, especially in summertime, of corn in flower and in ear, which impresses great gladness on those who direct their gaze there. There is the grove of lovely saplings growing so near the monastery, and bunches of grapes are entwined among them. As a joy to the throats of the thirsty, water gushes forth wonderfully beautiful and cold. . . .

112. But since I am responsible in every way for the conservation of this monastery with the help of God, and for the everlasting preservation of everything that is of advantage to it, I have come up with another thought: I hereby declare that all those men I selected from the *episkepsis* [fiscal district] of Neokastron whom I used in the role of *vestiaritai* [imperial bodyguards, courtiers closest to the emperor], who worked for me until my death on the construction of this holy monastery from its very foundations, and in other hired jobs and essential services—yes, and those who, after the completion of its construction, were also counted as *vestiaritai* together with the others, and summoned from the aforementioned *episkepsis* of Neokastron—these [men] should be altogether immune [from service], after my death and up until their death.

[They must] never be dragged into compulsory service or extra-compulsory service or *psomozemia* [a tax consisting of bread deliveries for the army] by the superintendent of the monastery villages, nor by its superior. Rather [they can] resettle all together, [leaving] the place in which they live today, with their entire household, and live near the God-protected fortress of the monastery, there where both Lykochorion and Tou Drachou, which I resettled, are located. These particular *vestiaritai* are at the same time to assist the monastery and ward off those who might try to harm it and ruin its possessions. For I wish and order these *vestiaritai* to be obedient to such action on the part of the superior [abbot of the monastery], and to be used for dispatch work whenever the superior is in need of them. [It is] for such things above all that I have bestowed upon them, as I have said, exemption and immunity from other compulsory services and *psomozemiai* after my death. If ever the superior has occasion to make use of one of them for some service, in the city or in another place, he must not fail to give the man being sent a horse to ride (since he is poor and without resources), for use on the prescribed route only, and such payment as corresponds to the distance to the destination. Should some of these particular *vestiaritai* wish at sometime or other to serve under some other master rather than work for this holy monastery and not to obey the most honorable superior (as I have ordered [them to do]), let them henceforth be deprived of all the privileges to which I entitled them, and be banished from the *episkepsis* of Neokastron, and sent away to another estate by the superior even if [they are] not willing. For they are at odds with my wishes regarding their benefits.

Questions: What did Isaac Komnenos have to gain from drafting this typikon*? What did the monks gain? How was the monastery to be regulated and governed, both by secular and by church authorities?*

57. THE "STATUTES" OF CONRAD OTTO II

The "Statutes" attributed to Duke Conrad Otto II of Moravia (1182–89) granted the first privileges to the increasingly powerful nobility in the Czech lands. In addition, the "Statutes" regulated the status of the "castle warriors," the lesser nobility, members of which were granted economic privileges. The original document (now lost) was adopted in 1189 at the court assembly in Sadská (near Nymburk, Czech Republic). This was one of the first introductions of written instruments into the local legal system. The document was issued in three versions, each for a different part of Moravia (Znojmo, Brno, and Břeclav). The Brno version, translated below, was amended in 1229 by King Přemysl I Otakar (1198–1230). Although local customs are mentioned in places, the legal language is heavily influenced by canon law (which is even mentioned at the end). Perhaps the most significant influence of Roman law is the idea that possession of merit (fiefs) became hereditary. This document therefore testifies to the emergence of the hereditary, landed nobility.

Source: trans. F. Curta from *Codex diplomaticus et epistolarius regni Bohemiae*, ed. G. Friedrich (Prague: Wiesner, 1912), vol. 2, pp. 329–32.

In the name of the holy and integral Trinity, amen. Otakar, who is also [called] Přemysl, king of Bohemia by the grace of God, together with the *župans* [barons] and all the noblemen, as well as the people of the province of Brno, forever. It is both worthy of and belongs to the majesty of the royal highness and honor to look over all in a just way and to make sure that nobody is punished against the rule of law, but that one's rights are preserved unaltered. For observance of the law keeps honor and glory in this world, and [for that] God gives to the soul a reward in the heavenly kingdom. So that the rights that have been established first by our predecessors, in memory of the good Duke Conrad and of others and then by us for the whole province of Brno, cannot be changed over time by any man, but will forever remain permanent and firm, let it be known both in the present age and in the future, that, after careful consultation of our faithful *župans*, both from Bohemia and from Moravia, wishing for all to respect them [the rights] unaltered forever, we established the law as follows: all *hereditates* [allodial properties, to be owned free of any obligations toward anyone else] that noblemen, both magnates and lesser nobles, held at the time of Duke Conrad without being contested, rightfully and peacefully until now, let them be kept in the same way in good peace. Let no chamberlain summon anyone except for the safe testimony of those concerned; in particular each one of them [the chamberlains in question] must take with him an envoy from the [local] castellan and [from] the judge, in addition to two good men from the surrounding manors; but if the chamberlain goes alone the second or the third [time] without messengers from officials, nobody can be made responsible if he is killed. If a thief is caught by a nobleman or by the one who owns the manor, let all his property and his neck [that is, life] be given to the prince. Moreover, if a thief is captured in a [particular] place, but hangs himself [that is, commits suicide, in order not to be caught alive], all that he has goes to the prince, except the crops that are left in the field. The same for what they call *narok* [Czech word meaning "claim, cause of action"], which is not to be admitted unless there is secure testimony about one's loss of the goods [that is, about the accusation of theft], except when it happens in the woods or some hidden place, or to a guest [that is, a foreign settler]; and a court notice is to be given before he is admitted [to bring the case] to the one concerned, namely the judge, the castellan, and the others. When some poor man comes to complain about something, let not his clothes be stripped away from him [that is, let not his money be taken away]. Let no *zok* [Czech word meaning "complaint, plaintiff"] accuse anyone, unless there is safe testimony from the neighbors about the damage; and if the *zok* is condemned by public testimony [that is, if the public testimony invalidates his own], let him be stoned. If anyone has to go through the ordeal of water, let nobody push him into the water except the priest and his assistant. And if God helps him, let him give to the judge two deniers, and fourteen to the priest; if he takes his clothes off, and refuses to undergo the ordeal, let him pay the chaplain seven deniers and the old woman two. If a *narok* is brought against a certain nobleman, and not a *druh* [Czech word for "retainer, companion"], then let a *puer* [servant] go to court for him; and if he fails to appear there, let him pay two hundred deniers for that. When what is called *zuod* [Czech word for "assembly"] is conducted, agents of the castellan, of the judge, of the steward, and of the chamberlain, as well as one or two from that [particular] neighborhood need to be present. And let them not overrule the three but remain on the third. And if there is someone found guilty, let [that man] pay two hundred deniers to the princely treasury and make satisfaction to the one who is called *powod* [Czech word for the one who first brought the accusation]. If someone steals horses, mares, oxen, or cows, or some other important things, let the magnitude of the damage be estimated with sure faith and the oaths of those who are entrusted with judgment, and let the plaintiffs follow that accordingly. Thieves should be given the same punishment as their accomplices and companions. If they steal something else, clothes or something of that nature, let it not be reported to the court; but if a bull or cattle are seized unlawfully, let it be reported to the court. And if someone is injured on the road coming from the market, or anywhere else, let it be reported to the court. When a nobleman is caught stealing and is punished by hanging, but has no offspring, his property reverts to the king; and if someone is caught stealing in the open, then his wife has a right to a third [of his property]. Any nobleman or peasant that kills anyone must pay to the court two hundred deniers, and let him go elsewhere [that is, be banished] and ask for mercy, while his wife can sit at home in peace, without any trouble [to her]. If a man has no son or sons, but has daughters, let them inherit in the same way the *hereditas*. If they do not, let the inheritance go to the closest heirs. If the cattle or the honeybees are stolen from someone, let [the thief] be tried by the iron ordeal, that is by the plow. Furthermore, if someone is robbed by *wiboy* [Czech word for "lightning," here in the sense of surprise attack], let him identify the perpetrator whom he wants, and out of *hirdozt* [Czech word for "pride"] let him name whom he wants, and let the old customs be preserved. Whoever does not pay the *theloneum* [toll, custom duty], and has no license from the toll officer, should not be punished in any other way than by paying double the amount of the *theloneum*, in addition to a fine of sixty deniers. If someone recognizes his own horse pulling a wagon, let him pay no more than sixty denarii for the wagon and the load. And if someone's horse is wounded by someone else, let the horse not be compensated by [the decision of] a judge, except only sixty deniers. Similarly, if someone is called and receives his judgment in court, let neither *wrez* [Czech word for "notch," here with the meaning of "sting"] nor *pohonce* [Old Czech word for "judicial sentence, punishment"] apply, only two deniers, namely that which is called *pomocne* [Czech word for "auxiliary, ancillary"] in the vernacular. And nobody is obliged to run to the general call, which is called *nestoyte* [Czech word meaning "do not stand"] in the vernacular, unless he wants to do so out of his own free will. If someone is sued for his movable or immovable property, namely those goods over which he has possession, let neither the judge nor the steward of the landlord claim to possess it; let him who is sued for his property keep it in peace until a sentence is pronounced [in court] over this matter. If things that have been stolen are found next to a village, let that village not be punished in any way for the investigated theft. Moreover, none of those who guard the forest should plunder anyone on the road or in the marketplace, unless they plunder the one whom they have caught cutting a tree. For that, let the judge never impose a fine of three hundred deniers, but only of sixty. In addition, a judge should never judge by himself, but in the presence of a castellan or of several nobles; and when a steward judges, he should not go out of court for advice, but let him judge in the presence of knights [castle warriors]. When it is time to go to trial, and everyone is in place, and the steward does not want to come, let the judge distribute justice in the presence of the knights. And let the judge or the steward hold trial always in the morning, never in the afternoon. When someone is killed on the road, whether he is a nobleman, or a judge, or a steward, there is great confusion; as usual, money, gold, and silver are brought there; he who accuses and the lord [of the slain] shall swear by the relics of the saints. If someone is sued for debt and does not show up in court the first time, let him be sold [as a slave], unless he can prove a legal impediment [for which he could not show up in court]. Moreover, none of the men in the service of nobles, who go to court on somebody else's behalf or on their own, should pay the new *theloneum*, but only the old one. Let no one appear in court who has not by law been summoned in the first place. Moreover, if the king's steward confiscates something from someone without a trial, let the king correct that by his own law. In the case of the chamberlain's steward, let him pay a mark of gold. In the case of a lord, let him lose his benefice. In addition, a duel, which is called *kiy* [Czech word for "club"] in the vernacular, should only take place between foreigners. In all of this, exceptions are the privilege of the churchman granted by princes and the right of the clergy with ecclesiastical gifts, which are governed by canon law. To that disposition, we raise the limitation and observance of order according to the law. And so that no one opposes the truth in those prescribed [above], preferring falsehood, and nobody obscures [its meaning] by raising doubts, we ratify our authority, as necessary, and we protect and confirm by the testimony of our seal that which we have [already] confirmed by justice and the truth of his Son.

Questions: Why were full rights to hereditates *confirmed in this document? Does that have anything to do with inheritance customs? What is the relation between the laws established by the "Statutes" and the "old customs"? Who may have been interested in the preservation of the latter and would have opposed the former? What are the circumstances in which someone found guilty had to pay two hundred deniers to the "princely treasury"? Why was that payment demanded in the first place?*

58. TREATY BETWEEN RIGA, GOTLAND, AND SMOLENSK

Although not the first agreement regulating trade along the Daugava River, from the Rus' lands to the Baltic Sea, the treaty between Smolensk, Riga, Gotland, and the other German towns is the most comprehensive text concerning that trade. It survives in seven variants, one of which is shorter than the other six. The Gotland recension translated below is the East Slavic copy (written in Cyrillic) of a text that was likely written down originally in Latin or in Middle German. The charter was written on parchment and is now in the State Archives in Riga, Latvia. To judge from the text below, Prince Mstislav Davidovich of Smolensk (1223–31) had sent his envoys to Gotland, where the actual treaty was signed. In Gotland, however, and specifically in the city of Visby, an association of German merchants had previously been formed, which would later be called Hansa. Several cities on the southern shore of the Baltic Sea, from Lübeck to Riga (and farther to Reval/Tallinn, in Estonia), had joined that association, the main purpose of which was long-distance trade with Rus', primarily in furs. The ratification of the treaty in Gotland was the last phase of the process of negotiation that started in Smolensk, where Mstislav had moved after having been prince of Novgorod between 1184 and 1187. The treaty of 1229 regulated not only trade, but also relations between the German merchants (called "Latins" in the Rus' text) and the Rus' people—merchants, prince, and commoners. In other words, a number of legal dispositions accompany what was fundamentally an act of economic cooperation. The legal dispositions seem to have mediated differences between the legal systems of Rus', on one hand, and of the German towns of the burgeoning Hansa, on the other, while in some cases, creating a basis for common legal action that may be regarded as a rudimentary form of international law. Much revolves around the Volok, a generic term for the land between two navigable rivers, over which ships or boats had to be dragged. Smolensk was strategically located on the Dnieper River, a major axis of trade with the south, and the upper course of the Daugava (Western Dvina, in Russian), which linked the Valdai Heights of inner Rus' to the Baltic Sea. Associations of carriers responsible for the transportation of goods across the Volok were a key component of the trade network established by German merchants in the heart of Rus'. Conversely, the treaty specifically allows Rus' merchants to travel freely all the way to Lübeck, at the mouth of the Trave River in northern Germany, an indication that the (later) Hansa had not yet monopolized trade across the Baltic Sea. Despite the mention of the year 1228 at the end of the treaty, its ratification likely took place after the death of Albert, bishop of Riga on 17 January 1229. The treaty is therefore dated to the spring of 1229.

Source: trans. F. Curta from A. Ivanov and A.M. Kuznecov, *Smoļenskas-Rīgas aktis 13. gs.–14. gs. pirmā puse: Kompleksa Moscowitica-Ruthenica dokumenti par Smoļenskas un Rīgas attiecībām* (Riga: Latvijas Valsts vēstures arhīvs, 2009), pp. 529–36.

What happens over time, as time [goes by], is often forgotten. That is why it [what happens] is committed to trustworthy men, or is confirmed in writing, so that it is known to all, even to those who live later. In the year in which Albert, the bishop of Riga died, the prince of Smolensk, Mstislav, son of David, thought about sending [and decided to send] to Riga his best priest Jeremiah and with him the prominent man Pantelei from his city of Smolensk. The two of them were sent to Riga, and from Riga they reached the Gothic Shore

[Gotland] to seal the peace in that place. They sealed the peace, because there was no peace for all merchants between Smolensk [on one hand,] and Riga and the Gothic Shore [on the other]. Good people strove for this peace—Rolf from Kassel, a knight of God, and Thomas from Smolensk—for the peace to be kept forever. They restored the peace to the advantage of the Rus' and of all Latins, who are involved in trade with Rus'. On the basis of this peace, so that it may be consolidated, it was convenient to the prince and to all Latins and all those, who travel across the eastern [Baltic] Sea, to establish the law and to set it in writing, as to how the Rus' should deal with the Latins, and the Latins with the Rus'. If, God forbid, conflict breaks out between us, and one man kills another, that man will have to pay, so that the peace is not broken [as well]. And that payment needs to be done in such a way as to be agreeable to both sides. If a free man is killed, then [a wergild, or man-price, of] ten *grivny* [ingots of standard form and weight] of silver per head [must be paid]. If a slave is killed, then one *grivna* of silver must be paid in Smolensk or in Riga or on the Gothic Shore. For an eye, a hand, a leg, or any other [limb], [one must pay] five *grivny* for each limb. For an eye, five [*grivny*] of silver, for a hand five [*grivny*] of silver; for a leg, five [*grivny*] of silver, and for a limb five *grivny* of silver; for each tooth, three *grivny* of silver—in Smolensk, as well as in Riga and on the Gothic Shore. When someone strikes another with a piece of wood [that is, a club or a polearm] and that one is either bruised or wounded, [the perpetrator] must pay one and a half *grivny* of silver. When one hits [another on] the ear, [he must pay] three-quarters of [a *grivna* of] silver. If anything like that happens to an envoy or to a priest, the amount is doubled, twice [he has to pay]. So are payments to be paid in Smolensk, in Riga, and on the Gothic Shore. When a Rus' in Riga or on the Gothic Shore falls in debt, one cannot put him in the stocks. When a Latin in Smolensk fails [to pay his] debt[s], one cannot throw him in prison. If there is no guarantor [around], [then] he can be shackled. When a Latin sells goods in Smolensk to a Rus' on credit, he [the Rus'] must first pay the German, even when he owes money to another Rus'. The same applies to a Rus' in Riga and the Gothic Shore. When the prince is angry with one of his men and he [the Rus' man of the prince] owes money to a German, and the prince enslaves everyone depending upon that man, his wife and his children, he [the prince] must first pay the Latin, after which the prince can deal with his man as he pleases. The same law applies to the Rus' in Riga and the Gothic Shore. A Rus' cannot bring a Latin to court with only one witness when two witnesses are not available, one German, the other Rus', good people. Similarly, a Latin cannot win [in court] against a Rus' without two witnesses, one Rus', the other German, either in Riga or on the Gothic Shore. A Rus' cannot force a Latin to [undergo the] iron ordeal; [only] if the Latin agrees, he can do that. And a Latin cannot force a Rus' to do that either; if the Rus' agrees, then he can do it. A Rus' cannot challenge a Latin to a duel in the land of Rus', and a Latin cannot challenge a Rus' to duel either in Riga or on the Gothic Shore. If Latin guests in the Rus' land strike each other either with the sword or with the wood [clubs or pole-arms], the prince has nothing to do with it, [for] they have to sort those things out among themselves. Similarly, if Rus' guests in Riga or on the Gothic Shore strike each other, the Latins have nothing to do with it; instead, let the Rus' straighten up those things by themselves. If a Rus' catches a Latin man [in the act] with his wife, he [the Latin] must pay for that ten *grivny* of silver. Similarly, if a Rus' does that, he must pay [the same amount] in Riga or on the Gothic Shore. If a Latin man forces himself upon a free woman, who had until then been blameless, he has to pay for that five *grivny* of silver. The same rule applies to a Rus' in Riga and on the Gothic Shore. If she had not been beyond blame, then she receives [only] one *grivna* for the rape. When (a Latin man) rapes an (unfree) maiden, and there are witnesses against him, he must pay one *grivna*. The same rule applies to a Rus' in Riga and on the Gothic Shore. If anyone among the Rus' and the Latins accuses the other falsely, then he has to pay three *grivny* of silver. When a Rus' must pay a Latin, but does not want to do so, the Latin can request [the assistance of] a *detskii* [policeman, executive deputy of the judge] from the *tiun* [judge, the prince's agent distributing justice in his name]. If he gives a loan to the *detskii* and he [the *detskii*], in [no more than] eight days, does not bring the affair of the merchandise [purchased] by the Rus' man to order, then he [the Rus' man] must provide a guarantor for him [the Latin man]. If the people of Smolensk prevent him [the Latin man] from doing that, then they themselves have to compensate for the damage. The same rule applies to a Rus' in Riga or on the Gothic Shore. If the *tiun* learns that Latin guests have arrived, he must send people with wagons to transport the merchandise, and he should not prevent [the Latins] from coming. For if he prevents them from coming, there will be damage. When a *vălăk* [*volok*, carrier, person who works with his own wagon to move things around for someone else] takes Latin merchandise for transportation, and some of that merchandise, which was entrusted to him, is lost, all *vălăks* have to pay. The same rule applies to a Rus' in Riga and on the Gothic Shore. If a Latin comes to the city [of Smolensk], he will be free to sell his merchandise [as he pleases], and nobody should say anything against that. The Rus' should do the same in Riga and on the Gothic Shore. If a Latin wants to move out of Smolensk together with his merchandise, neither the prince nor anyone else should prevent him [from doing so]. The same [applies to] a Rus' who [wants to] travel from the Gothic Shore to the Trave [the name of the river, at the mouth of which Lübeck is located]. If a Rus' buys merchandise from a Latin man and takes it [home] with him, the Latin does not need to take it back, [as long as] the Rus' pays for it. Similarly, a Rus' does not take his merchandise back from the Latin, [as long as] the Latin pays for it. A

Rus' cannot bring a Latin to the court of any [other] prince than the prince of Smolensk; but if the Latin agrees to that, he can do so. Similarly, a Latin cannot bring a Rus' to any court other than those of Riga and the Gothic Shore. A Rus' cannot call the *detskii* upon a Latin, without previously showing [the affair] to the Latin alderman; if the Latin refuses to listen to the alderman, then the Rus' can call the *detskii* upon him [the Latin man]. Similarly, a Latin should not call a *biric* [policeman, agent of the local judge] in Riga and on the Gothic Shore. If a Rus' has received merchandise from a German either in Riga or on the Gothic Shore or in any other German city, the two sides must come together, and the Rus' must be subject to the law that applies in that city. They should not prevent free trade. The same applies to Germans in the Rus' lands. A Latin does not need to join either the prince or the Rus' in war; if he wants to do that, [though], let him do it. Similarly, a Rus' does not need to go to war together with the Latins, either in Riga or on the Gothic Shore; if he himself wants that, let him do it. A Rus' cannot be summoned [in court, as a witness] either in Riga or on the Gothic Shore. Similarly, a Latin cannot be summoned in the Rus' land. If a litigation ends in Smolensk between a Rus' and one of the Latins, before judges and good people, then it cannot be reopened in Riga or on the Gothic Shore. And what ends in Riga and the Gothic Shore, before judges and good people, cannot be reopened in Smolensk. The Germans have to pay the *pud* [toll, transportation tax] to the *voloks* [carriers], who carry the merchandise of every guest. And if this expires, let the same apply in the German church, and one should institute another [provision] that is similar to this one. Every Latin man is free to travel from the Gothic Shore to Smolensk without paying any tolls. The same rule applies to the Rus' [man] traveling from Smolensk to the Gothic Shore. If it happens that the Latin guests come to the city [after paying the toll to the carriers], they have to give to the princess a piece of cloth and [a pair] of gloves to the *tiun* at the place where they pay the toll, so that they can transport their merchandise without any impediment. For every two *kapi* [weight measure] of wax, the Latin has to pay the wagoner a Smolensk *kuna* [monetary denomination, the equivalent of one twenty-fifth of a *grivna*]. If a Latin buys a *grivna* of gold and weighs it, he has to pay the wagoner a Smolensk *nogata* [monetary denomination, the equivalent of one twentieth of a *grivna*]. [But] when he sells, he does not have to pay anything. If a Latin buys silver vessels, he has to pay to the wagoner a Smolensk *nogata* for every *grivna* of silver. [However,] if he sells, he does not have to pay anything. If a Latin buys a *grivna* of silver, he has to pay to the wagoner two *vekshas* [*veksha*, the smallest monetary denomination, the equivalent of one one-hundred-fiftieth of a *grivna*]. [But] if he sells, he does not have to pay anything. If a Latin burns [that is, melts a quantity of] silver, let him pay a Smolensk *kuna* for every *grivna* of silver. If the *kap*, with which one weighs, is broken or too light [because of being worn], then let both [weights] be brought to the place, where the church of the Mother of God on the Hill is, and the second to the Latin church, and let them be compared. If both Latin guests and Smolensk people come to the toll stations, then let them draw lots as to who will go first to Smolensk. If people from another country find themselves there, let them go last. The same rule applies to the Rus' in Riga and on the Gothic Shore. The bishop of Riga, the grand master [of the Sword Brothers] and all the lords guarantee free traffic on the Daugava from upstream all the way to the sea, both on water and on land, both to Latins and to the Rus'. The honest merchant has free access from the sea onward, and [access is free] also for whomever wants to move up and down the Daugava. If, God forbid, one's ship or boat is broken, whether the owner is Rus' or Latin, in the parts of those who have guaranteed free access [to the Daugava River], his merchandise is free [to move] on water and on land, without damage to anyone. He is allowed to recuperate the merchandise with the assistance of his companions and to bring it to shore. If he needs further help, he must hire it before witnesses; whoever happens to be there can be a witness. Whatever one has promised [those being hired to help], one needs to pay, but no more than that. The same rule applies to the Latin in the Rus' land within the territory of the prince of Smolensk and in the territory of the prince of Polotsk and in the territory of the prince of Vitebsk. This charter was written in the year of the Lord 1228 under the bishop of Riga, the provost John, the master Folkwin, the knight, and under the townspeople of Riga and all [other] Latin merchants. The issue was dealt with by the wise merchants Regenbode, Dethard, Adam, who were from the Gothic Shore; Membern, Frederick Dumbe, who were from Lubeck; Henry the Goth, Hildeger, both from Soest; Konrad Scheel and Johann Kind, both from Münster; Bernhard and Volker, both from Groningen; Ermbrecht and Albrecht, both from Dortmund; Henry Zeisig from Bremen; Albrecht Sluk, Bernhard and Walter and Albrecht the Reeve, who were from Riga; and many other wise and good people. Whoever speaks against this treaty, whether Rus' or Latin, let him be regarded as an evil man. This charter was issued on the Gothic Shore in front of the Rus' envoys and the other Latin merchants.

Questions: Which conditions of the treaty favored the German merchants, and why? Why were such privileges being granted? Compare the regulation of criminal behavior in this text and in the "Statutes" of Conrad Otto II (Doc. 57). What does the document tell us about conditions in Rus' at this time? How would this treaty change the Rus' socially and politically?

59. CHARTER OF JOHN II ASEN FOR RAGUSA

In the aftermath of his victory at Klokotnica over Theodore Komnenos Dukas, the ruler of Epirus, John II Asen, the emperor of Bulgaria (1218–41), controlled practically all the important trade routes across the Balkans. He granted commercial privileges to the merchants of Ragusa (now Dubrovnik, in Croatia), a city that had been under Venetian control since the Fourth Crusade (1204). Taking advantage of the great degree of autonomy in economic policies that Venice had given to their city, Ragusan merchants made great profits out of the Balkan-Italian trade with land caravans and ships crossing the Adriatic Sea. By 1230, Ragusa was already at the center of an extensive trade network. The first in a long series of charters issued by rulers in the Balkans, John II Asen's charter secured the extraordinary commercial success of the city on the Adriatic coast. Rulers like John II Asen and the elites in the Balkans were interested in the luxuries that the Ragusan merchants brought to Balkan markets. The charter of 1230 is therefore a key component of a complex of economic policies that established a duty-free trade environment for the Ragusan merchants.

Source: trans. K. Petkov, *The Voices of Medieval Bulgaria, Seventh-Fifteenth Century: The Records of a Bygone Culture* (Leiden: Brill, 2008), pp. 482–83.

My tsardom gives this decree to the country of Dubrovnik [Ragusa] and to the beloved and loyal guests of my tsardom, so that they can travel over my tsardom's entire domain with any kind of goods, export and import any kind of goods, and transport any kind of goods, and come to any land and province of my tsardom, that is to Bdin [Vidin, in the northwestern part of present-day Bulgaria], Braničevo [on the Danube, in northern Serbia], or Belgrade; or go to Tărnovo and the entire Zagorie [northern Bulgaria], or reach even to Preslav and the territory of Kărvuna [the Black Sea coast in northeastern Bulgaria], or the territory of Krăn [northern Thrace, to the south of the Stara Planina Range of mountains], or that of Borui [Stara Zagora, in northern Thrace], or Adrianople [now Edirne, in southeastern Thrace] and Dimotika [now Didimoticho, to the south of Edirne], or the territory of Skopie [Skopje, in Macedonia], or that of Prilep or Devol [on the southern shore of Lake Ohrid, now in southeastern Albania], or Albania, or if they go to Thessaloniki. Everywhere they can buy and sell freely and without any harm and there will be no prohibitions against them in all provinces of my tsardom, but they should be able to buy and sell without problems as loyal and beloved guests of my tsardom. Whoever causes them any harm in any way in the passes or in the markets or anywhere else, against the law of trade, let it be known that he is an enemy of my tsardom and there will be no mercy [for him] but he will suffer the great wrath of my tsardom.

+ Asen, tsar of Bulgarians and Greeks +

Questions: Why does the Bulgarian emperor grant a trade privilege to the merchants of the Dalmatian city? How do you explain the precision of the geographic description of the area within which the privilege is granted? What is the "law of trade" mentioned in the text?

60. THE HENRYKÓW BOOK ON FEUDALISM

The history of the Cistercian abbey of Henryków (south of present-day Wrocław, in Lower Silesia) was written in the 1260s by its third abbot, Peter. Previously cellarer at Henryków, Peter had played an important role in several negotiations with the Piast dukes of Silesia and with other communities, urban and monastic. He was a well-educated man, most likely of German origin, but speaking both German and Polish. The Henryków Book, as Peter's history came to be known, is in fact a collection of stories about individual holdings that the abbey managed to obtain in the course of the thirteenth century. Another, unknown, author continued his work to the first decade of the fourteenth century. Peter's goal was to provide his fellow monks with arguments in order to help them respond to several kinds of legal claims to the monastic domains, especially by heirs and their successors, who had been dispossessed by means of donations to the abbey of Henryków. Unlike Peter, the later author relied on ducal charters, which he probably viewed as more reliable pieces of evidence to be used against legal challenges. The excerpt below is from the early fourteenth-century continuator of Peter.

Source: trans. F. Curta from *Księga Henrykowska*, ed. R. Grodecki (Poznań: Instytut Zachodni, 1949), pp. 342–43.

How [the estate of] Raczyce came [to owe] service [to the ruler] with a war-horse. While one prince came after another in this country [of Silesia], and that part of the country [where Henryków is located] fell to the famous prince Bolko [I, duke of Opole, 1282–1313], this estate [named] Raczyce was given to the prince's table by the older knights who divided the country, since it had belonged for a long time to [that table]. Duke Bolko therefore wanted to remove the claims [to that holding] of all those mentioned above, who regarded themselves as heirs of Raczyce. However, when several knights interceded for them, they ended up pledging themselves to serve the duke with one war-horse from the said estate. In this way they received the estate [back] from the hand of the prince [but] as a fief.

Questions: What does this text suggest about the relation between the Piast princes of Silesia and the local knights? Why did the heirs of Raczyce agree to serve the duke with one war-horse? What rights do you think that service implied? What is a fief, as described in this text?

CHAPTER EIGHT

FAITH, RELIGION, HERESY

Figure 8.1 Angel. Detail of the fresco in the altar niche, church of St-George, Kurbinovo, Macedonia.

61. THE INVENTION OF THE RELICS OF SAINT CLEMENT

Saint Clement was pope of Rome as disciple and successor of Saint Peter. He suffered persecution under Emperor Trajan (98–117), who exiled Clement to Cherson(esus) in the Crimea. After performing a number of miracles, converting locals to Christianity, and establishing numerous churches, Clement was condemned to death by being cast into the sea with an anchor tied around his neck. The cult of the saint is documented in Cherson during the sixth century, but by the ninth century it seems to have fallen into oblivion. On their way to the Khazars on a diplomatic mission from Constantinople, Constantine and Methodius stopped in Cherson in 860, where the younger brother began investigations into the whereabouts of Clement's tomb. The discovery of the relics happened on 30 January 861. They were placed in the cathedral of Cherson, but Constantine took some of the relics with him, first to the Khazars, then back to Constantinople, then to Moravia, and finally to Rome, where the relics were welcomed by Pope Hadrian II (867–72) in 867. According to a letter that Anastasius the Librarian wrote to Bishop Gauderich of Velletri in 875, Constantine himself wrote three texts in honor of Saint Clement: a short history, a sermon, and a hymn. In his letter, Anastasius told Gauderich that he had translated the first two texts into Latin, but had not touched the hymn, because of prosodic problems. Constantine likely wrote his short history in Greek while in Rome, probably at the request of Pope Hadrian II, as documentation for the invention of the relics. Shortly after that, however, he translated the text into Old Church Slavonic. The Slavonic version (translated into English below) survived in a few Russian manuscripts of the fifteenth and sixteenth centuries. Moreover, a canon (structured hymn) on the translation of the relics of Saint Clement of Rome was discovered in a Rus' manuscript dated to the twelfth or thirteenth century. This may well be the hymn written by Constantine that Anastasius refused to translate into Latin. The discovery of Saint Clement's relics was a major event in the history of his cult in eastern Europe. According to the Primary Chronicle, *in 988 Vladimir, prince of Kiev, moved the relics of Saint Clement from Cherson to Kiev, where the head of the saint was still preserved in the twelfth century.*

Source: trans. T. Butler, "Saint Constantine-Cyril's 'Sermon on the Translation of the Relics of Saint Clement of Rome,'" *Cyrillomethodianum* 17–18 (1993–94), pp. 30–37.

He [Constantine] roused some of the inhabitants of Cherson [now Sevastopil', in Crimea, Ukraine], plus the faithful pastor Georgius [most likely the bishop of Cherson] and the illustrious Nicephorus, who had then taken over the government of the city in a good and humble fashion, as well as many others, and one who rivaled the glorious clergy in fervor, even though he was inferior in station. And so the situation remained like that from day to day, and the feat had yet to be begun, when one day God allowed the saint [Saint Clement] to appear—it was the thirtieth [day] of January [861] when some of the fervent, as they were leaving the harbor [of Cherson, to go searching for the relics of Saint Clement at sea], set forth with the singing of psalms. And their prayerful song went like this: "Do not reject us in humiliation, O Clement, who approach your grave with faith, O holy one, but accept the hearts of your slaves, who approach the holy casket of your relics, praying that the [flock of the] blessed and generous may succeed in enjoying your chrism, God granting the faithful healing and remission of sins, and great mercy, through your prayers, O glorious one!" And so we came toward the blessed island, like an inseparable phalanx [an army of relic hunters], sustained not by weapons but by song. And when the desired island was already appearing before our eyes, the onset of a very nicely soaking, sudden downpour from the clouds overhead did not take away our daring. When we were getting ready to sing the second song, the clergyman who was speaking out the lines for everyone, Solomon by name—he was the priest of St-Procopius—was overcome with anguish and discomfort because he lacked the necessary light. And lo, suddenly, through the help of Saint Clement, the clouds dispersed, the moon was illuminated as well as the air, and there was a radiant glow around it. And the one who saw this, who was a witness for the man of the feat [the bishop], being together with him on a portable bench and listening attentively, cried out immediately: "Father, God knows how to illuminate gloriously and with grace the souls of those desiring sweet light through the prayers of Saint Clement!" And this joy illuminating us, we undertook the beginning of the second song, gloriously and freely, without any power preventing it. It went like this: "Overcome by fear of the Lord and trembling and tears. . . ." After the song we came with the bishop to the glorious island and the grave.

And when we had gathered around him, and had been enlightened by an appropriate teaching, after kneeling down on the cherished ground we did the whole morning service [orthros] and the beginning of the lauds [the morning prayers in the liturgy]. And when it was time for the middle song, there suddenly occurred a test from God of some benefit to those convinced in their faith. The clouds were thick and were advancing from the southern side of the island. When the bishop saw them, he sent one of the faithful to check—Digica by name—who had come there as one familiar with the area. And going there, he reported it was close to raining. Then, having begun our search, we ordered the singing of the kontakion [a thematic hymn], because we were not finding the location of the blessed tomb. Immediately, the cloud cluster moved off in a northerly direction, and a clear and translucent sky replaced the darkness with its own eyes, the stars, for seeing the sought-after relics of the blessed Clement, and by this feat it was preparing itself for the common endeavor.

And when the singer was singing the fourth song, which in one place says: "For the treasure is no longer hidden, and the light is in the candle holder"—like the morning star [in comparison to] some lamp—lo, a rib of the relics of Saint Clement began to appear! And being saddened, because some time passed and nothing more appeared, we were directing our eyes and mind, therefore, now toward God and now toward the grave. And while we were singing the sixth song, which in one place has: "For he guards the bones of the just, as David sings and celebrates in the psalms," there shone before us the holy and most glorious head of the most renowned Clement! Whereupon the one who saw it first, who is the present narrator, immediately cried out ecstatically: "Rejoice, fathers and brothers, in the Lord! Again, I say: rejoice! For lo, this blessed head has shone before us like the radiant sun from the depths of hell!" As soon as they all heard that voice, suddenly becoming joyful, they sent up a song of praise to God, gazing from the heavens to the holy casket. And pushing and being pushed, as toward some imperishable riches, they were coming forward as they sought to kiss or at least to see the pearly relics. And it was a joy for them and sufficient for their sanctification, to illuminate their persons just by touching them. And when the spiritual vision had illumined everyone and delighted them by a most glorious fragrance, suddenly there shone before us from the very depths the radiant stars of the other members which had been preserved—namely, his holy arms themselves, together with the thigh bones and all the attached members. And as though on the mystical firmament of a spiritual heaven, gathering everyone and beautifying the faces of the faithful by its worthy approach, suddenly, last of all there appeared the anchor, not making a sound—which is how it should be, in order of rank, after the blessed members. And even though it had rusted, in accord with its nature, still it had retained its hardness; and at once there began loud and universal singing of thanksgiving for even the tiniest of its fragments. There was continuous singing of praises to God all night long, until the appropriate hour for the spotless sacrifice and offering of Christ our God. And only a small number of people were silent, as would have been appropriate at such a service. And when the revered bishop had finished, he carried the blessed casket on his head to the boat, placing it there with one of the faithful.

They set out for the city of Cherson with this doxology: "Take now all you nations, just as in ancient times you took the four-sided ark! O divine congregation of Cherson, taken now the casket of the saint, as in song you invite everyone from the ends of the earth, to the divine holy day!" And when they had gone some ten stadia [about two kilometers] from the island, the God-loving governor of the city, together with some faithful and wise men who were there at the time, organized an appropriate welcome, signaling their approach on foot—not by fire, but by a multitude of candles. And they were singing this song around the holy casket: "Let us proceed around the casket, therefore, as around the ark of the covenant, not carrying in it today what Moses carried in the ark, but an apostle who sank the deceit of the invisible enemy." Having sung with us and given praise for the discovery of the island, he [Nicephorus] went with haste to the city, where he prepared and executed an appropriate welcome.

And after he kissed the blessed casket, he was imploring us to take it to a newly constructed tower of the fortress [of Cherson], built by him and named after Clement, and to put it there for a short time and to read there a homily of translation. We obeyed him and placed the casket there. But again a second time he implored us to take it along the wall of the city, to the church of St-Sozon, which was near the fortified wall, because it was evening and a multitude of people would be coming, and it would be difficult to carry the blessed casket to that place. And in the first watch of the night, when it was quiet, the bishop went in with some of the faithful and translated the most glorious Clement to the church of St-Leontius. And there being a congregation there, the bishop ordered all night singing until midnight by the men, and from midnight until morning by the monks and pious women, until the end, that being the custom of the faithful there. After that all-night singing, there was a procession of all the people the next morning, which gathered in that same church and went through the whole city. And in it there was to be seen every kind of person—faithful from every walk of life—jubilant and tearful in exultation of mind, spirit, and body, rejoicing with ineffable joy. And moreover, because of the early morning hour, it was impossible to distinguish or discern the rank of the joyful in that procession: rich and poor, nobleman and commoner, each and every one together, courageously oblivious to every danger, they went around the city with the holy relics and entered the cathedral.

Questions: Explain the reasons for Constantine's efforts to discover the relics of Saint Clement. What is the role that Constantine assigned to himself in these events? What are his merits, if any? How is the discovery celebrated in Cherson? Why were people in that city so excited about the discovery?

62. THE BOGOMILS

The only heresy in Orthodox Christianity outside Byzantium, and in the whole of eastern Europe before 1300, Bogomilism is known primarily from the Sermon against the Bogomils *written by a priest named Cosmas in the 960s or 970s. He is the only author to refer to Bogomil as the founder of the movement. The beliefs of the heretics that Cosmas described in some detail suggest a form of dualism, which links the Bogomils to both Manichaeans and Paulicians. That link is made stronger by Inquisition sources of the thirteenth century that clearly state that the origin of the Cathar heresy in western Europe was in Bulgaria. Like Manichaeans, Paulicians, and Cathars, therefore, the Bogomils believed that God had two sons, Christ and Satan, both being entirely spiritual beings. Satan rebelled against his father and created matter. He is therefore the creator of the world and everything in it, including humans. As a consequence, the Bogomils rejected the Old Testament. In their view, Christ was sent by God to earth with a message for the imprisoned human souls, to explain to them how to escape from matter and how to return to the spiritual kingdom. Since to them Christ was a purely spiritual being, the Bogomils denied any of his early experiences—the Incarnation, the Passion, and the Crucifixion. Christ, according to the Bogomils, taught abstinence from sexual intercourse, because reproduction perpetuated the prison of the soul: instead of joining Christ in the spiritual kingdom, the soul was reborn in an earthly body. Moreover, the Bogomils rejected baptism and any material objects related to Christianity (such as crosses, icons, and churches).*

Source: trans. K. Petkov, *The Voices of Medieval Bulgaria, Seventh-Fifteenth Century: The Records of a Bygone Culture* (Leiden: Brill, 2008), pp. 68–89.

It happened in the years of the Orthodox emperor Peter that a priest appeared in the Bulgarian land, by the name of Bogomil or, in truth, Bogunemil [pun on the name Bogomil, "loved by God"; Bogunemil translates as "not loved by God"]. He was the first one to preach heresy all over the Bulgarian land. Of his false teaching, we will narrate in due course. . . . Outwardly, the heretics are like sheep: meek, humble, and silent. Their faces are pale as if from long fasting. They would not utter a word and do not laugh, they are not inquisitive, and hide from another people's sight. On the outside, they do everything in such a manner as to be no different from the Orthodox Christians; on the inside, [though,] they are wolves and predators, as God said. . . . Heretics disparage them [relics] and laugh at us when they see us bow to them and ask for their help. They forgot the words of God, "Those who believe in me, they will accomplish the feats I do," and even greater ones. Not wanting to venerate the saints, they pour scorn on God's miracles performed by their relics through the power of the Holy Spirit. They say: "Miracles do not happen because of God's will; they are worked by Satan to deceive people." And many other bad words they say about them, nodding their heads like the Jews who crucified Christ. . . . This is how they speak of the cross, deceiving themselves: "How can we bow to it? The Jews crucified on it God's Son, and God hates the cross most." That is why they teach theirs to hate the cross and not to bow to it, saying this: "If someone killed the emperor's son with a wooden cross, how come that would be dear to the emperor?" The same is with God and the cross. . . . And what do they say about Holy Communion? "The Communion was not ordered by God, nor is it Christ's body as you say. It is like any plain food. . . ." Hearing these words, the heretics respond to us: "If you [the priests] are as holy as you say, why don't you live as you have been commanded? . . . But we do not see you to be like this. Priests do exactly the opposite: they drink, rob, and secretly do other things. . . ." Many do not even know what kind of heresy is theirs and think that they are suffering for the truth and God will reward them for the chains and the jail. . . . But how will they be dear to someone [pun on the name of Bogomil] although they suffer much, if they call the devil the creator of man and all of God's creatures? Because of their great ignorance some call him a fallen angel; others count him as a venial manager. Nonetheless, they esteem him so much as to name him the creator of God's creatures, and God's glory is for them Satan's glory. . . . As they hear God in the Gospels telling the parable of the two sons, they believe that the older son is Christ and the younger one, who deceived his father, the devil. They call him Mamon themselves. They also call him creator and manager of the earthly creatures; he had commanded people to marry, to eat meat, and to drink wine. In general, they slander everything that is ours and they proclaim themselves denizens of heaven, but people who marry and live secular lives they call servants of Mamon. Disgusted by all this, they reject it not out of abstention, as we would do, who do not count it for repulsive. . . . They slander the rich and teach theirs not to obey their lords; they hate the emperor and disparage the elders; they think that all who work for the emperor are hateful in the eyes of God and order all servants to stop working for their masters. . . . The heretics confess and absolve one another, although satanic chains bind them. Not only men, but women do that too, which is something worthy of condemnation.

Questions: Why does Cosmas the Presbyter call the Bogomils "wolves and predators"? What elements of the Bogomil faith does he choose to illustrate that characterization? Why do the Bogomils criticize the rich and call for disobedience to their lords?

63. THE MARTYRDOM OF SAINT LUDMILA

The Homily for the Feast of Saint Ludmila, Patroness of the Bohemians *is a Latin text to which historians refer by the first words,* Factum est. *The text survives in seventeen manuscripts, the earliest of which are from the thirteenth century. Since Daniel, bishop of Prague (1148–67) is mentioned in the text, historians agree that the* Homily *must have been written shortly before or after the year 1200, possibly upon the commission of Agnes, the abbess of the convent of St-George in Prague (1201–20), where Saint Ludmila's relics were kept. This is not a hagiographic text, but a sermon in which the saint's description is modeled after the Virgin Mary. The text and the Gregorian rhythm of the prose betray learned influences, which may in fact have contributed to turning Ludmila into a patroness not only of the Bohemians, but also of the Bohemian Church. Particularly relevant in that respect is the contrast between her and Drahomira, as well as the use of analogies with female characters from the Bible, such as Jezebel and Esther. Some even believe that the* Homily *is an adaptation of an older Marian hymn or homily. The overall goal of the author of the* Homily *was to give Ludmila the proper place among the saints venerated in Bohemia. Alongside Saint Adalbert, Saint Vitus, and Saint Wenceslas, she is the first and only female patron of the Czechs. In fact, the author of the* Homily *does not hesitate to regard her as more important than both Adalbert and Wenceslas. In relation to the latter, she was not just a grandmother, but the first Christian martyr of Bohemia.*

Source: trans. M. Kantor, *The Origins of Christianity in Bohemia: Sources and Commentary* (Evanston, IL: Northwestern University Press, 1990), pp. 209–11.

5. For when the prince of darkness, who is the devil, perceived that the darkness of disbelief among the people was diminishing on account of the light of Christ's handmaid, he inclined the heart of her daughter-in-law [Ludmila's daughter-in-law was Drahomira, Saint Wenceslas's mother], who hitherto maintained pagan customs, to yearn for her death. Thus, aflame with the spirit of Jezebel [1 Kings 18:4 and 19:2], she summoned two of the most contemptible members of her retinue, Tunna and Gommon, and commissioned them to carry out carefully the scheme that she designed in her heart, that is, to murder her mother-in-law. She did this so that after her murder the blessed youth Wenceslas, who was placed in her custody, more easily could be turned away from Christ's teaching and the Christian faith, and later, during her reign, it could be completely destroyed in the land. And after her death, she attempted to do this mercilessly. For having deprived the priests of their property, she expelled them from the land, and, under pain of death, prohibited them from appearing again in the land or from conversing with the holy prince. And now, after blocking the doors of the churches, she made offerings with impunity to idols and not to God, according to pagan manners.

6. Foreseeing her death, Saint Ludmila sought refuge at Tetín [now a village in the Beroun district of the central Bohemian region of the Czech Republic, to the southwest of Prague]. She thus followed the example of the Lord, who slipped away from those who wished to stone him and left the temple. For through this flight the Lord gave a sign to his beloved that they should flee from the bow, and that his beloved should save themselves thus. Indeed, I believe confidently, it was for the sake of the faithful, whose mother she was then in Bohemia, that she sought shelter in flight so that they would not lose their consoler in her. For though she yearned to die and to be with Christ, nevertheless she would still gladly remain in this world so as to protect and support the faithful. But because her soul pleased God, he [God] decided to take her away as quickly as possible from an ignoble and foolish people. And now, filled with the spirit of God, that pious lady made ready for her departure. Continually singing David's verses of praise in her heart and with her lips, she commended her struggle to the Lord so that he would deign to receive her soul in peace. Nevertheless, she strengthened herself, having also confessed and received the food of salvation for the journey, that is, the body and blood of our Lord Jesus Christ.

7. And thus the time came upon the executioners of the most criminal command. Insolently, maliciously, sharp of tongue, and filled with death-dealing

venom, they broke down the doors of the house where the handmaid of Christ was resting, and having altogether cast aside their shame, they were not frightened to drag their mistress down to their feet. But reminding them in a dove-like manner of the favors she had amply granted them, she strove to divert them from the crime they were about to commit and was distressed over their depravity rather than over herself. But like enraged dogs utterly devoid of compassion, they proceeded with the utmost savagery to do what they had begun and drew a rope around her neck. Then she said, "I earnestly beseech you to take my head with the sword so that I may lie in my blood; and permit me to depart to heaven in the manner of the holy martyrs, shedding blood for Christ's sake." But having stopped their ears to all her pleas, they tightened the rope until it began to cut her throat, and they squeezed the soul out of her body, like a serpent. Verily, this came to pass through the providence of the Lord, so that the crueler the death to befall her, the greater the grace she would attain.

8. Thus, by means of a rope she was pulled from the mire of this world, and by means of a rope she gained a golden chain for her neck. Thus, like Esther, she walked into the king's palace [Esther 2:8], having become a partaker in the dominion and radiant in glory. And through her prayers she shelters Christ's people so that they are not destroyed by their enemies. And as a wholly reliable sign that she was received in glory, this was what the follower of Christ was granted after her death: the very moment her blessed soul returned to God who created her, after it was drawn out from her contracted throat, rejoicing and triumphant, she gained a latitude not restricted by any limits. And, verily, all the saints, from the greatest to the least, came to meet her along with the most-high priest, Christ Jesus. And these spiritual luminaries surrounded her as if with kindled torches and congratulated the new arrival.

Questions: What is the attitude of Saint Ludmila's biographer toward Drahomira? What does the contrast between the two women tell us about social standards and ideals in early medieval Bohemia? Compare this account to that of Saint Wenceslas's assassination (Doc. 43). Why was Ludmila murdered with a rope?

64. INSTRUCTION ON LITURGICAL PRACTICES

Saint Luke the Younger was in constant search of an ascetic life. His vita, *which survives in several manuscripts, is an elegant and sophisticated text written in a rather elevated style, with allusions to biblical passages and use of the classical traditions. The latest event mentioned in the text is the conquest of Crete by Nicephorus Phokas under Emperor Romanus II in 961. The* vita *must therefore have been written at some point during the last third of the tenth century. The encounter between Saint Luke and the metropolitan of Corinth offers a unique glimpse into the liturgical practices in early tenth-century Greece. Perhaps the most important conclusion one can draw from this episode is that the performance of the eucharistic rite could take place in the small cell of a solitary. That is consistent with what is otherwise known about liturgy in Middle Byzantine churches. Judging from the size of the churches built in tenth- to early eleventh-century Greece, many of which are considerably smaller than late antique basilicas, the performance of the liturgical services may have appeared as "quasi-private," with little movement within a narrow space inside the church, especially in front of the sanctuary, and a greater emphasis on the symbolism of gestures and body posture. Since he was not a priest, Luke could not celebrate the divine liturgy. The Holy Communion that he was advised to take consisted of eucharistic bread previously sanctified elsewhere by an ordained priest. He would also have obtained from a church the incense which he was to burn when taking Communion. Unlike eucharistic bread or incense, it would have been much more difficult to obtain eucharistic wine since the metropolitan advises Luke to use ordinary wine instead. The exact meaning of the metropolitan's instructions is not easy to decipher, but it appears that in the absence of both priest and chalice, Luke was to receive the holy gifts separately—first the body, and then the cup. Before that, he was supposed to replicate in abbreviated form (the Trisagion and the Creed) the sequence of events in a standard liturgical service.*

Source: trans. C.L. Connor and W.R. Connor, in *The Life and Miracles of Saint Luke of Steiris* (Brookline, MA: Hellenic College Press, 1994), pp. 61, 63, and 65.

41. One day, he heard that the bishop [in fact, metropolitan] of Corinth was on his way to the queen of cities [that is, Constantinople] and was briefly pausing to rest nearby [that is, next to Mount Ioannitza, near Delphi in central Greece, where Saint Luke lived as a hermit]. He [Saint Luke] went to him not with empty hands, but bearing gifts, small ones, but great and ambitious in their intention, that is, he brought the finest that he had and kept for himself nothing that was better; he brought a variety of vegetables from his garden paradise for the bishop and the clerics and officials who were with him. When the bishop had been informed by them who this person was and where he lived and what sort of discipline he followed, he acted as a man who loves virtue and whose true affection is for the divine. Since he considered ostentation and the measure of his rank to be trivial, he made it a point to visit the hut of that poor man—although he was not poor in spiritual things.

42. When he arrived and saw how Luke lived, he marveled at what is truly worthy of marvel: not wealth and splendor, but voluntary and self-imposed poverty. For this reason he was eager to assist the man with gold, for we are more eager to gratify those who are above asking than those who request our help. He assigned one of the closer members of his entourage to present the gift, but Luke refused to take it, saying: "I came to you to ask for prayers and

instruction, O master, not for gold. For what is gold to us who have chosen such a life? Give me therefore what I need and exceedingly thirst after: teach me, ignorant and rustic as I am, how to be saved." The archbishop was very distressed at his rejection of the gift, thinking the action reflected contempt not of what was given, but of himself; he thought that Luke rejected it not because he was without need, but because he was not pleased with the gift. Sad of heart, he said, "Why do you reject us in this way along with our gift? For I am faithful, even if a sinner, and a bishop, even if unworthy. Why are you who want in every way to imitate Christ not willing to do so in this case, for he himself accepted the good intentions of those wishing to do a pious deed; the story of the money box is undeniable proof of this [John 12:6]. If you have no need at all for this gift, offer it to those who do need it. Now you seem to think the commandment to do good to others is empty and irrational, and you reject that nobility of mind that combines the love of God with the love of man. To sum up, you deny the basis that provides the alleviation of the burden of poverty and a road for many to salvation." When he heard this, the man of God concluded that he should no longer reject the gift lest he appear conceited and bring immeasurable grief upon the bishop. He accepted nothing more than a coin and reciprocated with prayers.

Then he asked the archbishop with all the humility that one could describe, "Tell me, O master, how those of us who settle in the mountains and the deserts on account of the great number of our sins—how may we participate in the divine and awesome mysteries? For you see that we lack not only a congregation but even a priest." He commended him for his inquiry and said, "Father, you do well to inquire about this good and important matter, for the good is not good unless the outcome is good. Now to begin with, a priest should be present, but if he is unavoidably absent, place a vessel containing what has already been sanctified upon the holy table, if it is a chapel, but if it is a cell, upon a very clean bench. Then, spreading out a covering, place it on the holy portions, and lighting the incense, sing the psalms of the *typika* or the Trisagion along with the Creed. After three genuflections, fold your hands and take with your mouth the esteemed body of Christ our God, saying the Amen. In place of eucharistic wine, you may drink a cup of ordinary wine, but this cup should not be shared afterward with another person. Next, put the remaining portions with the covering in the vessel, taking all care lest a pearl fall out and be trampled." The great one heard and gave thanks for this advice, then he turned to prayers and tranquility while the archbishop turned to his appointed road.

Questions: Why did Saint Luke reject the gift of the bishop in the first place? What elements of Christian rituals are emphasized in the instructions he received from the bishop? For whom did Saint Luke intend to perform the liturgy? What did he intend to achieve?

65. THE MARTYRDOM OF SAINT ADALBERT

Saint Adalbert was born c. 956 in Libice (Bohemia) into the Slavnikid family, the main political rivals of the Přemyslids. His name was Vojtěch, and he went to study at the cathedral school in Magdeburg, where he received his other name, Adalbert. The new name suggests that he took monastic vows, but instead of going to a monastery, he was appointed bishop of Prague in 983. While a bishop, he was confronted with political opposition, and he traveled much, especially to Italy, leaving his diocese unattended. In Rome, he met Emperor Otto III, whom he befriended. With the support of the emperor, Adalbert renounced his pastoral duties and embarked on a mission of Christianization among the Prussians, a tribe in the region of the Vistula delta in northern Poland. He was killed by the Prussians on 23 April 997. The cult of the saint played a very important role in Poland and Bohemia, and later in Hungary as well. Several hagiographic texts were produced within less than a century after his death; the one translated below was commissioned by Otto III or by someone else at the imperial court. The occasion may have been the translation of some of the relics of Saint Adalbert from Gniezno in Poland to Rome, where a church was built in 998 and dedicated to Saint Adalbert (the present-day basilica of San Bartolomeo all'Isola in Rome). The text is based on a now lost vita *written by a Benedictine monk named John Canaparius at the abbey of St-Boniface and Alexius on the Aventine Hill in Rome. That the* Life of Saint Adalbert, Bishop of Prague and Martyr *is based on John Canaparius's* vita *results, among other things, in the insistence on presenting Adalbert as an accomplished monk who could not be prevented by his episcopal duties from reaching his lofty goals. This suggests that the* Life *was also written in a monastery, most likely the same abbey of Saints Boniface and Alexius, possibly during John Canaparius's term as abbot (which ended with his death on 12 October 1004). The earliest surviving copies of the* Life *are all eleventh- and twelfth century manuscripts from the German lands, where the text was particularly popular, because the cult of the saint spread with imperial support.*

Source: trans. C. Gaşpar, "Life of Saint Adalbert Bishop of Prague and Martyr," in *Saints of the Christianization Age of Central Europe (Tenth-Eleventh Century)*, ed. G. Klaniczay (Budapest: Central European University Press, 2013), pp. 169, 171, 173, 177, 179, and 181.

27. Next, sharpening and making ready the sword of his preaching against the cruel barbarians, the godless, the idolaters, he started pondering with whom he should join battle first and with whom later, whether to go against the Lutizi [an alliance of Slavic tribes in the northeastern part of Germany which had come into being after the great revolt of 983 against Ottonian rule], who live on plunder taken from Christians and off the spoils extorted from unfortunate people, or into the territories of the Prussians, who workshop as god their stomach [Phil. 3:19] and avarice paired with death. At last, after swinging back and

forth between the two, he made up his mind: he would go and defeat the gods and idols of Prussia, since this land was closer and better known to the said duke [Bolesław Chrobry]. On his part, the duke, once he learned of Adalbert's intention, gave him a ship and a crew of thirty armed men to secure him a peaceful journey. Now, Adalbert went first to the city of Gyddanizc [Gdańsk, major port city in northern Poland], which stands on the border of the duke's vast realm and also touches the seashore. There, since divine grace rendered his arrival prosperous, numerous crowds of people were baptized. There he celebrated the ritual of the Mass and sacrificed Christ to the Father, [Christ] to whom he was to bring himself as sacrifice just a few days later. Whatever was left of the Host which he had shared with the newly baptized he had it collected and wrapping it in a very clean cloth, put it aside as provision for his journey.

28. Then, the next day, he said farewell to everyone, he took himself to a ship and onto the sea and disappeared from their eyesight, never to be seen again. From there, after a very rapid journey on the sea, a few days later he came ashore, while the ship went back together with his armed guard. As for him, he thanked the boatmen and the God of the boatmen for their help and remained there together with two brothers, of whom one was Benedict the priest and the other Gaudentius, his brother and beloved companion ever since the days of his childhood. Then, preaching Christ with great confidence, they went to a small island, which to the eye of the beholder presented a perfect circular shape, embraced from both sides by the curved branches of the river. But there came the owners of that place and kicked them out with blows. And one of them grabbing the paddle of his small vessel, came near the bishop, who, as it happened, was reciting psalms from his book, and gave him a terrible blow between the shoulders. The book flew out of Adalbert's hands, scattered all over the place, while he himself fell to the ground and lay there prostrated with his head and limbs spread out. Yet even though his body was suffering in this way outwardly, his mouth soon expressed what was going on inwardly, in his pious mind, namely the joyous laughter of his heart. "Thank you, O Lord," he said, "that, even if there should be no more than this, at least I have been found worthy to receive this single blow for the sake of my Crucified!" Then he crossed to the other side of the river and remained there on Saturday. When evening came, the owner of that property had our divine hero Adalbert brought over to his residence. The spineless crowd gathered from all sides and stood by watching with rabid snarls, like dogs, what would happen to him. Then Saint Adalbert, when asked who he was, from where, and for what purpose he had come there, replied in a meek voice as follows. "I am a Slav by birth, Adalbert by name, a monk by profession, and once a bishop by rank, but now by my function—your apostle. Your salvation is the purpose of our journey; that you abandon your deaf and dumb idols and recognize your maker, who alone is God and besides

whom there is no other; and that you may come to life, believing in his name, and be found worthy to receive the reward of celestial joys in the imperishable dwellings." Thus spoke Saint Adalbert. They, however, by now quite outraged, raised a terrible row shouting blasphemous words at him, and threatened to kill him. And right on the spot, they started hitting the ground with their sticks, giving his head a nudge or two with their cudgels, and for a long time gnashed their gruesome teeth at him. "You should think yourself very lucky," they said, "that you have made it so far undisturbed! Only a quick departure may give you some hope to stay alive; if you stay here even a little longer, you will not escape certain death! This entire realm, to which we stand as gateway, and we ourselves obey one common law and have one single way of life! But you, who have a different law, unknown to us, will lose your heads tomorrow if you do not go away tonight!" That very night [17/18 March 997] they were put in a small vessel and, going back, they stayed for five days in some village. . . .

30. The following morning had dawned all purple when they set off on their way, making their journey shorter with the help of the Davidic song [that is, Psalm] and never ceasing to invoke Christ, the joy of every well-pleasing life. Then, leaving behind them groves and haunts of wild beasts, when the sun was at midday, they arrived to some open country. There his brother Gaudentius celebrated Mass and our holy monk [that is, Adalbert] partook of the Holy Communion; after this, he accepted a few bites of food just to ease the labor of the journey. Then, reciting a verse [of the scriptures] as well as the psalm that followed it, he rose from the grassy turf, and went a little further—about a stone's or an arrow's throw—and sat down once more. Here he fell asleep and, since he was exhausted because of the long journey, sleep-bringing peace poured over him as if from a well-stocked horn. When, at last, they were all at rest, the pagan frenzy sprung up and [the Prussians] rushed against them suddenly [Josh. 11:7], throwing them all into chains. Then, Saint Adalbert, chained as he was back to back with Gaudentius and the other brother, said: "Brothers, do not lose heart! You know that we suffer this for the name of the Lord, whose power is above all other powers, whose beauty is above all ornaments, whose might is beyond words, and whose mercy is unmatched. What be so strong, what can be so beautiful as laying down a well-pleasing life for our most beloved Jesus?" Out of that frenzied crowd a fiery red-haired assassin sprang and, throwing a huge spear with all his force, pierced him deeply through his heart. That man, a priest of the idols and the leader of that sworn company, as if this were his duty, inflicted the first wounds. Then all the others came running and satiated their hatred by heaping wound upon wound amid a great melee. Adalbert's purple blood gushed forth from the wounds on both sides; he stood upright, his hands and eyes turned to the sky, and prayed. A red river kept flowing, a thick stream [Horace, *Ars poetica* 409], and, after the spears were taken out, seven huge wounds [Ovid, *Metamorphoses* 13.537] could be seen

gaping open. When they untied him, he spread his arms in the form of the cross and cried out to the Lord with ample, imploring prayers for his own salvation and for that of his persecutors. In this way, that saintly soul flew out of its prison; in this way, this noble body, spread out in the shape of a cross, took hold of the earth; and what is more, in this way, shedding much of his blood and his life with it, he could at last fully enjoy the blessed dwelling and [the company of] his most beloved Christ. O holy and most blessed man, on whose face there was always an angelic splendor, in whose heart Christ was always present! O pious [man] and most worthy of all honor, who embraced the cross, which he had always carried in his heart and in his thoughts, then also with his hands and with his entire body! Savage barbarians came running and armed from all sides and, with still unabated frenzy, cut off his noble head from the body and chopped off his bloodless limbs. They left the body in that place; the head they impaled and, boasting of their crime with joyful shouts [Virgil, *Aeneid* 3.523], they all returned to their dwellings.

And the holy and most glorious martyr of Christ, Adalbert, was martyred on the ninth day before the kalends of May [23 March, but the actual date is 23 April 997], when the emperor was lord Otto III, the faithful and most glorious caesar, on a Friday; obviously, this happened so that on which day our Lord Jesus Christ had suffered for the sake of humankind, on that same day that man would suffer for the sake of his God. Whose is all mercy forever, the honor, the glory, and the power forever and ever. Amen.

Questions: According to the author of this text, how did the locals in Prussia react to the mission headed by Saint Adalbert? Why were they so hostile to the group? Who killed Saint Adalbert and for what reason? What do we learn from this account about the lifestyle and the social organization of the locals? How does Saint Adalbert regard his assassins? Is there any difference between this attitude and that of his biographer?

66. THE MANY LIVES OF SAINT STEPHEN

No fewer than three different vitae *of Saint Stephen of Hungary are known, two of which are often called "legends." The earliest* (Vita maior) *was written at some point between Stephen's death in 1038 and his canonization in 1083 under King Ladislas I (1077–95). This is in fact the first medieval legend in Europe to make a saint out of a ruler who did not die a martyr's death. Stephen of the* Vita maior *is a "soldier of Christ" who, with the assistance of Saint Martin and Saint George, defeats pagans. The unknown author of the* Vita maior, *no doubt a churchman, used hagiographic clichés to create the portrait of Stephen as a warrior defending his country, as a legislator, and as the author of a work of moral edification (now known as the* Admonitions; *see Doc. 45). He is also described as the founder of episcopal sees, monasteries, and shelters for pilgrims. Stephen placed his kingdom, as well as his own person, under the protection of the Virgin Mary, a very early mention of the Marian cult that would appear in western Europe only a few decades later. By contrast, with the exception of the dedication of the church Stephen erected in Székesfehérvár, there is no mention of the Virgin Mary in the* Vita minor, *a shorter text written in Pannonhalma in the late eleventh century, probably during the early years of King Coloman (1095–1116). Besides describing that canonization and mentioning the subsequent miracles taking place in Székesfehérvár, the* Vita minor *depicts a harsher ruler, who does not hesitate to hang robbers two by two along the road, or to punish would-be assassins by blinding them and having their hands cut off. However, the author of the* Vita minor *also insists that Stephen learned to read and write as a young man and quickly gained a formidable reputation for wisdom. The portrait of a strong-fisted ruler at the center of the* Vita minor *may well be based on oral traditions, even though the text is clearly an elaborate piece of literature, with echoes of Horace and Persius.*

Source: trans. F. Curta from *Legendae sancti regis Stephani*, ed. E. Varjú (Budapest: Singer & Wolfner, 1928), pp. 6–7, 8–9, and 23–25.

Vita maior

In the meantime, as promised by the Lord, a son was born to the prince [Duke Géza, c. 970–97]. This child, according to the prophet, the Lord knew before he was conceived in the womb [Jer. 1:5]. And Bishop Adalbert [of Prague, 982–95; see also Doc. 47], the one beloved of God, baptized him according to the truth of his faith, and became his protector. The name given to him was Stephen, which was not without the knowledge of God. For Stephen in Greek means "crowned" in Latin. For God intended him to have the power to rule in this age and to bear forever the crown of blessedness, and he decided for him to receive eternal glory. The child grew up under royal care. After his childhood, when he was in his early teens, his father summoned the magnates of Hungary and those immediately below them. At the suggestion of the joint council, he placed his son Stephen at the head of the people as his successor. After that, at the end of his life, in the year 997 he exchanged the misery of this useless world for heavenly joy. In the same year, the blessed bishop Adalbert went to Prussia to preach the word of God and was crowned there with the palm of martyrdom.

As soon as the kingdom of Pannonia [modern-day Hungary] came under his care, the blessed young man reaffirmed his commitment to peace with the peoples from foreign countries, so that he could carry out more securely the plans that he had in mind for the tender nursery of Christianity. However, the enemy of all good things, Satan, full of envy and wickedness, in order to disturb the holy determination of the warrior of Christ, stirred a war against him, whereby his own people, not wanting to accept the yoke of the Christian faith, attempted with their noblemen to defeat him. However, shortly after defeating their leaders he [managed to] subdue all those people, having on his side the sign of the most glorious cross, the protection of the Virgin Mary, the Mother of God, and [working under] the banner of the God-loving bishop Martin [Saint Martin of Tours, c. 316–97, who was born in Pannonia] and the holy martyr [Saint] George. He pressed them to accept baptism to the glory of God and thus to receive salvation through the faithful priests. . . .

The most Christian prince serving God, sometimes consulting with all, other times with [only] some of them separately, divided his provinces into ten dioceses. He made the church of Esztergom the metropolis [that is, the archbishopric] and the guardian of the other [bishoprics] with the approval and consent of the Roman Apostolic See. Consequently, the aforementioned most honorable abbot Astrik [Anastasius, abbot of the Benedictine abbey of Břevnov, in Bohemia], adorned with the attire of the episcopal dignity, was appointed [archbishop] by canonical election and, on his advice, [the king] entrusted the other sees to the care and government of the fathers [bishops]. Everywhere foundations of sacred buildings were laid, convents of canons appeared, and cenobitic communities of those who live by rules flourished. Those who serve God gathered from all corners eager to enjoy the gracious hospitality of such a generous prince. And since Pannonia boasts of being the birthplace of the blessed bishop Martin [of Tours], with whose protection he [Stephen] had won the victory over the enemies of a king faithful to Christ, as we have said earlier, he built a monastery in the place called the Holy Mountain [abbey of Pannonhalma] dedicated to him [Saint Martin] on the counsel of those beloved by God. He endowed it with much income and all the other necessary things and made it [to be] like the bishoprics, by granting to it a tithe of all victors [that is, a tenth of all spoils of war, including prisoners of war as slaves or labor force].

Vita minor

As the fame of his name reached the ears of the whole world and the judgments of his lips were mentioned with great respect everywhere, sixty men from the aforementioned people [merchants] with all their belongings, abundant gold, silver, various jewels, and loaded wagons traveled to the Bulgarian border [of Hungary]. But a great number of serfs, whose souls are ready to die for the devil, stirred by the flames of greed, went before them, cut some down with swords, and robbed others, as many as they could [catch]. They [the merchants] were left without any property, half dead. They [therefore] came to the king's court to tell the story of what had happened [to them] and of what they had suffered. So, they continued their journey, came in a hurry to him [King Stephen], and fell at his feet. As soon as he saw them, he asked: "What is the cause of your misery?" "Milord," they replied, "we have set out on a journey without any evil intent, for we wanted to hear your exemplary judgments, but your subjects have taken away [from us] all the money that we have brought with us, and for no reason at all. And they seized much more in addition to that, and as soon as we came to our senses, we decided to appear before you." The king, who was quite reserved, used no look or word of threat. He restrained his anger, for it is written that he persists in his wrath to the end [Jer. 3:5]. He sent to the captain who had soldiers under his command and ordered him to gather before the appointed day all the people who had participated in the destruction. So, it happened as he had ordered, and they were brought before him for questioning. Turning to them, he said: "Why did you break the law of God? You have not known mercy, and you have brought innocent men to death. It is not the one who had followed the law that must be punished, but the transgressor. As you have done, so the Lord will do unto you this day." They received the verdict and were led away. They were hanged in pairs along the roads throughout the country. By this he wanted everybody to understand that that would happen to whomever does not respect the justice that the lord has established. And the inhabitants of the country heard of the king's judgment and were filled with fear. . . .

He died in the year 1038 of the incarnation of the Lord, on the sixth anniversary of the Roman emperor Henry [III, Holy Roman emperor 1046–56], and in the thirty-eighth year of his [own] reign (24 April). He was buried in the basilica of the Virgin Mary [in Székesfehérvár], which he had built with costly work. Many years passed, during which, whether because of the excessive malice of the people or because of some injustice in the church, the treasure of great wealth was hidden in the earth and from mortals, and [clear] only in the eyes of God. His elusive goodness was meant to show how precious he was to God, so he glorified him in the eyes of men with a series of miracles that came to light. And as he stood with praise and chanting to the Lord in heaven, so the church, here on earth, exalted him in praise and hymns in a worthy and memorable way. For his holiness, like the brilliance of a new star, shone in all the lands around him, and the pleasant fragrance [of his remains] filled the hearts of those present. A great number of people suffering from various ailments came [to his tomb] and were healed simply by touching the medicine of his goodness. Those who were about to perish, wailing and atrophied, returned [home] with strength.

When King Ladislas of good memory sat on the throne of the country, the bishops and abbots at the head of the holy church, after establishing his [Stephen's] holiness on the basis of testimony, proclaimed three days of strict fasting for consolation, while waiting in prayer for the supreme grace to descend upon the people. Then, lifting their hearts to God, they preached the praise of his name in the words of holy hymns and in that manner approached the place that enclosed his holy body. When [the tomb] was opened, an aroma exuded from there, like no other experienced before. The limbs of many wretched people gathered around were healed: the blind regained their sight, the lame regained strength [to walk], the skin of the lepers was cleaned, paralytics were saved [that is, could walk]. Whatever the illness, they were all healed. They lifted the inestimable weight [that is, the relics], gave thanks to the Almighty God, and then enclosed them in a silver reliquary.

Questions: Who are the opponents or enemies of Saint Stephen in the Vita maior *and* Vita minor, *respectively? How does Saint Stephen deal with them? How does the author of the* Vita minor *make the case for the sanctity of King Stephen? What does the author of* Vita maior *want the reader to remember about the king? How did the two authors see the role of the Virgin Mary? Which one seems to make a stronger connection between her and Saint Stephen?*

67. DEMONS, WINE, AND RELICS FOR A CHURCH IN SPARTA

Born at some point between 930 and 935 into a wealthy family in the theme of Armeniakon (in Asia Minor), Nikon spent twelve years in a monastery before moving to Crete, right at the time of Nicephorus II Phocas's conquest of the island from the Muslims. He remained on the island for seven years, working for the conversion of its inhabitants from Islam to Christianity. He then moved to continental Greece in 968 and visited Athens, Thebes, Corinth, Argos, Naupaktos, and many other places in the Peloponnese, before settling in Sparta, c. 970. He died c. 1000. His vita, *written in the mid-eleventh century at the earliest by someone who became an abbot of the monastery of Saint Nikon, describes him in strong terms: an unflinching, yet compassionate man with an incredible energy and an obsessive concern with repentance (hence his nickname, Metanoiete, which in Greek means "Repent!"). Those are the features captured in the earliest portrait of the saint, a mosaic in the northern arm of the cross-shaped church of the monastery of Saint Luke the Younger near Distomo (western Boeotia, Greece). Nikon had a strong physical frame and remarkable endurance: he crisscrossed the Peloponnese on foot several times, often traveling at a rapid pace on hot summer days, apparently without suffering from heat and thirst like everybody else. He had a loud voice, which could block out the racket produced by the game of* tzykanion, *in which the local* strategos *(general and governor) and his playmates engaged not far from the church of the monastery of Saint Nikon. He was also an impulsive man, eager to reproach not just demons but also brigands, even when he almost paid with his life for such brashness. Nikon did not avoid society, and, despite his ascetic habits, he gladly took a leading role in the community, being a manager and an arbiter at the same time. His was not the typical life of a solitary, for he constantly acted on behalf of the community in dealing either with the divine or with more earthly authorities.*

Source: trans. D.F. Sullivan, *The Life of Saint Nikon* (Brookline, MA: Hellenic College Press, 1987), pp. 125, 127, 129, and 131.

36. But it follows to relate fully in our story the miracles which occurred during the building of the holy church [in Sparta]. For the foundation was just being dug and had advanced to considerable depth when a very large stone was encountered which could not be moved. One might say that its removal was one of Hercules's labors. The stone was pushed by a boundless and numberless multitude and remained absolutely unmoved. But when the saint tried and only touched it with his hand, it seemed lighter than a feather and was easily removed from the foundations. At the removal of the rock, demons, who haunted the place to the great detriment of the inhabitants, and on account of whom, as I believe, it was ordained that the church be built there, leaped forth in the form of wasps from the foundation and struck violently and wounded those toiling in the task. But the blessed one immediately healed those so wounded by only prayer and the sign of the cross. And reproaching the wasps who had wounded them, he drove them from the place and sent them groaning into the bottomless depths. And so the stone was moved without bloodshed and the evil spirits were driven out by the holy man's censure. For all things will be subject and obedient to those who wish to live in God alone and do not debase the grace they have received. Since the number of those serving in the building of the holy house was not small and easily consumed the things brought to the holy man by the lovers of Christ, there was a complete scarcity of fresh and good wine. The holy man himself approached the vessel in which there was wine brought to him on the previous day by one of the poorest of the townspeople because the smell alone was repellant. He gave himself to prayer and called upon the master who can do all things to change the sour wine to a better one. So he prayed. And what did the God of miracles do, the God who has promised to glorify those who through their works have chosen to glorify him?

37. Of old he changed the great bitterness of Merra to a sweet richness by his divine and strong power, and again changed the water at Cana to wine. So even then for the holy man who had prayed he made the wine which had been like vinegar and was something to be avoided, very good and truly gladdening man's heart. The workmen, having drunk their fill for many days, or to speak more truthfully, much gladdened, were amazed and gave glory to God. By the same faith, even in the rest of the expenditures the great man was wealthy and, having nothing, he thought he had everything as the apostle says [2 Cor. 6:10]. For the providence of God and his wide-ruling and unstinting right hand, which is open and nourishes and fills all, was not unmindful of its own. One could then see unstinting wealth not only in the expenditures, but even in the daily progress and increase of the

work. In this work the saint himself, toiling with and joining the others, furnished great initiative, more of spirit than of body. So that each day what was found today seemed somewhat more than yesterday's building, [and] sometimes by a cubit or sometimes even more an invisible addition was seen on top of the earlier structure. Indeed, the material completely expended the day before at dawn was found abundant and more than enough for the building. It had been carried in unseen and entrusted to the holy man in the night. So, from this the work was believed to be divine and being accomplished in accord with God's plan, not least on account of the fiery pillar seen by night at the building site. This stretched from the earth up to heaven, and the local inhabitants could see it from afar and were confirming it with very great conviction. One day the saint wished to make a test of the love and faith which the prominent men of the city said they had for him, and in this area. From what he had he could not pay the workmen (he had the eyes that see all as witness that he did not have a single obol [copper coin of the smallest denomination]). [So] he proposed to the workmen that a chain be put about him and that like a slave he be dragged through the whole city by the neck. The faithful people of this [city] perceived the objective of the deed. With high spirits they lavishly paid what he owed to those who were dragging him and received in return a wealth of prayers. What, then, could be more holy, sanctified by the touch of his holy and pure skin, than this chain? And through the participation of the Holy Spirit in it, it is revealed as capable of setting people free from disease and weakness. Through it, evil spirits are driven daily from men and wondrous signs are worked and continuous cures abound for all who approach it with faith and place it on their necks. Even if its essence is iron, yet it is full of divine grace and power. The ranks of devils shudder before it, the angels reverence it, the divine and holy precinct rejoices in it. The chain is preserved there as if some golden necklace or elegant ornament and hung up within the holy shrine in which the divine body of the blessed one is treasured, together with the holy cowl he wore on his holy head. When touched for release from all kinds of disease, it is always and continuously an aid to those who are ill. We reverence these things, indeed, with much love and embrace them; we obtain sanctification and are deemed worthy of the grace of the Holy Spirit which resides in them.

Questions: What impression of Saint Nikon's abilities and character does this text give? What can it tell us about the beliefs of the population in the Peloponnese during the Early Middle Ages? Why was Saint Nikon successful? Compare the last section about the miracles performed by the chain of Saint Nikon to the account of the miracles at the tomb of Saint Stephen of Hungary (Doc. 66).

68. RULE OF THE LAVRA MONASTERY ON MOUNT ATHOS

Athanasios, the founder of the Great Lavra, was born in Trebizond c. 925–30 and came to Constantinople for his education under Emperor Romanus I Lekapenos (920–44). He became a professor there but felt a deep attraction to the monastic life. His inspiration was Michael Maleinos, the abbot of a monastery on Mount Olympos in Bithynia (northern Asia Minor). Athanasios arrived on Mount Athos in 958 and began living a solitary life, much like everybody else on the mountain. Only a few years later, however, the favored form of monastic life was not that of isolated anchorites coming together to celebrate the liturgy only on Sundays and on feast days (which is what a "lavra" actually is), but a more advanced form of "cenobitic" life. The rule that Athanasios drew for his foundation stressed the common life within the walls of the monastery, obedience to the abbot, and manual work. The total number of monks for this foundation was initially set at eighty, no more than five of whom were allowed to leave the monastery and live as hermits, if they proved themselves worthy of being granted that privilege. Monks at the Great Lavra ate together, and their food and rations were defined with great precision. The model for the rule that Athanasios drew up for the Great Lavra was the ninth-century rule of the monastery of Saint John Stoudios in Constantinople. The rule of the Great Lavra set provisions for the length of time necessary for testing newcomers, readings from the Gospels at mealtimes, clothing and diet, and the operation of monastic prisons—all in imitation of the Studite rule. However, there is a much greater emphasis in the rule of the Lavra Monastery on the diversity of manual labor required from monks, which in turn explains the dietary exceptions allowed for workers and craftsmen. There is also a much greater emphasis on reading than in the Studite rule.

Source: trans. G. Dennis, "Rule of Athanasios the Athonite for the Lavra Monastery," in *Byzantine Monastic Foundation Documents: A Complete Translation of the Surviving Founders'* Typika *and Testaments*, ed. J.P. Thomas and A. Constantinides Hero (Washington, DC: Dumbarton Oaks Research Library and Collection, 2000), vol. 1, pp. 223, 224–25, 226, 227–28.

9. Let it be noted that we do two hundred prostrations each day in the course of all the services during the day and night. This comes to forty at matins, twenty during each of the hours, thirty at vespers, and fifty at compline. During Great Lent, we even increase them by doubling the number at compline and matins and adding up to ten at the other services. . . .

17. It should be known that there are two disciplinarians, one in each choir, who are to remind the brothers to stand in an orderly manner in the choirs. After the wooden semantron [instrument used to call the faithful to liturgy] sounds, they urge on the slothful to run to the service. From those who have stayed behind they demand the reason for their doing so. By means of rather moderate

punishments they provide an incentive for those who have been tardy to do better. In addition, there is the wakener who at the matins readings goes quietly around to the brothers and wakes those sleeping. There is also the overseer who night and day wanders among the cells, places of service, and the other places of the Lavra, and with fitting severity and an appropriate penance breaks up those who are meeting at an improper time. There is also a doorkeeper who guards the entrance into the church, whose first task is to demand of those who come late a reason for their tardiness, and then, after one exit, he forbids those who want to leave at an inopportune moment from going out again. . . .

21. It must be known that at the signal given by the bell, when the brothers come down to the midday meal, they should carry a verse [of the psalms] upon their lips, just as [they should] after rising [from the table] until they have gone over to the narthex to perform the thanksgiving for the food they have shared. They take their seats in the order in which they have been received [into the monastery by seniority]. A monitor ensures that the tables are filled up in an orderly fashion without commotion. A reading then takes place. The ecclesiarch, that is, divides up the readings. He makes sure that none of the material that there was no time to read in the church is left out. The signal for the ending of this reading is the sound of the spoons at the last serving when all together toss them in their dishes. Similarly, at a signal, the wine is poured and at another signal food is served. . . .

24. It should be known that even though on the abovementioned three days of the week [Monday, Wednesday, and Friday] we do not use olive oil, the dishes are the customary ones, those which we always have, I mean vegetables and legumes. This rule also applies for the fast of Saint Philip, except that sometimes, as in Great Lent, we eat one meal a day. From the memorial of the holy apostles to that of Saint Philip, on Wednesday and Friday we do not partake of olive oil or wine. But if a feast of the Lord or the commemoration of a saint falls on one of these days, which grants us a holiday, then, if available, we eat cheese, eggs, and fish. As on the other days there are three servings of wine at midday and two in the evening. From the Nativity of Christ to the end of the twelfth day our diet is like that of the Pentecostal season. After that the rule of the previous days is again observed until Cheesefare Week [the week before the beginning of the Great Lent]. The week of Cheesefare is absolutely free [of fasting]. . . .

31. The arrangements to be made for those [who are] faint of heart and weak are left entirely to the judgment of the superior [abbot of the monastery]. On Wednesday and Friday during the fast before Christ's Nativity wine should not permitted except to the infirm, even though the superior may decide in favor of some receiving wine. On the remaining days of this fast, Monday, Tuesday, and Thursday, when the brothers eat only one meal a day, then before the meal workers, muleteers, carpenters, and shipwrights may be given two measures. When there is a memorial of a saint which frees us from reciting the hours, and

meals are served twice, then the abovementioned craftsmen receive an additional measure if they are laboring. If they happen to be without work, they too should be content with the diet of the community. For the brothers who are in ill health there is no fixed rule, but depending on the gravity of the illness of each we ought to give them proper care and encouragement. . . .

33. Remember that it is an ancient tradition and precept of the holy fathers that the brothers ought to lay before the superior their thought and hidden deeds, and they should conform to whatever the superior determines.

34. No brother is allowed to possess any personal property and private funds or coins or currency without the approval and knowledge of the superior. This is absolutely forbidden by our holy fathers and by the great [Saint] Basil [the author of the first monastic rule]. In the same way, the holy fathers have judged that secretly leaving the monastery is utterly alien to the monastic promise. Nobody, therefore, is allowed to leave secretly. But if a person finds that his soul is not at ease in our Lavra, let him inform the superior of the reason. If the man appears to have good cause to seek a change, then the superior should transfer him to another spiritual director or make some other arrangements for his welfare. In this way his departure from the monastery will be accompanied by prayer and blessing and will not be of the sort that was forbidden, cursed, and condemned by the holy fathers.

Questions: What notions of privacy and property did the rule institute in the cenobitic community at the Lavra Monastery? Why is the diet of the monks described in such detail? How is discipline to be maintained within the monastic community? What is the role of sounds in that regimen?

69. A HERMIT'S PORTRAIT: SAINT ANDREW-ZOERARD

The earliest preserved text of hagiography from Hungary is the legend of Zoerard and Benedict of Skalka written in or shortly before 1064 by Maurus, bishop of Pécs. Next to nothing is known about the author, except that he had been a monk in the Benedictine abbey of Pannonhalma (established in 996 by Duke Géza) before being appointed bishop, most likely by King Stephen I in 1029. He is responsible for building the cathedral in Pécs during the reign of Peter Orseolo (1038–41) and he participated in the coronation of King Andrew in Székesfehérvár in 1046. His name appears at the top of the list of witnesses in that king's charter for the abbey of Tihany. He mediated the peace between Andrew's son, Solomon, and his cousins Géza and Ladislaus, who met in Pécs in 1064. On that occasion, Géza expressed interest in the relics of Saint Andrew-Zoerard, and he apparently asked Maurus to write a biography of the saint, which also touched upon the life of the saint's disciple, Benedict of Skalka. Both hermits were canonized in 1083, a few years after Maurus's death. The text of the short legend survives in five manuscripts, all of a much later date. Zoerard was a hermit in the tradition of Eastern Christianity. Some have pointed out the clear association with Syro-Palestinian forms of ascetic life, most visible in such features as the strict diet of forty nuts for Lent, deprivation of sleep, and other forms of bodily mortification. Perhaps the most prominent of all is the chain tied around the waist, which is what Prince Géza wanted to obtain in 1064.

Source: trans. M. Miladinov, "Lives of the Holy Hermits Zoerard the Confessor and Benedict the Martyr by Blessed Maurus, Bishop of Pécs," in *Saints of the Christianization Age of Central Europe (Tenth-Eleventh Century)*, ed. G. Klaniczay (Budapest: Central European University Press, 2013), pp. 327, 329, 331, 333, and 335.

1. At the time when under the rule of the most Christian king Stephen the name and the religion of God, though still rude, was spreading in Pannonia, many clerics and monks from other lands, as the fame of the good ruler reached them, flocked to him as to a father, not forced by any necessity, but in order to gain the new joy of the holy way of life from their assembly. Among them, there was a man touched by the inspiration of the Holy Spirit, who had blossomed from rusticity like a rose from among the thorns, and bore the name of Zoerard; he came to this country [Hungary] from the land of the Poles, and having received the habit from Abbot Philip, whose monastery of Zobor [Benedictine abbey near Nitra established before King Stephen I, perhaps in the ninth century], dedicated to Saint Hyppolitus the Martyr, lay in the territory of Nitra, took the name of Andrew and determined to enter upon an eremitic life. And I have decided to give a brief account of the contrition of the heart and torment of the body he [Andrew-Zoerard] inflicted upon himself, from what I heard in conversation with his disciple, the blessed Benedict [of Skalka], who had kept company with him. I myself, Maurus, who am now bishop [of Pécs] by God's mercy, but was at that time a young pupil, beheld the good man, but what I have learned about his way of life I know by hearing, not by seeing. For the aforementioned monk Benedict often came to our monastery [in Pannonhalma, where Maurus was a monk before being appointed bishop] dedicated to the blessed bishop Martin [of Tours], and the following is what he told me about the hermit's venerable life.

2. After the venerable man Andrew entered the solitude of the desert, he always observed the practice of fasting until he achieved great exhaustion of the body, but also fortification of the life of the spirit. For three days, he used to abstain from anything that may be eaten, out of love for the grace of him who, having become man for the sake of humanity, fasted for forty days. And when the season of Lent came, he followed the example of the rule under Abbot Zosimas [a side character in the legend of Saint Mary the Egyptian], whereby each monk took forty-five dates for Lent; and thus he was given forty nuts by Abbot Philip, from whom he had received the monastic habit, and living contentedly on those provisions, he awaited with

joy the day of the holy resurrection. On those and other days, although such meager food that he ate was not only insufficient to invigorate the body, but also brought his very spirit to falter, he never ceased from his labor, except at prayer times, but used to take his ax and go into a solitary part of the forest in order to work. One day, as he lay there half dead, his body and spirit failing him because of excessive work and the rigors of fasting, a youth came to him most beautiful in appearance and angelic in likeness, who placed him on a cart and brought him to his cell. When the ecstasy he was in was over and he came to his senses, he realized what God's mercy had done for him; and he revealed all this to his abovementioned disciple Benedict (who told the story to me), binding him by an oath that he should not make it known to anyone before the day of his death. Moreover, after his daily work, he subjected his body to such nocturnal repose as should rather be called torment and affliction than rest. Around a leveled stump of an oak he constructed an enclosure, through which he fixed sharp canes from all sides. Then he would sit on the stump, using it as a seat to rest his limbs in such a posture that if his body, overcome by sleep, should perchance incline in any direction, he would be painfully pierced by those sharp canes and woken up. Moreover, he used to place on his head a crown made of wood, to which he attached four stones hanging on four sides, so that if his head bowed in any direction in sleep, it would be struck by a stone. Ah, what reward there is for this blessed man Andrew, what a blessed and eternal life, adorned a hundredfold by the crown that recompenses in heaven what was painfully earned on earth! Ah, what an unparalleled way of confessing faith, and how much more precious it makes the promised kingdom! Neither food nor repose could by their vain delight rob him of eternal life, and there was no way a wicked spirit could find a path to deceive him. . . .

3. As the time of his death was approaching, he [Andrew-Zoerard] made this known to those who were present and told them that they should not remove any piece of clothing that covered his body before the arrival of Abbot Philip, whom he had already sent for. As the abbot arrived in the place where the body of the venerable man, now dead, lay waiting to be washed [in preparation for burial], he discovered that a metal chain was squeezing his entrails. Ah, what a wondrous and incredible thing! The chain was causing the flesh to fester inside, though outside the skin had closed over it. But this manner of martyrdom might have gone unnoticed, had a knot joining the metal not been visible at the navel. As the chain was unfastened and drawn out of the body, the heavy sound of snapping ribs was heard. I asked the abbot for the middle part of the chain and kept it until now, when I could not deny the request of the most Christian duke Géza [the future king of Hungary, 1074–77], who had been pressing me with his heartfelt wish to have it.

Questions: What can we learn from this text about the conditions and challenges of those choosing the eremitical life? What forms of ascetic discipline did Saint Zoerard use to increase his concentration on spiritual matters? Compare Saint Zoerard with the Bulgarian hermit Saint John of Rila (Doc. 22). Compare the role of Zoerard's chain to that of Saint Nikon Metanoiete (Doc. 67).

70. THE *PASSION OF THE HOLY MARTYRS BORIS AND GLEB*

At the death of Prince Vladimir of Kiev (1015), power disputes between his sons led to the defeat of the eldest (Sviatopolk), who had meanwhile ordered the assassination of two of his younger brothers, Boris and Gleb. The story is told in the Narrative and Passion and Encomium of the Holy Martyrs Boris and Gleb, *which was written in the mid-eleventh century, more than fifty years after the events. The winner in the power struggle following Vladimir's death was Yaroslav the Wise, and he gets very good press in the* Narrative and Passion. *The author of the text is unknown, but he seems to have worked for Yaroslav, possibly during his reign (1036–54), for he took great care to depict the prince as the rightful exactor of revenge for his brothers' deaths. A Scandinavian saga,* Eymundar thattr Hringssonar *(which survives in a late fourteenth-century manuscript from Iceland) suggests a different solution. Eymundar is said to have fled his native Norway and traveled to Rus', hoping to be hired as a mercenary by one of three warring princes, all three sons of King Valdimar (Vladimir). He was taken on by Jarislafr (Yaroslav) and he helped the prince defeat his brother Burislafr (Boris?) who was ruling in Kiev. The saga specifically makes Eymundar and his men responsible for the murder of Burislafr. Whatever the true story behind Boris and Gleb's assassination, the author of the* Narrative and Passion *was apparently acquainted with at least one of the works dealing with Saint Wenceslas and perhaps with the* Life of Constantine *and the* Life of Methodius *as well. According to the* Narrative and Passion, *following the death of Boris and Gleb, their remains were placed in wooden coffins and a small chapel was erected on the grave site. Following his victory over a rival prince of Polotsk, Yaroslav's son Iziaslav ordered the remains of Boris and Gleb to be dug up and placed in stone sarcophagi. Around 1072, the remains were moved into a new church erected in Vyshhorod, near Kiev, and Boris and Gleb gained formal recognition as saints, thus becoming the first Rus' saints of the church. Since they were technically not martyrs, emphasis was placed on healing miracles performed at the grave site. The* Narrative and Passion *is the most popular and oldest East Slavic saintly biography.*

Source: trans. M. Kantor, *Medieval Slavic Lives of Saints and Princes* (Ann Arbor: University of Michigan, Department of Slavic Languages and Literatures, 1983), pp. 166–253.

The generation of the righteous shall be blessed, said the prophet, and their seed shall be blessed. Thus, these things came to pass before the time when the autocrat of the entire land of Rus' was Volodimir [Vladimir], son of Sviatoslav and grandson of Igor, he who enlightened this entire land with holy baptism. . . . Now this Volodimir had twelve sons, not by one wife, but by their several mothers. Among these sons, Vysheslav was the eldest, and after him came Iziaslav. The third was Sviatopolk, who conceived this evil murder. His mother, a Greek, was formerly a nun, and Iaropolk, Volodimir's brother, took her, and because of the beauty of her face, he unfrocked her, and begot of her this accursed Sviatopolk. But Volodimir, who was still a pagan, killed Iaropolk and took his wife, who was pregnant; and of her was born this accursed Sviatopolk. And he was of two fathers who were brothers, and for this reason Volodimir loved him not, for he was not of him. And by Rogneda he had four sons: Iziaslav, Mstislav, Yaroslav, and Vsevolod; and by another he had Sviatoslav and Mstislav, and by a Bulgarian woman, Boris and Gleb. And he placed them all in different lands as rulers. . . . He placed the accursed Sviatopolk as ruler in Pinsk, and Yaroslav in Novgorod, Boris in Rostov, and Gleb in Murom. . . .

And a messenger came to him [to Boris], informing him of his father's death: how his father Vasilii—for that was the name given to him in holy baptism—had passed away, and how Sviatopolk had concealed the death of his father, and at night in Berestovo [an estate near Kiev, which belonged to Vladimir], after taking up the floor and wrapping him in a rug, they had lowered him to the ground with ropes, took him by sledge and placed him in the church of the Holy Mother of God. And when the saintly Boris heard this he grew weak in the body and his entire face was covered with tears. And being choked with tears, he could not speak, but in his heart, he began to speak thusly: "Woe unto me, light of my eyes, radiance and dawn of my face, bridle of my youth, admonition of my foolishness! Woe unto me, my father and lord! To whom shall I turn, to whom shall I look, where shall I sate myself with the good instruction and admonitions of your understanding? Woe unto me, woe unto me! . . . My heart burns, my soul confuses my mind, and I know not to whom to turn, and to whom to show this bitter sorrow. To the brother whom I would have in place of a father? But he, methinks, has learned worldly vanities and contemplates my murder. If he sheds my blood and attempts to slay me, then a martyr shall I be unto my Lord. For I shall not resist, it is written: 'God resists the proud, but gives grace unto the humble' [James 4:6]. . . . Therefore, what shall I say or what shall I do? Lo, shall I go to my brother and say, 'Be a father to me. You are my brother and elder. What is your command, my lord?'" And musing thus in his mind, he set off to his brother, and he said in his heart: "Were I at least to see the face of my younger brother Gleb, as Joseph did Benjamin" . . .

Now after his father's death, Sviatopolk had settled in Kiev. Upon summoning the people of Kiev and giving them many gifts, he dismissed them. Then he sent to Boris, saying: "Brother, I wish there to be love between us and shall add to your share of father's possessions." But he spoke deceitfully and not the truth. He came secretly at night to Vyshegorod [Vyshhorod, a town just north of Kiev], summoned Put'sha and the men of Vyshegorod, and said to them: "Tell me in truth, are you loyal to me?" And Put'sha said: "We all are ready to lay down our lives for you."

But the devil, that hater of man's goodness from the beginning of time, upon seeing the saintly Boris place all his hope in the Lord, began to be even more active. And as once before he found Cain ablaze with fratricide, so now he found in truth a second Cain in Sviatopolk, and snared his thought, that he should kill all his father's heirs and seize all power for himself alone. Then the thrice-accursed Sviatopolk summoned to himself the counselors of all evil and the chiefs of all untruth, and upon opening his lips most foul, he emitted an evil voice, saying to Put'sha's people: "Since you promised to lay down your lives for me, go in secret, my friends, and where you find my brother Boris, watch for an opportunity and slay him." And they promised to do so. . . .

Now, upon returning, the blessed Boris pitches his tents on the L'to [Al'ta River, a tributary of the Trubezh River, to the southeast of Kiev]. And his retinue said to him: "Go, settle in Kiev on your father's throne, for all the troops are in your hands." But he answered them: "It is not for me to raise my hand against my own brother, and especially against an elder one whom I would have as a father." And when they heard this, the troops departed from him, and he remained with only his retainers. On the Sabbath day he was in distress and grief, and his heart was oppressed. And he entered his tent and wept with a broken heart but a joyful soul, sorrowfully lifting his voice: "Despise not my tears, O Lord. For as I have my hope in you, so shall I, together with your servants, accept my portion and lot with all your holy ones, for you are a merciful God, and unto you shall we render praise forever. Amen." He thought of the martyrdom and passion of the holy martyr Nikita [a Gothic martyr of the fourth century] and of Saint Viacheslav [Wenceslas, the prince of the Czechs], whose murders were similar to this. . . .

Then evening came. And he commanded that vespers be chanted and he himself entered his tent and began to say the evening prayer with bitter tears, frequent sighs, and much groaning. Afterward he lay down to sleep. . . . Upon awakening early, he saw it was the time of morning: it was holy Sunday. He said to his presbyter: "Arise, begin matins." And having put shoes on his feet and having washed his face, he himself began to pray to the Lord God. But those sent by Sviatopolk had arrived on the L'to during the night and drawing near they heard the voice of the blessed martyr chanting the morning psalter. . . . And at that moment he saw those running toward the tent, the flash of weapons, and the unsheathing of swords. And the venerable body of the most merciful Boris, Christ's holy and blessed martyr, was pierced without mercy.

Those who stabbed him with lances were the accursed Put'sha, Tal'ts, Elovich, and Liash'ko. . . . Then looking at them with tender eyes and a downcast face, and bathed in tears he said: "Brethren, end the service you have begun; and peace be unto my brother, and unto you, my brethren" . . . And at that moment he passed away and delivered his soul into the hands of the living God, in the month of July, on the twenty-fourth day, the ninth day before the kalends of August [24 July 1015].

And they slew many retainers. But since they could not remove the necklace from George, they cut off his head and tossed him aside, and for that reason his body could be recognized later. Upon wrapping the blessed Boris in a tent flap and laying him in a wagon, they drove off. And when they were in a pine forest, he began to raise his holy head. Learning of this, Sviatopolk sent two Varangians, and they pierced him through the heart with a sword. Thus he expired and received a crown everlasting. After having brought him to Vyshgorod [now Vyshhorod, on the northern outskirts of Kiev, Ukraine], they laid his body in the earth and buried it near the church of St-Vasilii. . . .

Having put this in his mind, that evil counselor the devil summoned the blessed Gleb, saying: "Come quickly, your father summons you and is very sick." He [Gleb] quickly mounted his horse and set off with a small retinue. And when he came to the Volga, the horse beneath him stumbled over a rut in the field and slightly injured his leg. And he came to Smolensk, and went on from Smolensk, and within viewing distance therefrom he boarded a small vessel on the Smiadin' [a river in the Smolensk region]. At that time, news of his father's death reached Yaroslav from Predslava [Yaroslav's sister]. And Yaroslav sent a message to Gleb: "Do not go, brother, your father has died, and your brother has been murdered by Sviatopolk." Upon hearing this, the blessed one cried out with bitter weeping and heartfelt grief: "O woe unto me, my Lord! With twofold weeping, I weep and moan, with twofold grief I grieve and groan. Woe unto me, woe unto me! I weep greatly for my father, but I weep even more and have despaired for you, my brother and lord, Boris." . . . And so, as he was groaning and weeping, and wetting the earth with his tears, and calling upon God with frequent sighs, those sent by Sviatopolk suddenly arrived—those evil servants of his, merciless bloodsuckers, the fiercest of fratricides, having the soul of savage beasts. The saintly one had set off in a small vessel, and they met him at the mouth of the Smiadin'. And when he saw them, he rejoiced in his soul; but they, upon seeing him, were covered with gloom and rowed toward him. And he expected to receive greetings from them. But when they drew alongside, the evil ones began to leap into his boat with bared swords in their hands, which glittered like the water. And immediately the oars fell from all hands, and all were numb with fear. When the blessed one saw this, he understood they wished to kill him. He gazed at them with tender eyes, his face bathed in tears, broken in heart, humbled in mind, frequently sighing, choked with tears, and weakened in body, and he lifted his voice in sorrow: "Let me be, my precious and dear brethren, for I have done you no evil! Leave me alone, brethren and lords, leave me alone! What wrong have I done my brother and you, my brethren and lords? If there be some wrong, take me to your prince, to my brother and lord. Have mercy on my youth, have mercy, my lords! You are my lords, I your slave. Reap me not from a life unripened; reap not the ear of grain still unripe but bearing the milk of innocence. . . ." But not a single word of this shamed them in any way, and like savage beasts they seized him. . . . Then looking at them, he said with a dejected voice and choking throat: "You have already done this in your thoughts; now that you have come, do what you are sent for." Then the accursed Goriaser ordered them to slay him quickly. Gleb's cook, Torchin by name, drew a knife, and seizing the blessed one, slaughtered him like a meek and innocent lamb. It was in the month of September, on the fifth day, on Monday. . . .

After Gleb had been slain, he was cast in a deserted place between two hollowed-out tree trunks. . . . And though the saintly one lay there a long time, he remained entirely unharmed, for he [God] left him not in oblivion and neglect but gave signs: now a pillar of fire was seen, now burning candles. Moreover, merchants passing by on the way would hear the singing of angels; and others, hunters and shepherds, also saw and heard these things. It did not occur to anyone to search for the body of the saintly one until Yaroslav, unable to bear this evil murder, moved against that fratricide, the accursed Sviatopolk, and fought many battles with him and was always victorious, with the aid of God and the help of the saintly ones. And as many battles as he waged, the accursed one always returned shamed and defeated. Finally, this thrice-accursed one attacked with a horde of Pechenegs. And having gathered troops, Yaroslav went forth against him, to the L'to River, and he halted at the place where the saintly Boris was slain. . . . They advanced against one another, and the field of the L'to was covered with a multitude of troops. . . . Toward evening Yaroslav triumphed and the accursed Sviatopolk fled. . . . And he could not endure being in one place and fled through the land of the Liakhs [Poland], pursed by the wrath of God. He fled into the wilderness between the lands of the Czechs and Liakhs and there forfeited his life in an evil manner. . . . And his grave exists even to this day, and from it issues an evil stench for the edification of men. . . .

And from then on discord ceased in the land of Rus'; and Yaroslav aasumed all power over it. And he began to inquire about the bodies of the saintly ones, how and where they were placed. And about the saintly Boris he was informed that he was placed in Vyshgorod; but about the saintly Gleb they knew nothing, as he had been slain in Smolensk. Then they told him what was heard from those coming from there—that they had seen a light and candles in a deserted place. And upon hearing this, he sent presbyters to Smolensk to search, saying: "That is my brother." And they found him where those things were seen. And they came with crosses and many candles and censers, and with great reverence placed him in a vessel. And upon arriving, they laid him in Vyshgorod, where also the body of the most blessed Boris lay. . . . For lo, it was most miraculous and wondrous, and worthy of memory, that though the body of the saintly one had lain for many years, it was harmed by no beast of prey, nor had it turned black as bodies of the dead usually do. Rather it was radiant, and beautiful, and whole, and it had a pleasing fragrance. Thus had God preserved the body of his martyr. . . .

But can I relate everything or tell of the miracles which occur? In truth, the entire earth cannot hold the most wondrous miracles which take place, for they are more numerous than the sand of the sea. And not only there, but in all the countries and in all the lands through which they pass, they cast out disease and illness, and visit those in prison and in fetters. And at the place where they were made worthy of the crowns of martyrs, churches were built in their names, and there too they do good and work many miracles.

Questions: What, according to the author of this text, were the reasons for the assassination of Boris and Gleb? What role did their retainers play? How do you explain that before his death, Boris thought of Saint Nikita and Saint Wenceslas as examples to follow? Compare the miracles at the tombs of Boris and Gleb to those at the tomb of Saint Stephen of Hungary (Doc. 66).

71. *TYPIKON* OF THE MONASTERY IN BACHKOVO

Gregory Pakourianos (d. 1086) rose to military and political prominence under Emperors Michael VII Dukas (1071–78) and Nicephorus III Botaneiates (1078–81). From the latter he received estates in the hinterland of Philippopolis (present-day Plovdiv, in Bulgaria), including land on which he later built his monastery. Gregory was granted even more estates in the central and southern regions of the Balkans by Emperor Alexios I Komnenos (1081–1118), who also appointed him grand domestic (chief commander of the troops) of the west in the circumstances surrounding the Pecheneg invasions of the 1070s and 1080s. The monastery that Gregory decided to establish was dedicated to the Mother of God Petritzonitissa. This epithet refers to the village of Petritzos (now Bachkovo, in the Rhodope Mountains, a few miles south of Asenovgrad). Gregory's may not have been the first monastic foundation in the area, for Georgian monks are mentioned there in several earlier sources. Nor was this the first time he acted as a monastic patron, for together with his brother Apasios (who is mentioned in the typikon *for the monastery in Bachkovo) Pakourianos made in 1074 a substantial donation to the Iviron Monastery, another Georgian community on Mount Athos. Established in 1083,*

Gregory's monastery at Petritzos remained under Georgian control for a relatively long time. Georgian monks were still present there in the thirteenth century. The typikon *for Gregory's monastery was written in three languages—Greek, Georgian, and Armenian, but only the Greek and Georgian versions have survived in manuscript. The translation below is from the Greek version. Gregory drew heavily on the* typikon *of the monastery of Panagios in Constantinople, with which he seems to have been closely associated. He therefore prescribed a disciplinary regime for his Georgian monks at Petritzos which, judging by the standards of the time, may be described as lenient. The choice of location may have something to do with the presence of large numbers of Paulicians (adherents of a set of beliefs regarded as heretical by the Orthodox Church) in the hinterland of Philippopolis. But Gregory was equally worried about the possibility of his foundation falling under bad influence. He therefore stipulated in his* typikon *complete independence for his monastery from any imperial, patriarchal, or metropolitan authority. Pakourianos wanted his monastery to have no more and no fewer than fifty monks, but he specifically forbade the inclusion of Greeks. The revenue from the many properties he donated to the monastery was expected to defer expenses involved in maintaining a school for six boys until they have "attained the proper age for the rank of priest." In order to allow the monks to procure for themselves goods that the properties he had donated to them could not possibly produce, Pakourianos instituted an annual fair beside his monastery.*

Source: trans. R. Jordan, "*Typikon* of Gregory Pakourianos for the Monastery of the Mother of God Petritzonitissa in Bačkovo," in *Byzantine Monastic Foundation Documents: A Complete Translation of the Surviving Founders' Typika and Testaments*, ed. J.P. Thomas and A. Constantinides Hero (Washington, DC: Dumbarton Oaks Research Library and Collection, 2000), vol. 2, pp. 519 and 524–26.

By the help and goodness of the revered and life-giving Trinity that has fashioned everything and sustains it, the Father without beginning and his word the Son without beginning and his life-giving Spirit of the same substance, the one divinity and power, into which we have been baptized and which we worship as our ancestors did, confident through our hope and sure trust in this we will begin to speak and write about the task which was prescribed to us and was the object of our desire and prayer, that is the formation of our newly established monastery, as will be revealed in what follows next concerning the limit and number of the monks in it and concerning the ordinance and rule by which they will live together to the honor and glory of our all-immaculate mistress the Mother of God.

In the locality of the fort called Petritzos all the monks knowing the Georgian script and language have been gathered and organized into the monastery recently built through the providence and with the help of the God of all by me, Gregory, by the goodwill of God the *sebastos* [court title indicating closeness to the emperor] and *megas domestikos* [chief commander of the troops] of all the west, the true son of Pakourianos now at blessed rest, the preeminent prince of princes, by birth from among those of the east from the most brilliant race of the Georgians. I add that I am the founder of this monastery and place of my burial established by God and newly built, which has been named for the honor and glory of the Mother of Christ our God, and of its far-famed and most beautiful holy church and in it the most beautiful tabernacle of God, built for my help, redemption, and salvation and in addition that of my own brother, the *magistros* [honorary rank] Apasios, of happy memory. . . .

2. We have given and established property from the possessions bestowed on us by revered chrysobulls [imperial charters with golden seals] with an inalienable right of family possession, complete ownership and true authority, properties established as free of tax by the terms of the revered chrysobulls; of these places, first and to begin with, is the fort situated in the same theme [Byzantine province] of Philippopolis [now Plovdiv, Bulgaria], that is, the village named Petritzos (generally called Basilikis by the common people) together with the hamlets below it—the field called Iannoba which has now been turned into a monastery, the field Batzakoba, the field Dobrolonkos, the field Dobrostanos, the field Bourseos, the field Lalkouba with that called Abroba—all these fields with the aforementioned fort together with all their territory, established tenure, ancient rights of possession and privilege of every kind and all revenue according to the summary of them in the previous delimitation.

In addition to these I have given the village situated next to these called Stenimachos [now Asenovgrad, near Plovdiv, Bulgaria] along with the two forts built by me in it, also their hamlets, that is, the field of Lipitzos and the field called Saint Barbara situated near to Prinezes together with the hermitages of St-Nicholas and St-Elias and St-George situated above and likewise the one situated below near the village, these places similarly complete with all their ancient territory and tenure and according to the delimitation made by me of the places between them and my fort of Bodena. In addition to these I have also given the fort called Baniska with Brysis and all the rest of its villages and hamlets, and further, the pastures with all their territory and ancient tenure. Similarly, I have also given in Topolinitza the village of Gelloba [known as] Praitorion with all its territory and tenure.

I have also given to our aforesaid monastery and the holy churches in it the estate called the estate of Zaoutzes with all its territory and ancient tenure in the theme of Boleron [a province in southwestern Thrace, a territory now divided between Bulgaria and Greece] in the locality of the military district of Mosynopolis [now near Komotini, in northeastern Greece], and inside the fort of Mosynopolis the building sites bought by me and the houses built on them at my own expense, also the buildings bought by our man and agent Vardanes out of our money and similarly the ones inside the fort of Mosynopolis, together with the monastery outside it, the one set up in the name and to the honor of Saint

George on the mount called Pappikion [a monastic mountain south of the Rhodope Range], with its vineyards and all fields and gardens and all the rest of its rightful landed property and its dependency inside the fort of Mosynopolis. . . .

In addition to this my blessed brother added the following in this written testament giving me in the form of a legacy out of the places bestowed on him by revered chrysobull, the village which is called Srabikion together with Kaisaropolis [unknown location in Macedonia, in the valley of the River Struma] which is situated in the theme of Serres [now a city to the northeast of Thessaloniki, Greece] in the military district of Zabalta with its lake and the fishing places and the hamlet called Glaunon under it. He made me owner, heir, and established commander of this fort and village. But because of my unbearable longing for him and because I do not need any worldly goods (for by grace of God and the favor of his goodness, by the help and joy of our mighty and holy emperors and because of my excessive zeal I needed nothing, as has been said), the aforesaid fort and village which he left me as a legacy I have assigned therefore to our aforesaid monastery and the holy church in it and to the family grave in which he was buried, for the salvation of his soul. All the names of the aforementioned forts, villages, and estates, all of which have been given to our holy church and the Georgian monastery called Petritzos, are all listed in the revered and honored chrysobull which has been issued for the monastery. . . .

Such properties as have been listed above in this rule were handed over by us to the aforesaid monastery with absolutely all the things in them, that is, the owners' plow animals, the dependent peasants, and all kinds of animals belonging to them, all kinds of land both hill and plain, mountain pastures, land for pasture and for plowing, vineyards, all kinds of plants fruiting and not fruiting, milling establishments worked by water or animals, lakes and the fallow land around them, forts and all kinds of buildings in them, and all articles and revenues from the immovable, movable, and animate property both inside and outside them.

In addition to these there are valuable icons, representations of Christ the Savior and all the saints, also valuable crosses with valuable relics of the divine life-giving cross, also holy Gospel lectionaries both in the Greek language and script and in that of the Georgians, which were made at very great expense with various stones and pearls and enameling, and sacred vessels for the holy church, patens, chalices, and various silver chandeliers and lamps of every kind, very precious imperial garments laid up in the church, also the garments given to me by our mighty and holy emperor Lord Alexios [I Komnenos] from among those which he put on his all-noble and most honored body on the occasion when with the great help and power of his divine right arm and with the good fortune of our holy emperor I crushed and destroyed his most terrible and most arrogant enemies who set themselves not only against the Roman empire but also every race of Christians—I mean the Patzinaks [Pechenegs] whose defeat and complete destruction is altogether one of the most difficult things to set down in writing. For I am convinced that even for many years after my death the miraculous act of Almighty God which happened then will in no way be forgotten.

Together with these are the very valuable imperial clothes which our almighty and noble emperor gave me when I returned from the capture by the Cumans and those which his most fortunate brother [Isaac] the *sebastokrator* gave me at that time. Also, there are other very valuable pieces of unsewn cloth and certain other different vessels of all kinds connected with the adornment and embellishment of the church which we donated in considerable numbers, wooden icons bearing large numbers of most pleasing figures of various saints, bronze chandeliers, and large numbers of candlesticks, all of which are listed carefully according to their type in this book [that is, the inventory at the end of the *typikon*].

Questions: Why did Gregory Pakourianos establish the monastery at Bachkovo? What would the monastery do with the forts mentioned in the document? How can the mention of the Pechenegs and the Cumans be interpreted? What were the languages used for liturgy in the monastery church at Bachkovo? Why are the icons considered objects of value, just as the church books, patens, and silver chandeliers are?

72. JEWS IN EAST CENTRAL EUROPE

Much of what is known about the religious life of Jews in medieval Hungary derives from commentaries on the Talmud and from rabbinical decisions (responsa) *on matters brought to their attention in the form of questions raised by various Jewish communities. At stake in all those cases was the correct application of Jewish law in specific circumstances and at specific moments in time. The earliest* responsa *concerning Jews in east central Europe are those of Rabbi Judah, son of Meir ha-Kohen, who lived in Mainz during the first half of the eleventh century. Rabbi Judah, son of Meir of Mainz, was his grandson, and the author of* Sefer ha-Dinim, *a collection of civil law that contains several* responsa *dealing with east central and eastern Europe. Two of the first three* responsa *translated below come from the* Sefer ha-Dinim, *while the third is attributed to its author and preserved in a later commentary. The attribution is largely based on the problem brought to the attention of the rabbi, which concerned two orphans from Przemyśl or its environs. The events in question are dated between 1018 and 1031, for the town is specifically mentioned as being in Poland. Between 1031 and 1069 (as well as after 1085), however, the town was under Rus' rule. The problem therefore was likely brought to the attention of Judah ha-Kohen at some point before the middle of the eleventh century. Kalonymos, son of Sabbati (c. 1005 to before 1096) was the leader of the local* yeshiva *(religious school for learning the Talmud) in Worms, c. 1070. His* responsum *is preserved in a thirteenth-*

century compilation of ritual law entitled Ears of Gleaning (Shibbolei haLeket) *by a prominent* halakist *(legal commentator on the Talmud) from Rome named Zedekiah, son of Abraham Anaw (1210–c. 1280). Given that Kalonymos moved to Worms from Rome in the mid-1060s, his* responsum *may be dated after that, perhaps to the late 1060s or early 1070s. Isaac, son of Moses (c. 1200–c. 1270) was a* halakist *from Bohemia who taught in Prague. He studied at prominent* yeshivot *in Germany and France. He settled for a while in Vienna before returning to Bohemia. He is the author of a long commentary on Talmudic ritual regulations entitled* Sefer Or Zaru'a.

Source: trans. N. Aleksiun from *Źródła hebrajskie do dziejów Słowian i niektórych innych ludów środkowej i wschodniej Europy. Wyjątki z pism religijnych i prawniczych XI–XIII w.*, ed. E.F. Kupfer and T. Lewicki (Wrocław: Zakład im. Ossolińskich, 1956), pp. 36–37, 39, 65–66, and 212.

Anonymous

Reuben and Shimon [generic, fictional characters, like X and Y] came to settle a dispute [in a rabbinic court]. Reuben stated: "He [Shimon] convinced me in the land of Hagar [Hungary] to speak to the queen [on his behalf], in order for her to ask the mint master to strike coins out of one hundred pounds of silver for Shimon. Shimon told me, 'I will share all my profit with you.' I told him: 'But you do not have any silver.' And he [Shimon] replied: 'I will try, perhaps God will give me some.' I agreed [to this arrangement] and spoke to the queen. She then ordered the mint master to strike coins for Shimon. After that, I left [the country] on a mission from the queen. I left my partner in my place, authorizing him to receive from Shimon my [share of the] profit, in the presence of witnesses. Shimon gave him [that is, to my partner] seven half-marks of silver, and nothing else. So, I am [now] asking for the remainder." Shimon replied: "Indeed, it came to my mind to ask the queen [to allow me] to strike coins, provided that God would help me obtain [some] silver. But I was afraid that you would slander me before the queen, and I therefore asked you to settle this matter for me. And you spoiled it for me as much as you could. So, I spoke to the queen myself, and did everything that I could [to make things work my way]. And even though you were away at the time, I gave your agent the one *zaquq* [either four or six ounces of silver], as I had promised to you. And in addition I also lent him [personally] six marks, as he [urgently] needed that money."

Anonymous

A certain Jew brought goods [to sell] from the country of the Poles. And Reuben and Shimon came and bought them [the goods] in secret. Meanwhile,

Levi [a fictional character, like Z] fell ill. Jehuda [another fictional character, like W] went to Reuben and told him, "Why did you commit fraud and buy the goods stealthily?" And Reuben had only a few golden jewels that he had given to his wife at the wedding ceremony [that is, out of those goods, Reuben had taken a few gold jewels which he had given to his wife as a gift at the wedding]. Shimon demanded that Reuben take the jewels back from his wife and give them to him.

Judah ha-Kohen of Mainz

Two brothers, little orphans, were raised by relatives. Riots broke out in the country, and their relatives fled, leaving them in a village with a Gentile [non-Jew] to look after them, for they have heard [news] about an army coming their way. They [the two brothers] remained there for a long time. And the[ir] relatives promised [to the non-Jew] to pay him for taking care [of the boys]. Eventually, the relatives returned and, when they wanted to pay the Gentile what they had promised, upon seeing them, he said to them: "One of your boys is dead, the other, behold, is right here standing in front of you." So, they gave to the Gentile some [money], took the boy and left. This boy was raised by them [his relatives], until he took a wife. He was married for one month . . . and at that time a certain man from our community, whose name was A, happened to arrive to that place. As people were sitting up with the deceased [for the wake], he began asking them questions in order to find out whether he [the deceased] had any brother or son. One of the sitters replied to him: "There were relatives, [namely] two brothers. At the time of emergency in . . . they took the captives from the city of Primut [most likely Przemyśl, in southeastern Poland, near the border with Ukraine]. At that time, those two [brothers] were still very young. They were taken, and when they led them out to the field, they were abandoned there, crying and moaning. Meanwhile, we saw a Canaanite [that is, a Pole] whom I [happened to] know. I begged him to take us into his house, including the boys. [And I said to him,] 'If heaven has will, have mercy upon us, and we will be redeemed. I will reward him accordingly and a payment for him will be prepared by me.' And [so] he did. [After that,] a miracle happened [when] I escaped [from my captivity] and went to the house of the Canaanite in order to inquire about the boys. He told me, 'One of the boys is dead, while the other, behold, is standing before you.' So, I took him and brought him to my house. After some time, we heard that Gentiles had brought a boy to Prague in order to sell him. He said he had been taken captive in the city of Primut. He was sold [in Prague] to a Jew from Javan [Byzantium]. Another [Jew] freed from slavery, who came from the land of Javan, said: 'I saw him [the boy bought in Prague] in Constantinople.'"

Kalonymos ben Sabbatai

And this is what Rabbi Kalonymos ben Sabbatai ha-Hazan of blessed memory in the land of Hagar ruled in the case of Abraham ben Hijja of Regensburg and his brother Jacob, who came from Rus' to the Jewish community [in Hungary] on the evening before Sabbath [Friday evening] with carts loaded by non-Jewish hired men and their Jewish companions. They remained on the other side [opposite bank, probably in Esztergom] of the River Dun [Danube], a little less than a mile away, because the wheel of one of the carts had broken. [So] they stopped there until they repaired [the cart]. And when they arrived in the community [of Esztergom], people had just left the synagogue on Sabbath night. And the community [of Jews in Esztergom] did not greet them and did not allow them to enter the[ir] synagogue until dawn.

Isaac ben Moses, Or zarua

I, the author of this text, arrived in the land of Hagar [Hungary] to Budn [Buda] and Ostrigos [Esztergom]. There are warm springs [there,] like those in Tiberias [in Palestine, to the west of Lake Genezaret,] and they sprout from the ground. I was asked if women could bathe in them [ritually], for they had doubts [about that matter], since they [the springs] were warm.

Questions: What aspects of economic and social life within Jewish communities do these texts reflect? What is the role of slavery? What do the last two texts tell us about the religious lives of the Jews in Hungary?

73. *RAZUMNIK*, A STUDY GUIDE

In Russian, Razumnik *means "clever, smart" and is the conventional title for a text described as apocryphal (of doubtful authenticity) despite its great popularity, as testified by more than forty manuscripts that contain copies of the text. The literary genre to which this text belongs is known in Greek as* eratopokriseis, *a series of questions and answers, the didactic value of which had long been recognized in Late Antique and Byzantine literature. Although surviving in miscellanies of a later date (fourteenth to eighteenth centuries), the* Razumnik *is most likely a product of early medieval Bulgarian culture and may be dated to the tenth century. The purpose of this text was definitely to teach, for both questions and answers are typically short, as if tailored for memorization.* Razumnik, *therefore, was an appropriate title for what seems to have been an instrument for testing the wit of the respondent as a suitable member of the Christian community. Some of the questions in fact suggest that the preferred instructional method was to make the student recognize that which he already knew. In other words, instead of being like a "For Dummies" book on the Creation, the* Razumnik *is more like flashcards, to be used by pairs of students taking turns in rehearsing questions and answers before the exam. The topics are arranged symmetrically, which suggests that, besides instruction and exercise, the* Razumnik *was intended to serve as a reference book on biblical history and chronology. The audience of this text was likely to have been the elite and literate social circles, primarily in monasteries. The* Razumnik *may well have been meant for the education of novices.*

Source: trans. K. Petkov, *The Voices of Medieval Bulgaria, Seventh-Fifteenth Century: The Records of a Bygone Culture* (Leiden: Brill, 2008), pp. 135–40.

Question: How did God create heaven and earth?
Answer: He took cream from the water, and it congealed, and [this is how] God created heaven and earth.

Q: And how did God make the sun and the moon?
A: After God made heaven and earth, he thought about how to make man, and how he will be born of him, and how he will be crucified and delivered to death. And when God thought about death, a tear dropped from the eye of the Lord, and that tear God called the sun. The moon, on its part, is [made] from God's throne. The stars are [made from] God's flesh and the angels are [made] of God's spirit and [from] fire. . . .

Q: Tell me what supports the earth.
A: Very high waters.

Q: What supports the water?
A: A large flat rock.

Q: And what supports the rock?
A: Four golden whales.

Q: And what supports the golden whales?
A: A river of fire.

Q: And what supports the fire?
A: An iron oak, planted before anything else, and its roots touch God's power. . . .

Q: How many are the human species?
A: Two—Adam and Eve.

Q: How did God make the devil?
A: When God made heaven and earth, God saw his shadow in the waters and said: "Come out, brother, and be with me." And it came out like a man and God gave it the name Samael.

Q: How did it fall from God?

A: When God was planting paradise and commanded it to be planted, Samael kept stealing everything. Then he went out, secretly, and heaped it all at another place. The Lord said: "You steal from me; you are banished!" And Samael came out and said: "Lord, bless what we planted. Let it be blessed, and I am here in the middle of it." Samael went to see the tree that he had stolen to plant. As he saw the tree, he became all black, and the tree banished him from paradise. Then God called him the devil. . . .

Q: What was the first language that Adam spoke?

A: Halleluiah, that is, in the Syrian language, "Praise God in heavens." . . .

Q: Who invented the Latin books?

A: Nunael, Umam, and Breitul.

Q: Who invented the Greek books?

A: Mercury.

Q: And who invented the Bulgarian books?

A: Cyril the Philosopher. . . .

Q: How large is earth?

A: The earth is as thick as the distance between the earth and the sky.

Q: Why is earth full of water?

A: Just as the body is full of blood, so the earth is full of water.

Q: How far is the sky from the earth?

A: As much as it is from east to west, so much it is from the earth to the sky. . . .

Q: How do the stars set?

A: The sky rotates, that is why they set. . . .

Q: From where did fire come?

A: An angel lit [it] up from the pupil of God and carried it to Adam.

Q: Why did God not make woman from clay, as he did man, but from his rib?

A: The angels requested this from God. The Lord said: "I did it so that they are dear to one another."

Questions: What are the main variations from Christian doctrine that one can recognize in the answers given in the text? How can one explain the answers given to the questions about Latin, Greek, and Bulgarian books? What can we learn about attitudes toward the devil from the Razumnik?

74. SOCIAL PROBLEMS IN THE *QUESTIONS OF KIRIK*

The Questions of Kirik *is a unique penitential (a book on the imposition of penance according to the canons of the church) of Orthodox Christianity. As such, it may rightly be considered as the most important source for the social history of medieval Rus', especially for the study of everyday life. The text is structured as 101 questions asked by a priest-monk named Kirik (most likely a deacon in the Antoniev Monastery in Novgorod, the author of a treatise on computus, entitled* Teaching on Numbers*), with twenty-four and twenty-eight more questions asked by two priests named Sava and Il'ia, respectively. The answers to all those questions are given by Bishop Nifont of Novgorod (1131–56). Many of the questions asked by the three priests have to do with the public and private lives of both churchmen and lay parishioners. Most prominent are family relations within urban communities, such as Novgorod. There is in fact an allusion to the use of birchbark letters, and Novgorod must have been the place where the Orthodox lived side by side with Catholics ("Latins"). Interdenominational relations prompted some of the questions addressed to Nifont, especially with regard to the conversion to Orthodox Christianity. Much attention is paid to such matters as motherhood, childhood, superstitions, and folk religion. Some of the questions addressed to Nifont seem to have originated with readers of apocrypha (religious writing not approved by the church, and not included in the canon of scripture). Sexual practices preoccupied both the clergy and the laity, and the bishop shows a surprisingly lenient attitude in many cases brought to his attention. He was conspicuously harsher in matters concerning the survival of pre-Christian practices. There is a greater penance for taking one's sick child to a sorcerer than for fornication. This text is dated to between c. 1140 and 1160, possibly to the late 1150s. The* Questions of Kirik *were very popular in subsequent centuries, as indicated by no fewer than thirty-six surviving manuscript copies, with the oldest dating to the late thirteenth century, and the most recent to the seventeenth century.*

Source: trans. F. Curta from *Kirik Novgorodec: uchenyi i myslitel'*, ed. V.V. Milkov and R.A. Simonov (Moscow: Krug', 2011), pp. 358, 363, 369, 371–72, and 383.

These are the questions of Kirik, who asked Nifont, the bishop of Novgorod, and others. God bless, father! . . .

10. If a Latin wants an Orthodox baptism. If there is anyone of the faith and with a Latin baptism who wants to come to us, let him go to church for seven days. You first give him a name and read four prayers every day, each repeated ten times. Give him neither meat nor milk. On the eighth day, let him wash and come to you, recite a prayer over him according to the custom, and put on him clean clothes, or let him put on his own clothes and put on him a baptismal vestment and a crown, and so anoint him with the holy myrrh, and give him a candle. And at liturgy, give him the Holy Communion, and treat him like a newly baptized [member of the congregation] for eight days, as the law commands. . . .

33. Where they offer crumbled bread, cheese, and honey to Rod and the Rozhanicy [pagan spirits or deities of the family], absolutely forbid that, for somewhere it is written: woe to those who drink to Rozhanica! . . .

39. And what they write about the heads of the three youths [in the fiery furnace, Dan. 3:19–90] and other prophets, this, he said, instead of a cowl, because that is what the Ephesians wore [Eph. 4:20–24].

40. The bishop monk Luka-Evdokim [Luka, bishop of Novgorod, 1035–c. 1059] told me this: "Prayers for the catechumens should be done in the following way: for a [Volga] Bulghar, a Cuman, or a Chud [Finnish-speaking inhabitant of northern Rus'], forty days of fasting before baptism, and let him go out of the church as a catechumen; for a Slav, eight days, and for a child, in a different way, it is good to do it within a few days. At baptism there are three to four prayers, which are to be read ten times; read them." . . .

69. He [Kirik] said to him [Nifont]: "Look, your eminence, some live in the open with concubines, even have children [by them], as if they were married, while others do it in secret with many [of their] slaves—which one is better?" "Neither one is good," he said.

Questions: How do you explain the varying number of prayers for catechumens? How were people of the Roman Catholic faith ("Latins") to be treated, if they expressed the desire to convert to Orthodox Christianity? What role did pre-Christian (pagan) rites play in the life of the population of northwestern Rus' during the High Middle Ages? Why was living in secret with one's slave not good, in the eyes of Nifont?

75. THE ASSASSINATION OF BISHOP STANISŁAW OF CRACOW

Duke Bolesław II (1058–79) continued his father's support for Benedictine abbeys in Poland and established the abbey in Lubiń (near Kościan, in west central Poland). In 1071, he nominated as new bishop of Cracow a young man named Stanisław, who was born in Sczcepanów (near Brzesko, in Lesser Poland) into a military family probably related to the Piasts. Stanisław was the canon of the previous bishop, Lambert Suła (1061–71), and his appointment by Duke Bolesław II was confirmed in 1072 by Pope Alexander II (1061–73). A few years later, Bolesław threw his support behind Pope Gregory VII in his struggle with Emperor Henry IV and was rewarded with a royal crown in 1076. However, his magnates organized a conspiracy, possibly headed by Bishop Stanisław of Cracow and the king's brother, Władysław Herman, who ruled at that time in Mazovia, most likely under Bolesław's supervision. In 1079, Bolesław ordered the execution of the bishop, which turned Stanisław into a martyr and a symbol of the independence of the church from the state. Since following the execution the body of the bishop was quartered, he later became a symbol for the reunification of the kingdom (in much the same way that the disparate parts of his body were miraculously put together again). Attitudes, however, varied. Gallus Anonymus, writing for Bolesław's nephew, calls Stanisław "a traitor bishop." In contrast, to Vincent Kadłubek, Bolesław was a "tyrant," for Vincent wrote for Casimir II, who by comparison was much more generous to the church. The assassination of Bishop Stanisław did not immediately turn him into a saint. In fact, the earliest evidence of a cult of Saint Stanisław cannot be dated before the early thirteenth century, when Vincent Kadłubek described the bishop's death as that of a martyr, followed by miraculous events. Stanisław was canonized in 1253 through a trial during which a collection of miracles was gathered in an official protocol now in the archives of the cathedral chapter in Cracow. Vincent of Kielcza (c. 1200–70) wrote a vita *(now known as* Vita minor, *from which a fragment is translated below) shortly before 1250, no doubt in preparation for the canonization process. He wrote a second* vita, *now called* Vita maior, *after the canonization (at some point between 1257 and 1261), at the specific request of Prandota, bishop of Cracow (1242–66), as an official biography of the saint for liturgical purposes. In the preamble of the* Vita maior, *Vincent presents himself as a Dominican friar, but he may have joined the mendicant order later in life. At any rate, in 1222 he was the chaplain of Bishop Iwo Odrowąż of Cracow (1218–29), then a cathedral canon between 1227 and 1235. Vincent traveled to Italy, the first time in 1237 as a member of an episcopal delegation sent to bring back the body of Bishop Iwo Odrowąż, who had died in Modena in 1229. The* Vita maior *may have been written in the Dominican priory in Racibórz; Vincent also authored a patriotic poem entitled "Rejoice, Mother Poland," as well as several hymns. His poetic skills may be recognized also in the fragment translated below. The* Vita minor, *which was written some 170 years after the events narrated therein, has no historical value. Vincent relied on earlier sources, especially on his namesake, Vincent Kadłubek, and added material from legends that circulated in the mid-thirteenth century. However, his is one of the most important sources for the cult of Saint Stanisław, for it shows a remarkable transformation of the bishop into a towering symbol of the Polish Church and state.*

Source: trans. F. Curta from "Vita Sancti Stanislai Cracoviensis episcopi (Vita minor)," in *Monumenta Poloniae Historica* 4, ed. W. Kętrzyński (Lwów: Akademii Umiejętności w Krakowie, 1884), pp. 257, 260–61, 262–63, and 279–81.

7. At that time, he [Bishop Stanisław of Cracow] often called for the correction of King Bolesław [II], who then ruled Poland and whose life was wicked. With paternal zeal, he asked him to repent, as if he were the prodigal son. But because the king was incorrigible, on his part the bishop had to endure mortal hatred and persecution for his righteousness. The holy man therefore avoided talking or staying with him [the king] under the same roof, so as not to give the impression that he was agreeing to his unjust laws and the oppression of the poor, [to which] he was witness. He also shuddered at the wicked way of

looting, grazing the meadows, and [harvesting] the corn of his subjects, which the king and his henchmen treated as the common law of the land. For such and similar reasons, he avoided their councils and any relations with them, and instead spent much time in his church, diligently and early performing God's service, devoutly and frequently celebrating the sacraments of Christ, whenever he could. He devoted himself most willingly to prayer, to reading and contemplation, and from the bottom of his heart he prayed to God for the people that had been entrusted to him. . . .

11. One day, Bishop Stanisław, wishing to increase the income of the church of Cracow, bought a certain village located on the bank of the [River] Vistula, called Piotrawin, from a count [named] Peter, [in exchange] for a certain amount of money, paid in silver according to the applicable weight. While Peter was still alive, the bishop held the village for several years as the rightful owner. However, when Peter left this world and was buried within the territory of that village, his brothers and closest kin, who were the legitimate heirs of the deceased, began to demand that the bishop return their hereditary property. And already King Bolesław disliked the bishop, because the saint had accused him of his crimes, but the venom in the king's heart had not [yet] raged against him. The brothers and relatives of the deceased, therefore, having waited for more than two years for the king's anger to flare up hotter, took advantage of the opportune moment. They first requested that the bishop return [what] was [rightfully] his, and if he refused to give up his right, they would take him to royal court, [to be judged] by the king and his princes. What more? The bishop stood before the king, a complaint was lodged, both sides were heard, the subject of the dispute was resolved, the verdict was considered, and finally, to put an end to the altercation, the decision of the king and of the judge was that the bishop had to give up his right to the property, if he [was not able to] present the person who had sold the village to him, to produce the sale contract, or to call on appropriate and reliable witnesses. When the decision of the king and the judges was announced, Bishop Stanisław read a list of witnesses publicly according to the custom. When the opposing party agreed with them, the bishop was ordered to come with the witnesses to the next meeting in Piotrawin. The deadline for the bishop to testify was approaching, but they [the witnesses], fearing the tyrant, dared neither to attend the trial, nor to bear witness to the truth.

12. The servant of God Stanisław, seeing that he lacked human help, and not wanting to lose the property of his church, sought refuge in God's protection as if in a fortified tower. But he came to the meeting, at the scheduled date, and before the council, he said [the following] to the king: "O worthy king, and all you righteous Polish princes! Since there is no truth in this land, give me a delay of three more days, and I will bring you the one who sold the village [to

me], to testify as to whose inheritance that is." Some people heeded the bishop's words, others were surprised, and many considered them mad nonsense. Overall, however, it was agreed to permit him a delay of another three days. . . .

13. Meanwhile, the third day came and the bishop went to the church in Piotrawin to celebrate Mass there, while the king, princes, and a great crowd of people gathered in the neighborhood. Bishop Stanisław, having finished the rites, as he stood in pontifical vestments and in full [attire], went out of the door of the church, [to the place near the church] where Peter's body had been buried, and ordered the tomb to be dug up and opened. Then he knelt [next to the tomb] and with tears said to the Lord: "Have mercy on us, Almighty God, who reigns over the living and the dead. . . . Call, we pray, your servant Peter from the dream of death [back] to life, raise him from the wretched dust after three years, to bear witness to the truth, for you have raised Lazarus from the tomb . . . Peter, arise, you who sleep, and come back from the dead. . . . Get up," he said, "and step out!" . . . And immediately Peter rose to his feet, and the bishop shook his hand, helped him come out of the tomb, and led him into the circle of the council. . . .

32. And when the bishop of Cracow, Saint Stanisław could not use a fatherly voice to keep him [the king] from his cruelty, first he rebuked him, threatening him with the destruction of the kingdom, and then hung a curse sword over him [placed an anathema on him] and forbade him to enter the church. And he, like a bent and dry branch that is easier to break than to straighten, fell into an even greater frenzy and persisted in stubbornness. And here, when Saint Bishop Stanisław was performing God's service in the church of St-Michael on Skałka [an outcrop in Cracow on top of which the church was located] and was praying for protection from the saints, he [the king], being in front of the altar, while the holy rites were performed, with no respect for the dignity of the state, place, or moment, and not fearing the saints or the divine majesty, ordered that the bishop be seized and taken away from the altar. But when the cruel perpetrators and henchmen tried to pounce on him [Stanisław], they fell so many times, and that many times repentance struck them. And the third time they fell to the ground, they were completely powerless. And the tyrant, cursing them, exclaimed: "O you degenerate cowards, can you not seize one priest?" Then he threw himself like Doeg the Edomite [1 Sam. 22:18–19], raising his criminal hand upon God's anointed, he severed the bridegroom from the bride's womb, the shepherd from his flock, and killed the father in the embrace of the daughter, and the son almost in the womb of his mother. What a pathetic sight it is! The wicked cruelly struck the saint with a sword, the criminal [killed] the pious, the robber of saints [finished] the bishop, and inflicting terrible wounds on him, with the sword stained with blood, he made him a victim of Christ. So the righteous die at the hands of the wicked, so the good shepherd lays down his life for his flock, so the seed of the grain is thrown into the ground to grow into a lush ear [of

corn], and after throwing away the straw, it enters the Lord's barn; so the soldier of Christ, so the athlete of God fought for justice, indeed like Naboth [1 Kings 21:1–16] he dies in his field, lest the vineyard becomes a vegetable garden. The voice of the blood poured out of heaven, the earth moist with a bloody rose is not silent [anymore], and the murderer's sword itself, stained with the blood of a martyr, demands vengeance on the perpetrator of the crime committed. Such a cruel man killed an innocent with his hands, making him a glorious martyr, [then] tears him into pieces, chopping individual members still and scattering [them] to the wild animals and birds of the sky in all parts of the world, as if individual particles should be punished, and as if he thought that in this way, he would remove the memory and his name from the world.

Questions: How did relations between the king and the bishop of Cracow affect the violence against the latter? How does Vincent of Kielcza feel about the events he describes? Why do you think he insisted upon the dismemberment of Saint Stanisław's body, as he was writing in the thirteenth century?

76. STEPHEN NEMANJA ESTABLISHES THE HILANDAR MONASTERY

After abdicating in favor of his son in 1196, the grand župan *of Serbia, Stephen Nemanja (1166–96) took monastic vows and withdrew to Studenica, a monastery built in central-western Serbia during his reign. Two years later, he moved to Mount Athos in order to join his other son, now named Sava, who was already there as a monk. In 1198, father and son established a new monastery on the Holy Mountain, in favor of which Stephen Nemanja (now the monk Simeon) issued a charter, as if he were still the grand* župan. *The charter lists with great precision the endowment that Simeon made to the new monastery. The original document was written on parchment and was in the archive of the Hilandar Monastery until some point in the late nineteenth century, when it was moved to Belgrade. It disappeared from Belgrade at the time of the Austro-Hungarian occupation of Serbia during World War I (1915–18). It is now known only from photographs of the original.*

Source: trans. F. Curta from A.V. Solovjev, *Odabrani spomenici srpskog prava: od XII do kraja XV veka* (Belgrade: G. Kon, 1926), pp. 11–14.

In the beginning God created the heaven and earth and men on it and gave his blessing to them. And he gave them power over his entire creation. And some of them he made emperors, others princes or rulers. And he left his flocks to pasture, keeping them from all kinds of evil assaulting them. Thus, my brothers, merciful God made the Greeks emperors and the Hungarians kings. And he set each nation apart, giving to it laws and establishing customs, and gave it rulers, and separated it [from others] by his wisdom. After that, out of his great and infinite mercy and his love for humankind, he granted for our great-grandfathers and our grandfathers to rule over the Serbian land. And this God did to make humans better, not to destroy them.

And he established me as the great *župan*, who received the name Stephen Nemanja at baptism. And I got what was mine by inheritance, and even more, and with the help of God and through the wisdom that God bestowed upon me, I made it stronger. And I built up my patrimony, which had been destroyed, and I gained Zeta with its towns in the land by the [Adriatic] sea. And from Arbanases [the northern part of present-day Albania] I took Pilot; from the Greek land, I took Lab [present-day Kosovo] with Lipljan [Lipjan, in central Kosovo], Globočica [in southwestern Kosovo], Reke, Zagrlata [the mountainous region in southern Serbia], Levče, Belica, and Lepenica [regions in central Serbia]. And all those lands I have obtained with the help of God and through my own efforts. And with God's assistance peace now reigns over my realm. . . .

. . . I left my beloved son, Stephen, great *župan* and *sebastokrator* [the ruler's son; Stephen the First-Crowned was king of Serbia between 1217 and 1228] on my throne, to take over the realm granted to me by Christ. [He is the] son-in-law of *kyr* Alexios, whom God crowned emperor of the Greeks [Alexios III Angelos, 1195–1203]. And even though I was [now] the unworthy servant of Christ named Simeon the monk, and I gave him [his son Stephen] all the blessings, just like Isaac had blessed his son Jacob, in order to assist him in all blessed deeds during his rule, and [to remind him] to be merciful to Christians and the churches and to those who serve in them, and not to be ashamed in front of the Creator and his Lord. . . . And I moved out of my fatherland and went to the Holy Mountain, and found there an earlier monastery named Hilandar, [which was dedicated to] the Presentation of the Mother of God. Of [that monastery] not a single stone [was left] upon another [Matt. 24:2], as it had long been destroyed. And in my old age I began working hard [to restore it], and with the help of my son, Stephen the great *župan*, God made me the *ktetor* [(re)founder]. Through the intercession of the Mother of God, I asked and obtained the restoration of pieces of this monastery, which had been destroyed. I asked and renewed it by the will of the Mother of God. From the emperor [Alexios III Angelos], I obtained Parici in Prizren, and I gave to the monastery on the Holy Mountain of the Mother of God in Melee [the region on Mount Athos where Hilandar is located] [the following] villages: Neprobišta [now Napërbisht, north of Prizren, Kosovo], Momuša [now Mamuşa, near Prizren, Kosovo], Slamodrava [now Samadraxhëter, near Prizren, Kosovo], Retivla [now Retimlja, near Rahovec, in the district of Gjakova, Kosovo], Trnje [now Tërrnje, near Prizren, Kosovo], Retivštica, Trnovac, Hoča and the other Hoča [now Hoçë e Madhe, near Orahovac, in the district of Gjakova, Kosovo], as well as the market there.

And I planted two vineyards there, as well as four beehives—one in Trpeze [now Trpeza, near Prizren, Kosovo], the second in Dabšore, the third one in Goliševo, and the fourth in Parici. And each beehive has two men. And [I gave also to the monastery the] Bogača Mountain [that is, pastureland on the Bogača Mountain, about eleven miles to the northwest of Peja, in western Kosovo]. And from the Vlachs, [I gave to the monastery] the jurisdictions of Rad and Djuradj. And altogether there are 170 Vlachs. And I gave cattle as many as I could, and from Zeta, mares and thirty *spuds* [about eighty-five pounds] of salt.

And if any men of the monastery [dare to] run away, or if [some] Vlach [runs away] either to the great *župan* or to someone else, they must be returned. And if one of the men of the *župan* joins the men of the monastery, he must go back. And I granted to the monastery on the Holy Mountain all of those [things], and established that my children, grandsons, cousins, or anybody else could not claim them. If somebody alters this [arrangement], may God judge him and have the holy Mother of God, as well as me, Simeon the sinner, at the Last Judgment.

Cross of Simeon and signature.

Questions: What motivated Stephen Nemanja to establish Hilandar? Why did he tell the story of his life in this charter? How did he view the monastic communities on Mount Athos? What is his attitude toward his own family? Compare the mention of the Vlachs here to that in Kekaumenos's Strategikon *(Doc. 33).*

77. SAINT SAVA'S SECOND TRIP TO THE HOLY LAND

Shortly after his death in 1236, Archbishop Sava of Serbia was buried in Bulgaria, but his body was later translated and reburied in the monastery church in Mileševa (near Prijepolje, in western Serbia), which had just been built by Sava's nephew, King Vladislav (1234–43). No evidence exists of the cult of Saint Sava until 1250. That he was venerated as a saint is proven, however, by the first vita *written in 1253 by Domentijan. The author was a monk at the monastery of Hilandar, which had been established by Sava and his father Simeon (Stephen Nemanja) in 1198. Domentijan was most likely Sava's disciple, and he also wrote the third (and latest)* vita *of Saint Simeon. Despite relying heavily on his own eyewitness experience of many of the events narrated, as well as on his conversations with Sava, Domentijan's work is a sophisticated literary construction, which deploys a panoply of rhetorical strategies to enhance the prominence of the central figure and his saintly character. In fact, the author consistently refers to his hero, Sava, as saint, an indication that, without declaring it, the* vita *was meant to solidify an already existing cult. But not all the details in the narrative, no matter how accurate they may appear, should be regarded as credible from a historical point of view. For example, while it is quite possible that Sava met al-Kamil in Cairo, it is very unlikely that he traveled all the way to Baghdad ("Great Babylon"). His visit at the site of the fiery furnace in which the three youths—Hanania, Mishael, and Azariah—were thrown by Nebuchadnezzar II, king of Babylon (Dan. 3:8–24), as well as his meeting with "the metropolitan bishop of the Christians in Babylon" (possibly Sabrisho V ibn al-Masihi, patriarch of the Church of the East, 1226–56) were most likely invented to create an aura of sanctity and a sacred landscape for Saint Sava's last trip to the Holy Land. The same is true for Sava's encounter with al-Mustansir, the penultimate Abbasid caliph (1226–42). Domentijan was correct to call the latter "the Turkish caliph," as al-Mustansir's great-grandmother had indeed been a slave concubine of Turkish origin. Despite the accuracy of such details, however, it is likely that Domentijan employed them rhetorically to enhance the veracity of his embellished account of Sava's trip.*

Source: trans. F. Curta from L. Juhas-Georgievska, *Stefan Prvovenčani, Domentijan, Teodosije* (Novi Sad: Izdavački centar Matice srpske, 2012), pp. 163–179; rev.

The saint [Sava], noting that his people prospered under a good administration, with rich and decorated churches, wanted to leave his homeland one more time, in order to finish his life in a foreign country. So, he invited the king [Vladislav] and in the presence of bishops, lords, and all churchmen assembled, he left to them his people, and asked them to take care of them, of religion, the church, and morals. After those instructions, he declared that he would be replaced as archbishop by one of his disciples [named] Arsenije [archbishop of Serbia, 1233–63], whom he had himself chosen, established, and appointed archbishop. Having done all of that, the saint told everyone words of peace and gave them the blessings, and left with some of his disciples, taking much gold and silver for the travel expenses, [as well as] for the charity to be distributed to the holy places [that is, churches in the Holy Land] and to the poor. Reaching the western sea, in Dioclea [present-day Montenegro], he boarded a ship prepared in advance [probably in Ragusa, now Dubrovnik, in southern Croatia]. The news of his departure for Jerusalem with so many riches having spread, some pirates who were roaming in that sea, embarking on their light boats, hurried to ambush [him] in a bay, where they were waiting for a good moment to plunder. But even in those circumstances, God came to his rescue and protection: fog covered the bay, and he passed without [the pirates] noticing [him]. As the fog disappeared, the pirates saw from a distance the saint's ship already entering the harbor. First angry and upset at their failure, and having pondered it, the ruffians recognized in him a man of God. So they went to him, confessed their ill intent, and asked for his forgiveness. The saint gave them something to eat, as well as some gifts of value, and after blessing and instructing them by means of a sermon most appropriate for the occasion, he let them go. Such perfect kindness astonished them to such a degree that they gave thanks to God for having prevented them from committing such a[n act of] sacrilege. Repenting for their sin, they went, each one to his own place. The saint continued his trip to Jerusalem, through an awful chasm. The storm began instantly, and the waves lifted the ship with such violence that the travelers rushed to the saint, crying: "Have mercy on us, O holy father, we are [all] going to die, unless you save us with your prayers!" Saint Sava stretched out his arm, made the sign of the cross in the air, and said: "In the name of our Lord Jesus Christ, I say to you, winds and sea, stop your fury and settle down!" At this last word, the wind stopped, and the calm sea returned. Those who witnessed this miracle, astonished and afraid, glorified God and his chosen man. With God's help, they arrived shortly after that to Acre, whence the saint took the road by land to Jerusalem. He was honorably and happily received there by Patriarch Athanasios [II, Greek Orthodox patriarch of Jerusalem, c. 1231–44].

When he entered the great church [of the Resurrection], he venerated the Holy Sepulcher as well as the holy places outside and inside the city [of Jerusalem], covering them in kisses [kissing icons or relics is a form of veneration among Orthodox Christians]. The patriarch blessed him and gave him guides to go to Alexandria, where the metropolitan [Nicholas I, Greek Orthodox patriarch of Alexandria, 1210–43] came out to meet him and introduced him to [his] city with great honor. They spent many days enjoying the sweetness of their pious conversations. Taking advantage of this great opportunity, they visited the churches and monasteries of the environs. After that, the saint accepted the offer of the patriarch to give him guides to visit the desert [monasteries] in the Mareot[is, a brackish lake in northern Egypt near Alexandria], Libya [generic name for the entire region to the west of the River Nile], Thebais [the region of Upper Egypt in which some of the earliest monasteries were organized in the fourth century by Saint Pachomius], Nitria [the desert region in northwestern Egypt, where monasticism was first established by Saint Ammon], and others. He [Sava] went to all, visiting the holy fasting fathers [of the desert], who appeared to him as shining with virtues as suns of the religious world. From there, he turned back in the direction of Jerusalem. On his way, he went down to Kalomna [now al-Muharraq, thirty-seven miles south of Asyut, in central Egypt] at the monastery of the Holy Virgin built on the very spot where she stopped with child Jesus and her husband, Joseph, as they were fleeing [to Egypt] to escape Herod. From Jerusalem, following a long and difficult route, our father entered the great Babylon [Baghdad], where the sultan, the Turkish caliph [al-Mustansir], welcomed him with honors in a house prepared for him and furnished with all that was necessary. Our saint first went to the church of the Three Youth in the Furnace, where he was welcomed with great respect by the metropolitan bishop of the Christians [possibly Sabrisho V ibn al-Masihi]. As for the sultan, he admired the courage of the old saint, coming from so far away with so much trouble, [only] to see Babylon. And he bestowed upon him everything that was necessary for his return and gave him guides [whom he instructed] to accompany him with all [due] respect to the sultan of Egypt [al-Kamil, the fourth Ayyubid sultan of Egypt, 1218–38] and to bring news about the saint's well-being [upon their return to Babylon]. The Egyptian sultan received Sava with honors: he accommodated him at his own expense and arranged for him to have a peaceful and agreeable sojourn. [After that,] he ordered his own officers to escort him to Mount Sinai, and to make sure that he would have everything that he needed. Upon his arrival at Mount Sinai, at the monastery of the Burning Bush and of Saint Catherine, the great martyr, he venerated and covered in kisses the relics of the saint and the place where the bush burned without being consumed. On top of Mount Sinai, where God talked to Moses, our saint prayed and wept for a long time. During Lent [in that year], which Saint Sava spent on [Mount] Sinai, he went up to the peak every Saturday, and did not return to the monastery but after saying the entire liturgy. He gave away much charity. Back in Jerusalem again, he departed for great Antioch, where the patriarch [Dorotheos, Greek Orthodox patriarch of Antioch, 1219–45] received him reverently. He remained [in Antioch] for a while, to get a rest. Our saint made rich donations to the church, to the patriarch, and to all churchmen. After that, he departed for Great Armenia [the Armenian Kingdom of Cilicia, at that time under the rule of King Hethum, 1226–70], looking everywhere for relics of saints that he could take back to his country.

Questions: How does Domentijan describe Saint Sava during the trip to the Holy Land? What is he trying to accomplish with that description? Why did Saint Sava visit some of the sites in the Holy Land, but not others? Judging by the evidence of this text, does Domentijan describe him as a simple pilgrim? What reasons might there be for insisting upon this pilgrimage to the Holy Land?

78. THE SYNOD OF 1211 CONDEMNS THE BOGOMILS

To distract attention from his military and political failures, the Bulgarian emperor Boril (1207–18) summoned in 1211 a church synod (assembly) in Tărnovo, the main purpose of which was to condemn the Bogomils. He wanted to pose as a Byzantine emperor and guardian of Orthodoxy and, as such, he seems to have led the debate in person. The final document of that synod, called synodikon, *placed an anathema (curse) on the priest Bogomil and his followers. However, the show trial of "those who had sown impiety" did not bring any substantive measures and no changes are known to have taken place in the organization of the Bulgarian church as a consequence of the 1211 synod. The translation below is not from the original document, which did not survive, but from the text rewritten under John II Asen in 1235 and preserved in two versions, with additions and changes made repeatedly until the late fifteenth century. That text is in fact a collec-*

tion of edicts adopted at previous church councils, to which the assembly of 1211 added a number of edicts concerning Bogomilism, all placing an anathema on the heresy and its supporters. A triple anathema was placed on Bogomil's disciples, about whom nothing else is otherwise known, but also on a certain dedec *("father") of Sredec named Peter of Cappadocia, who was most likely a Bogomil leader and who lived in the twelfth or early thirteenth century. According to the* synodikon, *Emperor Boril "sent out orders throughout his kingdom" for the Bogomils to be "gathered in sheaves like some kind of weeds." The heretics were put under guard, with the most recalcitrant being "given over to different punishments and sent into exile." However, nothing is known from sources pertaining to thirteenth-century Bulgaria that could be compared with the show trial of a Byzantine doctor named Basil, who was burned at the stake in Constantinople a century prior to the 1211 synod in Tărnovo. Nonetheless, some believe that the Bogomils persecuted in Bulgaria by Boril fled to Serbia, where a decade later Archbishop Sava summoned an assembly at the monastery of Žiča to persuade them back into the Orthodox Church. However, since there is no mention of the exact nature of the heresy that Sava combatted, the connection between the two assemblies taking place at a distance of ten years in Bulgaria and Serbia, respectively, is tentative at best.*

Source: trans. M. Paneva from I. Bozhilov, A.-M. Totomanova, and I. Biliarski, *Borilov sinodik: Izdanie i prevod* (Sofia: OOD, 2010), pp. 344–45, 349, and 353.

Because our most cunning enemy disseminated the Manichaean heresy throughout the Bulgarian land, mixing it with the Messalian, on those with whom this heresy originated, anathema! On the priest Bogomil who adopted the Manichaean heresy under the Bulgarian emperor Peter, adding that Christ, our God, was born of the Mother of God and ever-virgin Mary only as an illusion, and as an illusion he was crucified and rose the divine flesh with him, leaving it in the air; on his past and present disciples, who claim this and called themselves "apostles," anathema! And on all who maintain this heresy and their customs, and their nocturnal gatherings and mysteries, and their wicked teachings, as well as on those who associate with them, anathema! Upon those who love them and consciously eat and drink with them and accept gifts from them as like-believers, anathema! Upon those who, on the twenty-fourth day of the month of June, on [the feast of] the nativity of Saint John the Baptist, make spells and pick fruit and whatever foul mysteries they perform during that night, comparable to pagan rituals, anathema! Upon those who call Satan the creator of the visible things and master of rain, hail, and of everything that comes out of the ground, anathema! Upon those who say that Satan created Adam and Eve, anathema! Upon those who reject Moses the God-seer and Elijah the Tishbite and the rest of the holy prophets and patriarchs and say that their sacred writings come not from God, but from Satan, and that these men were prompted by him [Satan] to write what they wrote; and what they have said about Christ they have said involuntarily under duress. And therefore, on the Bogomils, who reject all the books of the Old Testament, and all the holy prophets, who shone forth in it, anathema! Upon those who say that the woman conceives in her womb through the agency of Satan and that Satan dwells there continuously until the delivery of the baby, and that the holy men cannot drive him out by baptism, but only by prayer and fasting, on those who say such things, anathema! Upon those who calumniate John the Baptist saying that both he and baptism with water come from Satan and who reject baptism with water and baptize without water, only saying "Our Father" once, anathema! Upon those who turn away from all divine singing in the holy churches and the very house of God, namely the church, and who say that one should only sing the "Our Father" wherever one might be, anathema! Upon those who reject and revile the holy and sacred liturgy and the entire saintly order, saying that these have been invented by Satan, anathema! Upon those who reject and revile the Communion with the holy body of our Lord Jesus Christ, as they reject the mystery of Jesus Christ, performed by him for our salvation, anathema! Upon those who reject the veneration of the holy and life-giving cross, and the holy and sacred icons, anathema! Upon those who accept any of these heretics in the holy church of God before they have confessed and cursed this entire heresy, as it has been said, anathema! Upon Basil the Physician, who sowed the thrice-cursed Bogomil heresy in Constantinople under the Orthodox emperor Alexios Komnenos, anathema! . . . Upon Peter of Cappadocia, the elder of Sredec [present-day Sofia, in Bulgaria], on Luke, and Mandeleus of Rodobol, anathema thrice! . . . Upon the thrice-cursed Bogomil and to his disciple Michael, and on Theodore and Dobre, on Stephen and Basil, and Peter, and on the rest of his disciples and adherents, who speak falsely that the incarnation of Christ was an illusion and that he had not accepted his flesh from our holy and immaculate lady, the Mother of God, on all of them, anathema!

Questions: How does the description of the Bogomil beliefs in the synodikon *compare to that of Cosmas the Presbyter (Doc. 62)? What do the beliefs and practices attributed to the heretics tell us about the society of early thirteenth-century Bulgaria and its values? Based on the evidence of the* synodikon*, how could one identify a Bogomil? How do you explain the mention of the heresy in Constantinople, the capital of the Byzantine Empire?*

CHAPTER NINE

CRUSADES

Figure 9.1 Hermann of Salza. Grand master of the Order of St-Mary (1210–39). Drawing from Christoph Hartknoch.

79. THE ARMY OF THE FIRST CRUSADE IN HUNGARY

The History of the Journey to Jerusalem *is the longest and most detailed account of the First Crusade. Its author is known by the name Albert (or Adalbert). Out of thirteen extant manuscripts, this name appears in only some of them, all dated to the thirteenth century. That he was indeed from Aachen (in western Germany, at the border with Belgium and the Netherlands) is beyond doubt, given his knowledge of the hinterland of the town and of its people. The first six books of the* History *were written a short time after 1100, after the events narrated therein. Albert used mostly oral sources, namely testimonies of participants. He was certainly not aware of any of the other three surviving accounts of the First Crusade—the anonymous* Deeds of the Franks (Gesta Francorum), *and the chronicles of Raymond of Aguilers and Fulcher of Chartres. However, his* History *later became one of the main sources used by William of Tyre for his narrative of the First Crusade. The account of the crusaders' passage through Hungary has been recently described as a carefully crafted narrative mirroring later events, for the lessons learned in Hungary could be useful for the entire crusade. Albert definitely saw the crusaders' tribulations in Hungary as being God's punishment for their sins and for their massacre of the Jews in the Rhineland. He put in King Coloman's mouth a speech for the envoys of the crusaders, in which he blamed the pilgrims for having been obsessed with material goods rather than with going to Jerusalem, and for acting with pride and tyrannical intentions. This is without doubt Albert's, not Coloman's, interpretation of events.*

Source: trans. S.B. Edgington, *Albert of Aachen: Historia Ierosolimitana, History of the Journey to Jerusalem* (Oxford: Clarendon Press, 2007), pp. 61, 63, 65, 67, 69, and 71.

2.1. Therefore, after Peter the Hermit's departure and the very great disaster which befell his army; and then a short while after the cruel massacre of the army led by Gottschalk the priest, indeed, after the misfortune of Hartmann, a count from Swabia, of Emicho and the other brave men and princes from the land of Gaul, namely Drogo of Nesle, Clarembald of Vendeuil; after the obliteration of his army which was cruelly carried out in the kingdom of Hungary at the gate of Meseburch [Moson, now in Mosonmagyaróvár, in the northwestern part of present-day Hungary, at the border with Slovakia and Austria]: after all this, Godfrey, duke of the realm of Lotharingia [1089–96, future ruler of Jerusalem as Godfrey of Bouillon, 1099–1100], a most noble man, and his brother Baldwin, who share the same mother, Warner [count] of Grez[-Doiceau, now in the Walloon Brabant province of Belgium], a relative of that same duke, Baldwin of Bourcq [future count of Edessa, 1100–18; king of Jerusalem, 1118–31] likewise, Rainald [III, episcopal] count of Toul, Peter [count of Astenois] his brother also, Dodo [lord] of Cons[-la-Grandville, today in the Meurthe-et-Moselle department of France], Henry of Esch[-sur-Sûre, now in northwestern Luxembourg] and his brother Godfrey, very brave knights and very illustrious princes, were making the journey by the direct route to Jerusalem in the middle of August of the same year [1096]. . . .

2.2. At last, after a lot of destructive talk as to what they should do first, and what would be a safe and wise way to investigate the truth of the affair and the cruelty the Hungarians had shown toward their fellow Christians when they had dealt with them on many occasions, it seemed to everyone a sensible plan that they should not send in advance any of the most renowned and chief men for an inquiry into the abominable murder and wickedness, except Godfrey of Esch, because he was known to Coloman, the king of the country [king of Hungary, 1095–1116], having been sent a long while before this journey on an embassy from Duke Godfrey [of Bouillon] to this same king of Hungary. They sent along with him twelve others chosen from the duke's household, Baldric [Godfrey's seneschal], Stabelo [Godfrey's chamberlain], and others whose names are not known, to disclose the mission of so many nobles in this way: "To King Coloman of Hungary, Godfrey, duke of Lotharingia, and the other nobles of Gaul [France] send greetings and every token of goodwill in Christ. Our lords and princes wonder why, since you are of the Christian faith, you have destroyed the army of the living God with such a cruel martyrdom, and you have in fact forbidden them to pass through your land and kingdom and have afflicted them with various false accusations. Because of this they are now shaken by fear and doubt, and they have decided to delay at Tulln [an der Donau, near Vienna, in Austria] until they learn from the mouth of the king why so cruel a deed was perpetrated by Christians persecuting Christians."

3. The king replied with all his assembled men listening, "We are not persecutors of Christians, but whatever cruelty we have displayed toward them, or death we have inflicted on them, we carried out because we were compelled by an overwhelming necessity. For in the first place when we prepared all good things for your army which Peter the Hermit assembled, a license was granted to buy goods in fair weight and measure, and we organized a peaceful passage for them through the land of Hungary. They returned evil to us for good [Gen. 44:4]; not only stealing gold and silver, horses and mules and herds from our territory, but even destroying our cities and castles and killing about four thousand of our men; they plundered possessions and clothes. After Peter's company unjustly committed these quite intolerable outrages against us, Gottschalk's army followed, and the one that was destroyed, which was put to flight and which you met, laid siege to the castle and fortification of our realm at Meseburch, wanting in their pride and in the tyranny of their strength [Eph. 6:10] to enter our domain to punish and drive us out, from whom with God's help we were only just protected." However, while the king was replying to these things, he ordered those same envoys of the duke to be entertained with honor in his own

palace in a place called Pannonhalma [the Benedictine abbey of Pannonhalma, near Győr, which was founded by Duke Géza in 996], where everything they needed was served to them lavishly at the king's very table for eight days. After those eight days the king, who had taken counsel with envoys from his nobles about the duke's embassy, sent back the envoys with envoys from his own court to carry the king's replies to the duke and the army commanders in this manner: "King Coloman sends greetings and unfeigned love to Duke Godfrey and all his fellow Christians. We have heard this about you: that you are a powerful man and prince in your land, and found to be trustworthy by all who have known you, and because you are always careful of your good reputation I have now chosen to see and acknowledge you, and accordingly I have come to a decision, that you may come down to us at our castle of Sopron [near Szombathely, in western Hungary, at the border with Austria] with no thought of any danger, and if our armies stay on either side of the marsh [at the southern end of Lake Neusiedler] we may safely hold a conference about all the things you have asked us about, and of which you suppose us guilty."

4. . . . He [Duke Godfrey] found the king there and greeted him in a friendly way and kissed him with humble devotion. Then they held various conversations between them about friendship and the reconciliation of Christians, until this consideration of peace and love made such good progress that the duke was convinced of the king's good faith, and he took twelve from the three hundred with whom he had come into Pannonhalma and the land of Hungary to see the king. . . . Therefore, the duke entered Pannonhalma, and he was received with honor by the king himself and his nobles. Everything necessary was served to them with goodwill and in quantity from the court and table of the king, as was fitting for such an illustrious prince. Then for eight days the king held many meetings of his men, who had also flocked to see such a very renowned prince, seeking to find a plan by which such an innumerable army, heavily armed, could be allowed in trust and confidence into his country, and yet his kingdom and his people's possessions be safe. At last, a plan was devised and was announced to the duke, that unless eminent men and leaders of the army were given as hostages, no passage would be granted to him and his men, so that the king would not lose his lands and kingdom, if some pretext arose, to the strength of such an infinite mass of people. When he heard this the duke acceded to the wishes of the king in all things and did not refuse to give the hostages he sought, making the condition, however, that after this the army of pilgrims [that is, crusaders]—in future as well as now—might pass through his land without any hindrance and obtain peacefully the necessities of life. Without delay, the king sealed a treaty with the duke, all the nobles of his kingdom sealed it also with a sworn oath not to harm the pilgrims further as they passed through. So, with all these matters settled thus on both sides in good faith, the king, on the advice

of his men, asked that Baldwin, the duke's own brother, should be a hostage, and his wife [Godechilde] as well, and all his household. . . .

6. Therefore, now that so illustrious a prince had become a hostage and the king had returned with him into Pannonhalma, all the army was allowed over the bridge across the marsh in accordance with the command and consent of the king, and they set up camp on the River Hantax [not identified]. When the camp had been established, and everyone settled down in their quarters, Duke Godfrey appointed heralds to announce throughout each and every household and tent that no one, under pain of death, should touch anything, or carry off anything by violence in the kingdom of Hungary, or cause any insurrection, but should purchase everything at a fair price. In the same way, the king also ordered it to be announced throughout the whole kingdom that the army might procure a plentiful supply of necessities: bread, wine, corn, and barley, beasts of the field, birds of the sky [Jer. 16:4]. And it was ordained, on pain of death, that the Hungarians should not burden the army by selling at an unjust price, or upset them, but rather they should offer all things for sale to them on lenient terms. So it was that the duke and the people crossed the kingdom of Hungary, every day in peace and quiet, buying in fair and just measure, and they arrived at the River Drava, where they made a heap of wood and joined together many reeds and got across the river, with the king continually watching on their left side with a strong troop of cavalry, together with Baldwin and the other hostages, until they arrived at the place which is called Francavilla [Manđelos, in northwestern Serbia]. They stayed there for three days and purchased the necessities of life and what the army needed at a fair price, then they went on down to Malevilla [Zemun, now in Belgrade, Serbia] with the whole army, spending five nights on the bank of the Sava. . . . For no more than three ships were discovered there, in which one thousand armored soldiers were sent across to take possession of the bank. The remaining multitude crossed over the riverbed by joining together wood and vines [for rafts].

7. Scarcely had the people and all the princes got clear, when they saw the king in all his state, with the duke's brother Baldwin and his wife and all the hostages, which he restored to the duke in that same place, and then he returned into his kingdom, having commended the duke and his brother with very great love, which he showed by many gifts and the kiss of peace.

Questions: According to Albert of Aachen, what is the explanation for the mistrust the crusade leaders had toward King Coloman? Why did he request Godfrey's brother and his wife as hostages? Why did the king of Hungary not provide the necessary means for the crusaders to cross the Rivers Drava and Sava? What were Coloman's goals when monitoring the movements of the crusaders "with a strong troop of cavalry"?

80. BERNARD OF CLAIRVAUX CALLS ON THE CZECHS TO TAKE THE CROSS

Pilgrims flowed to the Holy Land in the aftermath of the First Crusade, and many of them continued to use the "Bavarian Road" through Hungary (mentioned in the letter translated below). However, there is no clear evidence that people from east central or eastern Europe joined the armies of Peter the Hermit and Godfrey of Bouillon. The earliest evidence of participants from east central Europe is dated to the time of the Second Crusade. At some point in the summer of 1147, the German king Conrad III met near Nicaea with the Bohemian troops under the command of Duke Vladislav II (1140–52). However, neither the troops nor the duke followed the campaign to Damascus but returned home upon reaching Ephesus. Duke Vladislav stopped in Constantinople, where he was well received by Emperor Manuel I. Was the participation of the Czechs the result of the preaching done by Cistercians, as in other parts of Europe? To be sure, according to Vincent of Prague, Vladislav II took the cross after the public reading of a letter from Bernard of Clairvaux (1090–1153), which had been sent specifically to the duke of Bohemia and his noblemen. This must be the letter translated below, in which Bernard encourages the duke and his subjects to take the cross in exchange for a full remission of sins. Bernard announced to the Czechs that the crusading army was scheduled to depart on Easter 1147 and was to follow the "Bavarian Road." Bernard also asked the bishop of Olomouc, Henry Zdík, to exhort and instruct further all potential crusaders who lived in Bohemia. However, there is no indication of crusade preaching in Bohemia. The exact moment at which Bernard of Clairvaux wrote his letter to the duke of Bohemia and his subjects is not known, but it was before Easter 1147. If, as is probable, he wrote it after preaching the crusade at the Council of Vézelay (31 March 1146), the letter must have arrived in Bohemia after Easter (7 April 1146), for Bernard announced the departure of the crusading army on the "next Easter." The plans for that departure must have been finalized shortly after Conrad III took the cross in December 1146. However, at the diet (formal deliberative assembly) that took place in Frankfurt on 13 March 1147, Bernard's preaching of the crusade received an unexpected response. The idea was put forward that instead of going to the Holy Land, the Saxon noblemen in attendance would be authorized to launch a crusade against the pagan tribes east of the Elbe River. Bernard responded favorably to this commutation of the crusade vows and, at his specific recommendation, Pope Eugenius III issued Divini dispensatione consilii *on 11 April 1147. By that time, the crusading army under Conrad III and his nephew Frederick Barbarossa was supposed to have already departed, as Easter was celebrated in 1147 on 30 March. The army left only in May, and it is not clear whether the Czech contingent under Vladislav II marched along with the German troops or moved on its own, separately.*

Source: trans. B.S. James, *Letters of St. Bernard of Clairvaux* (Chicago: Henry Regnery, 1953), pp. 463–64.

To the Duke Vladislav, all the other nobles, and to all the people of Bohemia, greetings in Christ, from Bernard, styled abbot of Clairvaux.

I address myself to you in the cause of Christ, in whom lies our true deliverance. I say this so that the warrant of the Lord and my zeal for his interests may excuse my hardihood in thus addressing you. I am a person of small account, but my love for you in Christ is not small. This zeal of mine impels me to write in a letter what I would far sooner inscribe upon your hearts with my voice, if I had the power to follow my will in the matter. But the body is weak although the spirit is willing. My corruptible body cannot comply with the inclinations of my spirit, nor can the burden of my flesh keep pace with its speed. But although the great distance between us prevents me from reaching you in body, my heart stretches out to you, and this is what really matters. Hear then the good news I have to tell you, news of deliverance, and open your arms wide with devotion to receive the rich indulgence that is offered you. This time is not like any time that has gone before, new riches of divine mercy are descending on you from heaven, and happy are we to be alive in this year of God's choice, this year of jubilee [a special year of remission of sins], this year of pardon. I tell you, the Lord has never done the like for any former generation, never did our fathers receive so rich an outpouring of grace. See, you who have sinned, to what artifice God has had recourse in order to save you, consider the depths of his pity for you and be amazed! He places himself in need of you, or pretends to do so, in order to help you with the riches of heaven. The earth is troubled and shaken because the Lord is losing his land, the land in which he was seen amongst men for more than thirty years. His land, the land which he honored with his birth, made glorious with his miracles, sanctified with his blood, and endowed with his tomb. His land, the land in which the voice of the turtledove was heard [Matt. 3:16], the voice of the Virgin's Son calling men to a pure life. His land, the land in which the flowers of his resurrection first blossomed. This land evil men have begun to invade and, unless someone be found to withstand them, they will swallow up the holy sanctuaries of our religion, violate the couch on which our life fell asleep in death for our sakes, and profane the holy places adorned with the blood of the Immaculate Lamb. Hear something more, something well calculated to smite the hardest heart of any Christian. They accuse our King of betraying us, they charge him with pretending to be God when he was not. Let those of you who are loyal to him arise and defend their Lord against the shame of such an imputation. Safe is the battle in which it is glorious to conquer and a gain to die. Why do you hesitate, you servants of the cross? Why do you, who want for neither strength nor goods, make excuses? Receive the sign of the cross, and to all of you who have confessed their sins with truly contrite hearts, the supreme pontiff, to whom it was said, "What you shall loose on earth shall be loosed in heaven" [Matt. 18:18], offers a full pardon. Receive this proffered gift and hasten each to outstrip the other in taking advantage of this opportunity which will not come again. I ask and advise you to put this business of Christ before everything else and not to neglect it for what can be done at other times. And so that you may know when, where, and how it is to be done, listen further: The army of the Lord is to set out next Easter, and it has been determined that a large part of it shall pass through Hungary. It has been laid down that no one shall wear any colored, gray, or silk apparel, and use of gold or silver harness has been forbidden. But those who wish may wear gold or silver when they enter battle, so that the sun may shine upon them and scatter the forces of the enemy with terror. We have written in Latin because you have with you a learned and holy man in the lord bishop of Moravia [Henry Zdík, 1126–50]; and I pray to him that, according to the wisdom he has received from the Lord, he may with all diligence exhort and instruct in this matter. We have sent a copy of this letter to the lord pope, to whose admonitions you must listen with attentive ears and whose commands you must implicitly obey.

Questions: What arguments did Bernard use to stir up enthusiasm among the Czechs for the Second Crusade? Why did he call that crusade the "business of Christ"? How do you explain the concession Bernard made to those who wish to "wear gold or silver when they enter battle"? What could have prompted him to mention that a copy of his letter was sent to the pope?

81. HUNGARY AT THE TIME OF THE SECOND CRUSADE

Otto, bishop of Freising (c. 1110–58) was the half-brother of King Conrad III and the uncle of Emperor Frederick Barbarossa. His biography of the latter was written at the emperor's request to cover the main events of his reign between his coronation in 1152 and the events of 1156. The participation of Frederick together with Conrad III in the Second Crusade is covered in the first book of the Deeds of Frederick Barbarossa. *In addition to being favorable to Frederick, Otto made every effort possible to extol the virtues of the German aristocracy, its values and valor. The collectively negative portrait of the Hungarians must be understood as an effort to highlight the merits of the German imperial social and political configuration. The excursus on Hungary was inserted before Otto's account of King Géza II's 1146 campaign that led to his victory in the battle of Fischa against Duke Henry XI of Bavaria (11 September 1146). Because of that, Otto is therefore inclined to depict the Hungarians in the worst possible light. What is remarkable in Otto's effort to demonize the Hungarians, however, is his use of a claimant to the throne to justify the German conquest of Bratislava. Boris was King Coloman's son from his second marriage with Eufemia, the daughter of Vladimir II Monomakh. Coloman repudiated his second wife on a charge of adultery, and Eufemia returned to Rus'; her son, Boris, was born in Kiev c. 1114. Consequently, Boris was never regarded as a legitimate heir to the Hungarian throne.*

Source: trans. F. Curta from Otto of Freising and Rahewin, *Gesta Frederici seu rectius Cronica*, ed. F.-J. Schmale (Darmstadt: Wissenschaftliche Buchgesellschaft, 1965), pp. 190, 192, 194.

32. At that same time that, as mentioned, Duke Henry [XI Jasomirgott] of Bavaria [1141–56] was at war with Bishop Henry of Regensburg [1132–55] and the inhabitants of his city, as well as with Ottokar [III], margrave of Styria [1129–64], some knights from Austria snuck into Hungary and took by surprise, in the middle of the night, the castle of Bosan, known as Pressburg [Bratislava, in Slovakia], which Emperor Henry [V, 1099–1125] had once besieged [in 1108], and conquered it. They took some captives, others they killed, and others managed to flee. When the king of Hungary, Géza [II, 1141–62], the son of King Béla [II, 1131–41] learned about this, he immediately sent some of his counts to seek out why and how all that had happened. Then he followed them himself and hurried to the rescue of the castle with a large throng of Hungarians. The counts sent ahead were able to learn from those in the castle why they inflicted such a grave injustice upon the[ir] king. They explained that they had not acted either to the benefit of the Roman king or to that of their duke, but for their lord Boris. Boris, the son of the previous Hungarian king Coloman [1095–1116], claimed the Hungarian throne on the basis of the hereditary right, and had oftentimes appealed to both the Roman and the Greek emperors, and had gained with money many of our knights to his side. So, as he arrived at that place, the king of the Hungarians set up camp and besieged the castle, for which he used many siege engines and weapons, and surrounded the entire city with archers. Since the duke was in Upper Bavaria and the king in the distant parts of the empire, the Germans could not hope for any rescue and therefore opened peace negotiations with the Hungarians. In short, after much discussion, they gave up the castle, in exchange for the king paying them, under oath, no fewer than three thousand pounds of silver, and returned home. However, the king of the Hungarians was upset at the destruction caused by the Germans and suspecting that they had acted so at the instigation of the duke of Bavaria, he declared him his enemy and gathered a very large army from his entire land. Before we give the account of the expedition of those people, it seems right to provide some details about the location of the land and the life of the people who live therein.

33. The land is surrounded by forests and mountains, particularly by the Apennines [in fact, the Carpathian Mountains]. In ancient times, this land was called Pannonia. In its interior, there are fields in a very large plain, which is crisscrossed by rivers and streams and is rich in forests full of all sorts of wild animals. The land is delightful on account of the charm provided by nature. It is also rich because of the fertility of its arable fields, so that it appears as pleasant as the paradise of God or as Egypt. It offers, as mentioned, a beautiful landscape, but has only a few city walls and buildings, as expected from a barbarous nation. The boundaries of this

country are made up less of mountains and forests as of large rivers. To the east, where the famous river Sava flows into the Danube [in fact, that is the southern, not the eastern border of Hungary] is Bulgaria; to the west, Moravia and the German, Eastern March [Austria]; to the south—Croatia, Dalmatia, Istria, and Carinthia; and to the north—Bohemia, Poland, and Ruthenia [in fact those lands are to the northwest and northeast of Hungary, respectively]; to the southeast, Rama [Bosnia, which is in fact to the southwest of Hungary]; to the northeast [in reality, to the southeast] come the lowlands of the Pechenegs and of the Falones [Cumans], which are rich in game, but barely know any plow and hoe. Because the land has often been invaded by barbarians, there cannot be any surprise that the customs and language there are primitive and unpolished. First, as I explained in more detail elsewhere, the land was devastated by the Huns, who, according to Jordanes [*Getica* 24], were descendants of unclean spirits and harlots. After that came the devastation caused by Avars, who ate raw, unclean meat, and then finally, the conquest by the Hungarians coming out of Scythia, where some of them still live to this day. Those Hungarians have ugly faces with deep-set eyes, are short in stature, and wild barbarians in customs and language. One would be right to blame fortune or otherwise to wonder about the divine forbearance, which has given this beautiful land to such freaks, for one can barely call them humans. However, they imitate the shrewdness of the Greeks in that they do not take any decision without frequent and long deliberations. Finally, their villages and towns have only pitiful houses, mostly of straw, rarely of wood, and even less of stone, as during summer and autumn they prefer to live in tents. When they assemble at the court of their king, each magnate brings his own chair, and they deliberate at length and discuss the state of their state. In winter, they do the same thing, but inside one of their houses. All are in every respect obedient to their prince, and regard it as wrong to annoy him even with secret whispering, and even more so to anger him through some open opposition. So, even if the kingdom is divided into seventy or more counties, two thirds of the fees and fines for every suit are taken by the royal treasury, while another goes to the count. Despite the land being so vast, nobody except the king dares to strike coins or to collect customs duties. If anyone among the counts causes even the smallest offense to the king or is ever unjustly accused of such a thing, then he is arrested by some court servant of the lowest rank, who is sent by the king. Even if he may be surrounded by his retainers, the man is put in chains and under various forms of torture. Nobody asks the king, as it is customary with us, to make a judgment through his peers. Someone who is accused is not allowed to defend himself, and the will of the king is treated by all as law. If the king wishes to go to war, all gather without opposition, as if parts of one body. The peasants who live in villages give one man for every nine or seven or, when needed, even fewer men, and equip him with all that is necessary, while the rest are left at home to till the fields. The knights, however, do not dare to remain at home but for very serious reasons. In the royal retinue, there are many guests [foreigners], whom they call "princes." They are also ready to defend the king from all sides. Almost all of them march against us in an ugly manner and have horrible weapons, except those who are schooled by the guests, whom we now call mercenaries, or who are their descendants. So, they acquire not a natural, but a somewhat apparent valor, as they now imitate our princes and guests in both gallantry and splendor of weapons.

Questions: How did the German crusaders conduct themselves while transiting Hungary? What reasons does Otto of Freising give for their behavior and difficulties? What can one learn from his account about stereotypes that educated men like him entertained about Hungary? How does the description of Hungary that he gives compare to that of Abu Hamid (Doc. 50)? Why does Otto of Freising compare the Hungarians to the Greeks?

82. THE CRUSADE AGAINST LETTGALLIANS

The key source and the earliest narrative for the history of the early Baltic crusades is the Chronicle of Henry of Livonia, *written in Latin. Born in Saxony near Magdeburg in 1187 or 1188, Henry came to Riga (in what is now Latvia) in 1205 with Bishop Albert, under whose brother he had been educated at the monastery school at Segeberg. Three years later, he was ordained priest for the Lettgallians (the inhabitants of the eastern parts of present-day Latvia) around the village of Papendorf (now Rubene, some sixty miles to the northeast of Riga). It is not clear why he suddenly decided to write his chronicle between August 1224 and spring 1226, and then to add one final chapter in 1227 or 1228. He remained a parish priest for the rest of his life and probably died at some point after 1259. His chronicle tells the story of how the Livs, Latvians, and Estonians were conquered, and covers a period of about forty years. The largest part of the text is dedicated to the reign of Bishop Albert of Riga (1201–29). In his chronicle, Henry defends the rights of the church of Riga against its enemy, primarily the Danish king. Henry took part in many of the events described in his narrative and saw warfare and revolt in the lands of the Livs and Latvians. He took part in the crusading as a chaplain. He was outside Livonia for only brief periods of time: he went to Rome in 1215 for the Fourth Lateran Council, and then to Germany with Bishop Albert in 1222–24. His was therefore a vivid eyewitness account, which some historians now regard as an autobiography. Henry compares the crusade in Livonia with the wars in the Old Testament, as he regards the crusade as a response to the threat posed by pagans to Christians, and as revenge upon the enemies of Christianity.*

Source: trans. J.A. Brundage, *The Chronicle of Henry of Livonia* (Madison: University of Wisconsin Press, 1961), pp. 127–28.

[In 1212, Bishop Albert] called together the pilgrims [crusaders], the master of the Militia and his [Sword] Brothers, and the Rigans and Livonians who still remained faithful. They all assembled and collected a great army. Taking all the necessary supplies with them, they marched to Treiden [now Turaida, in Latvia, halfway between Riga and Rubene] and besieged the fort of Dobrel [an elder of the Latgallians], in which there were the apostate Livonians, not only the Livonians belonging to the Brothers of the Militia, but also the bishop's Livonians from the other part of the Aa [the River Gauja, in central Latvia]. The prince and elder of the latter was Vesike [a Liv chieftain, prince of Kokenhusen, now Koknese, in southern Latvia]. The Livonians left the fort from the rear and, after wounding some men in the army, they took their horses and loot and returned to the fort, saying: "Take heart and fight, Livonians, lest you be slaves to the Germans." They fought and defended themselves for many days. The Germans destroyed the ramparts of the fort and killed many men and beasts with the many large rocks which they shot into the fort with their paterells [siege engines]. Some forced the Livonians from the defenses with arrows, wounding a great many of them. Others put up a [siege] tower, which the wind knocked to the ground the next night. At this there was great noise and rejoicing in the fort and the Livonians sacrificed animals, paying honor to their gods according to their old customs. They immolated dogs and goats and, to mock Christianity, they tossed them from the fort, in the face of the bishop and the whole army. But all of the Livonians' work was wasted. The tower was put up more strongly, another wooden tower was quickly strengthened, it was pushed across the moat, and the fort was sapped from below. From the highest point in the fort, meanwhile, Russin [of Sotecle, an elder of the Letgallians] called Berthold, master of Wenden [a member of the Sword Brothers], *draugs*, that is, his fellow. Russin took off his helmet, leaned down from the wall, and uttered words about peace and their former friendship. Suddenly a bolt from a ballista struck his head. He fell and shortly thereafter he died. The Germans were digging day and night at the ramparts. They did not rest until they got near the top of the fort, until the rampart was cut in two, until it was expected that the whole fortification would tumble to the ground. The Livonians, seeing that the height of their strongest fort was being toppled, were bewildered in soul and confused in mind. They sent their elders, Asso and others, to the bishop. They asked for mercy and begged that they not be killed. The bishop, in order to persuade them to return to the sacraments of the faith, sent his banner into the fort. Some of them put it up; others then threw it down. Asso was bound for torture, war began again, and the final fight was worse than the earlier one. At length they gave up, raised blessed Mary's standard on high, and bowed their necks to the bishop. They humbly besought him to spare them and promised that they would immediately accept the neglected faith of Christ, that they would henceforth observe the sacraments faithfully, and that they would never again call to mind pagan rites. The bishop had pity on them . . . [and] returned to his city [Riga] with his men, taking with him the Livonian elders, enjoining the others to follow in order to renew the sacrament of baptism and to return to their former peaceful tranquility. The messengers of the Livonians followed the bishop to Riga, seeking pardon before the whole multitude.

Questions: How does Henry feel about the Letgallians? Does his view change as they are constrained to accept Christianity? How did they react to the attack on Treiden? Which of Russin's actions show that Henry had firsthand knowledge of the events?

83. THE ARMY OF FREDERICK BARBAROSSA CROSSES THE BALKANS

One of the most important sources on the German participation in the Third Crusade is a text entitled History of the Expedition of the Emperor Frederick, *which was written shortly after the events narrated therein, c. 1200. The* History *survives in two manuscripts, both from the early thirteenth century. However, the text in its entirety is known from two copies made in the mid-eighteenth century in Moravia. According to one of the two manuscripts, the author of the text was "an Austrian cleric," while a side note mentioned "Ansbertus" as that cleric's name. Nonetheless, the* History *is a composite text, written by more than one author. Much of the earlier part covering the years 1189 and 1190—including the account of the trip across the Balkans—was composed by a contemporary, most likely a participant in the expedition. The events of the Third Crusade narrated in the* History *had a great impact on east central and southeastern Europe. The army of Frederick Barbarossa included Czech troops, and some two thousand Hungarians joined the crusaders as well. In the Balkans, however, the crusaders were met with hostility both from the Byzantine officials (such as the duke of Braničevo) and the local population. Emperor Isaac II Angelos (1185–95) had ordered the restoration of forts in the mountain passes and of city fortifications by which the crusaders were to pass. Moreover, instead of following the military road across the Balkans, the crusading army was shown a secondary, much rougher tract, which had been previously blocked at key points in preparation for possible ambushes. The crusaders plundered the countryside in search for provisions. They were harassed by auxiliary troops in Byzantine service, who carefully avoided any direct confrontation with the entire army. The crusaders managed to repel the troops sent against them and even seized several forts in Thrace, including Beroe (now Stara Zagora, in Bulgaria) and Adrianople (now Edirne, in Turkey). They remained in Philippopolis for three months and left a garrison in the city once they decided to move farther on. It is important to note that, despite approaching Frederick Barbarossa with proposals of military assistance, neither Stephen Nemanja's nor Peter's offer was for the crusade properly speaking, but for an attack on Constantinople.*

Source: trans. F. Curta from *Quellen zur Geschichte des Kreuzzuges Kaiser Friedrichs I*, ed. A. Chroust, *Monumenta Germaniae Historica, Scriptores rerum Germanicarum*, n.s. 5 (Berlin: Weidmann, 1928), pp. 26–28, 29–31, 32–33, 39–40, and 45.

Crossing the entire army by boat over the River Drava, which is called Trâ in the vernacular, was a great trial, and some drowned along with their horses, swollen by the river in front of the eyes of all. We celebrated the feast of nativity of Saint John the Baptist [24 June 1189] in the province between Hungary and the border with Greece, at St-George [now Čalma, in Vojvodina, Serbia, near the Serbian-Croatian border], a mile away from Francavilla [now Manđelos, a village to the east of Čalma, in Serbia]. From there we marched to Sirmium [now Sremska Mitrovica, on the River Sava], which was once a famous city, but now is ruined and in a quite miserable state. On the eve of the feast of Saints Peter and Paul [28 June 1189], we crossed the Sava or Sovua River, at the point where it flows into the Danube. [We did that] more successfully than when crossing the Drava, and soon after that we were in the land under the rule of the Greeks. That was five weeks after entering the land of Hungary at Prespurch [Bratislava, now the capital city of Slovakia]. We celebrated the feast of the most holy apostles [29 June 1198] in that place, namely on the bank of the Sava, in a Greek town, partially destroyed, which is called in German Wuizzinburch and in Greek Pelgranum [Belgrade, now the capital city of Serbia], across [the river] from Goin [probably Zemun, now within the city of Belgrade]. We have crossed Hungary much more peacefully and in unusually mild weather, which was even greater, since we and our animals were spared the mosquitoes, the gadflies, flies, and snakes, which in Hungary [normally] follow and pester horses during the summer but were only rarely seen [during our journey].

On the kalends of July [1 July 1198], we crossed the river [Morava]. Traveling through the forest, in which we lost all our boats, so that we had to put all our equipment in carts and wagons, we reached Brandiez [Braničevo, now Golubac near Požarevac, on the Serbian border with Romania] on the sixth none of July [2 July]. . . . Even though the duke of Brandiez pretended to welcome the emperor, "the result proves the deeds" [Ovid, *Heroides* 2.85], as it soon became apparent, for he behaved perfidiously and altogether against the emperor [Frederick I Barbarossa] and the entire army, much like all the Greeks. He has misled us away from the usual route or the public road of Bulgaria, as they call it, while, in addition, blocking the rocky and difficult path on which he took us, at the order of his lord, the Greek emperor. However, the Hungarian crusaders and pilgrims, who knew this route and had gone two to three days ahead of the army, opened the road [for us] after much work. The Greeklings could not stop them and so, "false witnesses have risen against me" [Ps. 27:12], namely with the treacherous Greeks. Their malice did not stop there though, for Greeklings, Bulgarians, Serbs and semi-barbarian Vlachs were laying in wait in the large forest of Bulgaria, through which we were marching after leaving Brandiez on the fifth ides of July [11 July 1198]. With poisoned arrows shot from their hiding places, they were bent on killing the rearguard in the camp, but also the servants walking ahead [of the army] in search of food or fodder for the horses. When apprehended, many of them confessed that they had been ordered to do so by their lord, the duke of Brandiez, and especially through the edict of the emperor of the Greeks. They promptly received their punishment and were hanged. The entire army of pilgrims suffered greatly in the woods, when a great number of servants were killed, who had been sent to procure food, and when gangs of robbers broke in, stealing our horses and plundering carts without a military cover. Moreover, the road was exceedingly difficult, and there were many losses among the foot soldiers, especially the poor, who would eat whatever they could get. But despite all those dangers, our men were undeterred and marched ahead with increasing courage and determination. . . .

In those days an advanced guard [envoys] came from the great count of Serbia and Crassia [Ras or Raška, in what is now southern Serbia], as well as from his brother, who was an equally powerful count. They announced the arrival of their lords, those counts, who wanted to welcome the most illustrious emperor. They promised to provide whatever service [he needed from them] and to be obedient [to him]. The army finally made it to Nisa [Niš, in Serbia], which had earlier been a strongly fortified town, but had been in part destroyed by the king of Hungary Béla [III, 1172–96] at the time of the Greek tyrant Andronicus [Emperor Andronikos I Komnenos, 1183–85]. On account of the [local] market, our men remained for three days in that town. Neaman [Stephen Nemanja, grand *župan* of Serbia between c. 1170 and 1196] and his brother Chrazimerus [Stracimir, Nemanja's older brother] appeared with great pomp in front of the lord emperor and were honorably received by him and by the leaders of the army on the sixth kalends of August [21 July 1189]. As a sign of their allegiance, they brought to the lord emperor wine, barley, and flour, sheep and cattle in great numbers, and among other gifts, they gave him six sea cows or seals, as they are called [most likely Mediterranean monk seals], a tamed boar, and three live, equally tamed deer. They honored also the individual princes who were closer to the emperor, and gave them likewise wine, cattle, and sheep. They offered themselves and all their people under arms and declared that they were ready to come to the assistance of this expedition, especially against the emperor of Greece, if he would try to oppose the army of Christ. They believed [him capable of that] because of the road bandits, who, as mentioned, had attacked our people and caused many losses, both in people and in goods. Moreover, the counts, together with their third brother Merzilas [Miroslav] had taken the city of Nisa by sword and bow. They had removed from the dominion of the Greeks the entire territory around it, up to Straliz [most likely Sredec, the medieval name of present-day Sofia, the capital city of Bulgaria], and placed it under their own rule. As they wanted to extend even more their power and rule in all directions, they offered homage and fealty to the Roman emperor, for the everlasting glory of the Roman empire, in exchange for that land, which they had won by military valor and now wanted to receive from the hand of the emperor. They were moved not by fear, but only because of love for him and for the German empire. . . .

They brought to the emperor's attention another matter, which had been discussed earlier. They asked him to use his imperial authority and make possible the marriage of the daughter of Berthold, the illustrious duke of Dalmatia, Croatia, and Merania, who was also margrave of Istria, with the son of Merzilas [Miroslav], the duke and prince of Chelmenia [Hum, in what is now Montenegro] and Crassia [Ras], which are located next to Dalmatia. The emperor and the worthy council of princes responded favorably to this request, and Duke Berthold took an oath that by the next feast of Saint George [24 April 1190], his daughter would be betrothed in Istria to the young Tohu [Timoslav], provided that Tohu and his heirs born from the daughter of Duke Berthold, at the death of their father [Miroslav] will be considered first in the line of inheritance, before all his brothers, and with all the rights to rule. This agreement was then confirmed by the counts in person, who gave their right hands. . . .

Nonetheless, the power of the empire of the Greeks was declining day after day, and as it is truly revealed, "every kingdom divided against itself is brought to desolation" [Luke 11:17], so the empire was divided into four parts and, precisely at the moment when we were marching through, it was [thus] weakened and diminished. For one of the royal blood named Isaac [Dukas Komnenos, 1184–91] rose in Cyprus and declared himself emperor. A certain Theodore [Mangaphas, 1188–93] rebelled on the other side of the Hellespont, which is also called "the arm of Saint George," in the environs of Philadelphia. And over a large part of Bulgaria, as well as along the Danube up to where it flows into the sea, Kalopeter the Vlach and his brother Assanius [Peter and Asen, the Vlach leaders of the rebellion of 1185 in the Stara Planina Mountains of Bulgaria] ruled as tyrants together with their Vlach followers. Exactly when the crusading army crossed Bulgaria, the aforementioned counts of Serbia and Ras, taking advantage of the troubles of the Greek empire, seized the opportunity and placed a part of Bulgaria under their rule. They had previously struck an agreement with Kalopeter against the emperor in Constantinople. This Kalopeter greeted the lord emperor politely through letters and envoys, bowing in front of this majesty with due respect and with promises of loyal assistance against his enemies. . . .

On the seventh kalends of September [26 August], with great excitement we occupied Philippopolis [now Plovdiv, in central Bulgaria], as God had most likely established for us. We found there many things, which were both pleasant and useful for the army. And while the Greek emperor was denying us the crossing [of the Bosporus Strait] by ship, we decided to stay in that city for a while, as if it belonged to us. We therefore harvested the vintage in that region and pressed the grapes, put the crops in silos, and everyone took for himself whatever he needed to the assigned accommodation. We remained in that city for almost eleven weeks, as the "land rested [from war] before" us [1 Macc. 1:3] and, as the Lord had struck terror [in their hearts], there was neither Satan, nor any other evil. . . .

So, within a short span of time, as mentioned, the army of Christ and of the holy cross won three towns and about ten castles with their environs. The Armenians and a few Bulgarians who lived there and were paying tribute, humbly came to the lord emperor and the army leaders and begged him profusely. They swore fealty and obedience and obtained for themselves warranty of safety for themselves and their villages, provided that they would supply the army with market goods for the duration of their stay in Philippopolis. And they faithfully kept their promise.

Questions: What reasons are given in this text for the behavior of the German crusaders? Why were "Neaman" and "Kalopeter" eager to cooperate with them? What were the main problems Frederick Barbarossa was facing while crossing the Balkans? Why did the Armenians swear fealty to the emperor?

84. THE SWORD BROTHERS

After moving the episcopal see of his diocese from Üxküll (today Ikšķile, in Latvia) to Riga, Bishop Albert entrusted the defense of his diocese to a new military order, specifically created for the occasion—the Livonian Brothers of the Militia (also known as the Sword Brothers, because of their white cloaks decorated with red swords). To be sure, Henry of Livonia credited Theoderic of Treiden, the abbot of the Cistercian abbey of Dünamünde (now Daugavgrīva, a residential quarter of Riga), with the creation of the order. The knights, all of whom were of noble origin, lived in district castles, each with its own council and military commander. Within less than two decades after its foundation, the new order conquered almost all of the southern region of Estonia. The Sword Brothers then began conquering the lands south of the River Daugava. They were met with fierce resistance from the Curonians and the Semigallians. While returning through Semigallia from a raid into Lithuania, the army of the order was ambushed at Saulė (unknown location in northern Lithuania, in the environs of Šiauliai) in 1236 by a coalition of Lithuanians and Semigallians. The entire army was wiped out and its commander killed. The Sword Brothers never recovered from that disaster and were forced by the pope to disband, its members reorganizing in 1237 as the Livonian branch of the Order of St-Mary (Teutonic Knights). In that new capacity, the Livonian Knights, as they were now known, persisted until the sixteenth century.

Source: trans. F. Curta from Henry of Livonia, *Chronicon Livoniae*, ed. L. Arbusow and A. Bauer (Darmstadt: Wissenschaftliche Buchgesellschaft, 1959), pp. 22, 24, 298, 304, 306.

Four years after his ordination [Albert, bishop of Riga; the year is 1202], the city [of Riga] was entrusted to the few pilgrims [that is, crusaders], who were standing around the house of the Lord as if they were a wall [Ezek. 13:5], while the bishop, together with the other pilgrims went to Germany. After he left, his brother Engelbert arrived. He was a[n Augustinian] monk from Neumünster [in Holstein, north of Hamburg, in Germany] who brought with him the first townspeople of Riga and working with him [God], who gave the word to the evangelists [Mark 16:20], he began to spread the name of Christ among the pagans. He had [on his side] Brother Theoderic of Treiden and Alebrand and the other brothers, who were living in Livonia under the [Augustinian] order's rule. Shortly after that, the brothers of the convent of the Blessed Virgin Mary in Riga elected him to be their provost, as they liked both [the way he was conducting] his life and his [sense of] order. He was [a monk] of the same [canon] order as that of the abbey of Segeberg, from which Meinhard of blessed memory had come, who had been elected bishop of the Livs. Wishing to establish a similar house, Meinhard had first founded their convent in the parish of Üxküll. However, Bishop Albert, three years after his ordination [in 1201/02] had moved the convent of regulars, as well as the episcopal see from Üxküll to Riga. He also consecrated the cathedral [in that city] and dedicated it, as well as the entire land of Livonia, to Mary, the blessed Mother of God. In addition, he built a monastery of Cistercian monks at the mouth of the Daugava, which is known as Dünamünde or the Mount of Saint Nicholas. He appointed abbot Theoderic of Treiden, who had worked with him for the evangelization [of the natives]. As he predicted the perfidy of the Livs and feared that one could not withstand the multitude of pagans, and because he thus wanted to multiply the believers and to maintain the church [alive] among the pagans, at that time Brother Theoderic established the Brothers of the Militia of Christ. Pope Innocent [III, 1198–1216] gave them the rule of the Templars [to follow] and a sign to wear on their clothes, namely a sword and the cross. He placed them under the jurisdiction of the bishop [of Riga]. . . .

In the meantime, the brothers of the order [that is, of the Militia of Christ] and a few other Germans [presumably, crusaders] surrounded the fort of Dorpat [now Tartu, in eastern Estonia] and attacked it for five days. And because their number was so small and could therefore not take such a strong fort, they plundered the hinterland and returned to Livonia with the spoils. And again, the brothers of the order collected an army and invaded Estonia. They struck the Jerwanians [inhabitants of the region now known as Järva-Jaani, in northern Estonia] particularly hard, because they had often gone to war against the

Danes. The army of the brothers killed [many of them] and took many prisoners from among them and carried off many spoils. And the people of Jerwan came to them at Kettis, promising perpetual fidelity to the Germans and to all Christians. So, the brothers promptly left that place and returned [to their own land] with the entire booty. . . .

And the bishops [Albert of Riga and Hermann of Estonia] sent envoys to the prince [Viachko, the former prince of Kokenhusen, who had been sent from Novgorod to Dorpat] in Dorpat and asked for the extradition of those rebels inside the town, who had violated the sacrament of their baptism, had thrown away the faith in Jesus Christ, and had returned to paganism. Those rebels had driven out the brothers of the order, their brethren and lords, killing some and taking others prisoner. They had plundered daily the neighboring regions, which had converted to Christianity, and had laid them waste. However, the prince did not want to separate himself from the rebels, because the Novgorodians and the princes of Rus' had granted him the town and the lands around it in perpetuity and had promised that they would defend him against the attacks of the Germans. So, all criminals from the neighboring lands, as well as from Saccala [Sakala, a region of southwestern Estonia] had gathered in that same town around that same prince. They were the traitors and murderers of their brethren, the brothers of the order and the merchants. They had caused the evil attacks on the Livonian Church. They regarded this prince as their commander and lord, for he had been the old root of all [kinds of] evil [1 Tim. 6:10] in Livonia, the one who had broken the peace of the true peacemaker and of all Christians. He had secretly killed those faithful men, who had been sent from Riga to help him against the Lithuanians, and he had plundered all their goods. All those people therefore despised the peace with the Christians and putting their faith in their strong fort, they were every day seeking to harm them [the Christians]. In fact, this fort was stronger than all forts in Estonia, for the brothers of the order had fortified it earlier with much effort and expense and had supplied it with many weapons and ballistas, which the traitors had [meanwhile] stolen. The prince also had there [in Dorpat] with him a great number of Rus' archers. Moreover, they prepared paterells [trebuchets] in the manner of the Oeselians [that is, according to a method employed by warriors from the island of Saaremaa], as well as other instruments of war. . . .

For the Church of Livonia to set free from the present troubles her [own] daughter, the Church of Estonia, to which she had given birth for Jesus Christ, the most honorable bishop of Riga sent [in 1224] and called upon the brothers of the order, the vassals of the church, together with the pilgrims, the merchants, and the townspeople of Riga, in addition to all the Livs and the Letts. To all those who belonged to the Church of Livonia, he proclaimed a military expedition. And they all obeyed him faithfully and gathered with their troops at Lake Rastigerwe [Lake Rautina near Valga, in southern Estonia], and called to them the most honorable bishop of Riga, together with his brother, the no less honorable bishop Hermann, with all the men, priests, and knights. After they finished in that same place the mysteries of consultation and praying, they dispatched ahead the best and most capable men from the army, so that crossing Ugaunia [the province of southern Estonia around Tartu] by day and night, they could take the fort of Dorpat by surprise the next morning. Those people then divided their troops, sending some to attack the fort, and the others to plunder those in Wierland who were still in rebellion. After three days, they brought back many sheep, cattle, and everything else that the army needed. However, the bishops and the pilgrims, together with the greater part of the army followed [them] and reached the town [of Dorpat] on the day of the Assumption of the Blessed Virgin [15 August 1224]. A year before that, on that same day, the fort of Fellin [now Viljandi, in southern Estonia] had been taken. They now covered the field with tents and attacked the fortification of the town, setting up their small [siege] engines and paterells, preparing a great number of instruments of war, and building a bastion or a very strong wooden tower. They built that in eight days out of tall trees, and it was as high as [the walls of] the town, closer to which they pushed it over the moat. At the same time, they began digging underneath [the walls]. Half of the army was busy digging day and night, with some excavating, and the others hauling away the loose dirt. In this way, a large part of the masonry crumbled away from the battlement in the morning, and they immediately brought the tower closer to the fort. Meanwhile, envoys were sent to the prince—priests, and knights, as well as prominent men—who promised him free passage for his men, his horses and all his belongings, if he would surrender the fort and abandon the apostate people. Hoping to receive assistance from Novgorod, the prince firmly declared that he would never give up the fort. . . . Without any delay, they reached the bulwark. As the others from the army saw that, they rushed after them. What more? One hurried to be the first to go up to exalt the glory and praise of Jesus Christ and his Mother Mary, and so that he would win for himself the praise and the reward for his efforts. Another went up—who was first, I do not know, only God does—and a great multitude followed him. . . . By means of sword and lance they pushed the Estonians away from the rampart. . . . But the Rus', who resisted the longest, were finally beaten and fled to the citadel. They were drawn out of there and all killed together with the prince [Viachko], about two hundred men. . . . Therefore, of all men who had been inside the fort, only one was left alive, [namely] a vassal of the grand prince of Suzdal' [Iurii II, grand prince of Vladimir-Suzdal', 1218–38], who had been sent by his lord to the town together with other Rus' [warriors]. This man the brother of the order dressed up and, putting him on a good horse, they sent him to Novgorod and Suzdal' to announce to his lords what had happened.

Questions: What were the circumstances in which the Militia of Christ was established? How does Henry describe their duties? Can they be characterized as a monastic-military order? Compare the resistance of the inhabitants of Dorpat to the attitude of the Lettgallians in Treiden (Doc. 82)? How do you explain the difference?

85. THE CONQUEST OF ZARA

Geoffroy de Villehardouin, marshal of Champagne, was an experienced soldier (probably a veteran of the Third Crusade), and one of "the chief men in the army," as he himself describes the leaders of the Fourth Crusade. He was in fact among the first to take the cross at the tournament held by his lord, Count Thibaud III of Champagne, in 1199. He remained with the crusaders until the fall of Constantinople in 1204 and became a marshal of the Latin empire of Constantinople. At some point after 1207 he began writing his chronicle, the first crusade account written in a vernacular (Old French). The Conquest of Constantinople *survives in six manuscript copies, the earliest of which may be dated to the thirteenth century. The first two hundred paragraphs of the text are written in a dramatic style, with many examples of direct speech, several of which appear in the episode of Zara. Nonetheless, the information in those as well as in the subsequent chapters is invaluable, since the author was an eyewitness to almost everything that is narrated in the* Conquest: *he was at Zara in 1202, at Constantinople in 1204, and at Adrianople in 1205. Aware of his quality as an eyewitness, Villehardouin often uses "I" or "we" to introduce himself into the narrative. However, there are also cases in which he writes about himself in the third person singular, or, as in the episode of Zara, skillfully effaces himself. This narrative technique, in which the author has multiple voices, is typical for the epic genre, and the* Conquest *was in fact modeled after the* chansons de geste. *Its purpose may therefore have been to entertain, and not just to inform, an aristocratic audience.*

Source: trans. F. Curta from Geoffroy de Villehardouin, *La conquête de Constantinople*, ed. J. Dufournet (Paris: Flammarion, 2004), pp. 70, 76, 78, 80, 82, and 84.

62. Then the doge [of Venice, Enrico Dandolo, 1192–1205] spoke to his people and said: "Sirs, these people [the crusaders] cannot pay us anymore. Everything that they have paid is ours entirely, according to the covenant that they [had with us, but] now cannot keep. However, our good right [deriving from the agreement] will not be recognized everywhere, and [should we try to pursue it,] we would be greatly blamed, both us and our country. Let us therefore seek an agreement with them.

63. The king of Hungary [Emeric, 1196–1204] has taken from us Zara [now Zadar, in Croatia] in Sclavonia, one of the most fortified cities in the world. We would never recover it, whatever our forces, without those people [the crusaders]. Let us ask them to assist us in conquering that city, and [in exchange] we

will postpone the payment of the 34,000 marks [silver coins], which they owe us, until God will allow us all to take that city—them and us." So was this agreement proposed, but it was met with much opposition from those who wanted to disband the army. Nonetheless, the agreement was [eventually] accepted and put in action. . . .

77. On the eve of [the feast of] Saint Martin [10 November 1202], they reached Zara in Sclavonia, and saw the city defended by tall and large walls. One could not have asked for a more beautiful, richer, and better defended [city]. When the pilgrims [that is, crusaders] saw it, they were amazed, and they said to each other: "How could such a city be taken by force, if God himself would not allow it?"

78. The first ships to come before the city cast anchor, in order to wait for the others [to arrive]. The next morning was a beautiful and clear day; and that is when all the galleys and others ships that had stayed behind [finally] arrived. They stormed the harbor and broke the strong and well-made chain [blocking access to the harbor]. They landed where the harbor was between them and the city. And then one could see many knights and sergeants coming out of the ships, bringing out of the galleys many beautiful horses and many rich tents and pavilions. Thus, the army camped [there] and put Zara under siege on the feast of Saint Martin [11 November].

79. By that time, however, not all barons had [yet] arrived, for the marquis [Boniface] of Montferrat [the commander of the expedition] was not yet there. He had delayed his departure because of some business [of his own]. Stephen du Perche who was sick had remained in Venice, much like Matthew of Montmorency. As soon as they recovered, Matthew of Montmorency joined the army at Zara, while Stephen du Perche did not behave that well, for he abandoned the army and went to Apulia [southern Italy], where he remained for a while. Together with him went also Rotrou of Montfort and Yves de la Jaille, as well as many others who were strongly blamed. They all went to Syria with the expedition in March [of the following spring].

80. On the morning of [the feast of] Saint Martin, the inhabitants of Zara came out of the city to talk with the doge of Venice who was in his pavilion, and they told him that they would surrender the city to him, along with all their possessions, if their lives would be spared. The doge answered [and told them] that he could not reach either this or any other agreement [with them], without consulting with the counts and the barons, and we went to talk to them about it.

81. While he was on his way to talk to the counts and the barons, this group of men that you have learned about earlier [from my story], which wanted the army disbanded, told the envoys [of the inhabitants of Zara], and said: "Why do you want to surrender this city? The pilgrims will not attack you, and you have nothing to fear from them. If you could defend yourselves against the Venetians,

your problem is solved." And they chose one of them named Robert of Boves, who went to the walls of the city and repeated what had already been told to the envoys. So, the envoys returned to the city, and the negotiations were left where they were.

82. When reaching the counts and the barons, the doge of Venice said to them: "Sirs, it so happens that those inside the city would like to surrender it to me, provided that their lives be spared, but I would not agree to those terms or any other, for that matter, without your consent." And the barons answered: "Sir, we advise [you] to accept those terms. [In fact,] we even ask you to do so." So he told them he would do so. After that, they all gathered at the doge's pavilion to ratify the agreement, only to find out that the envoys had left at the advice of those who wanted the army to be disbanded.

83. Then an abbot of Vaux, from the order of Cîteaux [that is, a Cistercian abbey] stood up and said to them: "Sirs, in the name of the pope I prohibit you from attacking this city, for it is a Christian [city] and you are pilgrims [crusaders]." When the doge heard that, he was very angry and said to the counts and the barons: "Sirs, I had an agreement with this city according to my own will, but your people destroyed that deal. As for you, do not forget that you have promised to help me conquer this city, and now I order you to do it."

84. The counts and the barons discussed the matter together with those who were on their side and said: "What a great insolence on the part of those who have broken this deal! No day has so far passed without them making all efforts to disband this army. Here we are in danger of losing our honor if we do not take this city." And they said [to the doge]: "Sir, we will help you take it, despite those who would try to prevent us from doing so."

85. That was the decision they have taken. In the morning, they went to camp right in front of the city gates, where they set up their petraries [stone-throwing siege engines], mangonels [traction trebuchets], and other machines, of which they had many. On the seaward side, they put up their ladders on the ships [most likely "castles" or platforms to shoot from the ships]. And then the petraries began to pound the city, the walls, and the towers. This attack lasted for five days. During that time, they put sappers to work in order to bring the wall down. When those inside the city noticed that, they offered the same terms that they had rejected on the advice from those who wanted to disband the army.

86. That is how the city was surrendered to the doge of Venice, and the people were spared. The doge went again to the counts and the barons, and said: "Sirs, we have conquered this city by the grace of God and your efforts. Winter is already here, and we will not be able to move again from here before Easter, for we will not find supplies elsewhere. However, this city is rich and well supplied with all goods [that we need]; we will divide everything among ourselves equally—you will take one half, and we will take the other."

87. So they did as they have decided. The Venetians took the side next to the harbor, where the ships were, while French [crusaders] took the other side. And each group was given the appropriate accommodation on its side. The army decamped and took up quarters within the city.

88. Once everybody was accommodated, a serious mishap took place around vespers [in the evening]: a brawl broke out between the Venetians and the French, both ugly and violent, and they all took up their weapons. So serious was the brawl that few were the streets on which there was no fighting with swords, lances, and spears. Many were wounded, and many died.

89. But the Venetians could not withstand the attack and they began to suffer great losses. The good men, who did not want anything bad to happen, came fully armed in the midst of the melee and began to separate the combatants. But when done with separating combatants in one place, the fighting would start again somewhere else. The confrontation continued well into the night. They had a hard time and much trouble when attempting to separate the two sides fighting each other. Know that it was the greatest misfortune that ever happened or fell upon the army. A little more, and that army would have been entirely destroyed. But God did not want that to happen.

90. There was much damage on all sides. It was at that time that a noble man from Flanders was killed, named Gilles of Landas; he was struck in the eye and died in the melee, just like many others, about whom no more will be said. So, the doge of Venice and many a baron put a lot of effort during that week into bringing back the peace after that brawl. And thanks be to God, they succeeded in bringing back the peace.

Questions: How does Villehardouin explain the circumstances leading to the conquest of Zara? What was the role of the Venetians, especially of their doge Enrico Dandolo? What were his arguments to convince the crusaders to attack the city? How did the people of Zara view the crusader force? How was this a crusade?

86. THE CRUSADE OF KING ANDREW

Thomas of Spalato wrote his History of Salona *in the 1250s or 1260s. A notary of the commune of Spalato (now Split, in Croatia), canon of the cathedral, archdeacon, and candidate for the position of archbishop of that city, Thomas wanted to write a* gesta episcoporum, *that is a chronicle of the deeds of the archbishops of Salona and Split. In the process, however, he managed to produce a uniquely valuable source for the history of eleventh- and twelfth-century Dalmatia. Because he had access to numerous sources that are now lost, his* History *has been used primarily as a source for the earlier periods. More recently, the work of Thomas of Spalato became the object of intensive study as a literary text and a mirror of Thomas's views of the world around him. Under examination, therefore, have been sections of the* History *that cover events closer to*

Thomas's lifetime. One of the most salient features revealed by recent studies is a strong feeling of urban patriotism and the admiration that Thomas had for the republican government of Split, which in turn seems to have been the source of Thomas's rather dismissive, if not outright critical, views of other political or ethnic communities. The Slavs, Hungarians, and Mongols who populate the History *are either primitive, or cruel, or simply foreign and incapable of understanding the superior civilization of Dalmatia. Chapter 25 on the "passage" (crusading expedition) of King Andrew II of Hungary is a good illustration of those features. While admiring the king, Thomas saw the Spalatins in much more favorable terms, and did not hesitate to denounce the "evil and audacious men" who tried to poison Andrew. Thomas wrote in elegant Latin and made extensive use of rhetorical figures to strengthen the effects of antithesis, parallelism, and rhyme. An admirer of Isidore of Seville, he therefore wrote his* History *in the "Isidorian style," as illustrated by his use of rhyme created by repeating certain parts of words or sentences. In keeping with literary fashions at that time, Thomas often engages in etymologizing to explain events.*

Source: trans. M. Matijević-Sokol, J.R. Sweeney, and D. Karbić, *History of the Bishops of Salona and Split* (Budapest: Central European University Press, 2006), pp. 159, 161, 163, and 165.

During this time King Andrew of Hungary had taken the sign of the cross, desiring to fulfill the vow of his father [Béla III, who took the crusading vow in 1195 but died shortly after that], and set out on a journey to go to the aid of the Holy Land. He therefore sent word and hired large vessels from Venice, Ancona, Zadar, and other cities along the Adriatic coast. He directed them all to set their course for the harbor of the city of Split. Moreover, he sent ahead all the equipment, arms, and provisions on a great number of carts and pack animals. So, when they arrived, they filled the entire city to overflowing. In advance of the king and the Hungarians a huge crowd of Saxons [most likely Bavarian and Austrian crusaders under the leadership of Otto VII of Andechs-Merania and Duke Leopold VI of Babenberg] arrived. They were all peaceable and well-behaved and were looking forward with eagerness and devotion to sailing with the king, for each had taken the sign of the cross. At the king's request, the Spalatins [that is, the citizens of Split] gave over the entire area outside the walls to the pilgrims [that is, crusaders] for lodging. Indeed, they vacated their houses and turned them over to their guests. Soon, however, these quarters were so densely filled with men and beasts that there was no room to pass in or out. And even so the suburban houses could not hold all of them, no matter how tightly they were crowded together and packed in. The greater part of the retinue of the royal court remained outside the city in tents scattered over the fields. As for the citizens, some were terrified, while others marveled to see the unaccustomed throng of people.

And so, in the year of our Redemption 1217, on the twenty-third day of the month of August, King Andrew arrived at the city of Split. All the citizens and foreigners and the whole crowd of his army marched out in procession to meet the lord king, loudly sounding his praises. Then all the clergy robed in silk vestments over their surplices [a white liturgical vestment worn by churchmen for the mass] proceeded with crosses and censers as far as the Pistura Square, chanting together in a manner worthy of the king's majesty. Upon seeing the solemn assemblage in procession, the illustrious king at once dismounted from his horse. Surrounded by a large company of his magnates, he went on foot, flanked on either side by the assembled bishops, to the church of St-Domnius [the cathedral]. Then, after Mass had been celebrated and the offering had been given on the altar, he retired to his quarters. On that day, the community bestowed a most generous procuration [a great amount of money most likely to offset the costs of the crusade] on the king in the house called Mata, outside the walls at the northern gate. There were then said to have been more than ten thousand horsemen in the royal retinue, not including a host of commoners, who were almost without number. . . .

While King Andrew delayed his departure for some time as the fleet was being readied, Archbishop Bernard [of Split] died and was buried next to the church of St-Domnius. . . . Meanwhile the king boarded ship and set out on his prearranged journey. The Spalatins even gave him an escort of two galleys as far as Dyrrachion [Durrës, in Albania]. Yet, as the king had been unable to obtain a sufficiently large fleet to transport all the crusaders, some were compelled by necessity to return home, while others were obliged to wait until the following year. . . .

Now King Andrew had crossed to Syria and struck great fear into the Saracens. After he had deployed his numerous forces he advanced a good distance inland from the coast, storming castles and towns and crushing underfoot every obstruction that stood in his way. But fate's envious course [Lucan, *Phars.* 1.70] hampered the prince's noble undertakings and did not permit his worthy successes to be advanced further. For behold, evil and audacious men, whether his own or strangers I know not, schemed at the king's death, and armed with diabolical cunning, treacherously passed him a poisoned drink! As a result of this villainy, he but narrowly escaped the threat of death. In fact, even before he was fully recovered, he began to think of returning. Fearing to expose himself and his kingdom to such risks and believing his vow to the Lord to be fully satisfied, he commenced the return march to the frontiers of his country, accompanied by his entire retinue. Moreover, he had no wish to entrust himself further to the fortunes of the sea; but making the journey by land, he arrived at Antioch [in January 1218]. From there he passed on to Greece [the empire of Nicaea, the borders of which were far removed from Antioch; from Antioch, King

Andrew had to cross through the Seljuk territory to reach Nicaea] where, before advancing further, he contracted a marriage alliance with [Theodore I] Lascaris, king of the Greeks [emperor of Nicaea, 1208–22], accepting the king's daughter [Mary] as a wife for his firstborn son Béla [future King Béla IV, 1235–70]. From there he traveled through Greece and went up [through the Latin empire of Constantinople] into Bulgaria. There he was detained by [John] Asen [II], the king of the Bulgarians [emperor of Bulgaria, 1218–41], who did not permit him to depart until Andrew gave full surety that his daughter [Mary] would be united in marriage to the Bulgarian king. Thus did King Andrew complete his pilgrimage and return to his own kingdom.

Questions: What is Thomas's view of King Andrew? What does his History *reveal about crusader ideals and realities in east central Europe? What seems to be the source of the conflict between the king and the "evil and audacious men"? What were Andrew's concerns and motivations in accepting the two marriages for his daughter on his way back home?*

87. THE TEUTONIC KNIGHTS IN TRANSYLVANIA

The Teutonic Knights are commonly associated with the Baltic region and the crusades in Prussia and Lithuania. However, their first presence in Europe is linked to Transylvania. Because of increasingly aggressive Cuman raids across the eastern frontier of his kingdom, Andrew II (1205–35) invited the Teutonic Knights to Hungary in 1211 in order to protect the southeastern border of Transylvania. However, when the Knights began to assume political independence and to build stone castles without royal approval, they were expelled in 1225. The document below is the first in a series of royal charters for the order. The original charter is now lost, but the text is preserved in the papal registers as a copy of the documents that the envoys of Pope Gregory IX took with them to Hungary in 1231, in order to negotiate the return of the Knights and the reconciliation between them and King Andrew. The initial grant for the Knights treated them as "guests," much like earlier royal grants had treated groups of immigrants upon whom the Hungarian kings had bestowed certain privileges. In other words, although mentioning their role as crusaders, King Andrew regarded the Knights exactly as his grandfather, Géza II (1141–62), had regarded the "Saxon" (German-speaking) colonists he had first brought to Transylvania (and for whom King Andrew issued in 1224 a special privilege known as the Andreanum*). However, the primary task of the Knights was military, which is why the 1211 grant offered privileges not granted to other "guests." For example, the Knights were allowed to take possession of the land of Borza "in perpetuity," a promise that King Andrew would break only fourteen years later.*

Source: trans. F. Curta from H. Zimmermann, *Der Deutsche Orden in Siebenbürgen. Eine diplomatische Untersuchung* (Cologne: Böhlau, 2011), pp. 162–63.

In the name of the Holy Trinity and indivisible unity. Andrew, by the grace of God, king of Hungary, Dalmatia, Croatia, Rama, Serbia, Galicia, and Lodomeria [Vladimir-in-Volhynia, that is, Volhynia] in perpetuity. Among the signs of royal distinction, which have marked the memory of our unforgettable ancestors, the most distinguished of all, and deserving of praise, is the desire to lend to guests an intercessory hand of generous liberties; for their activities are recognized as beneficial to the kingdom, and prayer to God is commendable. Because of that, piously wishing to follow in the footsteps of our venerable parents, and striving together with them to win the eternal reward at the end of our present tribulations, out of mercy, we have sent the crusaders of the hospital of St-Mary, which was at one time located in Jerusalem, but now, because of our sins, is in Acre, to the land called Borza [now Ţara Bârsei, the region around the city of Braşov, in central Romania], which is beyond the forest in the parts toward the Cumans. Though it is now deserted and uninhabited, they can settle [that land] in peace and they can freely have it in perpetuity, so that their activities will contribute to the expansion of [our] kingdom, and with that, our act of charity will become known to God the almighty through their prayers, for the salvation of our soul and of those of our parents. In addition, should gold or silver be found there, in the said land of Borza, we allow them to appropriate the part remaining after paying that which belongs to the royal treasure [that is, the royal tax]. Moreover, we give them complete freedom to set up markets in the said land, and [we grant them] exemptions from custom duties and allow them to build timber forts and timber towns, in order to protect the kingdom from the Cumans. We also decide that no voivode [governor of Transylvania] should request hospitality from them, and we let them use freely both money and weights, granting them immunity and exemption from any taxes. They are going to be subject to no judicial authority or power [other] than that of the king. We order our bailiff Fekete János to give the mentioned crusaders the said land of Borza in possession. He is the one who marked the boundaries of the said land and transferred it to them within the limits set by Voivode Michael [governor of Transylvania, 1209–14]. The first boundary of that land begins at the frontier castle at Almagia [now Hălmeag, near Făgăraş, in central Romania] and continues to the frontier castle in Noilgiant [now Ungra, between Făgăraş and Odorheiu Secuiesc, in Romania]. From there it reaches the frontier castle [at] Nicolai [near Micloşoara, between Braşov and Odorheiu Secuiesc, in Romania], where the river flows that is known as Alt [now Olt], and going upstream up to [the point where] the Tortillou [now Prejmer River] flows into the Alt. And then from there up to the source of the Tortillou [River], and from the water called Timis [now Timiş] to the source of the water called Borsa [now Bârsa River], and from there, since the [Carpathian] mountains surround that land, it extends [back to] Almagia. All this land, surrounded in such a manner by mountains and rivers, is called Borza. Notwithstanding the fact that our charitable offer will not be hidden in oblivion from him [God], who is charity, we decided to back up our present offer with a certifying seal, as a precaution for the future. Written by the hand of Master Thomas, the chancellor of the royal court and provost of Veszprém, in the year 1211 from the incarnation of the Lord. [Given at the time] the venerable John, was archbishop of Esztergom [1205–23], the esteemed Berthold, elected archbishop of Kalocsa (1206–18) and *ban* [of Croatia, Dalmatia and, Slavonia], Kalán, bishop of Pécs [1186–1218], Boleslaus, bishop of Vác [1193–1212], Katapán, bishop of Eger [1198–1215], Simon, bishop of Oradea [1202–17], Desiderius, bishop of Cenad [1204–28], Wilhelm, bishop of Transylvania [1204–22], Gothard, bishop of Zagreb [1206–14], Peter, bishop of Győr [1206–18], and Robert, bishop of Veszprém [1209–25]. [Given at the time] Poth was count palatine and the count of Moson, Michael was voivode [of Transylvania], Peter was count of Bač, Gyula was count of Bodrog, Bánk was count of Bihar and count of the royal court, Marcellus was count of Keve and count of the [royal] court, and Nicholas was count of Bratislava. [Given] in the seventh year of our reign.

Questions: What were the relations between King Andrew and the Teutonic Knights? How are the dealings between them and the voivode of Transylvania defined in this charter? What obligations did the Knights have in exchange for the land and rights granted by the king? Why are the boundaries of the territory given to the Knights described with such precision? What can one tell about the significance of this document from the list of witnesses?

88. THE CONQUEST OF PRUSSIA AND SAINT BARBARA

The earliest account of the conquest of Prussia by the Teutonic Knights is a text known as the Hermann of Salza Letter. *Although long attributed to the fourth grand master of the order (who died in 1239), the text is in fact of a later date. It was probably commissioned by the seventh grand master of the order, Heinrich von Hohelohe (1244–49), most likely in the circumstances surrounding the Treaty of Christburg (1249), at the end of the First Prussian Uprising (1242–49), although there is still much debate about the compilation of this document. The text survives in an early sixteenth-century manuscript, but was known to Peter of Dusburg, whose* Chronicle of Prussia *(written in Latin) used the information therein for his history of the Teutonic beginnings in Prussia. Written in German, not Latin, the* Hermann of Salza Letter *is the first narrative of the Teutonic conquests and the first account of the transfer of knighthood (as associated with the military-monastic orders) outside the Holy Land. The excerpt here describes the discovery of the relics of Saint Barbara in the winter of 1242. Between the thirteenth and the fifteenth centuries, those were among the most sacred objects in the region, attracting visitors from France, Bohemia, and Lithuania.*

Source: trans. G. Leighton from *Scriptores rerum Prussicarum*, ed. T. Hirsch (Leipzig: S. Hirzel, 1876), vol. 5, pp. 159–68.

In the name of the blessed Lord, amen. I, brother Hermann, master of the hospital of St-Mary of the German House in Jerusalem, wish to make known to all people of God how the land of Prussia came to us, as we have learned it from our wise brothers, who were there and know it completely. Conrad was the duke of Masovia and Kuyavia [1194–1247], and he ruled several other lands of Poland. There was in the land at this time a bishop, a Cistercian, known as brother Christian [bishop of Prussia, 1215–45]. He took on the task to bring to Christianity the heathens in the land of Conrad. The pagans took this as a joke, something not serious, and they rode into the duke's land [plundering it] for the whole day, as they wished. Since the duke held it under his protection, the land was settled with three hundred churches, some parish churches, other [simple] churches, and chapels. The heathens overran Conrad's land so much that when they sent some of their men, Petrarten, Prerch, and Thorand, along with their aides, the duke offered them many fine robes, geldings, and horses [hoping] to appease them. They had more than what they could [have possibly] wanted. So, the duke made a truce and sent all the knights and women from Poland [as hostages], and sent gifts to the heathen legates, so that their demands might be fulfilled. When they received the gifts, they did not appear to be too nice to them after all. They were not satisfied, and so the pagans brought [the same] misery as before, and took booty and people away from [Conrad's] land. Those who could not follow them were killed. As for women carrying their children, the pagans took them from the arms of their mothers and impaled them on spears, and so they died. They wreaked so much havoc and cruelty to priests and churches, slaying and burning, that people hoped that these pagans had sent many of them to God as martyrs. The heathens destroyed the duke's land to such an extent that not a single castle remained, save for Płock, which lay on the Vistula.

Conrad then saw that he could not hold his land any longer. So, he consulted with Bishop Christian as to how he should go about keeping it, and Christian told him of a group of knights in Livonia [the Livonian Brothers of the Sword], who fought against the pagans, and took much land from them. Christian told him [also] that they had formed a military order [established by Bishop Albert of Riga in 1202], in order to stand firm against the pagans. So, Conrad and Christian found a man of honor, named Bruno [future master of the Knights of Dobrzyń]. And they asked him if he wanted to establish a similar order [for Prussia]. Its members would wear a white mantel, the same as the Knights of Livonia, with a red star. They also asked him if he wanted to build a castle and furnish it with all that was necessary. So, Christian established the order [of the Knights of Dobrzyń], and they were no more than fifteen men. Conrad learned of this and built a castle on the bank of the Vistula, called Dobrin [now Dobrzyń nad Wisłą, near Włocławek, in the voivodship of Kuyavia-Pomerania, Poland] and gave it to the order together with a settlement called Szadłowice [near Inowrocław, in the voivodship of Kuyavia-Pomerania, Poland]. The [members of the] Order [of Dobrzyń] made an oath to the duke, and promised that whatever lands they won back from the heathens, they would be divided equally [between them and Bishop Christian]. When the pagans heard of this order of knights, they were angered and ran before the castle of Dobrin. They could take nothing from it, so they rode for four, five, or ten days in the region, slaughtering as they pleased.

Then the abovementioned duke saw that this order of knights was not successful. He then heard of the brothers of the Teutonic House, that they might be able to help him. The duke sent for his counts and all of his men, and [decided to send out] legates to accomplish this task. He told them: "You must bring these brothers of the German House to me, so we might fight the heathen well with the help of God." And he said to the assembly [of counts and his men] that these brothers of the Teutonic Order were noblemen and well known in the papal and imperial courts. In light of those connections, they could easily acquire the privilege of preaching the cross against the heathens, and [secure] papal protection [for their lands]. And so the duke bade all of the bishops who were under his command, and their men, who were barons, to ride and fulfill his demands. These men all spoke with one mind, [saying] that the duke had found the best way to solve the problem of the pagans, and all agreed that the duke should send envoys to the brothers of the German House. The bishops then gave letters with their seals. As a consequence, the brothers were summoned and sent to the land of Prussia. Conrad gave the brothers of the German House the land up to Kulm [now Chełmno, in northern Poland] and Löbau [now Lubawa, near Iława, in the voivodship of Warmia-Mazuria, Poland]. This was done together with his wife, Agafia [the daughter of Sviatoslav III, the Rus' prince of Peremyshl], and children, Bolesław [future duke of Mazovia, 1247–48] and Siemovit [future duke of Mazovia, 1248–62], in addition to the bishops and the noblemen of the lands with all rights, and they did this willingly. The knights therefore acquired this land [in June 1230], in addition to that that they would recover from the heathens, settling in the surrounding areas. Bishop Gunther of Masovia, Michael of Kuyavia, Bishop Christian, Provost Berthold, William the deacon, Pribisław the Elder and the Younger [possibly father and son], who were counts of Dyrsaw [now Tczew, in the voivodship of Pomerania, northern Poland], Chancellor Nicholas and other good people, both churchmen and laymen, confirmed [the donation]. This happened in the year 1200 [in reality, 1230].

And so the brothers came to the land of Prussia and established themselves there with the assistance of the duke and other noble pilgrims [that is, crusaders]. And they crossed the Vistula to the land of Kulm, which Conrad had given to the brothers. They first built there a fort out of an [enormous] oak tree, and God sent them aid in the form of the pilgrims, who brought many things with them. From this first expedition, with God's help, a castle was built along with a town, known as Marienwerder [now Kwidzyn, in the voivodship of Pomerania, northern Poland]. From that town, armies attacked the land of Reisen [Pomesania, the region in the vicinity of the modern cities of Elbląg and Malbork, in northern Poland], where the [pagans] were forced to give tithes. From there, Christburg [now Dzierzgoń near Malbork, in the voivodship of Kuyavia-Pomerania, northern Poland] was built. And so the Christians established themselves alongside the people of Reisen, and baptized them, and they [the Pomesanians] pledged to undertake Christianity. After Christburg, another castle was built, which was known as Honede, and now is called Balga [now Znamenka near Gogolevo, on the southern shore of the Vistula Lagoon, in the modern region of Kaliningrad, Russia]. From that castle the lands of Allirlant, Natangia [the southwestern part of the present-day region of Kaliningrad, Russia], Clein-Barten and Gross-Barten, and the land of Pogesania [the region of northern Poland between the Elbląg and the Pasłęka Rivers], of Wytaen, and the land of Weweden and Schlunien were attacked and baptized into the faith. All of the people took baptism and became the order's allies. From the land of Barthen, [the knights moved to] the land of Samland, [which] was baptized. In that place there was a land called Gerdauen.

When these castles had all been built with God's help, Swantopolk [II, duke of Pomerania, 1215–66] took charge of the enemy, [and decided] that they should attack secretly the Christians on the Vistula. At that time there was a legate of the pope in Prussia, who was bishop of Modena [William of Modena, c. 1184–1251], but he could be of no assistance to them. [In 1242], Swantopolk drove against our people and killed so many people, that it became a real danger in the eyes of the legate. He demanded [complete] obedience [to the pope] from us, and called us to defend Christianity, lest all Christians who had come to the land of Prussia would be killed by pagans, together with their followers, and all their people would flee to Balga and Elbing [now Elbląg, in northern Poland]. Shortly thereafter, Swantopolk led a great heathen army into the Kulmerland and took great spoils, killing some three thousand Christians. The land was so burned, that no places remained save for Kulm, Thorn [now Toruń, Poland], and Rehden [now Radzyń Chełmiński near Grudziąz, in the voivodship of Kuyavia-Pomerania, Poland].

Brother Dietrich von Bernheim, who at that time was grand marshal, met with a few brothers to decide what course of action to take. They realized that they could not hold the land if Swantopolk continued to dwell in it, and [concluded from that that] it would be to their advantage to take it from him, or [else] it would be bad for Christianity. So, they decided to attack a castle called Scheidenitz [Schardewitz, now Sartowice, near Świece in the voivodship of Kuyavia-Pomerania, Poland], seeing that no one was there to help them. They stealthily began to assault the castle on the night of the feast of the holy virgin Barbara, who had been martryed in Antioch [4 December]. For that reason, they regarded it as a great honor to the Christian faith to engage in battle on her feast day. Therefore, the knights hoped to see a miracle on that night, and they scaled the walls of the castle with [only] twenty-four men. Inside the castle, they found fifty men, whom they slew, fighting all night long, until the sun rose above a high tree. With God's help and with that of his blessed Mother, as well as the assistance of the holy virgin Saint Barbara, the knights killed all the men who were in the castle. The brothers had no idea that the relics of Saint Barbara were there. One knight was searching the castle for its treasure, when the brothers entered the cellar. There, they found a chest with two locks and with the seal of Swantopolk on it. They brought out the chest [to daylight], and [inside it they] found a box plated in silver. The knights opened the box, and [inside it was] a head with a braided plait of hair. Next to it was a letter, explaining that the head was that of Saint Barbara. The brothers fell to their knees and gave great thanks to God. Those whom they had taken captive saw how happy the brothers were to find the relics of Saint Barbara. Among those captives was an old woman, who told the brothers, "I can make you [even] happier, as all the honor that you [now] have is from the blessed virgin." When the brothers asked how she knew about that, she answered, saying: "I have prayed to our Father. One night, I had three visions, in which the saint came to me as a beautiful woman, who wanted to go on a pilgrimage. When she left me, I spoke with a sob and was mute: 'O loving virgin, where are you going? Take me with you!' She answered me, saying: 'I will go to Kulm and will hear a Mass.' Then three more times I went out of my bed and to the door. When coming to the door, I saw her no more. Then I became aware that the brothers were in the castle, and I spoke: 'You have arrived here. Then I knew that it was her who had helped you.'" The brothers left the castle and went to Kulm with great honor and the relics of Saint Barbara. There was a noble entrance with the relics and a procession, and all went to Kulm.

Questions: What is the author's opinion about Bishop Christian and Duke Conrad of Mazovia? How does he describe the local populations, the "pagans"? Who are these "pagans"? What is the role of castles in the conquest of Prussia? How is the discovery of the relics of Saint Barbara in Scheidenitz linked to that conquest? Compare this account to that of Henry of Livonia about the crusade against Letgallians (Doc. 82).

89. POPE GREGORY IX CALLS FOR A CRUSADE AGAINST JOHN II ASEN

As early as 1225, Pope Honorius III (1216–27) asked Ugrin, archbishop of Kalocsa to preach the crusade "against the unfaithful" of Bosnia. One of those who took the vows in the Bosnian crusade was King Andrew II's nephew, John, whom the same pope urged in

1227 to fulfill his pledge. A second crusade was proclaimed by Pope Gregory IX (1227–41) in 1234 in Bosnia and Slavonia, with the same indulgence granted to participants as that offered to those taking the cross for the Holy Land. Unlike the previous crusade, that proclaimed by Gregory IX was quickly organized by King Béla IV and lasted for four years, with some notable success. The crusade was barely finished when John II Asen, emperor of Bulgaria (1218–41), abandoned Catholicism and allied himself with the empire of Nicaea against the Latin empire of Constantinople. Disappointed and furious, Pope Gregory wrote to King Béla to ask him to launch another crusade against a schismatic ruler, who had harbored heretics in his country, a probable hint at refugees from Bosnia entering Bulgaria. In Hungary, churchmen were to offer indulgences to participants in the crusade against John II Asen, which, again, were just as those for the crusade to the Holy Land. In subsequent letters to the king, the pope made use of Pope Innocent III's decretal Vergentis in senium *(1199) regarding the confiscation of the property of heretics, to allow Béla to occupy Bulgaria. However, the crusade against John II Asen never materialized. The fall of the Latin empire in 1261 caused a renewal of crusade calls, with Pope Urban IV (1261–64) deploying for the last time the crusading rhetoric and mechanism against the Orthodox Christians.*

Source: trans. F. Curta from *Les registres de Grégoire IX*, ed. L. Auvray (Paris: Albert Fontemoing, 1907), vol. 2, col. 875 (no. 4056).

Lateran, 27 January 1238. He [Pope Gregory IX] calls on the king of Hungary [Béla IV] and the archbishops of Strigonium [Esztergom] and Kalocsa, Bishop Perusino, the legate of the Holy See, and to all bishops of Hungary, ordering them to preach the word of the cross against the treacherous Asen and his land. To him who takes the cross in person and labors [toward the success of the crusades], the pope will grant an indulgence, like that granted to those who go to the assistance of the Holy Land. The pope asked and demanded him to come to the help of Christ. And, if he is truly repentant and confessed his sins, and he comes in person and of his own labor does everything, and at his own expense, he granted him a full remission of sins, as well as the land of the said Asen, which is infected with the heretical wickedness, as he explains it, insofar as it was laid down in the general council, [it is granted] to him and the other Catholics to take possession of it.

Questions: Why did Pope Gregory IX send this letter to Hungary? How did he justify a crusade against a Christian country (Bulgaria)? Why is Emperor John II Asen called "treacherous"? What did Gregory hope to achieve by proclaiming this crusade?

CHAPTER TEN

LAW

Figure 10.1 Law Code of Vinodol. A page from the sixteenth-century copy of the Law Code of Vinodol (1288).

90. FIRST LAW CODE IN EASTERN EUROPE

Restored to his position as bishop of Moravia (which was now elevated to the rank of archbishop), after being released from captivity in Reichenau Abbey in 870, Methodius continued his brother's program of translations. He may have thought about making himself useful to the ruler of Moravia, Svatopluk, when translating from Greek into Old Church Slavonic a portion of the collection of ecclesiastical laws known as Nomokanon, *namely the* Collection of Fifty Canons *compiled in the sixth century by John Scholastikos. He also used an adaptation of the* Ekloga *of the Byzantine emperors Leo III (717–41) and Constantine V (741–75) for a body of civil law known as the* Court Law for the People. *Two versions of this text exist, one long, the other short. The short version of the* Court Law *has thirty-one articles and has been dated to the late ninth century on the basis of a number of archaic features of the language used therein. Various forms of punishment that appear in the* Ekloga *(death penalty and mutilations) are replaced in the* Court Law *with flogging and selling into slavery, probably under the influence of western European legal practices. Unlike the* Ekloga, *however, the* Court Law *has more articles related to pagan practices. Moreover, it contains an original article (no. 3 below) on the spoils of war.*

Source: trans. K. Petkov, *The Voices of Medieval Bulgaria, Seventh-Fifteenth Century: The Records of a Bygone Culture* (Leiden: Brill, 2008), pp. 48–54.

1. Before all justice God's justice should be discussed. That is why Saint Constantine [the Great, Roman emperor, 306–37], as he wrote the first law said this: any village in which pagan sacrifices and oaths are performed is to be given over to God's temple [to the nearby church], with all of its properties. If there are lords in the village and they perform sacrifices and swear oaths [in pagan fashion], sell them with all of their property and give their price to the poor [as charity].

3. Of spoils. When someone goes out to fight the enemy, he has to guard himself against vile and satanic words and deeds, he has to have God in his mind, to pray and seek God's guidance in the battle; for God helps those whose hearts seek advice, and victory is not won by overwhelming force, but it is God's fortress that gives victory. The prince takes the sixth part [of the spoils after war], and all the people take the rest. Let great and small share equally. The *župans* [noblemen] should be content with [what is given to them from] the prince's share. All other spoils are the people's share. If there are some, be they *kmets* [perhaps members of the social elite], [or] be they commoners, who were courageous and accomplished heroic feats, then if there is a prince or a commander there, let them give [to the heroes] from the prince's share dividing it into whatever is proper, for those who fought and for those who stayed in the camp. Because this is what the prophet David said, wrote, and enjoined.

7. If someone weds his godmother, according to secular law they should be separated and have their noses cut off; according to church law they could be separated and do penance for fifteen years. Their penance should be as follows: for five years they should stay outside [the church, that is, be excommunicated], weep, and listen to the liturgy [from a distance]; for [the next] four years [they should be allowed to] stay in the church until the [the readings from the] holy Gospel; for [the next] three years, [they would have to leave the church] at [the Creed, which begins with] "I believe in one God"; and for [the remaining] three years, they can attend to the end, but still stay on bread and water. And so their term will end, and in the sixteenth year they can receive everything [including Communion]. The same punishment applies to anyone who copulates with his goddaughter, as well as to the one who is found with a married woman.

9. Whoever forces himself upon a virgin girl in a deserted place where she cannot be helped should be sold and his property given to the girl.

16. No one should forcefully drive out from the church those who sought sanctuary in it. Those who fled there should explain the affair and their guilt to the priests, who will accept them as fugitives until an inquiry is done according to the law and the accusations are investigated. If someone attempts to use force to take the fugitive out of the church, whoever he might be, let him suffer 140 [lashes until he] bleeds. Then let there be a due inquiry into the accusation against the one who fled.

19. If someone buys a prisoner of war with all his chattels from foreigners and the former can pay his price, let him be set free. If he cannot ransom himself let him work as a slave until he ransoms himself. . . .

21. A soldier who has [been captured and] abandoned our Christian faith [while in captivity] and returns to his land should be given to the church.

30. Whoever steals someone else's slave, hides him, and does not let him go, he is guilty before the master of the slave and either has to give another slave or pay his price.

Questions: Compare these regulations with the provisions of the treaty between Riga, Gotland, and Smolensk (Doc. 58). What types of violations are highlighted in the Court Law*? How restrictive is this law? What is the role of slavery in the society for which the* Court Law *was written?*

91. CHURCH AND SECULAR LAW IN THE *STATUTE OF YAROSLAV*

The Statute of the Grand Prince Yaroslav *is, in fact, a charter that survives in six redactions, the earliest of which was written down in the twelfth or early thirteenth century, most likely based on an initial version drawn up between 1051 and 1054. Issued for the benefit of the church in Rus', the* Statute *considerably expands the jurisdiction of ecclesiastical courts, far beyond canon law. In that respect, the* Statute *is different from legal standards in Byzantium, because it combines crimes otherwise under secular law with modified punishments most typical for Rus'. Most provisions of the* Statute *pertain to criminal law: definitions of offenses and the appropriate penalties. In fact, the* Statute *expands upon an earlier code attributed to Vladimir, which bestowed tithes upon the church in Kiev and granted jurisdiction to the church in such matters as divorce, adultery, abduction, incest, and rape, as well as domestic disputes. By contrast, the* Statute of Yaroslav *contains a very elaborate schedule of monetary fines to be paid primarily to the metropolitan, in fewer cases to the victim or the victim's family (as wergild). In that respect, the* Statute *is not very different from the dyadic (or "archaic") lists of primarily secular rules issued by Rus' princes, the most famous of which is* Russkaia Pravda. *The "Greek Nomokanon" mentioned in the introduction of the* Statute *is most likely the* Nomokanon in XIV Titles, *a collection of ecclesiastical laws compiled by Patriarch Photius in 883, and translated into Old Church Slavonic in the eleventh century as the first (or "Efrem")* Kormchaia *("Book of the Pilot").*

Source: trans. F. Curta from *Rossiiskoe zakonodatel'stvo X–XX vv.*, ed. O.I. Chistiakov (Moscow: Iuridicheskaia literatura, 1984), vol. 1, pp. 139–40.

I, Grand Prince Yaroslav, the son of Vladimir, according to the behest of my father [and] after consulting with Ilarion, the metropolitan of Kiev and of all Rus', understood from the Greek Nomokanon that litigations should not be tried by the prince, neither by his boyars or his judges. I [therefore] established the right of the metropolitan and the bishops to resolve cases of divorces in all towns [of Rus'], as well as the right of the church and the metropolitan to get income from the *myt* [custom duty] every tenth week. And the people [that is, personnel] of the metropolitan do not pay tax anywhere, nor [do they pay] travel or trade duties.

In the case of someone kidnapping a girl in order to marry her: if the victim happens to be a boyar's daughter, then [the perpetrator must] pay five *grivny* [ingots, the monetary standard of twelfth- and early thirteenth-century Rus'] of gold for her shame, and [another] five *grivny* of gold [a *grivna* of gold was the equivalent of fifteen *grivny* of silver] to the metropolitan. If the victim happens to be the daughter of a lesser boyar, then [the perpetrator must pay] her a *grivna* of gold [for shame], and to the metropolitan a[nother] *grivna* of gold. If she turns out to be [the daughter of] good people, then [the kidnapper will have to pay] two *rubly* [a thirteenth-century monetary unit that was the equivalent either of an entire *grivna* of silver or of just half that, or about one hundred grams of silver] for shame to her, and another two *rubly* to the metropolitan. (In addition to that), each one of the girls who participated in the abduction [must pay] sixty *kuny* [*kuna* was a monetary denomination, the equivalent of one twenty-fifth of a *grivna* of silver] to the metropolitan, and the prince will prescribe punishment to [each one of] them as behooves his authority, regardless of the punishment [mentioned] above.

If someone rapes the daughter or the wife of a boyar, [he will pay] her five *grivny* of gold for shame, and [the same amount] to the metropolitan as well. Should [she] be [the daughter or wife of a] lesser boyar, [the perpetrator will have to pay to her] one *grivna* of gold, and another one to the metropolitan. [If the victim turns out to be from among] good people [most likely the rich in the towns], [the perpetrator has to pay] two *rubly* [to her] and two *rubly* to the metropolitan. [If she is from among] commoners, [the perpetrator has to pay to her] twelve *kuny*, and twelve *kuny* in addition to the metropolitan. And the prince will prescribe to them punishment according to his authority, regardless of the [other] punishment [mentioned] above. . . .

Also, if a wife, with or without husband, gives birth to an illegitimate child and destroys him in any way—feeding him to the pigs, causing an early, unnatural abortion, or drowning [the child]—then, after she is exposed as guilty, she will be sent to the monastery [to do the required penance] until her relatives [can] redeem her.

If the parents of a girl from a family of great boyars do not want their daughter to marry, even if the girl wants that, then [they have to pay for such an offense] to the metropolitan five *grivny* of gold. If the perpetrators are from among lesser boyars, [then they have to pay for such an offense] one *grivna* of gold to the metropolitan. If they turn out to be from among good people, [they will have to pay] the metropolitan two *rubly* or twelve *grivny* [most likely, *kuny*]. If they are ordinary people, they will have to pay one ruble.

If the husband is unfaithful to his wife, the metropolitan cannot collect money from him, but the prince must impose [on him] the punishment [appropriate] for an adulterer.

If a man enters into a second marriage without dissolving the first, then he is responsible for that to the metropolitan. He should live with his first wife and send the second to the monastery.

If a wife, having a husband, arbitrarily enters a second marriage, or begins to cheat on her husband, then this wife [should be sent] to a monastery, and the metropolitan should fine her second husband [for that].

A serious illness of a wife, even if it continues for a long time and leads to her disability, cannot be grounds for divorcing her.

The same rule applies to a husband who is ill. . . .

If someone sets fire to a threshing floor or a courtyard, or anything else [on the estate of the church], [the perpetrator will pay] the metropolitan forty *grivny*. [Moreover,] penance will be imposed [upon the perpetrator], and the prince will prescribe [for that person an additional] punishment. . . .

If either a Jew or a Muslim enters into a relationship with a Rus' woman, then fifty *grivny* [will be collected] from the infidel for the metropolitan, and the Rus' [woman] will be sent to the monastery. . . .

If someone commits fornication with a nun, [he will have to pay] the metropolitan forty *grivny*, and moreover penance will be imposed [on the perpetrator]. . . .

If someone cuts off the hair on the head or beard [of some other man], [the perpetrator will have to pay] the metropolitan twelve *grivny*, and the prince will prescribe [to that person] an additional punishment. . . .

If someone steals hemp, flax, or anything [else] from the grain harvest, then [he will pay] three *grivny* to the metropolitan. . . .

If a wife was engaged in witchcraft in the form of spells, making amulets, or potions and poisons of various kinds, then that is not a [sufficient] reason for divorce, but the husband, after exposing her, will have to punish [his] guilty [wife] according to his power [over her]. . . .

If a wife beats her husband, [then she will have to pay] three *grivny* to the metropolitan. . . .

If a man beats someone else's wife, [then he must pay her due for shame] according to the law, and, in addition, six *grivny* to the metropolitan. . . .

If someone eats any of the meats that are forbidden to Christians—horse, bear, or some other [kind of meat]—that person will be held accountable to the metropolitan, who will determine the punishment for the perpetrator. . . .

One should neither eat nor drink with someone who is unbaptized, whether a foreigner or a fellow countryman, until [the time] they are baptized. And if it becomes known that someone has eaten or drunk with such people, the perpetrator will be responsible to the metropolitan. . . .

If someone commits fornication with a Muslim or a Jewish woman, and does not break that bond, let him be excommunicated from the church and from among Christians; the perpetrator will have to pay twelve *grivny* to the metropolitan.

Questions: Which of the crimes above is most serious? How does one know? Where is canon law clearly applied, and why? Why is the punishment for cutting someone's hair or beard so high? Does the Statute of Yaroslav *explain why divorce is rarely, if ever, an option? Why is the metropolitan designated to execute those laws that pertain to sexual relations of Christians either with Muslims or with Jews?*

92. THE LAWS OF KING COLOMAN

In the history of medieval Hungary, King Ladislas I (1077–95) is known for having issued a large number of statutes, which were meant to adapt and often modify the legislation introduced by his predecessor, Stephen I (1000–38). One of the most obvious features of Ladislas's legislation is the emphasis on property and public order. None of his laws survive in the original form, and all are from fifteenth- and even sixteenth-century transcriptions. Because of that, it is impossible to date any of the legislative documents attributed to Ladislas's reign with any degree of certainty. His successor, Coloman (1095–1116) is also known for the development of criminal law during his reign. The compilation of decrees issued in his name is dedicated to Seraphin, archbishop of Esztergom (c. 1095–1104), and it may therefore be dated to the early twelfth century. However, the effort to put together those royal decrees was most likely the work of an assembly of both laymen and churchmen convened at Tarcal (now a village in northeastern Hungary) shortly before or shortly after the year 1100. It may well be that the assembly was meant to discuss the existing legislation going back to King Stephen and to propose amendments. This, as well as the mixed composition of the assembly, explains why the laws collected were for both the church and for secular society. In fact, some of the laws even presume the ongoing cooperation between churchmen and royal officials in establishing a well-ordered Christian society.

Source: J.M. Bak, G. Bónis, and J.R. Sweeney, *The Laws of the Medieval Kingdom of Hungary, 1000–1301* (Bakersfield, CA: Charles Schlacks, 1989), pp. 25–30.

But here begin the laws of Coloman, by the grace of God, king of Hungary . . .

1. It pleased the king and the general council that possessions given to monasteries and churches by the holy king Stephen shall remain undisturbed.
2. Since our people are often as much burdened by the hardship of travel as by poverty, and cannot come to the royal court whenever necessary, we order that twice yearly, namely on the feast of the apostles Philip and James [1 May] and during the octave of Saint Michael [eight days after Michaelmas, on 6 October] a synod be held in each bishopric at which the [local] count and [other] counts as well as authorities in other offices shall assemble with their bishops, and whoever does not appear, even if summoned without a seal [by means of a verbal citation, through an agent] shall be deemed guilty. . . .

17. The vineyards, fields, and lands granted by any king shall remain forever with those to whom they were given. . . .
18. Dispossessed former peasants shall, if they have no land elsewhere, return to their own place. If their land was given to monasteries or churches, and they have other land, this grant shall remain inviolable. . . .

32. If someone who unjustly usurped possession of the land of another is found guilty by ordeal, he shall give the same amount of his own land and pay additionally ten [gold] *pensae* [money of account equal to ten Byzantine gold coins, or the value of ten steers (young oxen), or four hundred pennies].

33. Merchants entirely devoted to business for the purpose of growing rich shall pay double the old customs levy, but the poor who live from trade shall pay the usual levy. . . .
47. We command that each village of the Ishmaelites [Muslims, most likely of Khwarazmian origin, who lived permanently in Hungary] shall build a church, and from each of these villages an endowment shall be given. After it has been built, half the Ishmaelites shall leave the village and settle in another place, and that shall henceforth live united in custom together with us in that house, which is one and the same Church of Christ, harmoniously in one religion. . . .
48. If an Ishmaelite has a guest, or anyone invited to dinner, both he and his table companions shall eat only pork for meat. . . .
59. The bishop or the archdeacon shall be the judge in cases of abduction of women. . . .
67. Bigamous [priests] or the husbands of widows or of women repudiated by their husbands shall give up these illicit marriages or be excluded from the clergy. . . .
70. No one recognized to be a clerk shall wear secular clothing, namely: a slit fur cloak or spotted tunic, pale yellow gloves, a red striped coat, a green mantle, boots or a fur cap, painted or silken footwear, silk shirts and tunics, and these are not to be held together at the breast by knots or fibulae, but are to be such as embrace the neck, as it were. . . .
73. Burials of Christians shall take place only in a churchyard.
74. No Jew should dare to buy or sell Christian slaves, nor may he retain any in his service; and he shall lose those, which he has now, if he does not sell them in the allotted time.
75. If, however, one of them has agricultural land, he shall farm it with pagan slaves. Jews, if they can afford it, are permitted to hold property, but they themselves may not reside outside episcopal sees.
77. No one should dare to sell or convey outside Hungary a male or female slave of Hungarian origin or anyone born in Hungary, even one of foreign parentage, except for slaves of other languages who were brought in from other regions, nor [should they export] any animal except male cattle. If a count should violate this decree, either he shall be deprived of his office, or he shall lose two-thirds of his property; a third of his wealth, however, shall remain for his wife and heirs.

Questions: In what ways it is apparent from the laws that this is a society recently converted to Christianity? How are Muslims and Jews treated? Compare the treatment of both groups in the Statute of Yaroslav *(Doc. 91). What violations were deferred to churchmen to be dealt with under canon law?*

93. *RUSSKAIA PRAVDA*

The short version of the law code now known as Russkaia Pravda (The Rus' Law) *was discovered in the early eighteenth century. The first eighteen articles in this version (which are otherwise known as "the oldest Pravda") are believed to have been issued by Yaroslav the Wise in 1016 (or, more likely, 1019), with the remaining articles issued jointly by his sons, Iziaslav, Sviatoslav, and Vsevolod, after their father's death. An earlier generation of scholars believed that after 1113, Yaroslav's grandson, Vladimir Monomakh, expanded upon the short version and added a series of articles of his own, which resulted in the longer version of the* Russkaia Pravda; *this was further enlarged in the 1140s and 1170s. However, it is likely that the short version actually emerged long after the text of the longer version had taken its present shape. Unlike most medieval law codes, the surviving text of the short version was incorporated into the text of the* Novgorod First Chronicle *as a charter issued by Yaroslav specifically for Novgorod and its citizens in recognition of the outstanding services that they have rendered to him in the war with Sviatopolk. However, the provisions of the short version seem to be out of place and date for the eleventh century. Therefore, it has recently been suggested that the short version is in fact an adaptation of the longer version (first attested in the late thirteenth century) written as late as the fifteenth century.*

Source: trans. F. Curta from *Pamiatniki russkogo prava*, ed. L.V. Cherepnin and S.V. Iushkov (Moscow: Gosudartsvennoe izdatel'stvo iuridicheskogo literatury, 1952), vol. 1, pp. 77–78.

1. If a man kills a man, the brother is to take vengeance for his brother; the son for his father, or the father for his son, or the nephew for his uncle; and if there is no one to take vengeance, [then the murderer] is to pay forty *grivny* [silver ingot used as monetary unit] for the head [of the person killed]; if [the victim] is a Rus', or a young warrior in the prince's retinue, or a merchant, or a bailiff, or one of the prince's bodyguards, or a freeman of the prince, or a [Novgorodian] Slav, then [the murderer] has to pay forty *grivny*.
2. If a man is beaten [so badly that] he is covered in bruises and bleeds [from his wounds], then he does not need any eyewitnesses [to confirm what happened to him]; if he has no sign [of injury], then he has to have an eyewitness; if he cannot [produce that eyewitness], then that is the end of the case; if he cannot take vengeance by himself, then he is to receive three *grivny*, in addition to payment for the physician [who takes care of his wounds].
3. If someone hits someone else with a cudgel, or a rod, or a fist, or a cup, or a [drinking] horn, or the back of the hand, then [he must pay a compensation of] twelve *grivny*; if the offender is not caught [for the victim to take revenge], then he must pay, and there the matter ends.
4. If someone strikes someone else with an unsheathed sword, or with its hilt, then [he must pay a compensation of] twelve *grivny* for the offense.

5. If someone hits someone else's arm and the arm is severed or withers, then [he must pay a compensation of] forty *grivny*.
6. If [someone hits someone else on the leg, but the] leg is not severed, [yet the victim] becomes lame, then the children [of the victim will have to] humble [the perpetrator of the crime].
7. If someone cuts off the finger [of someone else], [he must pay a compensation of] three *grivny* for the offense.
8. For the mustache, twelve *grivny*; for the beard, twelve *grivny*.
9. If someone unsheathes his sword, but does not strike [anyone, only threatens], then he [must] pay one *grivna*.
10. If someone shoves someone else away from himself or pulls toward himself, then [he must pay] three *grivny* [compensation], provided that [the victim] brings two witnesses; if [the victim] is Varangian or a Kolbiag [foreign resident], then [he] takes an oath [and that will be sufficient to prove his claim].
11. If a slave is [taken and] hidden either by a Varangian or a Kolbiag, and does not bring [the slave] back for three days [after the loss of the slave was announced by the owner], and [the owner] finds out [where the slave is hidden], then on the third day [the slave owner] gets back his slave, in addition to three *grivny* for the offense.
12. If someone rides someone else's horse without asking for [the owner's] permission, he must pay three *grivny* [to the owner].
13. If someone steals someone else's horse, or weapon, or clothes, and [the owner] recognizes it [as his property] within his own community, then he gets back his own [property], in addition to three *grivny* for the offense.
14. If someone recognize [his stolen property], he should neither take it back nor say to someone else [who has it], "This is mine"; but he should say, "Come to a [judicial] meeting, to show where you got it"; if he [who is thus asked to appear in that meeting] does not show up, he must provide surety within five days.

Questions: What violations did the Russkaia Pravda *attempt to restrict or control, and why? How can one explain the serious nature of attempts to cut someone's facial hair (beard or mustache)? Vengeance is not excluded, at least in principle; however, what is the basis of solving conflicts caused by violence?*

94. LAW CODE OF VINODOL

In the mid-thirteenth century, the counts of Krk, who had exercised control over that island since the twelfth century, took over the region facing the island in continental Croatia, known as Vinodol. In the twelfth century, Vinodol was a Hungarian march on the border with the Holy Roman empire and with Venice. Count Bartol II entered in the service of the Hungarian king Béla III (1172–96) and was granted Modruš, next to Vinodol, in 1193. When Bartol II died without male heirs, King Andrew II (1205–35) allowed the transfer of Modruš to his nephew Vid II, who at that time was ruling as count in Krk. This was in fact the basis for the claims of the counts of Krk to the lands on the continent. When in 1271 the citizens of the town of Senj (in the Lika-Senj county of modern Croatia) elected Count Vid IV as their podesta (chief magistrate), the road to Vinodol was open. Shortly after that, the counts introduced changes in the administration of the region and the rights of local towns, which provoked the reaction of the local population. Many of the castles in the region had been manned by "castle warriors," as they were in Hungary. With the coming of the counts of Krk, those members of the lesser nobility lost their freedom and became subjects of the counts. In order to regulate their relations with the counts, and to confirm the changes in the administration of the region that they had introduced, the Law Code of Vinodol was enacted in 1288. Issued in the form of a charter with seventy-five articles, this is the first law code of the western region of the Balkan Peninsula. The Law Code is in the vernacular language, and the oldest manuscript copy dates to the late fifteenth or early sixteenth century, written in Glagolitic script.

Source: trans. F. Curta from *Vinodolski Zakon, 1288*, ed. J. Bratulić (Zagreb: Globus, 1988), pp. 51, 52–53, 57, 59–60, 62, and 63.

In the name of the Lord. Amen. In the year of our Lord 1288, the first indiction, on the sixth day of the month of January. At the time of the King Ladislas [IV], the most glorious king of Hungary [1272–90], in the sixteenth year of his reign. At the time of the great men Frederick, John, Leonard, Dujam, Bartol, and Vid, the princes of Krk [the northernmost island in the Adriatic Sea, in the Kvarner Bay], Vinodol [the region facing the island of Krk in continental Croatia], and Modruš [the region to the east of Vinodol, in continental Croatia]. Since people often realize that they need to guard the old and tested laws, each and all the people of Vinodol, wanting to hold on to those good old laws, which their ancestors had kept intact, gathered at a meeting in Novi Grad, both churchmen and laymen, in the presence of the same prince Leonard, mentioned above, and elected from each town in the Vinodol town, not all old people, but those known to have a better memory of the laws of their fathers, and had heard from their grandfathers.

1. First of all, if any of the public churches in the Vinodol has to be consecrated or is consecrated by the lord bishop, in whose diocese that church is located, he cannot receive for that said consecration more than forty *soldins* of petty Venetian currency, in addition to one lunch and one dinner, and that from the very people who [are about to] consecrate the church. The deacon, whom they call *malik* in Croatian, and *macarol* in the language of the Vlachs, and who

assists the bishop in that same church, may receive for that same consecration only a *bolanča* [medieval coin] worth fifteen petty Venetian coins. . . .

5. Furthermore, if the lord prince of Vinodol or the said bishop [happens to] visit the county of Vinodol, in whichever of the towns he arrives, he may confiscate for the support of himself and his company, and [he may ask] the hundredman of the town [head of a group of one hundred town dwellers] to bring him the cattle or small livestock, which may happen to be closest, and that from the stock of *kmeti* [former "castle warriors"], of nobles, of priests, and of all other people. Nevertheless, the lord prince must always pay for that, while he may have his *permani* [princely servants or retainers] seize for himself, his family, and for his court the nearest cattle available in that same town, from any of those mentioned above.

29. Furthermore, if anyone kills any of the vice-counts or a servant in the company of the prince or a *perman*, and if he flees without being caught, let the prince know how to collect the compensation money in the form of a fine (obligation) in whatever form and as much as he wants, with only half of that from the family of the criminal, as the family is obligated to pay only half, and the criminal the other half. But if the criminal is caught, then the same prince or someone else in his place can extract revenge from him as he pleases, but his family is not to be punished in any way. . . .

42. Furthermore, no *ključar* [bailiff] is credible and can be trusted about anything that he says he has given to someone or given away or borrowed or that he has given in any manner from his warehouse, which would be worth more than twenty *soldins*, unless he has credible witnesses. And also, for that to be worth twenty *soldins*, he must take an oath on the holy Gospel.

43. Furthermore, no innkeeper can be trusted without testimony for any claim that he would make for [the payment of] his own wine, except for a value up to ten *soldins*. And *podružnik*, that is, the one who sells somebody else's wine, up to fifty *soldins*. And they still have to take an oath on it.

44. Furthermore, no trade book is credible without good witnesses, except up to fifty pounds for each debt. And for this, one has to take an oath on the Gospels to verify his trade books. . . .

53. Furthermore, if anyone points out that a bailiff or a witness is guilty, there should be no litigation against the accuser or against the witness or against anyone else acting in their name. And if anyone claims that a bailiff or a witness is guilty and promises to prove that with witnesses and those witnesses are not ready to testify or their statements do not support the claims of the accuser, then he should not raise any lawsuit against them in advance. That is, if a witness is called before the court because of some case, and one party would like to refute his testimony, he can do so if he has witnesses. If witnesses are called against him or against his testimony, and they testify as he was about to prove, henceforth he may not bring witnesses against any of those witnesses in advance. That is,

let him or anyone else oppose that testimony. Or, because of his testimony, no lawsuit can be filed against him for any reason. . . .

57. Furthermore, no assembly, municipal or individual, in the town or elsewhere, may be held for any business that concerns the community, if the prince's agent is not present. And if they should act contrary to that, they shall lose all their property in favor of the abovementioned prince.

Questions: Whose interests are defended by the stipulations of the Law Code of Vinodol? Why can no bailiff's testimony be trusted? Under what circumstances and by whom was an oath taken? What is the role of witnesses in the legal system of northern Croatia during the Middle Ages?

95. MAKING A WILL

Although commonly dated to 1305 (on the basis of the year 1302 mentioned in the last chapter of Book 5), the elaborate text of the Statute of Zadar *was drawn up in the 1260s. The version preserved is in a fifteenth-century manuscript from the library of the Franciscan convent in Dubrovnik; it shows the heavy influence of Venetian law, for the city fell to Venice in 1409. Judging from fourteenth-century court records, articles from legal books of Venetian origin were added to the original late thirteenth-century* Statute *to address issues such as the job descriptions for different urban magistrates. No fewer than 160 "novels" (new stipulations) were added at a later time, perhaps in the fifteenth century, all of them edited into a single text in 1458. The Venetian influence is also evident in the careful organization of the text into five books, each with its own titles and chapters. The first book deals with regulations pertaining to the communal officials, their election, and their oaths of office. The second book deals with communal magistrates and judicial procedure in civil cases. Book 3, from which a fragment is translated below, covers such diverse matters as property, trade, contracts, loans, and inheritance. The fourth book is entirely dedicated to maritime affairs, while the fifth deals with rebellions against the count, black markets, and other pernicious matters.*

Source: trans. F. Curta from *Zadarski statut sa svim reformacijama odnosno novim uredbama donesenima do godine 1563*, ed. J. Kolanović and M. Križman (Zagreb: Ogranak Matice hrvatske, 1997), pp. 348 and 352.

3.23.105. Everyone is allowed to write his own will with his own hand, seal it with a well-known seal, and deposit it in places specified in the statute.

The last provision of every testator is rightly called the holy law: according to that law, that is, according to the last will, we desire and command that every inhabitant of the city and of the district of Zadar walks safely on the paths of the teaching below. Therefore, when someone, of whatever condition or sex, wants or decides to draft a last will, and if that person wants to write it with his [or her] own hand, let him [or her] be free to do what he [or she] wants, and let such a will be valid, and let his [or her] judgment not be in vain, but let it be taken as firm and valid, if the said will states the year, month, and day of drawing up the will. Also, if the said will is provided with its own or usual seal, or if its copy, without any addition, subtraction, or modification is stored in one of the six places listed below, namely the chamber or office of the procurator of the commune of Zadar, the sacristy of the monastery of the Friars Minor, the sacristy of the Dominican priory, the sacristy of the convent of the nuns of St-Nicholas of the Order of St-Clare, or the sacristy of the convent of the nuns of St-Mary de Melta outside the city, or the sacristy of the monastery of St-Mary inside the city.

3.23.109. Drawing up a will in the countryside and its form.

When a person from Zadar or its county finds himself in a village or town on an island of the Zadar district and wants to make a will there, we want him [or her] to be free to make a will in front of four witnesses; after these four witnesses have been called for the will of such a testator, they shall be obliged within fifteen days after the death of the said testator to appear in court to testify to the truth without any admixture of falsehood, of all the details claimed to have been said, that the testator ordered, mentioned, and disposed. And then, if it seems to our lord the count and to the judicial court that witnesses are lawful and credible, let the lord count and the judicial court order that a public document be drawn up on the basis of their statements. The procurator or judge or examiner is obliged to lay his hand on the document and let such a document be taken by all together and respected in everything instead of a will, and as a will. And we want that document or will of any citizen of Zadar, which is drawn up in a village, on an island, or in any other place in the district of Zadar, or an abbreviated transcript of a witness statement worded in the aforementioned manner, to be as valid and have full force as if that citizen of Zadar who drafted the will in one of the aforementioned places died in Zadar. Otherwise, if the person survives and leaves the place where he [or she] made his [or her] will while alive, let his [or her] will made in a village, on an island, or in another place in the Zadar district not be valid by law. However, the abbreviated testamentary record of a person who permanently and always resides in a village, on an island, or [some] other place in the district of Zadar, or his testament drawn up on the basis of an abbreviated transcript of a witness statement, shall be valid and firm in all respects, whether he [or she] who made the will dies in that same place and of that same disease, or if he [or she] dies elsewhere or of a different disease.

Questions: What institutions served as archives of public records in early fourteenth-century Dalmatia? How was the validity of a will guaranteed? Why was drawing up a will in the countryside different from the practice in the city? How did the last stipulation of the Statute *influence the relations between the city of Zadar and its hinterland?*

CHAPTER ELEVEN

LITERACY AND LITERATURE

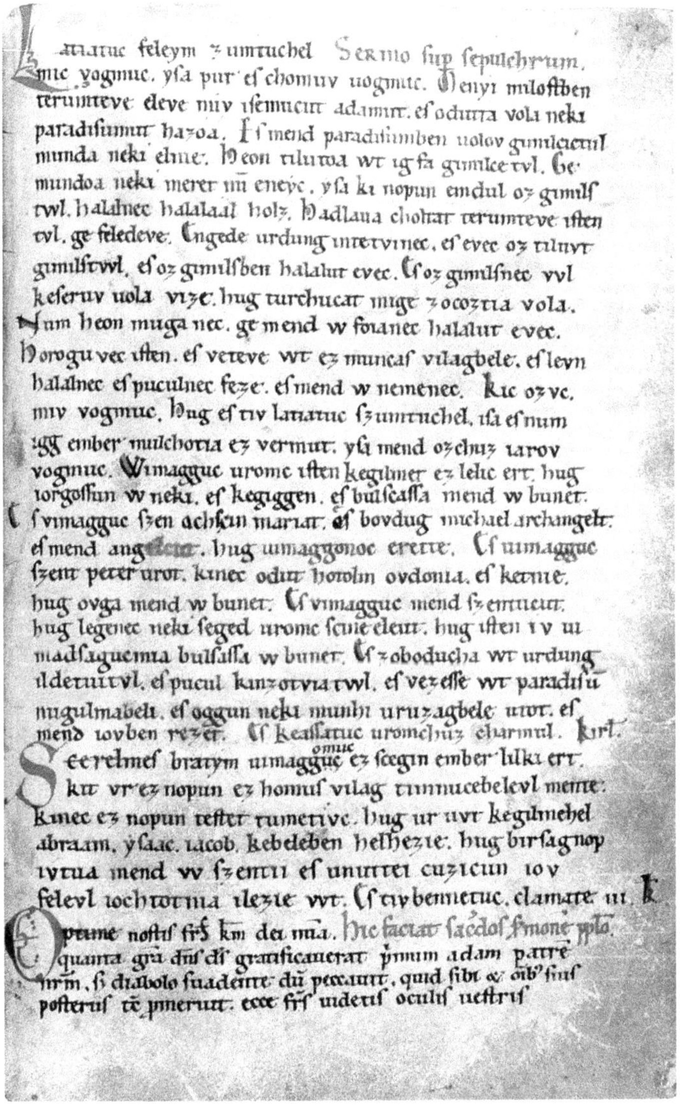
Latiatuc feleym zumtuchel Sermo sup sepulchrum.
mic vogmuc. yſa pur eſ chomuv uogmuc. Menyi milostben
terumteve eleve miv iſemucut adamut. eſ odutta vola neki
paradiſumut hazoa. Eſ mend paradiſumben uolov gimilcectul
munda neki elnie. Heon tiluvtoa wt ig fa gimilcetvl. Ge
mundoa neki meret nu eneyc. yſa ki nopun emdul oz gimilſ
twl. halalnec halalaal holz. Hadlaua choltat terumteve iſten
tvl. ge feledeve. Engede urdung intetvinec. eſ evec oz tilvvt
gimilſtwl. eſ oz gimilſben halalut evec. Eſ oz gimilſnec vvl
keſeruv uola vize. hug turchucat migé zocoztia vola.
Num heon muga nec. ge mend w foianec halalut evec.
Horoguvec iſten. eſ veteve wt ez munkaſ vilagbele. eſ levn
halalnec eſ puculnec feze. eſ mend w nemenec. Kic ozvc.
miv vogmuc. Hug eſ tiv latiatuc ſzumtuchel. iſa eſ num
igg ember mulchotia ez vermut. yſa mend ozchuz iarov
vogmuc. Wimagguc uromc iſten kegilmet ez lelic ert. hug
iorgoſſun w neki. eſ kegiggen. eſ bulſcaſſa mend w bunet.
Eſ vimagguc ſzen achſcin mariat. eſ bovdug michael archangelt.
eſ mend angelcut. hug uimaggonoc erette. Eſ uimagguc
ſzent peter urot. kinec odut hotolm ovdonia. eſ ketnie.
hug ovga mend w bunet. Eſ vimagguc mend ſzentucut.
hug legenec neki ſeged uromc ſcine eleut. hug iſten iv ui
madſagucmia bulſaſſa w bunet. Eſ zoboducha wt urdung
ildetuitvl. eſ pucul kinzotviatwl. eſ vezeſſe wt paradiſu
nugulmabeli. eſ oggun neki munhi uruzagbele utot. eſ
mend iovben reſet. Eſ keaſſatuc uromchuz charmul. kirl.
omnic
Szeretlmeſ bratym uimagguc ez ſcegin ember lilki ert.
kit vr ez nopun ez homuſ vilag timnucebelevl mente.
kinec ez nopun teſtet tumetivc. hug ur uvt kegilmehel
abraam. yſaac. iacob. kebeleben helhezie. hug birſagnop
ivtua mend w ſzentii eſ unuttei cuzicun iov
felevl iochtotnia ilezie wt. Eſ tiv bennetuc. clamate. iii. K
Optime noſtris frs km dei mia. Hic faciat ſacdoſ ſmone pplo.
quanta gra dns ds gratificauerat primum adam patre
nrm. ſi diabolo ſuadente du peccauit. quid ſibi et oibus ſuis
poſteris te pmeruit. ecce frs uidetis oculis ueſtris

Figure 11.1 Funeral Sermon and Prayer. A text in Hungarian preserved in the Pray Codex, a late twelfth- or early thirteenth-century manuscript.

96. KHRABR DEFENDS THE SLAVONIC LETTERS

At some point during the tenth century, most likely in Preslav, a new alphabet was introduced in Bulgaria to replace the Glagolitic. Unlike the alphabet invented by Constantine, this was an adaptation of the Greek uncial to the needs of Old Church Slavonic. The adaptation is now known as the Cyrillic alphabet, which is currently used for writing many Slavic languages (Russian, Belarusian, Ukrainian, Bulgarian, Macedonian, and Serbian). The two systems of writing Old Church Slavonic coexisted for a while and were sometimes used within one and the same manuscript, a phenomenon known as "synchronic digraphia," the concurrent existence of two writing systems for the same language. However, such a synchronic use of the two alphabets did not last long. While several palimpsests exist of Cyrillic over Glagolitic, there is none of Glagolitic over Cyrillic. Moreover, the innovation seems to have caused some controversy, for around 900, a monk named Khrabr ("the Brave") composed a treatise entitled On the Letters *to defend the Glagolitic letters as better suited to rendering the sounds of Old Church Slavonic. He mentions thirty-eight letters, but the Glagolitic alphabet has thirty-nine letters, with some letters (such as* izhe, kher, *and* jer*) having more than one form. Khrabr may have been familiar with late Glagolitic, which relied on a total of forty-two letters. In his defense of the "Slavonic letters," he drew upon the Cyrillo-Methodian tradition. He explicitly attributed the invention of the alphabet to Constantine, and the translations into Old Church Slavonic to him and his brother Methodius. Khrabr even alluded to naysayers, who believed that only Hebrew, Greek, and Latin were sacred languages (to the exclusion of Old Church Slavonic), a reference lifted directly from the* Life of Constantine. *There is no mention in Khrabr's treatise of the new alphabet, Cyrillic, but he mentions the historical circumstances in which the "Slavonic letters" had been invented, and even gives the exact year for that (6363, which in the Alexandrian chronology corresponds to the year 863). The text of Khrabr's treatise survives in multiple manuscripts (a clear sign of its popularity) written in Bulgaria, Serbia, Russia, and Moldavia, the earliest of which is from 1348. Ironically, despite Khrabr's defense of Glagolitic, his work survives only in Cyrillic manuscripts.*

Source: trans. K. Petkov, *The Voices of Medieval Bulgaria, Seventh-Fifteenth Century: The Records of a Bygone Culture* (Leiden: Brill, 2008), pp. 65–68.

To begin with, in the past the Slavs had no books, but, being pagans, they read and augured with strokes and notches. After they converted, they were forced to write down the Slavic speech with Roman and Greek letters, without adapting them. . . . Then God, who loves humanity, who arranges everything, and who does not leave the human species without wisdom but brings everyone to reason and salvation, took mercy on humanity and sent down Saint Constantine the Philosopher, called Cyril, an orthodox and truth-loving man, and he invented thirty-eight letters for them, some modeled after the Greek letters, some according to the Slavic speech. At first, he began as in Greek. They say *alpha*, and he said *az*. Both alphabets begin with A. And just like the Greeks created their letters after the Hebrew [letters], so did he [invent the Slavonic letters] after the Greek [letters]. . . .

Others say: "What need is there for Slavonic books? God did not create them, nor did the angels, nor have they been there from the beginning, like the Hebrew, the Roman, and the Greek letters, which have been around from the beginning, and are accepted by God." Still others think that God created our letters. They do not know, poor wretches, what they are talking about and believe that God commanded that books be written down solely in three languages, as it is written in the Gospel: "There was a board with writings in Hebrew, Roman, and Greek" [Luke 23:38; John 19:20]. There were no Slavic [writings] there, therefore, the Slavic books are not from God. What can we say or tell to such brainless [people]? But let us respond to them first of all that, as we have learned from the holy books, God and no else is the source of everything. The first [language] God created was neither Hebrew, nor Hellenic, but Syrian, which was spoken by Adam, and from Adam to the Flood, and from the Flood until God separated the languages at the making of the Tower, as it is written: "The languages were confounded" [Gen. 11:7]. And as the languages were confounded, so were the traditions and the customs, as well as the rules, the laws, and the arts, according to the people. . . .

And if you ask the Greek writers, saying: "Who created your letters or translated your scriptures, and when?" there is scarcely anyone among them who knows. But if you ask the Slavic schoolchildren, saying: "Who created your alphabet or translated your books?" they all know, and will answer thus: "Saint Constantine the Philosopher, called Cyril; he invented our alphabet and translated our books, he and his brother Methodius." And if you ask when that was, they know, and will say, in the time of the Greek emperor Michael, and Boris, the Bulgarian prince, and Rastica [Rastislav], the Moravian prince, and Kocel, the prince of Blaten [Mosapurc, now Zalavár, at the western end of Lake Balaton in Hungary], in the year of the creation of the world 6363 [863]. There were other replies [to the detractors of the Slavonic letters], but of them there will be word elsewhere, for now there is no time. This is how, brothers, God gave understanding to the Slavs. To him be glory, and honor, and power, and worship now, and always, and to the ages of ages. Amen!

Questions: What is the justification for the invention of the Slavonic letters? How does Khrabr describe their relation to the Hebrew and Greek letters? How does he use the Bible in support of promoting the Slavonic letters? What is his view of Constantine (Saint Cyril)?

97. SAINT CLEMENT OF OHRID ON SAINT CYRIL

Clement was a disciple of Constantine (Cyril) and Methodius, who together with Naum and Angelarius fled from Moravia and came to Bulgaria in 885. He was sent by King Boris (852–89) to the frontier province of Kutmichevica, a region in the central Balkans now divided between Macedonia, Greece, and Albania. That region had recently been taken over by the Bulgarians, and Boris was most likely concerned with the conversion of its inhabitants to Christianity. Clement began preaching to the inhabitants of Kutmichevica, particularly to commoners, which may explain why the majority of his works belong to the homiletic genre (sermons). No fewer than sixty-three sermons survive, some of them with more certain attribution than others. Clement's sermons have a simple, tripartite structure, with an introduction addressing the congregation, a detailed description of the celebrated event, and a moralistic part asking the members of the audience to purge their wickedness and live their lives piously. In addition to sermons, Clement wrote eulogies delivered as sermons on specific feast days associated with important saints. Those sermons were more elaborate, with a narrative part in the middle dedicated to the life of the saint. The prose of the narrative is combined with poetic passages, and also employs anaphora (a rhetorical device that consists of repeating a word or a phrase at the beginning of successive sentences). Clement's Eulogy of Cyril the Philosopher, *the first work to consecrate the image of an "apostle of the Slavs," is an excellent example of Clement's technique. The eulogy was written sometime during the last decade(s) of the ninth century in Ohrid, for the feast day of Saint Cyril (14 February). The text employs anaphora in a very subtle way. The word for "bless(ed)" (*blazhe*) occurs repeatedly throughout the text, in the introduction to draw attention to the subject of the sermon, but no fewer than twelve times in the last third of the text, each time at the beginning of the sentence. Each sentence is addressed to Saint Cyril, as if on behalf of (or together with) Clement's audience. Finally, "blessed" appears two more times in the conclusion, where Clement wanted his audience to focus on Cyril's death on the day that became the feast day of the saint. The goal of this sophisticated technique was therefore to introduce the "blessed" Cyril as a saint, and to direct the attention of the audience to that particular aspect in such a way as to make the message of the sermon memorable.*

Source: trans. K. Petkov, *The Voices of Medieval Bulgaria, Seventh-Fifteenth Century: The Records of a Bygone Culture* (Leiden: Brill, 2008), pp. 93–97.

Lord, bless! Lovers of Christ! Here shines for us the resplendent memory of our most blessed father Cyril, the new apostle and teacher of all the lands. . . . By the mercy and love of humanity of our Lord Jesus Christ he became the shepherd and teacher of the Slavic people, who wallowed deeply in ignorance and spiritual darkness. . . . He translated the ecclesiastical order from the Greek into the Slavic tongue and went to Rome, leading his chosen flock to perfection. The Lord God willed that his most honorable body rested in Rome.

When we take stock of his accomplishments, labors, and travel there is really no one else who can be similarly praised. Verily, even though he shone in later times, he surpassed everyone else. Just like the morning star, which up late, illuminates the entire sky spreading light with its luminous rays, so the most blessed father and teacher of our people who was brighter than the sun through the light of the Holy Trinity illuminated innumerable people sunk in the depth and darkness of ignorance. What place remained hidden, what place did he not illuminate with his steps? What art remained unknown to his blessed soul? He proclaimed to all peoples the secret mysteries, explicating them clearly with expressions easy to understand. To some he wrote, to others he preached; for the divine grace has been poured into his mouth. For this God blessed him forever. . . .

On account of this, O most blessed father Cyril, blessed are your lips, which poured forth spiritual sweetness for my lips. Blessed is your tongue of many languages, through which the dawn of the eternal Trinity without beginning shone forth for my people and dispersed the sinful darkness. Blessed is your very shiny face, illuminated by the Holy Spirit through which the light of the knowledge of God dawned for my face and polytheistic error was destroyed. Blessed are your gold-rayed eyes, through which the blindness of ignorance reigning over my eyes was shattered and the light of the knowledge of God shone through. Blessed are your angel-like pupils lit up by the divine glory that eliminated the blindness of my heart and enlightened me with God-inspired utterances. Blessed are your most honest hands through which the divine cloud of knowledge of God descended upon my people and watered with divine dewdrops our hearts charred by the draft of sin. Blessed are your God-moved fingers through which my people were set free from the sinful yoke. Blessed is your gold-gilded bosom from which life-giving water from on high poured forth for my people spurred by your prayers. Blessed are your resplendent feet, on which you, like the sun, speedily traversed the whole world, preaching the God-inspired doctrine. Blessed are your resplendent footsteps, through which our misguided steps learned the right way. Blessed is your most holy soul through which the sinful wounds of my soul healed and whose spiritual sermons implanted reason in our hearts. Blessed are your God-moved fingers through which the supreme wisdom, hidden from many, was written down to reveal the secrets of the divine knowledge. Blessed is your most honorable church, in which your wisest and God-exuding body reposes.

Questions: Is there any evidence of the cult of a saint in this text? What is the source of Saint Cyril's many talents and skills? In what way does Saint Clement use light metaphorically? What other forms of poetic language can one recognize in this text?

98. BIRCHBARK LETTERS

One of the most extraordinary sources for the history of medieval eastern Europe is the ever-growing body of letters written on birchbark. Found since the 1930s during archaeological excavations on several sites in Russia, Belarus, and Ukraine, over one thousand letters so far have been dated between the first half of the eleventh and the mid- to late fifteenth century. Those dates are not based on internal evidence, but on the dendrochronological analysis of the remains of timber walkways on the sites on which the letters have been found. After being read, the letters were commonly thrown in the middle of the street, to be washed away with all the garbage, which is why many ended up "sandwiched" between layers of reconstruction of the timber walkways. The largest number of letters come from Novgorod, but several other sites have produced birchbark letters; one of them, from Pskov, is reproduced in translation below. The letters are typically short, as they are written on small pieces of birchbark, usually 8 × 25 cm. To prepare the bark for writing, the coarser layers were stripped away in order to leave a smooth and flexible strip, which was soaked and boiled to add elasticity. Letters of the Cyrillic alphabet were scratched onto the inner (sometimes also the outer) surface with a sharp-pointed instrument made of bone, metal, or wood. The birchbark letters are an invaluable source for economic history and shed light on social life in medieval Rus' towns. Most were written by laymen, predominantly by people of some means, many of whom could afford to hire scribes capable of writing these messages for them. Some addressees appear in more than one letter. For example, Olisei Grechin, to whom a priest wrote Novgorod 549, is known from another letter as a court official. However, the priest writes to him as an icon painter, and Grechin appears in that quality in the entry of the First Novgorod Chronicle *for the year 1196. Some authors may be identified even in the absence of a name. For example, Novgorod 607/562 was most likely written by a court official reporting to a superior. Author(s) and addressee(s) could be in neighboring cities. For example, Mikula, who is mentioned in Novgorod 109, was most likely a Novgorodian who had bought a slave woman in Pskov, had left with her, and had sold her somewhere else to a third party ("that man"). Someone in Pskov, however, complained that the slave woman in question had been stolen from him, so Zhiznomir was arrested for Mikula's crime and imprisoned. His traveling companions, however, put up bail for him. He was now trying to find out from Mikula what had happened to the slave woman in order to show up at the hearing where, backed by a highly ranked official (the "prince's man"), he would try to prove that Mikula had purchased the slave in good faith. Gostiata, the woman who wrote Novgorod 9, had been abandoned by her former husband. She must have been living not in Novgorod, but somewhere else, for she does not seem to have been aware that her ex-husband had "struck hands" (a ritual gesture for making a contract, in this case a betrothal agreement) with another woman. She was now asking for Vasil', possibly a male family member, to come to her assistance. Sometimes, the network revealed by the birchbark letters can be geographically very wide. Giurgii wrote his letter (Novgorod 424) either from Smolensk or from Kiev. He wrote to his parents living in the territory of Novgorod, between four hundred and nine hundred kilometers away from him. That Giurgii wanted "all of you" to join him implies that, when moving, his mother and his father were supposed to be accompanied by the entire household, including servants and probably slaves. In Pskov 6, the calligraphy and the text arrangement suggest careful planning. The ending is formulaic and conveys the idea of the author putting his trust in the addressee, with the expectation of a favorable outcome. The dialect used is the same as that employed in letters written in Novgorod, which may indicate that Kiurik and Gerasim were from that city, famous for its fur trade. The fur trade is also at the center of the conflict between Novgorod and the principality of Vladimir-Suzdal' concerning the collection of tribute (in the form of arctic fox pelts) from the northeastern periphery of the Novgorod lands (the region around the town of Volok on the River Msta). Zakhariia, who is mentioned in Novgorod 724, was the* posadnik *(mayor) of Novgorod between 1161 and 1167. Andrei Bogoliubskii was the grand prince of Vladimir (1157–74) who apparently took advantage of a conflict between the prince of Novgorod (Sviastoslav Rostislavich) and* posadnik *Zakhariia to occupy the region around Volok. Consequently, Sava was forced to give him the tribute that he had collected on behalf of the prince of Novgorod.*

Source: trans. J. Schaeken, *Voices on Birchbark: Everyday Communication in Medieval Russia* (Leiden: Brill, 2018), pp. 61, 64, 72–73, 81, 102, 120, 131.

Novgorod 607/562, *c.* 1075–1100

Zhiznobud has been killed by (or among) the Sychevichi [clan]; (he was) a Novgorodian peasant. And they have (his) inheritance.

Novgorod 109, *c.* 1100–1120

A letter from Zhiznomir to Mikula. You bought a slave woman in Pskov. Now the princess [the wife of the prince of Pskov] has arrested me in that [matter], and [my] companions have gone surety for me. So, now send a letter to that man: does he have the slave woman? And there is what I will do: after buying horses and mounting one of the prince's men, then on to the hearing. And you, if you haven't collected that money, don't take anything from him.

Novgorod 424, *c.* 1100–1120

[A letter from Giurgii to] father and to mother. After selling the farm, come [all of you] here, either to Smolensk or to Kiev. Grain is cheap. If you don't come, send me a note, so that I know that you are well.

Novgorod 9, *c.* 1160–1180

+ From Gostiata to Vasil'. What [my] father gave me and [my] relatives gave, that is with him. Now, taking a new wife, he won't give me anything. Having struck hands [in a new marriage contract], he has sent me away and has taken another. Please come!

Novgorod 724, *c.* 1160–1180

From Sava, a bow to [my] brethren and companions. The people have left me, although they were supposed to collect the rest of the tribute before autumn and send it as soon as the road was passable, and go onward. But Zakhariia, having sent [a man], had declared an oath: "Do not let Sava collect even a single fox pelt from them. I myself am responsible for that." And that is why he has not immediately afterward settled accounts with me and has neither been with you, nor here. And therefore, I stayed on. After that, peasants came; they had got a man from Andrei [Bogoliubskii], and [his] people took away the tribute. And eight [men], who [were] under Tudor, violated [their oath of fealty]. Be cautious in dealing with him, brothers, in case there is any difficulty about this there [in Novgorod] for him and his companions.

Novgorod 549, 1180–1200

A bow from the priest to Grechin. Paint for me two six-winged angels on two small icons above the Intercession. And I salute you. God [will be the guarantor] for the reward, or else we two can come to terms.

Pskov 6, *c.* 1260–1280

From Kiurik and from Gerasim to Anfim. About the squirrel skin: if you [plural] haven't traded [it yet], send [it here] immediately, because squirrel skin is selling well here. And about ourselves: if you [Anfim] are free, come to us; Ksinofont has done us harm. And about this man: we don't know him. In this, [may] God's will [be done], and yours.

Questions: What concerns pertaining to daily life are reflected in these letters? How are those letters different from others (Docs. 12, 14, 88)? What problems specific to Rus' can one identify here?

99. *SERMON ON LAW AND GRACE*

Ilarion was a Rus' priest in the church of the Holy Apostles in Berestovo (now Berestove, in Kiev), where the prince of Kievan Rus' had a large and well-furnished residence.

Well educated, Ilarion must also have been a monk, for he became metropolitan of Kiev (1051–55) during the last years of Yaroslav the Wise (1019–54). Shortly before that (possibly in 1048 or 1049), he wrote and delivered a homily entitled Sermon on Law and Grace. *The language of this homily is Old Church Slavonic, and without any known precedent, its author produced a highly sophisticated text, in which anaphoric repetitions, doublets and triplets of word and clause, agglomerations of balanced antitheses, and syntactic parallelism create rhythm and skillfully link style to the overall message. Contrasting the Old (the "Law") and the New Testaments (the "Grace"), Ilarion dwells upon the history of salvation, which concludes with the moment when "grace and truth should shine forth upon new people." That serves as a transition to a discussion of the conversion of the Rus' under Vladimir, which is detailed in the fragment translated below. To Ilarion, the Christianization of Rus' was an integral part of sacred history, a piece of the divine plan for humankind. Vladimir is compared to Nebuchadnezzar but is also called* khagan *(much like Vladimir's son, Yaroslav). Nonetheless, to Ilarion, the Rus' ruler was another Constantine the Great. Much like the Roman emperor and his mother Helena brought the cross from Jerusalem to Constantinople, Vladimir and his grandmother Olga took the cross even farther when transporting it, figuratively speaking, from Constantinople to Rus'. While the parallel between Olga and Helena did not necessarily turn the former into the saint that she would become later, on behalf of the Rus', Ilarion seeks the intercession of Vladimir, as if he were a saint.*

Source: trans. F. Curta from *Il sermone di Ilarion "Sulla legge e sulla grazia,"* ed. I.P. Sbriziolo (Naples: Istituto universitario orientale, 1988), pp. 70, 72, 74, 78, and 80.

The Roman land, then, glorifies Peter and Paul with voices of praise, praises Peter and Paul, since because of them the Romans came to believe in Jesus Christ, son of God. Asia and Ephesus and Patmos glorify John the Theologian. India, Thomas; and Egypt, Mark. All lands, cities, and nations honor and glorify their own teachers, who taught them the Orthodox faith. Therefore, we also glorify to the best of our abilities, albeit with humble praises, the one who did so many wondrous and great things, our teacher and mentor, the great *khagan* of our land, Volodimer [Vladimir], the grandson of Igor' of old [913–45], and the son of the famous Sviatoslav [d. 972]. When in power during their years of rule, those became famous among several nations through their vigor and courage. To this day they are still remembered for their victories and might. They were not rulers of a poor, unknown country, but in the land of Rus', which is known and renowned at all four ends of the world. Famous people are thus born to famous people, and noblemen to noblemen. Our *khagan* Volodimer grew up, and later passed his teenage years and became an adult, mature in strength and might, distinguishing himself through vigor and wisdom, then became the ruler of his land and subdued all the neighboring lands all around, some peacefully, others, who were rebellious, with the sword. And he lived his life in such a manner, ruling over his country with justice, valor, and wisdom, until he was visited by the Most High. God the compassionate turned his most merciful eye to him, and he was able to understand all things: he understood the emptiness of the lie that is in idolatry, and he moved on the path of seeking the one God, the Creator of all things visible and invisible. In addition, he has often heard about the godly Greek land [Byzantium], pious and strong because of faith. [He has heard] that [in that country] they honor and worship the only God of the Trinity, that many works and miracles and [divine] signs happened there, that churches [there] were full of people, that all [their] cities were devout, and that they were all zealous in prayer, standing before God. Having heard all of that, with strong desire in his heart, he got inflamed with the spirit: he had to become Christian, and with him, his country as well. And so it came to happen. God has chosen in this manner the human creature; our *khagan*, therefore, took off the clothes of the man he had been before, removed [all] transient things, shook off the dust of faithlessness, and entered the holy font, being reborn through the Holy Spirit and the water [John 3:5]. After that, being baptized in Christ, he clothed [himself] with Christ [Gal. 3:27], and came out of the font now made white, for he was now a son of eternity, the son of the resurrection [Luke 20:36]. He took the name of Basil [after Emperor Basil II, whose sister he married], a name forever celebrated, from one generation to another, which was written for him in the books of life, which are in the heavenly and eternal city of Jerusalem [Rev. 20:12–21:3]. So it was until he began his deeds of devotion, and that was not the only way in which he showed the love that he had for God, but he did much more than that. He ordered throughout his country that everybody be baptized in the name of the Father, the Son, and the Holy Spirit. [And he also commanded] that the Holy Trinity be glorified openly and loudly in all cities, and that all should become Christians—commoners and the great, slaves and free men, the young and the old, the noblemen and the humble, the rich and the poor. And nobody opposed his noble will, and if someone accepted baptism not out of love, then [that person did it] out of fear of him who had given the order, since in him faith had been joined to authority. And at the same time all our land began to glorify Christ, the Father, and the Holy Spirit. And at that point, the darkness of idolatry began to move away from us and the dawn of faith to appear. At that point, the fog of slavery to the demons cleared, and the word of the Gospel brightened our land. Temples were destroyed, and churches were built [instead]. Idols were smashed, and icons of saints were put up [instead]. Demons ran away, and the cross shone upon the cities. The shepherds of Christ's flock, namely the bishops, standing in front of the holy altar, offered the bloodless sacrifice before the holy altar; the priests and the deacons and all the clergy embellished the holy churches and clothed them in beauty. The echo of the trumpet of the apostles and of the thunder of the Gospels could be heard in all cities; the incense offered to God purified the air. Monasteries were built on mountains, [and] monks appeared [in them]. Men and women, small and great, all [now] filled the holy churches, singing praises and saying: "One is holy, one is our Lord Jesus Christ, to the glory of God the Father, amen!" Christ is victor! Christ triumphed! Christ is king! Glory to Christ! Great are you, O Lord and marvelous are your works! Glory to you, our God! You, therefore, we praise, O noble [ruler] and famous among rulers of the earth, most powerful Basil. We are certainly not surprised at your goodness, strength, and might. How should we thank you, for through you we came to know our Lord and we escaped the lies of idolatry, for because of your will, Christ is praised in all [our] land? And how should we call you, O beloved of Christ, O friend of righteousness, cradle of mercy? . . . O emulator of Constantine the Great [Roman emperor, 306–37], of like intelligence, of like love for Christ and his ministers! With the blessed fathers of the Council of Nicaea [in 325], he [Emperor Constantine the Great] established the law for the people. You, [in turn,] in frequent meetings with our new fathers and with the bishops, with utmost humility requested their advice on how [best] to establish the law for those people, who had just learned about God. [Constantine] obtained the submission to God of the reign of the Hellenes and the Romans, you have done the same with the kingdom of Rus'. Now, therefore, Christ is king both for them and for us. Together with his mother Helena, Constantine strengthened the faith when bringing the cross from Jerusalem and spreading its glory throughout their entire land. You and your grandmother Olga have strengthened the faith after bringing the cross from the New Jerusalem, [namely] from the city of Constantine, and after that exalted it throughout your entire land. Much like his imitator [Constantine], the Lord has granted you to partake with him in like honor and glory in heaven because of the piety you have showed in your life.

Questions: What is the image of Volodimer (Vladimir) in Ilarion's sermon? Why is he called a "khagan"*? How are biblical citations employed in the text? What can one make of the comparison of Olga and her grandson Volodimer (Vladimir) on one hand, to Saints Constantine and Helena, on the other?*

100. *ON THE LAME AND THE BLIND*

The Tale of the Body and the Soul *is an allegorical story of a lame man and a blind man who conspire to enter their lord's vineyard. In several manuscripts, the text is attributed to an author named Kiril, but only a few add to that "bishop of Turov." Turov (now Turau, in Belarus) was a town in northwestern Rus', and several bishops of that see are known from the sources. None of them mentions Kiril. On the other hand, the works attributed to "Kiril of Turov" on the basis of style betray the mindset and interests of a monk in a monastery. The existence of Kiril of Turov and the authorship of the works attributed to him have therefore been the subject of much debate. The* Tale *has a relatively simple structure. The author introduces the "basic text" (the story of the lame man and the blind man set to guard a vineyard), and then goes through that text, line by line, or word by word, to explain the meaning of the allegory. The lame man is the soul, the blind man is the body. Their lord (God) asks them to guard a garden, which could be Eden or a monastery, in general. They enter the garden and steal the fruits (human transgression) and are punished (Last Judgment). There is a clear emphasis upon hierarchs holding office unlawfully. Some have taken that to be a denunciation of Bishop Fedor of Rostov, who had attempted to set up a metropolis in Vladimir with the assistance of Grand Prince Andrei Bogoliubskii (1169–74). But there is little political in the* Tale, *a purely allegorical commentary about the nature of man (both soul and body).*

Source: trans. F. Curta from *Pamiatniki literatury Drevnei Rusi, XII vek*, ed. L.A. Dmitrieva and D.S. Likhacheva (Moscow: Khudozhestvennaia literatura, 1980), pp. 296, 298, and 300.

Listen closely, as I will deliver my speech in [good] order, so that you [can] follow it [easily]. Even though my mind is scattered, and my tongue is coarse, hoping that your prayers [will help], I nonetheless ask for the gift of words. Even though I am not worthy to speak about this [matter], I will nonetheless write [the following words] for the benefit of those who listen. If someone listens with anger [in the heart], that person does not look for something that would benefit his own [soul], but for something [that could be used] against us, a reason to scold us.

After they sat for a while, the blind man said to the lame: "What is this fragrance [coming] from the gate of the vineyard that wafts over me?" The lame man answered: "Our lord has many good things inside the vineyard, and there are no words to describe how good their taste [really] is. But since our lord is wise, he put the two of us here, you a blind and me a lame man, and we cannot in any way draw pleasure from [tasting] those good fruits." The blind man answered, saying: "Why have you not told me about this before? We would not have tolerated it, but [instead] what was given to us in possession would have long been destroyed!" (Understand that sin is a spiritual burden; therefore, the prophet says: "A heavy burden weighed me down" [Ps. 37:5]). And the blind man said: "Take the basket and climb on me; I will carry you, but you will show the way, and we will take the goods of the lord. I do not think he will come [around] here [anytime soon]." Those are not the ideas of people who seek God, but of those who care about worldly power, who care about the body, who are not expecting any retribution for their actions, and who act as if letting the vain steam of their souls into the wind! That is why Isaiah says: "Jealously will seize an untaught people" [Isa. 26:11]. We sinners envy the honor and glory of the righteous, instead of emulating their deeds. "However," the blind man continued, "if our lord does come here, we will hide our deeds from him. If he asks me about the theft, I will say, 'You know, my lord, that I am blind'; and if he questions you, you will say, 'I am lame and cannot walk.' And so we will outwit our lord and receive the reward for our efforts." And the lame man climbed onto the blind man, and entering the vineyard, they plundered all the goods of their lord that they could find there.

However, brethren, do not scold me for my ignorance, because of which the story takes an unworthy appearance. For just as a bird with tied legs cannot soar up into the air, so it is impossible for me, mired [as I am] in the desires of the flesh, to talk about spiritual things. The words of a sinner, deprived of the grace of the Holy Spirit, cannot achieve anything. Nevertheless, let us return to what was said before, explaining the meaning of this parable.

INTERPRETATION. They say, as [already] said, "for a long time." What does "a long time" mean? Is it contempt for God's commandments and concern for the body, as well as indifference toward one's own soul? For nobody who fears God will care for the flesh, no man of true faith attempts to obtain an office unlawfully, nobody who awaits death and the resurrection after death, except those two in their worst deeds. And again, I will say the same thing, in order for you to understand it better: "The blind man said to the lame: 'What is this fragrance [coming] from the gate that wafts over me?'" and so on. Here one can see the self-centered and conceited arrogance of Adam, who although he owns everything on earth, the animals, the sea, and the creatures within it, sated in Eden with goodness, nonetheless dared to take for himself that which was sacred before sanction was granted, for from Eden he entered [the garden of] paradise. Therefore, the scripture says: "The Lord God sent him out of the garden of pleasure to cultivate the ground from which he was taken" [Gen. 3:23]. Think about that: it was not there that he was commanded to live, from where he was expelled. But he entered [in that place] like a churchman unworthy of the priesthood and hiding his sin, who ascended to the episcopal rank, while disregarding God's covenant for the sake of high rank and earthly glory.

COMPARISON. For that, God condemned Adam to death, because he touched the tree of the knowledge of good and evil. The tree of the knowledge of good and evil represents one's knowledge of one's sin and exercising free will, something that that is pleasing to God. For it is written: "Woe to those who knowingly sin!" [Isa. 5:21] This is what destroys the breath of the life-giving spirit, which God had breathed onto him [Adam], the unfulfilled goodness of sanctification. For it is written: "And he breathed in his face the breath of life" [Gen. 2:7]. Likewise, Christ, blowing on the faces of the apostles: "Receive," he said, "the Holy Spirit" [John 20:22]—the imperfect grace, merely a warranty of sanctification, for he commanded them to wait for the Holy Spirit itself, "which will come," he said, "and sanctify you to the end" [Acts 1:4–8]. Similarly, bishops consecrated subdeacons, readers, and deacons—an incomplete gift, but a warranty of consecration, so that they can prepare themselves for the final consecration [into the priesthood]. Nothing pleases God more than elevation in rank, and nothing is more disgusting than arrogance boasting of getting into office, instead of being like God.

Now take a [good] look at the same blind man with a lame man, how they disregarded their lord's order and prohibition. Taking up the lame man, as well as the load, [t]he [blind man] carried it away, and going inside [the vineyard], approached the tree, ate the fruit, which was very good, and so with that the thing that he was supposed to guard.

CONTRAST. From that tree Cain [also] tasted: not being consecrated, he violated the hierarchical order and showing envy for Abel, who was consecrated, he killed him out of envy. The sons of Korah who were with Dathan and Abiram ate from that [same] tree: they were not consecrated, but nonetheless they took the censers and went into the tabernacle, and the earth swallowed them up [Num. 16]. And this was the tree that was tasted by Eli the priest: for though he knew that his sons had transgressed in their priesthood, yet he did not expel them from the priesthood [1 Kings 2:22–25]. And that was [also] the tree which heretics tasted, who, in deceit, as if knowing the spiritual path, went astray and died without repenting. But enough of this. Let us return to [our] story. Although my tongue is exhausted, the prophet inspires me when saying in the same way, "I am weary with crying, my throat is hoarse" [Ps. 68:4].

CONDEMNATION OF SINS: The lord learned that his vineyard had been robbed, [so] he ordered that the lame man be cast out of the gate, and that the blind man be removed from the watch. Understand [that], you most foolish dignitaries, you most inept priests! When will you come to your senses? Did he not give you ears to hear; did he not make your eye to see? Could he, who teaches all nations, not reprove? Does not he who teaches humans to understand comprehend our error? The Lord, after all, sees deceiving thoughts for what they are, and will remove the unrighteous from power and will drive the wicked away from the altar. For no dignity in this world will save from torment those who violate God's commandments.

Questions: What kind of story is that of the lame and the blind? How are biblical citations employed in the explanation of the story? What is the "Contrast" section meant to do and why does Kiril bring up the heretics in that context? Why is he referring to someone who is unworthy of being elevated to the rank of bishop?

101. THE *PRIMARY CHRONICLE* ON THE ORIGINS OF THE SLAVS

The Primary Chronicle *is the only medieval source that contains a story about the origin of all Slavs. Compiled by several authors and finished c. 1113, the* Chronicle *places the*

Slavs within the story of Babel and brings them to the lands of Rus' by means of a migration from the Danube region. This is a story with clear biblical models, for the Slavs are described as being divided into many "tribes," to which the Chronicle *refers as* plemena, *a word meant to denote the twelve Hebrew tribes of the Old Testament. There are in fact twelve Slavic "tribes" mentioned in the story, and the description of the territory of each one of them is modeled after the description of the share of the Promised Land apportioned to each Hebrew tribe. Two of the tribes (the Slovenes and the Polyanians) may have simply been made up, as they are not mentioned anywhere else. On the other hand, the mention of Noricum, the "Carinthians" (Carantanians), and the "Lutichians" (Lutizi), as well as the story of the Avar oppression of Dulebian women (which is very similar to what Fredegar has to say about Avar-Slavic relations), suggests that at least one other source for the story of Slavic origins in the* Primary Chronicle *must have been of central (if not western) European origin, perhaps mediated by the Cyrillo-Methodian tradition.*

Source: trans. S.H. Cross and O.P. Sherbowitz-Wetzor, *The Russian Primary Chronicle: Laurentian Text* (Cambridge, MA: Medieval Academy of America, 1953), pp. 52–53 and 55–57.

After the destruction of the Tower [of Babel] and the divisions of the nations, the sons of Shem occupied the eastern regions, and sons of Ham those of the south, and the sons of Japheth the western and the northern lands. Among those seventy-two nations, the Slavic race is derived from the line of Japheth, since they are the Noricians [inhabitants of Noricum, a Roman province in what are now Austria and Slovenia], who are identical with the Slavs.

For a long time, the Slavs dwelled beside the Danube, where the Hungarian and Bulgarian lands now lie. From among these Slavs, parties scattered throughout the country and were known by appropriate names, according to the places where they settled. Thus, some came and settled by the River Morava, and were named Moravians, while others were called Czechs. Among these same Slavs are included the White Croats, the Serbs, and the Carinthians [Carantanians]. For when the Vlachs attacked the Danubian Slavs, settled among them, and did them violence, the latter came and made their homes by the Vistula, and were then called Lyakhs. Of these same Lyakhs, some were called Polyanians [probably Poles], some Lutichians [Lutizi, a tenth- to twelfth-century federation of Polabian Slavs in northeastern Germany], some Mazovians, and still others Pomorians [Pomeranians]. Certain Slavs settled also on the Dnieper and were likewise called Polyanians. Still others were named Derevlians, because they lived in the forests [*derevo*, in Russian, means tree, wood]. Some also lived between the Pripet and the Dvina and were known as Dregovichians. Other tribes resided along the Dvina and were called Polotians on account of a small stream called the Polota, which flows into the Dvina [the Palata, which flows into the Pskov region of Russia and the northern part of Belarus, merges with the Western Dvina at Polatsk]. It was from this same stream that they were named Polotians. The Slavs also dwelt about Lake Ilmen' [in northwestern Russia, near Novgorod] and were known there by their characteristic name. They built a city, which they called Novgorod. Still others had their homes along the Desna, the Sem', and the Sula, and were called Severians. Thus, the Slavic race was divided, and its language was known as Slavic. . . .

Now while the Slavs dwelt along the Danube, as we have said, there came from among the Scythians, that is, from the Khazars, a people called Bulgars who settled on the Danube and oppressed the Slavs. Afterward came the White Ugrians, who inherited the Slavic country. These Ugrians appeared under the emperor Heraclius [610–41], warring on Chosroes [Khusro II], the [last] King of [Sassanian] Persia [590–628]. The Avars, who attacked Heraclius the emperor, nearly capturing him [in 620], also lived at this time. They made war upon the Slavs and harassed the Dulebians, who were themselves Slavs. They even did violence to the Dulebian women. When an Avar made a journey, he did not cause either a horse or a steer to be harnessed but gave command instead that three of four or five women should be yoked to his cart and be made to draw him. Even thus they harassed the Dulebians. The Avars were large of stature and proud of spirit, and God destroyed them. They all perished, and not one Avar survived. There is to this day a proverb in Rus' which runs, "They perished like the Avars." Neither race nor heir of them remains. The Pechenegs came after them, and the Magyars passed by Kiev later during the time of Oleg. . . .

These Slavic tribes preserved their own customs, the law of their forefathers, and their traditions, each observing its own usage. For the Polyanians retained the mild and peaceful customs of their ancestors, and showed respect for their daughters-in-law and their sisters, as well as for their mothers and fathers. For their mothers-in-law and their brothers-in-law, they also entertained great reverence. They observed a fixed custom, under which a groom's brother did not fetch the bride, but she was brought to the bridegroom in the evening, and on the next morning her dowry was turned over.

The Derevlians, on the other hand, existed in bestial fashion, and lived like cattle. They killed one another, ate every impure thing, and there was no marriage among them, but instead they seized upon maidens by capture. The Radimichians, the Vyatichians, and the Severians had the same customs. They lived in the forest like any wild beast and ate every unclean thing. They spoke obscenely before their fathers and their daughters-in-law. There were no marriages among them, but simply festivals among the villages. When the people gathered together for games, for dancing, and for all other devilish amusements, the men on these occasions carried off wives for themselves, and each took a woman with whom he had arrived at an understanding. In fact, they even had two or three wives apiece. Whenever a death occurred, a feast was held over the corpse, and then a great pyre was constructed, on which the deceased was laid and burned. After the bones were collected, they were placed in a small urn and set upon a post by the roadside, even as the Vyatichians do to this day. Such customs were observed by the Krivichians and the other pagans, since they did not follow the law of God, but made a law unto themselves.

Questions: How does the concern with the origin of peoples compare with earlier authors (Docs. 2 and 7)? What role does biblical history play in this notion of origins? Why are foreign rulers (Heraclius, Chosroes) mentioned in this context? What is the relation between tradition and history?

102. QUEEN VANDA OF THE POLES

Little is known about the life of Vincent Kadłubek (1150–1223), except that he was born in Poland into a knight's family, he may have been of noble origin, and that he was educated, perhaps in France or in Italy, before returning to his homeland in the 1180s to serve in the cathedral of Cracow as canon. In the dynastic struggles that followed the death of Bolesław IV (1146–73), Vincent took the side of Casimir II, who probably commissioned the Chronicle of the Poles. *Vincent became bishop of Cracow in 1208 and was confronted with the military and political aspirations of his patron. He participated in the Fourth Lateran Council (1215) together with Archbishop Henry Kietlicz. He also favored the Cistercians and withdrew to their abbey in Jedrzejów after resigning from office in 1217 or 1218. The first four books of the* Chronicle *take the form of a dialogue between John, archbishop of Gniezno (1149–67), and Matthew, bishop of Cracow (1143–66). Matthew introduces episodes from the history of Poland to which John then replies with parallels from ancient history, as well as philosophical, moral, and juridical reflections. Vincent had a concept of Polish history that was completely different from that of his predecessor, Gallus Anonymus. He augmented Gallus's mythical account of Piast origins and invented an ancient Polish state rivaling the Roman empire. He also introduced a host of fanciful characters, such as Gracchus, the dragon-slaying founder of Cracow, and his daughter Vanda, the queen of the Poles. Vincent approached the problem of power and rulers through the lens of the rhetorical category known as* de virtutibus et vitiis, *in which the moral evaluation of the characters takes precedence over chronological order in guiding the flow of the narrative. Vincent, in other words, wrote to provide examples both to the people of his present time, as well as to those of future times. He was concerned not so much with the Piasts as with the realm of Poland, the body politic to which he referred as* res publica. *The main enemies of* res publica, *according to him, were ambition, pride, intemperance, and immorality. Failure to live by virtue would lead to disaster, and no dynasty was safe if tarnished by vice. The text of Vincent's chronicle is written in "difficult ornaments"* (ornatus difficilis), *a very elaborate style of prose, one of the key characteristics of which is the insertion of citations from classical authors. Those citations were meant to be "gems" to be discovered by the educated reader, who would recognize that citations had been subtly adapted to a new context and would thus generate a new meaning, parallel and auxiliary in relation to that of the main story. Thus, a verse from Virgil's* Aeneid *that refers to a woman (Camilla of the Volsci, a warrior virgin) can be applied to a man who commits suicide because of another woman (Vanda, another warrior virgin).*

Source: trans. F. Curta from *Die Chronik der Polen des Magisters Vincentius*, ed. E. Mühle (Darmstadt: Wissenschaftliche Buchgesellschaft, 2014), pp. 100 and 102.

No, for on the rock of Holophagus [a dragon], a remarkable city was built immediately after that, and was called Graccovia [Cracow] after the name of Gracchus, so that he will forever be remembered. And his funeral had barely ended when work on the city finished as well. Some, [however,] have called [that city] Craccovia after the croak of ravens, who according to them gather on the corpse of the monster [that is, Holophagus]. But the love of the senate, of the noblemen, and of the people for the deceased prince [Gracchus] was so great that they elected in his place his only daughter named Vanda, to rule over the country [of Poland]. She so surpassed all other [women] through her beauty and the perfect appeal of her charm, that one could say that nature had not [just] given to her generously but had actually been quite prodigal [in showering] her with gifts. For even the smartest [people] marveled at her carefully thought-out counsel and the worst enemies were tamed by her stare. As a certain tyrant of the Lemanni [Germans] concocted a plan to plunder this people [the Poles], so that he could grab this almost vacant rule [over Poland] for himself, he was defeated rather by a miraculous, until then unknown power rather than by weapons. For his entire army, as soon as they gazed at the queen [Vanda], was struck to the ground as if by sunlight. Similarly, as if by command of the divine power, all their ill intentions were taken away, and they gave up fighting, hoping [by such means] to avoid not a battle, but a sacrilege. For they did not [only] have respect for a human being [Vanda] but were [also] terrified by that human's superhuman majesty. Their king, however, whether out of love, a bad mood, or both—who knows—spoke with frustration in his voice: "Vanda could rule over the sea, the earth, and the air! She could sacrifice her people to the immortal gods. But I offer myself for you all, noble men, as the beast to be festively sacrificed for the gods of the underworld, so that both you and your descendants may live long lives under a woman's rule." He spoke, threw himself onto [his] drawn sword, and died. He let his "spirit [go] forth with wrath and moaning to the world below" [Virgil, *Aeneid* 11.831, in reference to Camilla].

This Vanda, they say, gave her name to the River Wandalus [Vistula], which flows through the middle of the kingdom [of Poland]. That is why all those who submitted to her authority were called Vandals. But [Vanda] died, for she had rejected carnal union, and had preferred instead to remain a virgin in marriage, without children, so that after her, power [in Poland] dwindled for a long while, in the absence of a king.

Questions: What is the attitude of Vincent Kadłubek toward "Lemanni"? What accounts for his point of view? What were Vanda's qualities that recommended her for queen? What is one to make of the effort to derive the name of the city of Cracovia from that of the Roman tribune Gracchus? Why might this account have value for historians?

103. THE *HUNGARIAN-POLISH CHRONICLE* ON A MEETING OF RULERS

The Hungarian-Polish Chronicle *is a name conventionally given to a relatively short text written in the late 1220s or early 1230s by an unknown author at the court of Prince Coloman, the younger brother of King Béla IV (1235–70). The* Chronicle *survives in five manuscripts, all from Poland, where the initial text was most likely taken in 1241 by Coloman's widow, Salomea, the daughter of the prince of Sandomierz, Leszek I (1194–1227). The author of the* Chronicle *directly and explicitly equated Huns with Hungarians. Some have therefore dismissed the* Hungarian-Polish Chronicle *as a made-up history of Huns and Hungarians. In reality, there is no mention of Árpád, only of Attila ("Aquila"), who leads the Hungarians trekking through Europe from Lithuania and Scotia to "Dacia" (Denmark), Lombardy, and Apulia. In Rome, Aquila is ordered to go to Sclavonia in order to revenge a certain king Casimir, who had been killed by his subjects. After establishing Aquileia (named after himself), Aquila battles the Slavs and the Croats for eight days, and creates a new state, which he names Hungaria. Aquila's descendants are then introduced to the narrative—Coloman, Béla, and Géza ("Yesse"), as well as Géza's wife, Adelaide, the sister of the Polish prince Mieszko, who lives in Cracow. The third and final part of the chronicle is largely based on Hartvic's* Life of King Stephen of Hungary, *but includes some original elements, presumably based on oral traditions, such as a critique of the Polish way of life and an account of the meeting of the Polish and Hungarian rulers at the border, near Esztergom. The story is full of errors and anachronisms: Mieszko II Lambert was the son of Bolesław Chrobry, not the brother of Géza, King Stephen's father; Lambert Suła became bishop of Cracow twenty-three years after King Stephen's death. Nonetheless, the knowledge of geography and the precision of the place names makes this a good indication of what was known in Poland about Hungary and its rulers.*

Source: trans. F. Curta from "Chronica Hungaro-Polonic: Pars I," in *Acta Historica* 26, ed. B. Karácsonyi (Szeged: Acta Universitatis Szegediensis de Attila József nominatae, 1969), pp. 40–44.

7. After accepting the sign of royal dignity [that is, the royal crown], the blessed, Stephen, king of the Hungarians [1001–38], generously endowed the episcopal churches and decorated [them] with [a] sufficient [number of] crosses and [liturgical] vessels and many other things, articles pertaining to the divine service, according to every need. Three months after [his] coronation, the bishop of Cracow, Lambert [Suła, 1061–71,] came to him to ask for a treaty and in order to

renew the peace and friendship [between the two countries]. And without delay, he [Stephen I] sent Astrik, the [arch]bishop of Strigonium [now Esztergom, in northern Hungary] and the commander of the army named Alba to his uncle the prince of Poland Mescho [Mieszko II Lambert, duke of Poland between 1025 and 1031 and again between 1032 and 1034] to ask him to come to the border between Hungary and Poland together with his magnates. And [Mieszko] gathered his entire army and came to King [Stephen] before Strigonium, pitching his tent at the border between Poland and Hungary. For the frontier of the Poles stretches as far as the bank of the River Danube by the city of Strigonium, and from there goes to the city of Agria [Eger], and from there to the river called Tizia [now Tisza], going around along the river called Cepla [Topľa, in eastern Slovakia], down to the castle Galis [probably Várhegy, near Prešov, in Slovakia], where the Hungarian, Ruthenian [Rus'], and Polish borders meet.

On the morning of the next day when the sun was up, they met [at the border], and having accepted the kiss of peace [from each other], at the same time joining hands, they entered the cathedral in Strigonium, which had just been built in honor of the saint martyr Adalbert, the apostle of the Poles and of the Hungarians. And the high priest [was] dressed for the holy Mass with the deacons of the holy altar and other churchmen, dressed in garments like bright stars shining in the sky, and King Stephen dressed in sacred garments and crowned with the royal diadem, shining like the sun among the stars, following the sacred procession, standing taller than all people with [his] head and shoulders. Once the procession came to a halt, the word of God was preached, and [the king] confirmed the privileges of the holy Roman Curia, and heard all people speaking, each in his own right. And he declared confirmed the peace and friendship for both peoples [Poles and Hungarians]. Everybody was pleased and confirmed [what had been decided] by an oath with their own hands. After the Mass, the hymn of the Holy Trinity was intoned: "Blessed be the Holy Trinity . . ." And the holy Host was offered by bishop Astrik to the king and to Prince Mieszko and to all the people. Once peace was accepted, and the Mass ended, they returned to their tents, where in happiness and joy, food and drinks, with strings and pipes, drums and choirs, lutes and charms, they were [all] merry for eight days. When this was successfully done, all in the Polish army, from the higher to the lower rank, received gifts, and the prince [Mieszko] was offered many great presents. After that they separated, the duke of the Poles returning to the castle of Salis [most likely the same as Galis mentioned above], while the king of the Hungarians went back to his beloved city of Alba [Székesfehérvár, to the southwest of Budapest, Hungary].

Questions: What is the role of Saint Adalbert in the story? In what forms is the power of the Hungarian king represented? Compare the role of gift giving in this story to that in the account of the Gniezno Summit (Doc. 44). What defines the frontier between Hungary and Poland?

CHAPTER TWELVE

THE NEW POWERS IN THE THIRTEENTH CENTURY

Figure 12.1 Seal of Grand *Župan* Stephen Nemanja (1198).

104. BENJAMIN OF TUDELA ON THE VLACHS

The travelogue of a rabbi named Benjamin of Tudela, who journeyed between 1160 and 1172 between his native Navarre (northeastern Spain) all the way to Baghdad and back, is most likely not the result of his travel or personal experiences, but of (at least) two redactions, the earliest of which was done by an editor living in thirteenth-century Spain, who also added a prologue. This text belongs to a genre of Jewish medieval literature known as "travel narrative," and consists of a list of entries, each with the following structure: "And from there, there are x (number) of days to y (place name), which is called z (Jewish name)." To this basic structure, comments are often added concerning the size, social structure, and specific details about the Jewish community in "y," as well as the names of its leaders, where there was a sufficiently large number of Jews to constitute a minyan *(a quorum necessary for worship). Benjamin crossed Greece from Corfu to Thebes, Halmyros, and Thessaloniki in 1161. One of his stops, two days' journey from "Rabonica" (Ravennika, an unknown location somewhere south of Lamia in central Greece), was in Sinon Potamo, near present-day Lamia. There were about fifty Jews in that place, but Benjamin did not give any details on them, except the names of their leaders. Instead, he focused on the Vlachs, who are described as mountain people, much like the Druses of Lebanon who are mentioned later in the text. In fact, the accounts of Vlachs and Druses are so similar that one may well have served as model for the other. The image of Vlachs swooping down from the mountains is also similar to that of Jews in the country of Baden, who appear in the context of news that Benjamin learned from Egypt and the countries in east Africa. Those Jews, believed to be the Falasha communities of northern Ethiopia, were "not under the yoke of the Gentiles, but possess[ed] cities and castles on the summits of mountains, from which they made descents" to raid the Christian kingdom of Amatum, or Nubia (Sudan). However, since no mention of Ethiopian Jews exists prior to 1300, the note on affairs in east Africa may well be a later interpolation. The same is probably true about the Vlachs of Sinon Potamo, the account of whom is probably a thirteenth-century interpolation in Benjamin's* Book of Travels. *In that case, the author of the interpolation (who was someone other than Benjamin, who died in 1173), transferred to the country of the Vlachs near Sinon Potamo the political and religious features associated with military turbulence in the other Vlachia, much farther to the north, in Bulgaria. That the Vlachs were as swift as deer when descending from the mountains to plunder and loot "the country of Greece" applies best to the rebels of 1185 led by Peter and Asen.*

Source: trans. M.N. Adler, *The Itinerary of Benjamin of Tudela* (New York: Philipp Feldheim, 1907), p. 11.

From there [Rabonica, located somewhere near Thermopylae, in central Greece] it is a two-day journey to Sinon Potamo [near Lamia, in Phthiotis, central

Greece], where there are fifty Jews, at their head being Rabbi Shelomoh and Rabbi Ya'akov. This [place] is at the foot of the mountains [of] Vlachia [Mount Othrys, in central Greece], on which mountains dwell the people called Vlachs, and they are as swift as deer and descending from the mountains to plunder and loot the country of Greece. And no man can climb up to them to fight, and no king can rule over them, and they do not hold fast to the faith of the Nazarenes [Christians] but call themselves Jewish names. And it is said that they were Jews and call the Jews "our brothers," [and that] when they meet them, they steal from them, but do not kill them the way they kill the Greeks, and they do not accept any religion. From there it is a two-day journey to Gardiki, which is in ruins and contains but a few Greeks and Jews.

Questions: What is the relation between Jews and Vlachs? What could have been Benjamin of Tudela's sources of information for this account? Why are Vlachs hostile to the Greeks? How would the (Jewish) reader of this text regard the fact that the Vlachs give themselves Jewish names?

105. THE VLACH REBELS IN BULGARIA

Niketas Choniates was still working on his History *when he died in or shortly after 1217. With the protection of his brother Michael, the archbishop of Athens, Niketas was appointed governor of Philippopolis (now Plovdiv, in Bulgaria), and he was there when the army of Frederick I Barbarossa crossed the Balkans on its way for the Third Crusade. He was in Constantinople when the city fell to the Latins in 1204, but he fled to Nicaea together with the other Byzantine refugees, both laymen and churchmen. He wrote the* History *in Nicaea, covering the period between the reign of Emperor John II Komnenos (1118–43) to the sack of Constantinople in 1204. Much of what he had to say about the reign of Emperor Isaac II Angelos (1185–96, 1203–04) is based on detailed knowledge obtained from official documents, testimonies from participants, and, last but not least, his own experience as eyewitness. As secretary to the emperor, he participated in the battle near Beroe (now Stara Zagora, in Bulgaria) in October 1187 in which the Byzantine army was routed by the Cumans. However, the* History *is not a report from the field, but a very sophisticated piece of Byzantine literature. In addition to many citations from ancient authors (such as Homer, in the passage below), Niketas often wants to show off his knowledge of ancient geography, for example when claiming that the Vlachs who rebelled in 1185 used to be called "Mysians"—a reference to the imperial Roman province of Moesia (inferior).*

Source: trans. H.J. Magoulias, *O City of Byzantium: Annals of Niketas Choniates* (Detroit: Wayne State University Press, 1984), pp. 203–04 and 205–06.

He [Emperor Isaac II Angelos, 1185–95, 1203–04] did the wedding rites penuriously [at the end of 1185 or in early 1186], using public money freely collected from his own lands. Because of his stinginess, he escaped notice as he gleaned other cities which were joined together around Anchialos [now Pomorie, on the Black Sea coast in Bulgaria], provoking the barbarians who lived in the vicinity of Mount Haimos [the Stara Planina Mountains], formerly called Mysians and now named Vlachs, to declare war against him and the Romans.

Made confident by the harshness of the terrain and emboldened by their fortresses, most of which are situated directly above sheer cliffs, the barbarians had boasted against the Romans in the past; now finding a pretext like that alleged on behalf of Patroklos [*Iliad* 19.302]—the rustling of their cattle and their own ill-treatment—they leaped with joy at rebellion. The instigators of this evil who incited the entire nation were a certain Peter and Asan, brothers sprung from the same parents. In order to justify their rebellion, they approached the emperor, encamped at Kypsella [now Ispala, near Keşan, Turkey, close to the Greek-Turkish border], requesting that they be recruited into the Roman army and be awarded by imperial rescript a certain estate situated in the vicinity of Mount Haimos, which would provide them with a little revenue. Failing in their request—for the punitive action of God supersedes that of man—they grumbled because they had not been heard; and with their request made for naught, they spat out heated words, hinting at rebellion and the destruction they would wreak on their way home. Asan, the more insolent and savage of the two, was struck across the face and rebuked for his impudence at the command of John [Dukas], the *sebastokrator* [senior court official].

Thus, did they return, unsuccessful in their mission and wantonly insulted. What words could possibly describe and embrace the endless string of Trojan woes inflicted on the Romans by these impious and abominable men? But none of this now; let us proceed with the narrative in historical sequence. . . .

When the Vlachs were afflicted with the disease of open rebellion, the leaders of this evil being those I cited above, the emperor marched out against them [in the spring of 1186]. These events, therefore, must not be overlooked and unrecorded. At first, the Vlachs were reluctant and turned away from the revolt urged upon them by Peter and Asan, looking askance at the magnitude of the undertaking. To overcome the timidity of their compatriots, the brothers built a house of prayer in the name of the good martyr Demetrios. In it they gathered many demoniacs of both races [that is, Vlachs and Bulgarians]; with crossed and bloodshot eyes, hair disheveled, and with precisely all the other symptoms demonstrated by those possessed by demons, they were instructed to say in their ravings that the God of the race of the Bulgarians and Vlachs had consented to their freedom and assented that they should shake off after so long a time the yoke from their neck; and in support of this cause, Demetrios, the martyr for Christ, would abandon the metropolis of Thessaloniki and his church there [both recently conquered by the Normans] and the customary haunts of the Romans and come over to them to be their helper and assistant in their forthcoming task. These madmen would keep still for a short while and then, suddenly moved by the spirit, would rave like lunatics; they would start up and shout and shriek, as though inspired, that this was no time to sit still but to take weapons in hand and close with the Romans. Those seized in battle should not be taken captive or preserved alive but slaughtered, killed without mercy; neither should they release them for ransom nor yield to supplication, succumbing like women to genuflections. Rather, they should remain as hard as diamonds to every plea and put to death every captive. With such soothsayers as these, the entire nation was won over, and everyone took up arms. Since their rebellion was immediately successful, all the more did they assume that God had approved of their freedom. Freely moving out a short distance without opposition, they extended their control over the lands outside of Zygon [the lands on the northern side of the Stara Planina Mountains]. Peter, Asan's brother, bound his head with a gold chaplet and fashioned scarlet buskins [tall, laced boots] to put on his feet. An assault was made upon Pristhlava [Preslav] (this is an ancient city built of baked bricks and covering a very large area), but they realized that a siege would not be without danger, and so they bypassed it. They descended Mount Haimos, fell unexpectedly upon the Roman towns, and carried away many free Romans, many cattle and draft animals, and sheep and goats in no small number.

The emperor marched out against them, and they, in turn, occupying the rough ground and inaccessible places, stood their ground for a long time. But unexpectedly a blackness rose up [that is, the solar eclipse of 21 April 1186] and covered the mountains which were guarded by the barbarians, who had laid ambushes at the narrow defiles; the Romans, undetected, came upon them unawares to send them scurrying in panic. The originators of this evil and commanders of the army, that is, Peter and Asan, and their fellow rebels ran violently to the Istros [the River Danube] like the herd of swine in the Gospels [Luke 8:33] who ran into the sea, and sailed across to join forces with their neighbors, the Cumans. The emperor was hindered by the vast wilderness from making his way through Mysia. Many of the cities there are in the vicinity of Mount Haimos, and the majority or practically all, in fact, are built on sheer cliffs and cloud-capped peaks. Thus, he posted garrisons and did nothing more than set fire to the crops gathered in heaps. Subjected to the trickeries of the Vlachs, who observed him closely, he turned back forthwith, leaving matters there to continue in turmoil [probably in July 1186]. As a result, he encouraged the barbarians to sneer even more broadly at the Romans and emboldened them all the more.

On arriving at the queen of cities [Constantinople], [Emperor] Isaac plumed himself on his achievements, so much so that one of the judges (this was Leon Monasteriotes) said that the soul of Basil the Bulgar-Slayer [Emperor Basil II, 976–1025, who defeated Samuel] was aggrieved because the emperor had utterly cast aside his *typikon* [monastic rule for the monastery that the emperor had established] and all the writings he had lodged in the monastery of Sosthenion [now Istinye, a neighborhood of Istanbul on the European side of the city], among which he had prophesied the revolution of the Vlachs. Isaac continued apace, deriding and ridiculing the prediction as being apparently mistaken, contending that he had won over the rebels by persuasion and had instantly led them back to their former subordination and bondage, while it took Basil a very long time to do so, and that Basil had belched forth empty lies and vain prophecies as from the bay-eating throat and tripod [allusion to Pythia, the high priestess of the temple of Apollo in Delphi].

Asan and his barbarians crossed the Istros [into Walachia, the southern region of present-day Romania] and met the Cumans, from among whom he enlisted a large number of auxiliaries. Then, as was their intention, they returned to their country of Mysia [after summer 1186]. Finding the land swept clean and emptied of Roman troops, they marched in with even greater braggadocio, leading their Cuman auxiliaries as though they were legions of spirits [Mark 5:9]. They were not content merely to preserve their own possessions and to assume control of the government of Mysia; they were also compelled to wreak havoc against the Roman territories and unite the political power of Mysia and Bulgaria into one empire as of old.

Questions: According to Niketas Choniates, how did the Vlachs go about establishing their power over formerly Byzantine territories? What can one learn from this text about the Vlach lifestyle and military tactics? How does Choniates see the two brothers, Peter and Asen? Compare the image of the Vlachs in Choniates to that in Kekaumenos (Doc. 33) and Benjamin of Tudela (Doc. 104).

106. STEPHEN NEMANJA SUBMITS TO EMPEROR MANUEL I

John Kinnamos was an imperial secretary who rose to prominence in the days of Emperor Manuel I Komnenos (1143–80), whom he seems to have followed in several military campaigns, including that in Italy (1155–56). He certainly witnessed Manuel's siege of Zemun in 1165. Much like in the case of the invasion of Serbia in 1172, this was an opportunity for John to express his admiration for Manuel's personal daring in battle. John's History *was written after the emperor's death, perhaps in reaction to the policies of the regency ruling in the name of Manuel's son, Alexios II, or in an attempt to regain favor with the new rulers. He seems to have been back in the imperial entourage under Andronikos Komnenos (1183–85).*

Source: trans. F. Curta from *Joannis Cinnami historiarum libri VII*, ed. J.-P. Migne (Paris: J.-P. Migne, 1864), cols. 662–63.

As he put Béla [III, king of Hungary, 1172–96] on the throne, he [Emperor Manuel I, 1143–80] turned against the Serbs, eager as he was to punish their insolence. To my permanent admiration, without waiting for all his troops to be assembled, the emperor with [only] a few thousands crossed a steep country, well defended by nature, and rushed to engage the grand *župan* [Stephen Nemanja]. Even though the latter had gathered numerous forces of allies from all corners, he started to flee. Then, as fear beset his spirit, he sent envoys to the emperor to ask for his forgiveness. Since he could not convince him [in that respect], he demanded a safe-conduct in order to come and see him in person. The emperor agreed to that, and he arrived in front of the imperial authority with his head uncovered and his arms bare to the elbow, his feet unshod, and a rope around his neck. He gave to the emperor the sword that he was holding in his hand, so that the emperor could do with him what he wished to do. Impressed by this attitude, Manuel granted him his mercy. After obtaining this victory, the emperor left Serbia taking the grand *župan* with him.

Questions: What is the significance of the manner in which Nemanja appeared in front of the emperor? In addition to military victory, what did Manuel hope to achieve by granting Nemanja "his mercy"?

107. SAINT SAVA ON STEPHEN NEMANJA'S ABDICATION

Born c. 1175, Rastko was the youngest son of Grand Župan *Stephen Nemanja of Raška. While still a boy, his father gave him a province to govern, namely Hum (present-day Montenegro), on the Adriatic coast in the region of Dubrovnik. However, Rastko fled the country and went to Mount Athos, where he was tonsured as a monk in the monastery at Vatopedi, taking a new name—Sava. After Stephen Nemanja abdicated in favor of his son Stephen at an assembly specially summoned in Ras in 1196, he withdrew to the monastery of Studenica (near Ušće, in the Middle Ibar region of central Serbia), his foundation of c. 1183. He took monastic vows and a new name—Simeon. Soon after that, he left that monastery and went to Mount Athos to be with his son. A few years later, Simeon and Sava established a new house at Hilandar, which soon became a major monastery at Mount Athos. Simeon died on 13 February 1199 and was initially buried in his foundation at Hilandar. A few years later, however, Sava's brothers Stephen the First-Crowned (Prvovenčani) and Vukan asked him to bring back home their father's remains. Late in 1206, Sava returned to Serbia with Simeon's relics, which he reburied at Studenica. On that occasion, Simeon was proclaimed a saint, and Sava wrote an order of service in his honor. In 1208, Sava also wrote the* Life of Lord Simeon, *which depicted his father as a ruler and as a monk.*

Source: trans. M. Kantor, *Medieval Slavic Lives of Saints and Princes* (Ann Arbor: University of Michigan, Department of Slavic Languages and Literatures, 1983), pp. 263, 265, 269, 271, and 273.

And after the thirty-seventh year of his reign had passed [1196], the all-merciful Lord, receiver of labors and giver of rewards to all who wish to be saved, scorned not his supplication which issued from the depths of his heart, and was compassionate. For clearly, when the time had come, this obedient man thought nothing of the glory and honor of this world and considered the beauty of this life as smoke. But love for Christ grew in him and ignited his heart, which was like a temple prepared for him, and a vessel most pure for his Holy Spirit. And by some inclination Christ inclined his mind and instructed him. And so, he sent to gather his noble children and all his chosen boyars, both the high and low in rank. And having gathered them to himself, he began to instruct them, saying: "My beloved children, whom I have reared! Behold, all of you know how in his wisdom God appointed me to rule over you, and how our land was ruined when first I acquired it. And all of you know how as long as I had strength with the help of God and our holy lady, the Mother of God, I was neither indolent nor allowed myself rest until I set everything in order. And with God's help I added to this land for you, both in length and breadth, as all of you know. And I have reared all of you as my own children, even to this day, and I have taught you how to keep the Orthodox faith. Many foreigners have risen against me and swarmed over me like a beehive, yet I resisted them and overcame them. Therefore, my beloved children, forget not your instruction and the Orthodox law, which I have established. For he who keeps this will have God as his helper, and our holy lady, the Mother of God, and my prayers, though they be sinful. Let me, your lord, now depart in peace, so that my eyes may see the salvation which he [God] has prepared before the face of the whole world as a revelation to all nations, and to your glory as well, my flock. For I see how all that is of man is vanity, that nothing remains after death; neither wealth remains nor is glory attained. For death comes and all this is lost. Thus, our restlessness is in vain. Short is the path which we walk, and our life is but smoke, vapor, decay, and dust. It appears for a little time, and then quickly vanishes away. Verily, all is vanity. For life is but shadow and dream, and our restlessness over everything earthly is for nothing, as it is written: 'When we gain the whole world, we then settle in our grave where together lie both king and knave' [Matt. 16:26]. Therefore, my beloved children, release me forthwith, that I may go to see the consolation of Israel" [Luke 2:5].

And with these admonitions the good lord and gentle shepherd admonished them. And they all wept much and said: "Leave us not as orphans, O lord, for you have illumined us, and you have instructed us, and you have enlightened us, O gentle shepherd, who lays down his soul for his sheep! For never during your days has the wolf carried off a lamb from the flock which God entrusted to you, O shepherd [John 10:11–17]. And throughout all your thirty-eight years were we sheltered and nurtured, and we have known no other lord and father save you, O master."

Now he, the venerable patriarch, with words most wise entreated them like a father to desist from weeping and tears, for it was God's will. And he chose his noble and beloved son Stephen Nemanja [Stephen Prvovenčani, grand *župan* in 1196–1202 and 1203–17, king in 1217–27], the son-in-law of the Greek emperor Alexios [III Angelos, 1195–1203, whose daughter, Evdokia, married Stephen Prvovenčani, Nemanja's son, in the 1190s], who was crowned by God, and handed him over to them, saying: "Take him in my place: a good root who issued from my loins. I am setting him on the throne of the dominion granted me by Christ." And having crowned him himself and blessing him abundantly just as Isaac blessed his son Jacob with ample blessings, he began to instruct him to concern himself with every good deed in his dominion, and to be kindhearted to the Christian community, the God-sheltered flock which he entrusted to him; and he said: "O my beloved child! Shepherd them, my Israel, give heed to them, and lead them like Joseph the lamb."

He commanded him to look after the churches and those serving therein, to listen willingly to the prelates and church servants, to respect the priests, and to protect the monks, "so they may pray for you, and you will be ashamed of nothing in the sight of God and man." Now he blessed his other noble and beloved son, Prince Vukan, appointed him grand *župan*, and turned over sufficient land to him. And upon giving the same commands, the good father placed them both before himself, and he said to them: "My sons, forget not my laws, but let your hearts preserve my words: for length of days, and long life, and peace shall they add to you. Let neither mercy nor faith forsake you; bind them about your neck and write them upon the table of your heart. So shall you find favor and good understanding in the sight of God and man. Trust in the Lord with all your heart and be not proud of your own understanding. Be mindful in all your ways that your way be the right one, lest your feet stumble. . . ."

And after he accomplished all these things—so that the work of this most wise and wonderful of men should be revealed to all—and blessed his community, he left the dominion given to him by God and his special and sundry accumulations, for it was the will of Christ the Lord and the most holy lady, the Mother of God, to fill him with an unutterable and sacred desire. He gave all his possessions to the poor, took leave of his dominion, his children, and his God-given wife of the first marriage (for he did not marry twice), and joined himself to that ineffable and honorable, holy angelic and apostolic station of the upper and lower form [monastic life of two different degrees]. And he was given the name Simeon on the twenty-fifth day of the month of March, on the feast of the Annunciation, in the year 6703 [1195, obviously a mistake; the correct year is 1197]. On that same day his God-given wife Anna, the former lady of the entire Serbian land, also assumed this holy station [that is, she became a nun]. And she was given the name Anastasia.

Questions: What does Saint Sava's biography suggest about the relationship between Nemanja's faith and his decision to abdicate? What is Sava's view of that decision? What point is he making about Stephen Prvovenčani and Vukan receiving parental advice on how to rule?

108. JOHANNITSA KALOYAN WRITES TO POPE INNOCENT III

In 1199, Pope Innocent III (1198–1216) wrote to Johannitsa (also known as Kaloyan, "Fair John"), the ruler of the polity that had emerged after the 1185 rebellion of the Vlachs and the Bulgarians. In his first letter dated between 1199 and January 1200, the pope claimed that he had "heard that the lineage of your ancestors has its origins in the noble city of Rome, and that you have taken from them, as if by hereditary right, both the generosity of the blood and the inclination toward the sincere devotion that you have for the Apostolic See." He therefore decided to send letters and envoys. The pope most likely wanted to entice Johannitsa into recognizing papal primacy, and thus contributing to the papal plans of expanding Catholic Christendom to the Balkans. The ruler of Serbia, Vukan (1202–04), would also be included in those plans. Johannitsa, on the other hand, saw the pope's move as an excellent opportunity to obtain recognition of his power from the outside. He requested an imperial crown and the elevation of his archbishop (Basil, based in Tărnovo) to the rank of patriarch. Between 1199 and 1204, the pope and Johannitsa exchanged many letters, copies of which have been preserved in the papal registers. It is likely that Johannitsa's letters were not written in Latin but translated into that language from the original Old Church Slavonic, probably through a Greek intermediary. Nonetheless, the line of communication between Rome and Tărnovo was maintained even through the turbulent year of 1204. That year witnessed the conquest of Constantinople by the crusaders, but also the rapid deterioration of the relations between Johannitsa and his neighbors to the northwest and to the south—Hungary and the Latin empire of Constantinople—that were also under papal jurisdiction. The letter below was sent by Johannitsa to the pope in November 1204, seven months after the conquest of Constantinople.

Source: trans. K. Petkov, *The Voices of Medieval Bulgaria, Seventh-Fifteenth Century: The Records of a Bygone Culture* (Leiden: Brill, 2008), pp. 227–29.

Kaloyan, king of Bulgaria and Vlachia, to the God-elevated, most holy, beloved of Christ and most respected father of my tsardom, Innocent the Third, most holy pope of Rome and successor of the prince-apostle Peter.

The envoy of the Apostolic See, the lord cardinal Leo [Brancaleone, appointed cardinal of the holy cross in Jerusalem in 1202] brought to my kingdom your holiness's writings [on 15 October 1204]. When I found out that you are sound and healthy, I praised God almighty and his most holy Mother. Let the writings of my kingdom find your holiness alive and residing in joy and delight. By the grace of

God almighty and the most blessed Mother of God and through the intercession of your holiness my kingdom is healthy and very well with every joy and delight.

Let it be known to your holiness and spiritual father of my kingdom, lord pope, that Lord Leo [Brancaleone], envoy of the Apostolic See arrived before my kingdom and brought me a crown, and after blessing it [on 8 November 1204], placed it on the head of my kingdom and placed in my hands a scepter and a banner, and blessed the most holy patriarch of my kingdom and all Bulgaria as your holiness had ordered. We praised much God and the most blessed Mother of God as well as your holiness's perceptiveness for granting to our kingdom what we desired according to our request, for which the entire Bulgaria and Vlachia and the domain of our entire kingdom much praised and glorified your holiness.

I am also writing on account of the Hungarian [King Emeric, 1196–1204]. My kingdom has nothing to do with his domain or anything else that belongs to him, nor are we causing him any harm. On the contrary, it is he who attacks and harms the domain of my kingdom [and let your holiness decide] whether I am not respecting the Hungarian or whether he is not respecting my kingdom. Let your holiness write him to stay away from my kingdom because my kingdom has no intention either to disrespect him or to go against his territories. However, if he goes against the territories of my kingdom and with God's help he gets vanquished, let your holiness have no suspicions [of foul play on the part] of my kingdom, but let me be free [of blame].

Also, about the Latins who entered Constantinople [on 13 April 1204]. I am writing to your holiness to [request that you] write them to stay away from my kingdom and not show us disrespect so that my kingdom would not cause them any harm. In case they initiate something against my kingdom, disrespect us, and kill some of the people subject to us, let your holiness not suspect my kingdom, but everything be free [of blame].

I did send to your great holiness two boys, one called Basil, the other Betlehem. Let your holiness give orders that they be put to school to study the Latin letters, for we have no grammarians here who could translate the letters that you send us. When they complete their studies, let them be sent back to my kingdom. I also sent, for now, as a sign of remembrance, two pieces of samite [luxurious and heavy silk fabric], two double episimies [expensive, gold-woven liturgical vestments], the one white, the other red, and a cameo. Indeed, every time I send to your holiness, I will always remember your holiness.

Questions: Why does Johannitsa ask the pope to write to the king of Hungary and "the Latins who entered Constantinople"? Why and in what manner does the pope seek to use Johannitsa's power in the region? What is the relation between coronation and elevation of an archbishop to the rank of patriarch? Is there anything in this letter that could indicate Johannitsa's misapprehension toward the pope?

109. ROBERT DE CLARI ON THE BATTLE OF ADRIANOPLE

Robert de Clari was a simple knight from Picardy (northern France) who, following his lord Peter of Amiens, participated in the conquest of Constantinople (1204), but who had already returned home by the time of the battle of Adrianople (14 April 1205). The account of the battle and its aftermath, including the marriage of Emperor Henry to the Bulgarian princess, was added in Picardy to the rest of the text that may have been drafted in Constantinople. Clari's chronicle has often been contrasted with that of Geoffrey of Villehardouin, the former representing the point of view of the knights, the latter a representative of the barons. Unlike Villehardouin, Clari explains the disaster at Adrianople as divine retribution for the arrogance of the barons toward "the poor people of the army" (like himself) and for the horrible sins committed in Constantinople after the conquest of the city. In and by themselves, the Vlachs have no significance: to Clari, they are only God's instruments for punishing sinners. That is why, unlike Villehardouin, Clari has nothing bad to say about Johannitsa Kaloyan ("John the Vlach," as he calls him). That is also why Henry I needs to be convinced by his barons that it is in his own interest to ask Boril for the hand of his stepdaughter. Robert de Clari's Boril lives in a savage country and may have barbarian features, but eventually sends his stepdaughter to Constantinople with a large retinue and an impressive dowry. Ultimately, Clari must have agreed with the barons, advising Emperor Henry that the Vlachs were now the most powerful and feared people in the empire, if not the world.

Source: trans. E.H. McNeal, Robert of Clari, *The Conquest of Constantinople* (New York: Columbia University Press, 1936), pp. 125–26 and 127–28.

Then it happened afterward that a city which the emperor [Baldwin I, 1204–05] had conquered rebelled against him; Adrianople [present-day Edirne, in the European part of Turkey] was the name of this city. When the emperor knew of it, he sent for the doge of Venice [Enrico Dandolo, 1192–1205] and Count Louis and the other barons and told them that he wanted to go and besiege Adrianople, which had rebelled against him, and that they should help him conquer this city, and the barons answered that they would gladly do so. So the emperor and the barons made ready to go to this city. When they came to this city, they laid siege to it, and while they were encamped there, behold one day John the Vlach [Johannitsa Kaloyan, 1196–1207], he and the Cumans, with a great force, came into the land of Constantinople [that is, of the Latin empire of Constantinople], as they had done before, and found the emperor with all his host encamped before Adrianople. When they of the host saw the Cumans clothed in their sheepskins, they had no more fear or care for them than for a troop of children. And these Cumans and this horde came at a great pace and they rushed upon the French and slew many of them and defeated them all in this battle. And the emperor was lost [in fact, taken prisoner], so that it was never known what became of him, and Count Louis [of Blois, 1172–1205] and many other high men, and so many others that we do not know the number of them, but fully three hundred knights were lost there. And those who escaped came fleeing to Constantinople, and the doge of Venice came fleeing and many people with him, and they left their tents and their harness just as they were when they were encamped before this city, because they never dared turn that way, so great was the rout. And thus truly did God take vengeance on them for their pride and for the bad faith which they had kept with the poor people of the host, and for the terrible sins which they had committed in the city [of Constantinople] after they had taken it.

When the emperor was lost by this disaster, the barons who were left were greatly dismayed. Afterward they assembled one day to choose an emperor, and they sent for my lord Henry [of Flanders], the brother of the emperor Baldwin who was, to make him emperor [Henry I, 1205–16]. . . .

It was not long after this that John the Vlach and the Cumans rode into the land of the marquis of Salonika [Boniface of Montferrat, king of Thessaloniki, 1205–07] and finally he fought with these Vlachs and Cumans, and he was slain in this battle and all his people were defeated. Then John the Vlach and these Cumans went and besieged Salonika and had their engines set up to assault the city. And the wife of the marquis [Margaret of Hungary, the daughter of King Béla III] had remained in the city, and knights and other people remained with her to defend the city. Now there lay in this city the body of my lord Saint Demetrius, who would never suffer his city to be taken by force. And there flowed from this holy body such great quantities of oil [that is, myrrh], that it was a fair marvel. And it came to pass, as John the Vlach was lying one morning in his tent, that my lord Saint Demetrius came and struck him with a lance through the body and slew him. When his own people and the Cumans knew that he was dead, they broke camp and went away to their land. And then afterward, the kingdom of Vlachia [that is, the Second Bulgarian Empire] fell to a nephew of John, Boris [in fact, Boril, emperor of Bulgaria between 1207 and 1218] was his name. So, this Boris became king of Vlachia, and he had a beautiful daughter [the princess was Boril's stepdaughter]. Then it happened that the emperor Henry, who was a right good emperor, took counsel with his barons as to what he should do about these Vlachs and Cumans, who were thus making war on the empire of Constantinople, and who had slain the emperor Baldwin, his brother [who most likely died in prison in Tărnovo]. Finally, the barons advised him to send to this Boris, who was king of Vlachia, and ask him to give him his daughter to wife. The emperor answered that he would never take a wife of such low lineage. And the barons said: "Sire, you should do so. We urge you to make peace with them, for they are the most powerful people and the most dread enemy of the empire and of the land." The barons talked so much that the emperor finally sent two knights, high men, and he had them very finely arrayed. The messengers went very fearfully to this savage land, and when they came there the people wanted to slay them. Nevertheless, the messengers talked with this Boris and he replied that he would gladly send his daughter to the emperor.

Then Boris the king had his daughter attired very richly and very nobly, and many people with her. And he sent her to the emperor, and he commanded sixty packhorses to be sent to him all loaded with treasure, with gold and silver and cloth of silk and precious jewels, and there was no horse that was not covered with a cloth of vermilion samite [a rich silk fabric dyed bright red and interwoven with gold and silver threads], so long that it trailed behind fully seven or eight feet, and never did they go through mud or by evil roads, so that not one of the samite cloths was injured, all for daintiness and nobility. When the emperor knew that the maiden was coming, he went to meet her, and the barons with him, and they made great welcome for her and her people, and then afterward the emperor married her.

Questions: What, according to Robert de Clari, were the reasons for Johannitsa's victory at Adrianople? What role do the Cumans play in the story? What were the relations between Boril and the Latins? What can the dowry Boril bestowed upon his daughter tell us about the resources of the Bulgarian emperor?

110. HENRI DE VALENCIENNES ON ALEXIUS SLAV

Little is known about Henri de Valenciennes other than what he says about himself. He was probably a cleric, not a knight, in the service of Peter of Douai (1145–1225), one of the most important barons of Henry of Flanders, the Latin emperor of Constantinople between 1205 and 1216. He must have followed his lord to Constantinople in 1204 and was clearly a witness to some of the subsequent events, including the battle of Philippopolis (31 July 1208) in which Henry of Flanders defeated Boril, the emperor of Bulgaria (1207–18). Henri de Valenciennes finished his History of Emperor Henry of Constantinople *by September 1209, when Peter of Douai returned to Flanders. Because it appears in five manuscripts (the earliest of which are dated to the thirteenth century) following Geoffrey of Villehardouin's* Conquest of Constantinople, *many believe that Henri's* History *was a continuation of Villehardouin's work. In reality, it is an independent, highly original work, which is very different from Villehardouin's because of its vividly epic style and the many speeches introduced into the narrative. Its coverage is also restricted to a little more than a year, from 25 May 1208 (the day of Emperor Henry's coronation) to July 1209. Despite the lack of dates, the* History *is quite precise in terms of personal and place names, many of which are confirmed by other sources. Henri de Valenciennes wrote for an audience of aristocrats in early thirteenth-century France, as indicated by some of the narrative strategies he used in the text of the* History. *For example, he compared the Vlachs in the armies defeated by Henry of Flanders to larks scattered at the approach of the sparrow hawks, or with* bruhiers *(falcons) that cannot be tamed for hunting. Both comparisons suggest an audience familiar with falconry, especially with falcons used as a sign of social distinction and treated as prizes at tournaments. On the other hand, the Vlachs and their Cuman allies are depicted as enemies of both empire and church, which has rightly been interpreted as crusading propaganda. Henri de Valenciennes regarded "Blaquie" as the country of its ruler Burile(s) but calls it Great Vlachia ("Blakie la Grant") in anticipation of its conquest by Emperor Henry of Flanders. There are two Vlach characters in the* History. *One, Burile(s), is in fact Boril, the emperor of Bulgaria, described as a usurper who has made himself king against God and reason. Some have seen in Burile(s) the villain of the* History, *the exact opposite of its hero, Emperor Henry. The other Vlach character is Esclas, who appears in the passage translated below. Esclas is the French version of Slav, a nephew of Peter and Asen, who sometime before 1208 had become lord of a district in the Rhodope Mountains. His first residence was at Tzapaina (now Cepina, near Pazardzhik), but he later occupied Melnik near Sandanski, in the Pirin Mountains of southwestern Bulgaria. He became an independent ruler of a principality centered upon Melnik, where he rebuilt the church of St-Nicholas and established a monastery nearby at Rozhen. His residence, a two-storied palace with a private chapel, is still standing in the center of the town. Following his marriage to the daughter of Emperor Henry, Alexius Slav received the title of despot (and the surname Alexius) and was recognized as ruler of Melnik until his death in or shortly after 1229. He remained a faithful ally of Emperor Henry but got married a second time to the daughter of Theodore Angelos Komnenos Dukas, the ruler of Epirus between 1215 and 1230. After Slav's death, the principality of Melnik was incorporated into Bulgaria under Emperor John II Asen (1218–41).*

Source: trans. F. Curta from Henri de Valenciennes, *Histoire de l'empereur Henri de Constantinople*, ed. J. Longnon (Paris: P. Geuthner, 1948), pp. 48–54.

Esclas, one of the noblemen against whom Buriles was waging war, and who was his cousin—for Buriles said that the land that Esclas had ought to be his, while Esclas said that he would never have it, and for that they fought against each other, so that Esclas often overcame him and took many people, friends, and fortresses from him—that Esclas, because he wanted to have on his side the power and the assistance of Emperor Henry, sent [envoys] to him to offer peace.

So, it all happened as I told you. After that, Esclas, who was very wise, came to the emperor, whom he found sitting in his tent in the company of the great barons. Esclas entered the tent and in front of all the barons who were there, he threw himself at the feet of the emperor, and kissed them, and then he kissed his hand. What else would I tell you? The peace was made and confirmed, and Esclas became a man [vassal] of Emperor Henry, to whom he swore fealty and loyalty from that moment onward, as appropriate to one's lord. And then he told the marshal in private that he was asking the emperor for [the hand of] one of his daughters [most likely born out of wedlock, as Henry's only wife, Agnes of Montferrat, had died in 1207 or 1208, and Henry had no children]. And Esclas fell again on his knees in front of the emperor and said: "Sir, I heard that you have a daughter, whom I ask, if you so please, to give to me in marriage. I am a man rich in lands and with a treasure of silver and gold; and I am regarded by many in my country as a genteel man [that is, a man of high social status]. So, I ask you, if you so wish, to give her to me."

And all those who were present there were pressing [the emperor] to give [the girl] to him, so that he would serve him more fervently and with greater will. And the emperor said: "My lords, if you advise me [to do so], I will follow [your advice]." And then he began to smile; and he called upon Esclas and told him: "Esclas, I give you my daughter in the manner in which God will make you enjoy that; and you will acquiesce all the conquest that we have done here, in such a manner that you will be my vassal and you will serve me. And if you obey my will, [you will have] Great Vlachia [most likely the rest of Bulgaria at that time under the rule of Boril], of which I will make you lord, with God's will and if I live [until then]."

And so, Esclas rose to his feet and he thanked him with tears in his eyes. And Esclas went back, and our men returned to a castle called Estanemach [Stenimachos, near Plovdiv, central Bulgaria]; and there Esclas met again with our men. And he discussed with the baron where he would marry the girl, and when. . . .

Esclas went straight to Salembrie [Selymbria, now Silivri, on the western outskirts of Constantinople] for his [promised] wife. He took her by the hand and told her that he wanted her to come [with him] to Constantinople; and she said she was ready to go. Esclas, who had fallen in love with the girl ever since he had seen her, went with her to Constantinople; for he wanted very much to marry her; and he could not wait another day before that would happen.

When the emperor learned the news about Esclas, he came out to meet him; and they came together to Constantinople, and he let him marry the woman. And he was so happy and relieved that he did not want anything else: for he had plenty and all the goods that belonged to him as a wealthy man, and everything was coming out [for him] as from a fountain where they all sprang out. And Esclas remained in Constantinople for the entire week, and then he bid farewell to the emperor and went away with his wife. The emperor bestowed upon him all the honors he could, and he treated him grandly, like all important people; and when he was about to leave, he told his daughter in private: "My beautiful daughter, be wise and courteous. You have taken as your husband a man with whom you will now leave: he is somewhat savage; for you do not understand his language, nor can he understand yours. In the name of God, make sure that he does not take umbrage at you, do not change your talents, and do not become mean. For there is a great shame for a genteel woman to be despised by her husband, and to be harshly blamed by God and by her own time. Above all, by God, do not replace your good upbringing with bad customs. If you are simple, sweet, affable, and tolerant, your husband will desire you; and thus honored, all his people will honor you. But especially make sure that by all means either of love or of friendship that they will have for you, you do not remove from your heart our people, from among whom you are now taken." "Sir," she said, "know that, God willing, you will not get any bad news from me. But dear father, we are about to leave, this is my wish: I will pray to God that, if he wills, you will have the power to overcome all your enemies and to increase your honor." And they hugged each other, and then they [Esclas and his wife] departed from them [the emperor and his men].

Questions: According to Henri de Valenciennes, what were the merits of Esclas that guaranteed his success? Why did Emperor Henry eventually decide to give his daughter in marriage to Esclas? How did the emperor regard Esclas?

111. JOHN II ASEN BOASTS OF HIS VICTORY AT KLOKOTNICA

John II Asen's victory at Klokotnica (near Khaskovo, in Bulgaria) firmly established the Bulgarian hegemony in the Balkans. Taken prisoner, Theodore, the emperor of Thessaloniki, was later blinded as punishment for his inciting a rebellion against the Bulgarian ruler. The victory allowed John Asen to occupy much of the territory under Epirote rule, and to extend Bulgarian rule across the Balkan Peninsula, from one sea (Black) to the other (Ionian). This feat is described in some detail in a Cyrillic inscription on a column in the church of the monastery of the Forty Holy Martyrs that John Asen built in Tărnovo to celebrate his victory. The list of territories in the text below is very similar to that in a charter that John Asen issued at some point after 1230 for the merchants of Ragusa (now Dubrovnik, in Croatia), to whom he granted free access to the cities of Bulgaria. The political prestige and economic prosperity of Bulgaria during his reign are well illustrated in the building program in Tărnovo, dominated by the large church of the monastery of the Forty Holy Martyrs, in the oblong narthex of which John Asen was buried at his death in 1241. The victory at Klokotnica also turned Bulgaria into a great threat to the Latin empire of Constantinople. One by one, the Thracian cities controlled by the Latins opened their gates to the Bulgarians. In each one of them John Asen replaced bishops or priests appointed by the Latin (Catholic) patriarch of Constantinople with suffragans of the metropolitan of Tărnovo. This is most likely the context in which, shortly after Klokotnica, the Bulgarian emperor established contacts with Patriarch Germanus II in Nicaea for the return of the Bulgarian church to Orthodoxy and the recognition of the archbishop of Tărnovo as patriarch of Bulgaria. Only five years after Klokotnica, John Asen laid siege to Constantinople together with the Nicaean emperor John III Dukas Vatatzes (1222–54).

Source: trans. K. Petkov, *The Voices of Medieval Bulgaria, Seventh-Fifteenth Century: The Records of a Bygone Culture* (Leiden: Brill, 2008), p. 425.

In the year 6738 [CE 1230], I, John Asen, in Christ God faithful emperor and ruler of the Bulgarians, son of the old emperor Asen, built from the foundations and adorned with paintings the whole of this most honorable church in the name of the Forty Holy Martyrs with whose help in the twelfth year of my reign, in the year this temple was being painted, I went to war in Romania [the European part of the Byzantine Empire] and routed the Greek army [at Klokotnica, on 9 March 1230] and captured emperor Theodore [Dukas] Komnenos [despot of Epirus between 1215 and 1230 and emperor of Thessaloniki between 1224 and 1230] himself and all of his boyars. I conquered his entire land, from Adrianople [present-day Edirne, in the European part of Turkey] to Drach [Durrës, in Albania], the Greek [part], as well as the Serbian and Albanian parts. The cities round about Constantinople and the city itself were ruled by the Franks, but even they obeyed the hand of my imperial [majesty], because they had no other emperor but me [the newly elected emperor, John of Brienne, did not reach Constantinople before 1231; at the time of the battle of Klotkotnica, he was still in France], and they lived their days thanks to me. God ordained it to be so, because without him neither word, nor deed can be accomplished. Glory to him for all ages! Amen.

Questions: What aspects of ideal rulership does the inscription from Tărnovo reveal? Why does he mention Adrianople in the context of his conquest? Compare his description of the lands he has conquered and the description of the territory within which he has granted a commercial privilege to the Ragusan merchants (Doc. 59).

112. SERBS DEFEAT THE BYZANTINES, A SERB ON THE BULGARIAN THRONE

The History *of George Akropolites (1217–82) is the main contemporary Greek source for what happened in the lands of the former Byzantine Empire between 1203 and 1261. He was born and raised in Constantinople under Latin rule. He received his education in Nicaea, with teachers paid by the emperor. He accompanied Emperor John III Dukas Vatatzes (1222–54) on his 1246 campaign in the Balkans, which ended with the conquest of the Struma and Maritsa valleys, from Adrianople all the way to Skopje and Prilep. Akropolites was responsible for drafting imperial letters and therefore knew about the plans and strategy of the emperor. He was a member of the imperial delegation that sealed the treaty with Michael II, despot of*

Epirus, in Larissa. Akropolites traveled again to Thrace and to Macedonia with John III's son and successor, Theodore II, during the first Bulgarian campaign of 1254–55. At that time, the emperor bestowed upon him the title of grand logothete. During the second campaign (1256), to which the first fragment below refers, he was appointed praitor, *an office that came with military and fiscal responsibilities in Albania and western Macedonia. However, without any experience in the matter, Akropolites was soon overwhelmed. He was in charge of the fortress of Prilep, which he was forced to surrender to Michael II of Epirus, who took him prisoner and kept him in Arta for two years. He was released only after the Nicaean victory at Pelagonia (1259). Upon his return from captivity, Akropolites traveled again to the Balkans, as envoy to the Bulgarian court in Tărnovo in the winter of 1260–61. Upon his return to Constantinople, he decided to dedicate himself to teaching philosophy, geometry, arithmetic, and syllogistics. His reputation as an intellectual may have been responsible for his selection for the Byzantine delegation to the Second Council of Lyon (1274), where the Byzantine Church was supposed to accept the primacy of the Roman Church in exchange for papal support against Emperor Michael VIII's enemy, Charles of Anjou. A few years prior to this important diplomatic mission, Akropolites began working on his* History, *using both written sources (letters, treaties, and other documents) and his own experience. He had firsthand knowledge of the military and political events in the Balkans.*

Source: trans. R.J. Macrides, *George Akropolites: The History* (Oxford: Oxford University Press, 2007), pp. 328–29 and 334.

70. Not very many days had yet gone by and, since the emperor [Theodore II Dukas Laskaris, emperor of Nicaea, 1254–58] realized that affairs in the west were in great disorder and that most of the territory had been taken by the rebel Michael and it was necessary for a general to be sent with any army in counterattack, he chose the said Michael Komnenos [Michael Palaiologos, the future emperor Michael VIII, who at that time was a general in the Nicaean army], giving him also an army from Macedonia, which was very small in size and worthless in quality. But Michael Komnenos could not object to the order he had been given and so, taking that paltry and unwarlike army, he went to Thessalonike [in 1257] and from there, after crossing the Vardar, which the ancients call the Naxeios [in fact, Axios], he joined Michael Laskaris [the brother of Emperor Theodore II's grandfather]. When they had deliberated, they proceeded against Beroia [now Veroia, in northern Greece], not in order to fight against it, for it was not possible for them to do such a thing, but to plunder the surrounding area. And they plundered a great deal, for their followers carried off a quantity of animals whose number is not easily counted.

While they were doing these things, the ruler of the Serbs [King Uroš, 1243–76]—they are a race which violates treaties and never shows gratitude to those who have been good to it, but for a small gain they cast aside and trample on the cup of friendship—learning of the rebellion of the renegade Michael, assembled an army numbering in the thousands and sent it against the Roman lands. Passing by Kytzavis [now Kičevo, in western Macedonia], they plundered the area around Prilep. The *skouterios* Xyleas [one of the "new men" promoted by Emperor Theodore II, who bestowed upon him the title of *skouterios*], who was near the town with the army which was under his command, saw that the army of Serbs was plundering the land and setting fires everywhere. He was a man ignorant in matters of war and with no military experience at all, for he did not have spies at a distance so as to learn from afar of the advance of the enemy, nor did he know how to array an army in battle order. He released each man to rush against the Serbs as he wished. Since their battle order had been broken up and they were few, they fell into the grip of the Serbs, who were more in number, and they were caught. Some were put to the sword, others were taken alive and carried off as captives. Later, when Xyleas himself, the *skouterios*, charged against the Serbs with the remaining soldiers, he barely escaped with his life, crossing mountains, hills, and precipitous places, pursued by the enemy. Thus, the army at Prilep [in central Macedonia] was destroyed in this way and we [George Akropolites was in command of the fortress] were shut up in the town of Prilep, as if incarcerated. . . .

73. Now the ruler of the Bulgarians, Michael [I Asen, 1246–56], the brother of the emperor Theodore's wife [who married Michael's sister, Helen, the daughter of John II Asen], a man who nurtured a great hatred against his brother-in-law the emperor and against the Romans, was mortally wounded by his first cousin Kaliman [Coloman Asen II, 1256], with the knowledge of certain inhabitants of T[ă]rnovo, when he [Michael] was staying somewhere outside this town; he died immediately. The man who murdered him, Kaliman, married Michael's wife and expected to make the realm of the Bulgarians his own, but the Russian Ouros [Rostislav Mikhailovich, son of the Rus' ruler of Chernigov, Michael I Asen's father-in-law, and duke of Mačva under Hungarian rule] came to T[ă]rnovo with an army and took his daughter [Anna], Michael's wife. Some men had already killed Kaliman, as he fled from place to place. Since the Bulgarian realm was left without a legitimate heir, the leading men met in deliberation and determined to accept Constantine, the son of Toichos [Tih, a Serbian aristocrat from Skopje], to rule them [Constantine Asen, 1257–77]. But so that the office should appear attractive to him and so that he might appear to govern by inheritance, they sent an embassy to the emperor Theodore requesting that he send his eldest daughter, who was named Eirene, for union with Constantine, son of Toichos, and be joined in lawful wedlock, as she was a granddaughter of the former ruler of the Bulgarians, John [II] Asan [1218–41], and was fitted for this realm. But since it happened that Constantine Toichos [already] had a lawful wife, they separated [her] from her husband and sent the woman to the

emperor Theodore. This was the state of Bulgarian affairs; thus, also the emperor Theodore had peace from them, and affairs were quiet for both sides.

Questions: For Akropolites, what is the cause of the Byzantine defeat at the hands of the Serbs under King Uroš? What is Akropolites's view of the political situation in Bulgaria?

CHAPTER THIRTEEN

MONGOL CONQUESTS AND *PAX MONGOLICA*

Figure 13.1 The Battle of Legnica (1241) in which the Mongols defeated Henry II the Pious, duke of Silesia, and his allies. Illumination from the *Vita beatae Hedwigis* (Hedwig Codex), a fourteenth-century manuscript.

113. THE *QURILTAI* OF 1235 (JUVAINI)

Ala-ad-Din Ata-Malik Juvaini was born in 1226 in the province of Khorasan, north-eastern Iran, into a distinguished family, the members of which held high office under both the Seljuks and the Khwarazm-Shah (sultans of the Anushtegin dynasty that ruled Iran between 1077 and 1231). His brother Shams-ad-Din became the sahib-i divan *(vizier) of the Illkhans, the Mongol rulers of Persia after the conquest of Baghdad and the destruction of the caliphate in 1258. One year later, Juvaini himself was appointed governor of that city. By that time, he had already distinguished himself as a historian. At age twenty-six, Juvaini traveled to Karakorum, the Mongol capital, where he remained until September 1253. It was during his sojourn there that he began writing a history of the Mongol conquests, on which he was still working in 1260 by the time he was governor of Baghdad. The information about the assembly (*quriltai*) of 1235 was most likely gathered during the sojourn in Karakorum. Despite the generally glorifying tone, Juvaini treated the Mongols with irony in his writings, although he blamed the Khwarazm-Shah for the Mongol onslaught on Persia. His attitude toward the Mongols was ultimately one shaped by his Muslim faith, especially by the* hadith *that refers to horsemen sent by Allah to exact vengeance on the wicked. In other words, Juvaini saw the Mongols as an instrument of Allah's plans for humanity, for despite their destructive role, the Mongols contributed to the expansion of Islam, including those territories, such as Mongolia, that the Muslim faith had never reached before. The destruction of fellow Muslims such as the Bulghars was simply a punishment of rebels (much like that of the Khwarazm-Shah), while the Rus' and the Hungarians were infidels who received the appropriate retribution for their disbelief.*

Source: trans. T. May from 'Ala' al-Dīn Aṭa Malik ibn Muḥammad Juvaynī, *Ta'rīkh-i-Jahān-Gusha*, ed. Mīrzā Muḥammad Qazvīnī, vol. 1 (Leiden: Brill, 1912), pp. 154–57, and vol. 2 (Leiden: Brill, 1916), pp. 224–25.

When the emperor [Ögedai, great khan between 1229 and 1241], who was a Hatim [of Tayyi, a pre-Islamic Arab famous for generosity and hospitality] in generosity and a Khusro [II, the last Sassanian king, 590–628] in affability, with his mind at rest regarding the conquest of Khitai [northern China under the Jin dynasty, 1125–34], had proceeded in triumph to his place of residence [Karakorum, the capital he founded in the Orkhon Valley of central Mongolia], and the princes and emirs [commanders] whom he had dispatched to all ends of the habitable quarters of the world, had all of them achieved their objectives and returned pleased with their triumph, his high counsel and lofty resolve required that he should again call his children and kinsmen together so that by conferring with them he might confirm the old and new *yasas* [wartime decrees, Mongol law] and ordinances, and they might again deploy armies to such countries as they saw fit, and all the princes and armies, noble and base, might share in the gifts of his goodness and liberality, which were like the spring rain. Thus, he sent messengers to summon them [to the meeting], and they all set out from their [respective] places of residence and came to the court. . . .

The emperor of the world welcomed those of his family that were his elder brothers and uncles with every mark of respect and deference, honor, and veneration. For his younger brothers and sons, who were like his own children, nay, like pieces of his liver [believed to be the fundamental organ in the body and the seat of one's passions and emotions], he honored them with all manner of benevolence and excess of kindness. For a complete month in agreement with his like-minded relatives and with the assistance of incomparable kinsmen, he joined dawn to dusk and morning to evening in constant partaking of bowls and goblets and the handing round of cups by the hands of handsome cupbearers. And they had their hearts' desire of the flower and fruit of false fate and they enjoyed all kinds of wanton pleasures. . . .

When the feasting had come to an end, he [Ögedai] turned to affairs of state and army organization. And since there were many parts of the climes [regions of the world] where the wind of rebellion had not left the brains of men, he tasked each one of his sons and kinsmen with a different campaign and resolved, once again, to take part in person [in the war] and to set his reins in motion. . . . Thus, each one of the princes and *noyans* [military commanders] was assigned to a different campaign and they were deployed to the east and the west, to the south, and the north. And since the tribes of the Qifchak [Cumans] and the Keler [Hungarians] had not yet been completely defeated, the chief attention was paid to the conquest and destruction of these peoples. Of the princes Batu [second son of Jochi—the eldest son of Genghis Khan—and grandson of Genghis Khan, khan of the Golden Horde between 1227 and 1255], Mengü Khan [Möngke, son of Tolui—youngest son of Genghis Khan—and grandson of Genghis Khan, emperor between 1251 and 1259], and Güyük [eldest son of Ögedai and grandson of Genghis Khan, emperor between 1246 and 1248] were appointed to conduct this campaign. Each departed to his own encampment with a larger army of Tajiks [Iranian-speaking people of the Fergana Valley in present-day Tajikistan and Uzbekistan] and Turks [non-Iranian nomads], intending to march at the beginning of the coming spring [of 1236]. They prepared for the journey and started out at the appointed time. . . .

When [Möngke] Khan held the great *quriltai* for the second time, they conferred together concerning the destruction and subjugation of all the remaining rebels. It was decided to seize the lands of Bulghar [Volga Bulgharia], the As [Alans, the semi-nomadic Iranian population of the north Caucasus region], and the Rus', which bordered on the camping grounds of Batu; for they had not completely submitted being deceived by the extent of their territory. He thus appointed certain princes to provide assistance to Batu: Mengü Khan and his [half-]brother Böchek; [Ögedai's] own sons Güyük Khan and Qadagha; of the other princes, Kölgen [son of Genghis Khan], Büri [son of Mutukan and grandson of Chaghadai Khan—the second son of Genghis Khan], Baidar [son of Chaghadai Khan]; Batu's brothers, Hordu [Jochi's eldest son] and Tangut [Jochi's fifth son]; and several other princes, as well as Sübetei Bahadur [great general of Genghis Khan, c. 1175–1248] from amongst the great commanders. The princes returned each to his own place of residence to muster their forces and armies; and in the spring, each set forth from his own territory and hastened to carry out his orders. They came together in the realm of Bulghar. The earth echoed and reverberated from the multitude of their armies, [and even] the beasts stood amazed by the size and tumult of their armies. First, they stormed the city of Bulghar [Bolgar], famous throughout the world for the strength of its position and its ample resources [particularly its dominance of the fur trade]; and as a warning to others, they killed the people or took them captive.

Questions: What does this document suggest about the organization of the Mongol empire? According to Juvaini, what was the reason for planning a western campaign at the quriltai *of 1235? What was the objective of that campaign?*

114. MONGOLS IN NORTHEASTERN RUS'

The Novgorod annals (known as the Novgorod First Chronicle*), one of the most important sources for the history of Rus', survive in many manuscripts. The oldest is a compilation of at least two lists, the later of which covers the years 1234–1330 and was written during the first half of the fourteenth century. This segment contains accounts of the battle on the Kalka River in 1223 (albeit under the year 1224) and of the Mongol invasion of northeastern Rus' in 1237 (under the year 1238). The sources for the latter seem to have been oral, although there is evidence of the use of such written sources as the newer version of the* vita *of Alexander Nevsky, which is reflected in fragments of a later date. That the account was written down later than the events narrated therein can be seen from the occasional reference to the Mongols in 1237–38 as "Ishmaelites," although Islam was not adopted by the Mongols in the Golden Horde before 1313. In other words, the annalist(s) projected onto the past the relations between native Rus' and the Mongols at the time of writing. The interest that the Novgorodian annalist had in the earlier, thirteenth-century Mongol conquest of Riazan', Moscow, and Vladimir was probably related to concerns about the situation of Novgorod in relation to the khans of the Golden Horde during the early fourteenth century. The annalist explains that at almost the same time as the Mongols took the cities in the principalities of Riazan' and Vladimir, they also attacked Torzhok in the principality of Novgorod. However, for reasons that have not been satisfactorily explained to this day, instead of marching* *on Novgorod, they turned south and took Kozel'sk in the principality of Chernigov. Novgorod was spared the destruction and devastation that had affected the neighboring principalities to the south and southeast.*

Source: trans. R. Michell and N. Forbes, *The Chronicle of Novgorod, 1016–1471* (London: Offices of the Society, 1914), pp. 81–84.

That same year [*anno mundi* 6746, or 1238, but in fact 1237], foreigners called Tartars [Mongols] came in countless numbers, like locusts, into the land of Riazan, and on first coming, they halted at Nukhla [unidentified fort or town in the southern region of the Riazan' principality] and took it. From here they sent their emissaries to the princes of Riazan, a sorceress and two men with her, demanding from them one-tenth of everything—of men and princes and horses—of everything one-tenth. And the princes of Riazan, Iurii Igorevich [grand prince of Riazan', 1235–37], Oleg, the brother of Ingvar [I, grand prince of Riazan', 1218–35], Roman Ingvorevich [Ingvar's younger son], and those of Murom and Pronsk, without letting them into their town, went out to meet them [the Mongols] to Voronezh. And the princes said to them [to the emissaries]: "Only when none of us remains, then all will be yours." . . . And the princes of Riazan sent to Iurii [II] of Vladimir [1212–15 and 1218–38], asking for help, or himself to come. But Iurii neither went himself, nor listened to the request of the princes of Riazan, but he himself wished to make war separately. . . .

And then the pagan foreigners surrounded Riazan [Staraia Riazan', located some thirty-one miles to the southeast of the modern city], and fenced it in with a stockade. Iurii of Riazan shut himself up in the town with his people of the city, but Prince Roman Ingvorevich began to fight against them with his own men. Grand Prince Iurii of Vladimir sent Eremei as military commander with a patrol and joined Roman. Then the Tartars surrounded them at Kolomno [now Kolomna, near Moscow, Russia], and they fought hard, and drove them to the ramparts. And there they killed Roman [Igorevich of Riazan'] and Eremei, and many fell here with the prince and with Eremei. And the men of Moscow ran away having seen nothing [that is, they did not fight with the Mongols]. And the Tartars took the town [of Riazan'] on 21 December [1237], and they have advanced against it on the sixteenth of the same month. They likewise killed the prince [Iurii Igorevich] and the princess [Agripina], and men and women and children, monks, nuns, and priests, some by fire, some by sword, and violated nuns, priests' wives, good women, and girls in the presence of their mothers and sisters. But God saved the bishop, for he had departed the same moment when the troops invested the town. And who, brethren, would not lament over this, among those of us left alive, when they suffered this bitter and violent death? And we indeed, having seen it, were terrified and wept with sighing day and night over our sins, while we sigh every day and night, taking thought for our possessions and for the hatred of brothers.

But let us return to what lies before us. The pagan and godless Tartars, then, having taken Riazan went to Vladimir[-on-Kliazma], a host of shedders of Christian blood. And Prince Iurii [Vsevolodich of Vladimir] went out of Vladimir and fled to Yaroslavl, while his son Vsevolod with his mother and the bishop and the whole of the province shut themselves in Vladimir. And the lawless Ishmaelites approached the town and surrounded the town in force and fenced it all round with a fence. And it was in the morning that Prince Vsevolod and Bishop Mitrofan saw that the town must be taken and entered the [cathedral] church of the holy Mother of God and were all shorn into the monastic order and the *schema* [highest monastic rank], the prince and the princess [Agatha, sister of Prince Michael of Kiev], their daughter and daughter-in-law and good men and women, by Bishop Mitrofan. And when the lawless ones have already come near and set up battering rams and took the town and fired it on Friday before Sexagesima Sunday [8 February 1238], the prince and the princess and the bishop, seeing that the town was on fire and that the people were already perishing, some by fire and others by the sword, took refuge in the church of the holy Mother of God and shut themselves in the sacristy. The pagans, breaking down the doors, piled up wood and set fire to the sacred church; and slew all, thus they perished giving up their souls to God. Others [Mongols] were in pursuit of Prince Iurii to Yaroslavl. And Prince Iurii sent out Dorozh to scout with three thousand men; and Dorozh came running, and said: "They have already surrounded us, prince." And the prince began to muster his forces about him, and behold, the Tartars came up suddenly, and the prince, without having been able to do anything, fled. And it happened when he reached the River Sit [a river in the Yaroslavl region of Russia, which empties into the Rybinsk Reservoir] they overtook him and there he ended his life. And God knows how he died; for some say much about him. And Rostov and Suzdal went each its own way [that is, they were taken by the Tartars]. And the accursed ones having come thence took Moscow, Pereiaslavl, Iur'ev [now Iur'ev Polski, in the region of Vladimir], Dmitrov, Volok [now Volokolamsk, near Moscow], and Tver. And thence the lawless ones came and invested Torzhok on the festival of the first Sunday in Lent. They enclosed it all with a fence as they had taken other towns, and here the accursed ones fought with battering rams for two weeks. And the people in the town were exhausted and from Novgorod there was no help for them; but already every man began to be in perplexity and terror. And so, the pagans took the town and slew all from the male sex even to the female, all the priests and the monks, and all striped and reviled gave up their souls to the Lord in a bitter and a wretched death, on 15 March [1238], the day of the commemoration of the holy martyr Nikon, on a Wednesday in the Easter week. And there, too, were killed Ivanko, the *posadnik* [mayor] of Novi Torg, Iakim Vlunkovich,

Gleb Borisovich, and Mikhailo Moisievich. And the accursed godless ones then pushed on from Torzhok by the road of Sergeri right up to Ignati's cross, cutting down everybody like grass, to within one hundred versts [about sixty-six miles] of Novgorod. God, however, and the sacred and apostolic cathedral church of St-Sophia, and Saint Cyril, and the prayers of the holy and orthodox bishop [Spiridon, 1229–49], of the faithful princes, and of the very reverend monks, of the hierarchical *veche* [assembly], protected Novgorod. And who, brothers, fathers, and children, seeing this, God's infliction on the whole Rus' land, does not lament? God let the pagans conquer us for our sins. God brings foreigners onto the land in his wrath, and thus crushed by them they [the Rus' people] will be reminded of God. And internecine war comes from the prompting of the devil; for God does not wish evil among men, but good; but the devil rejoices at wicked murder and bloodshed. And any land which had sinned, God punishes with death or famine, or with infliction of pagans, or with drought, or with heavy rain, or with other punishment, to see whether we will repent and live as God bids; for he tells us by the prophet: "Turn to me with your whole heart, with fasting and weeping" [Joel 2:12]. And if you do so, we shall be forgiven all our sins. But we always turn to evil, like swine ever wallowing in the filth of sin, and thus we remain; for this we receive every kind of punishment from God; and the invasion of the armed, too, we accept at God's command; as punishment for our sins.

Questions: According to the Rus' annalist(s), how did the Mongols manage to obtain so many victories so quickly? What can one learn from this account about Mongol tactics? How did Novgorod manage to escape the Mongol onslaught?

115. THE BATTLE OF MUHI

Hungary was the main target of the Mongol military operations of 1241. Together with his experienced general Sübetei, Batu led the main corps that entered Hungary from the Rus' principality of Halych-Volhynia, using the Verets'kyi Pass across the inner eastern Carpathian Mountains, which King Béla IV had just fortified. The Mongols broke through on 12 March 1241 after special units had cleared the way. The Hungarians who manned the fortification were either massacred or dispersed. On 11 April 1241, Batu inflicted a crushing defeat upon King Béla IV's army at Muhi. A great number of noblemen, magistrates, archbishops, and bishops died on the battlefield. The king barely escaped alive, while his brother Coloman later died from his wounds. The most detailed account of the Mongol invasion and the battle at Muhi is that of Thomas of Spalato. It is most likely based on oral testimonies of participants, some of whom took refuge in Dalmatia together with the king. To Thomas, the Mongols were a plague, a "pestilential nation." On one hand, he regarded the invaders as subhuman and monstrous; on the other, he recognized their extraordinary military skills, their resilience, and their cunning. He also described their weapons and armor in great detail, most likely after examining some with his own eyes. The battle of Muhi was not won by Mongols entering the combat to fight hand to hand, but by archers raining arrows upon their enemies. Thomas knew the names of the victors—Batu and Qadan, whom he (wrongly) believed to be brothers (they were in fact cousins). Qadan is constantly called an "uncivilized commander," but besides mentioning him by name, Thomas has nothing else to say about Batu. The comparison between Mongols and locusts suggests that to Thomas the invaders were an instrument of divine punishment. When commenting upon the defeat of the Hungarians at Muhi, he quoted the psalmist: "Your judgments are a great deep" [Ps. 35:7].

Source: trans. M. Matijević-Sokol, J.R. Sweeney, and D. Karbić, *History of the Bishops of Salona and Split* (Budapest: Central European University Press, 2006), pp. 253, 255, 257, 259, 261, 263, 265, 267, and 269.

In the fifth year of the reign of Béla, son of Andrew, king of Hungary [1235–70], and the second year of Gargano [de Arscindis, podesta of Split, 1239–42], the noxious race of the Tatars [Mongols] drew near the land of Hungary. Already for many years fearful rumors of this people had been crossing the world. For they had come out of the lands of the east, laying waste the regions through which they passed as far as the borders of Ruthenia [Rus']. . . . So when rumor of the fatal coming of the Tatars reached the ears of the people of Hungary, they treated it as some kind of joke or an empty dream: partly because such rumors had been heard many times before, and nothing had come of them, partly too because they had confidence in the great military forces of their kingdom. . . . At last, roused by their loud protests, the king stirred himself and set off for the furthest bounds of his realm. He came to the [Carpathian] mountains that run between Hungary and Ruthenia as far as the borders of Poland. There he went about inspecting all the easiest entry points to breach, and cutting down much woodland, he had long barricades built, blocking with felled trees all the places where transit seemed easiest. Then on his return he sent out messengers and summoned all the leading men, barons, and eminent figures of his realm, and gathered into one place the whole strength of the armed forces of Hungary. . . . They were gathered at the king's encampment like lambs to the slaughter. A general council was then held, and a number of days were spent debating how best to deal with the approach of the Tatars. Different persons had different ideas, and they would not come to agreement and settle on one plan. Some were simply paralyzed by fear and thought that they should retreat before them for the time being and not come to blows with the barbarous enemy, men without scruples who roamed the world fighting not to win a kingdom, but simply from greed for plunder. Others, foolishly untroubled and heedless of the danger, declared that the enemy would turn and flee at the very first sight of our vast forces. Thus those doomed to a swift destruction were unable to agree on any course of action. So as time passed with their discussions and long and pointless delays, lo, suddenly there came an unexpected messenger. He hastened to the king with the news that for certain a countless multitude of Tatars had entered the kingdom and was now near at hand. Thereupon, the king and the leading men of the realm broke off their council and began to ready their arms, to assign leaders to the various contingents, and to call together the larger part of the fighting men. . . . The period of Lent went by, and it was close to Easter [31 March 1241] when the entire host of the Tatar army burst upon the realm of Hungary. They had forty thousand men with axes who went in advance of the main host cutting down forests, laying roads, and removing all [obstacles] from the places of entry [into the kingdom]. They were thus able to surmount the barricades that the king had prepared as easily as if they were made of chaff rather than of great fir trees and oaks piled high. It took little time to trample and burn them down, and they offered no barrier at all to their passage. . . . The host was led by two brothers, the older called Batu and the younger Qadan. They sent on ahead of them a squad of cavalry. Those rode up to the Hungarian camp, making repeated shows of themselves and challenging them to battle. They wanted to test whether the Hungarians had any stomach to come out and fight them. The Hungarian king chose select knights and commanded them to go out and attack them. They set out in armed units and in good order. But the Tatar battle line did not stay around to engage in hand-to-hand combat, but rode off in rapid flight, firing arrows at the enemy as they went, according to their custom. The king then set out with the whole army, thinking that he was pursuing a fleeing enemy. Reaching the River Tisza, they crossed the stream. They were in high spirits, for they imagined that the enemy forces were being driven outside the bounds of the kingdom. Then they reached another stream, called the Solo [Sajó or Slana River]. However, on the other side of this stream the whole multitude of the Tatars was encamped in a concealed place among thick woods. The Hungarians could glimpse some but not all of them. When they saw that the enemy brigades had encamped on the other side of the river, they set up their camp on the nearer side [outside the village of Muhi, near Miskolc, in northeastern Hungary]. The king ordered the tents to be pitched close together, not scattered all over the place. The result was that they were all crowded together as though in a pen, and in defense of the camp they placed their carriages and shields in a ring around. The tents were pitched so close together and the tent ropes were so entangled and running across each other that there was no clear pathway at all. So it was impossible to move about the camp; it was as if the whole army were caught inside a net. . . .

At this point, Batu, the elder of the two leaders of the Tatar host, . . . had all his forces drawn up in their customary manner and ordered them to seize the bridge that spanned the two banks of the river not far from the Hungarian camp. . . . King Coloman [Béla's brother, who was "king" of Slavonia, Dalmatia, and Croatia between 1226 and 1241] then ordered his battle units to arm and proceeded from the camp, followed by Archbishop [of Kalocsa] Ugrinus [Csák, 1219–41] and his company; for he too was a man of warlike spirit and ready and bold to take arms. So, around midnight they came to the bridge; but already a part of the enemy host had crossed over. Seeing them, the Hungarians at once fell upon them. They fought them most bravely and killed a great number of them. Others were driven back to the bridge, forced off and drowned in the river. So they set up a guard at the head of the bridge and returned to their fellows in great exultation. The Hungarians were greatly cheered by the victorious outcome, as if they achieved an outright victory, and throwing aside their arms slept the whole night through without a care. The Tatars, however, set up seven war engines at the bridgehead, and by hurling large stones at them and harrying them with spears and arrows drove the Hungarians some distance off. With the guards put to flight, the Tatars could cross securely and freely, some over the bridge, some across fords in the river. So, at the very break of day the whole multitude of the Tatars appeared, spread over the plain. The guards from the bridge fled back to the camp, but their loud and urgent shouts could scarcely rouse their soundly sleeping comrades. . . .

Nevertheless, King Coloman, Archbishop Ugrinus, and a master of the Order of the Knights Templar [James of Monte Regali, master of the Templars in the province of Hungary and Slavonia, 1240–41] behaved as proper soldiers should. For rather than giving themselves over to rest and sleep they had spent the whole night awake and in arms, and as soon as they heard the shouting, they at once burst out of the camp. Girding on their battle gear, they formed into a close formation and charged at the enemy lines, fighting with great courage for some time. But they were very few in comparison with the vast numbers of Tatars, who kept appearing like locusts emerging one after the other from the ground [Exod. 10:2]. When a number of their company had been killed, the Hungarians retreated to the camp. Ugrinus, being ever outspoken and without fear, raised his voice and began to rebuke the king for his negligence and to upbraid all the Hungarian barons for their slowness and idleness, remarking that when faced with such peril they had no concern for their own lives or any resolve to defend the country as a whole. So those who were ready went out and joined them. But the others were paralyzed with fear and the unexpected, and as if they had lost their minds had no idea what they should put their hands to or where to turn. The three aforementioned leaders, brooking no further delay, sallied forth again to engage the enemy. Ugrinus launched himself with such daring among the densest ranks of the enemy that they cried aloud and fled from him as if he were a thunderbolt. Likewise, Coloman and the master of the Templars with his fellow Latin [French] knights wrought great slaughter among the enemy. All the same, they were unable to sustain the overwhelming numbers, and Coloman and the archbishop, both now seriously wounded, made it back to their fellows with difficulty. The master of the Templars and all his company of Latins were slain, and many Hungarians too perished in that fray. It was now around the second hour of the day [between 5:00 and 6:00 a.m.], and now the entire host of the Tatar army completely surrounded the Hungarian camp, as if in a ring dance. They drew their bows and set about firing arrows everywhere, while others circled the camp and sought to set it on fire.

The Hungarians, seeing that they were surrounded on every side by bands of the enemy, lost all sense and reason. . . . And when all hope of saving their lives was spent, and death, as it were, passed through the camp gazing in their faces, the king and the leading men, abandoning their standards, turned to seek refuge in flight. Then the rest of the army, terrified at the swift toll of deaths and stunned with fear of the devouring flames all around them, set their hearts on nothing else but flight. . . . But when the Tatars perceived that the Hungarian army had turned to flight, they left a door open for them, so to speak, and allowed them to depart. They did not pursue them with all their force, but followed them cautiously, on two sides, not allowing them to turn aside. All over the paths lay the wretched Hungarians' valuables, their gold and silver tableware, their crimson garments, their wealth of arms. But the Tatars, with their unparalleled savagery, paid little heed to all the rich plunder, intent only on human carnage. When they saw that their enemies were exhausted from running and unable to stretch out their arms to fight on their legs in flight, they began to rain spears upon them on all sides and to cut them down with swords, sparing no one, and butchering them like animals. Left and right they fell like leaves in winter; the whole way was covered with their wretched bodies; blood flowed like the stream of a river. The hapless country far and wide was red, stained with blood of her sons. Then the pitiful multitude, those whom the Tatar sword had not yet devoured, by necessity came to a certain marsh. They were not given the chance to take a different way; pressed on by the Tatars, almost the whole of the Hungarians entered the swamp and were there dragged down into the water and the mud and drowned almost to a man. There perished the most illustrious Ugrinus; there perished Matthias [Rátót, archbishop of Esztergom, 1239–41] and Bishop Gregory of Győr [1233–41]; there many a prelate and crowd of clerics met their fate.

Questions: What is Thomas the archdeacon's explanation for the defeat of King Béla IV and the Hungarian army? How did the Mongols obtain the victory? In what way were the Mongols an unusual enemy? Why did no Christian ruler, such as the Piast princes from across the Carpathian Mountains, come to the rescue of the Hungarians?

116. THE MONGOL SACK OF ORADEA

A prelate of Italian origin (most likely from Apulia), Roger of Torre Maggiore came to Hungary with Cardinal Giacomo di Pecorari, the legate whom Pope Gregory IX (1227–41) sent to the court of King Andrew II (1205–35). He obtained first the position of chaplain, then that of archdeacon of the cathedral chapter in Oradea. He traveled with the cardinal in Italy but was back in Hungary when the Mongols attacked Hungary in 1242. He left a dramatic description of the invasion in his Song of Lamentation on the Destruction of the Kingdom of Hungary by the Tatars. *The* Song *was written a few years after the events, many of which the author witnessed. Roger was in Oradea when the Mongols took the city, but fled to Cenad (in the Banat, south of Oradea) with a few companions. He found Cenad in ruins and devastated by the attack of another Mongol army. He sought refuge in the surrounding countryside, but eventually fell into the hands of the Mongols, from whom he escaped only during their retreat in 1242. He returned to Rome and was later appointed archdeacon in Sopron (western Hungary). He most likely wrote the* Song *as an epistle to his former patron, Bishop James of Sopron, who died in 1244. Roger attended the First Council of Lyon in 1245, when he was a canon in Zagreb. In 1250, he was appointed archbishop of Split by Pope Innocent IV (1243–54). He died in that office and was buried in the cathedral in Split.*

Source: trans. M. Rady and L. Veszprémy, *Anonymus and Master Roger* (Budapest: Central European University Press, 2010), pp. 199 and 201.

As we said before, King Qadan [the second son of the great khan Ögödai, and a grandson of Genghis Khan, was a general in the Mongol army led by Batu], having taken Rodna [a mining town in northern Transylvania] and captured Count Aristald, selected the best six hundred armed Germans ["Saxons," German-speaking "guests" invited by the Hungarian kings to settle in Transylvania] who were under the said count. Guided by them, they crossed forests, woods, rocks, and gorges and arrived beneath the city of Oradea [now in northwestern Romania, next to the Romanian-Hungarian border]. The city was very famous in Hungary; therefore, many nobles, ladies, and peasant women had gathered there. Even though the bishop had left with some canons, I stayed there with the remaining people. We had the castle [the citadel], which we saw damaged on one side, repaired with a strong wall, so that we could find refuge there should we be unable to defend the city. But when one day the Tatars [Mongols] suddenly arrived and my situation in the city was precarious, I did not want to go to the castle, but ran away into the forest and hid there as long as I could. They, however, suddenly took the city and burnt down most of it and left nothing outside the walls of the castle. Having collected the booty, they killed men and women, commoners and nobles alike, on the streets, houses, and fields. What more? They pardoned neither sex nor age. That done, they suddenly retreated, gathered up everything in the retreat, and settled five miles from the castle. They did not return for days, and those in the castle thought that they had left because of the strength of the castle that was protected by a deep moat and wooden towers on the walls; there were many armored warriors there, and whenever the Tatars came scouting from time to time, the Hungarian warriors chased them on fast horses. When the Tatars did not come to the castle for several days, and everyone thought that they had completely withdrawn from there, many of the warriors and others who were in the castle, confident that they had withdrawn, left the castle and moved together into the houses that still remained outside of it. Then, one day at dawn, the Tatars, whose whereabouts they could not know, rushed upon them and killed most of those who did not manage to flee to the castle. Then they immediately surrounded the fortification, set up seven siege engines across from the new wall and bombarded it ceaselessly with stones day and night until the new wall collapsed totally. They did not stop at all, and with the towers and walls demolished the castle was taken by storm. They seized the warriors, canons, and others who had not been killed by the sword in the attack. The ladies, damsels, and noble girls tried to escape into the cathedral. The Tatars ordered the warriors to hand over their weapons and from the canons they extorted by the cruelest tortures all that they owned. Because they could not easily enter the cathedral, they set fire to it and burnt the church, together with the women and whatever there was in the church. In other churches they perpetrated such crimes to the women that it is better to keep silent lest people get ideas for most evil deeds. Then they ruthlessly beheaded the nobles, citizens, soldiers, and canons on a field outside the city. They violated the saints' graves [such as the tomb of the king, Saint Ladislas], trampled upon the relics with their sinful feet, smashed to pieces the censers, crosses, golden chalices, and vessels, and whatever else was designed for the service of the altar. They dragged men and women alike into the churches and shamefully mistreated and then killed them there. After they had destroyed everything, and an intolerable stench arose from the corpses, they left the place empty. People hiding in the nearby forests came back to find some food. And while they were searching among the stones and the corpses, the Tatars suddenly returned and of those living whom they found there, none was left alive. And this slaughter was repeated day after day. They finally left for good only when there was no one else to kill.

Questions: What stratagem did the Mongols use at Oradea? What (false) assumptions about the invader does this text demonstrate? When the Mongols got into the city, what signs of destruction does Roger mention primarily?

117. THE CAMP OF BATU KHAN ON THE VOLGA

William of Rubruck was a Flemish Franciscan who went with King Louis IX on the Seventh Crusade (1248). He was at the king's side in Acre after the disastrous expedition in Egypt. He was in Constantinople on 13 April 1253, when he preached in the church of St-Sophia, and may have departed on a mission to the Mongols a month later. He was carrying a letter from King Louis IX to Sartaq, most likely asking the Mongol prince to allow William and his companions to remain in his territory (the ulus, *or territory, of Jochi, later known as the Golden Horde) and to preach the Gospel. Upon receiving the envoys, however, Sartaq decided to send them to his father, the ruler of the* ulus *of Jochi, Batu Khan (1241–56). Under the false impression that William of Rubruck was on a diplomatic mission, the purpose of which was to gather Mongol support against the Muslims (for a Christian-Mongol alliance with crusading goals), Batu Khan decided to send him to the great khan Möngke in Karakorum (near present-day Kharkhorin, in the Övörkhangai province of Mongolia). He was granted audience to the great khan on 4 January 1254, and he began his return journey on 10 July of that same year. He arrived in Tripoli (now Tirebolu near Trabzon, on the southern shore of the Black Sea in Turkey) on 15 August 1225. It is there that he drafted his report addressed to King Louis IX and entitled* Journey of Friar William of Rubruck from the Franciscan Order to the Eastern Parts in the Year 1253. *The work survives in five manuscripts, four of which are from England. Rubruck related his journey as an eyewitness account of his own mission, for the glory of Christianity and of the Franciscan order. In his work, he insists many times upon the idea that he was not an official messenger, but a brave friar on a mission to convert the Mongols. The audience of this text was King Louis IX and his entourage. It is to them that Rubruck described the Mongols as "no people and a foolish nation," with disgusting customs and arrogant claims to world domination. Although not written in elegant Latin, Rubruck's account is of the utmost importance, because it is the first European report based on direct observation of the lands of eastern Europe and central Asia. The good quality of this report turned it into a major source for Roger Bacon's* Opus maius *(1267).*

Source: trans. P. Jackson, *The Mission of Friar William of Rubruck: His Journey to the Court of the Great Khan Möngke 1253–1255* (Indianapolis: Hackett, 2009), pp. 130–34.

19. At the spot where we reached the Etilia [the Volga River] lies a settlement newly established by the Tartars [probably south of Saratov, Russia, on the site of the later Mongol town of Uvek], with a mixed population of Rus' and Saracens [Muslims], who take envoys across [the river] on their way to and from Batu's court, since Batu is to be found on the far bank, to the east. When he moves upstream in the summer, he does not go further than the point we reached;

and he was already beginning to head downstream. He moves up—as do all the rest—to the cold regions from January to August, and in August they begin to turn back.

We sailed down by boat, then, from the village to his camp. From that locality to the towns of Great Bulgaria [Volga Bulgharia] in the north it is five days' journey, and I wonder what devil took there the religion of Mahomet [Muhammad, the Prophet of Islam]. For from the Iron Gate [Derbent Pass across the Caucasus Mountains], where one leaves Persia, it takes more than thirty days, moving up along the Etilia as far as Bulgaria, to cross these wilds, and there are no cities, only some villages near the point where the Etilia flows into the sea. Yet these Bulgars are the worst sort of Saracens and adhere more strictly to the religion of Mahomet than do any of the others.

On sighting Batu's camp, I was struck with awe. His own dwellings had the appearance of a large city stretching far out lengthwise and with inhabitants scattered around in every direction for a distance of three to four leagues [between six and eleven miles]. And just as every one of the people of Israel know on what side of the tabernacle to pitch their tent [Num. 2:1–34], so these people know on what side of the residence to station themselves when they are unloading the dwellings. For this reason, the court is called in their language *orda*, meaning the "middle" [the Turkish word *orta* means "middle," but the Mongolian word *ordu* means "camp"], since it is always situated in the midst of his men, except that nobody takes up his station due south, this being the direction toward which the doors of the residence open. But to the right and the left they spread themselves out as far as they like within the limitations imposed by the terrain, provided that they refrain from alighting directly in front of the residence or opposite it.

First of all, we were taken to a certain Saracen, who failed to provide us with any food. On the following day, we were brought to court. Batu had had a large pavilion set up, since his dwelling could not accommodate the number of men and women who had assembled. Our guide warned us not to speak at all until ordered to by Batu, and then only briefly. He asked also whether you [Louis IX, king of France between 1226 and 1270] had ever sent them an embassy. I told him how you had sent to Keu Chan [Güyük Khan, great khan between 1246 and 1248] but you would not have sent envoys to him or a letter to Sartach [Sartaq, Batu's son and successor] had you not believed that they were Christians, inasmuch as you had not been somehow cowed into sending them but had done so to felicitate them on hearing they were Christian. Then he conducted us before the pavilion, and we were warned not to touch the tent ropes, which for them represent the threshold of the dwelling. We took up our stand there, with bare feet, wearing our habits but with our heads uncovered, and presented quite a spectacle to them. Friar John of Policarpo [John of Plano

Carpini, c. 1185–1252] had been there [before us], but had adapted his garb, so as not to incur contempt, since he was the ambassador of the lord pope.

Then we were brought in right to the middle of the tent but were not required to show some sign of respect by genuflecting, as is the usual practice with envoys. We stood before him [Batu Khan] for as long as it would have taken to recite the *Miserere mei Deus* [Ps. 51], during which time everyone observed total silence. He was seated on a throne that was deep and broad like a couch, completely overlaid with gold, and with three steps leading up to it, and one of his wives was at his side. Men were sitting around on his right and ladies on his left, and the space on their side not taken up by women—since the only ones there were Batu's wives—was filled by men. At the entrance to the tent stood a bench with *comos* [*kumys*, mare's milk, a traditional Mongolian drink] and large gold and silver goblets decorated with precious stones. He regarded us with a keen gaze, as we did him. He struck me as being of the same build as the lord John of Beaumont [King Louis IX's chamberlain] (may his soul rest in peace), and his face was covered at this time with reddish blotches.

Eventually he ordered me to speak, at which our guide told us to genuflect and begin. I went down on one knee, as one does to a man, but then he indicated that I should kneel on both, and I did so, being unwilling to make an issue of it. Then he told me to speak. And reflecting to myself that I could be at prayer, seeing I was on both my knees, I took my first words from a collect, saying: "My lord, we pray God, from whom all good things do proceed, that having conferred on you these earthly possessions, he will in time grant you heavenly ones, without which these are nothing." And as he listened attentively, I added: "Be absolutely sure that you will not possess the things of heaven without having become a Christian. For God says, 'He who believes and is baptized will be saved; but he who does not believe will be condemned.'" At these words he gave a slight smile, and the other Mo'als began to clap us in derision. My interpreter was dumbfounded, and I had to reassure him not to be afraid. Then when silence was restored, I said: "I came to your son because we heard he was Christian, and I brought him a letter from my lord the king of the French. He sent me here to you. You must know the reason."

Then he made me stand up and asked your name [the name of King Louis] and mine and those of my colleague and the interpreter and had it all written down. He also asked with whom you were at war, since he had learned that you had left your country with an army [for the Seventh Crusade]. "With the Saracens," I replied, "who are profaning Jerusalem, the house of God." He asked, again, whether you had ever sent him an embassy. "To you," I said, "never." Then he made us sit down and had us given some of his milk to drink—they make much of it when someone drinks *comos* with him in his own dwelling. While I sat gazing around, he ordered me to raise my face, as he wanted to have another look at us—or possibly with witchcraft in mind, since they view it as a bad omen or sign, or foreshadowing evil, when someone sits in their presence with his head as if he were sad, and especially when he leans his cheek or chin on his hand.

Questions: What concerns did Batu Khan have about the envoys, especially William? What aspects of power representation did the latter notice in the camp of Batu Khan? Why are parts of or the positions of the body mentioned so many times in this account? Compare the behavior of William in front of Batu Khan to that of Adalbert among the Prussians (Doc. 65).

118. KIEV AFTER THE MONGOL INVASION

John of Plano Carpini was born in 1182 in a small town near Perugia. He joined the Franciscans and traveled across Europe, to Germany, as well as to Spain on behalf of his order. On 16 April 1245 he departed from Lyon on a mission from Pope Innocent IV to the Great Khan Ögedai. The goal of this mission was to gather information about the Mongols, particularly about their goals and reasons for the devastation of eastern and east central Europe in 1241, and, if possible, to co-opt them into participating in the crusading projects against the Muslims. The envoys reached the Volga River in early April 1246 and Karakorum a month later. Khan Ögedai had meanwhile died, and the envoys found little understanding of their mission by the new khan, Güyük. The envoys returned and arrived in Kiev on 10 June 1247. For his merits as papal envoy, John was appointed archbishop of Bar (in what is now Montenegro). The Book of the Tartars (or History of the Mongols, Whom We Call Tartars) *was written as a report for the pope, upon John's return to Lyon. However, in his report John addressed all Christians, whom he wanted to warn against the new threat from the east. If the mission to convert the Mongols to Christianity failed (and John was forced to recognize that), he nonetheless reported the decision of "Duke Vasilko" to recognize papal primacy, after receiving the news that the envoys brought from Karakorum.*

Source: trans. W. Woodville Rockhill, *The Journey of William Rubruck to the Eastern Parts of the World, 1253–1255, as Narrated by Himself, with Two Accounts of the Earlier Journey of John of Pian de Carpine* (London: Hakluyt Society, 1900), pp. 2–4.

At that time, through God's special grace, the lord Vasilko [Romanovich], duke of Rus' [prince of Volhynia, 1231–69] had come there [to Poland], from whom we learned more accurately of the Tatars; for he had sent his ambassadors to them, who had come back to him and to his brother, Daniel [Romanovich, prince of Halych between 1205 and 1255], bearing to the lord Daniel a safe conduct to go to Batu [Khan, founder of the Golden Horde, 1241–56]. And he told us that if we wanted to go to them (and this is quite true), an ambassador could not conduct his business satisfactorily with them; and that furthermore he was looked upon as a mere nothing. Not wishing that the affairs of the lord pope and of the church should be obstructed on this account, with some of that which had been given to us in charity, so that we should not be in want and for use on our journey, we bought some skins of beavers and of some other animals. Duke Conrad [of Mazovia, 1194–1247], the duchess of Lenczy [generic term for Poland, here Conrad's wife, Agafia, the daughter of Sviatoslav III of Peremyshl], some knights, and the bishop of Cracow [Jan Prandota, 1242–66], hearing of this, gave us some more of these skins. Furthermore, Duke Conrad, his son, and the bishop of Cracow besought most earnestly Duke Vasilko to help us as much as he could in reaching the Tatars; and he replied that he would do so willingly.

So he took us with him to his country; and as he kept us for some days as his guests that we might rest a little, and had called thither his bishops at our request, we read them the letters of the lord pope, in which he admonished them to return to the unity of the holy mother church; we also advised and urged them as much as we could, as well the duke and the bishops, and all those who had met there, to that same end. But as at the very time when this duke had come to Poland, his brother, Duke Daniel, had gone to Batu and was not present, they could not give a final answer, but must wait his return before being able to give a full reply.

After that the duke sent one of his servants with us as far as Kiev. Nevertheless, we traveled ever in danger of our lives on account of the Lithuanians, who often committed undiscovered outrages as much as possible in the country of Rus' and particularly in those places through which we had to pass. And as the greater part of the men of Rus' had been killed by the Tatars or taken off into captivity, they were unable to offer them [the Lithuanians] the least resistance. We were safe, however, from the Rus' on account of this servant. Thence then, by the grace of God, having been saved from the enemies of the cross of Christ, we came to Kiev, which is the metropolis of Rus'. And when we came there, we took counsel with the *millenarius* [the leader of one thousand men, most likely a local Mongol commander or official] and the other nobles who were there, as to our route. They told us that if we took into the land of the Tatars the horses which we had, they would all die, for the snows were deep, and they did not know how to dig out the grass from under the snow like Tatar horses, nor could anything else be found (on the way) for them to eat, for the Tatars had neither straw nor hay nor fodder. So, on their advice, we decided to leave our horses there with two servants to keep them; and we had to give the *millenarius* presents, that he might be pleased to give us packhorses and an escort. Before we reached Kiev, when in Danilov, I was ill to the point of death; but I had myself carried along in a cart in the intense cold through the deep snow, so as not to interfere with the affairs of Christendom.

Having settled then all these matter at Kiev, on the second day after the feast of the Purification of Our Lady [4 February 1246], we started out from Kiev for other barbarous peoples, with the horses of the *millenarius* and an escort. We came to a certain town which was under the direct rule of the Tatars and is called Canov [now Kaniv, in the province of Cherkasy, Ukraine]. The prefect of the town gave us horses and an escort as far as another town, in which was a certain Alan prefect who was called Michaes, a man full of all malice and iniquity, for he had sent to us to Kiev some of his bodyguard, who lyingly said to us, as from the part of Corenza [a Mongol general], that we being ambassadors were to come to him; and this he did, though it was not true, in order that he might extort presents from us. When, however, we reached him, he made himself most disagreeable, and unless we promised him presents, would in no wise agree to help us. Seeing that we would not otherwise be able to go farther, we promised to give him some presents, but when we gave him what appeared to us suitable, he refused to receive them unless we gave more; and so we had to add to them according to his will, and something besides he subtracted from us deceitfully and maliciously.

Questions: How does the author characterize the situation in the steppe lands of present-day Ukraine? How does he suggest that the nominal power of the Mongol khan was exercised in the locale? While William of Rubruck tried to depict the Mongols as "a foolish nation," how does John of Plano Carpini describe the local rulers?

ACKNOWLEDGEMENTS

I would like to thank the following publishers for permission to reproduce text extracts from the following books and articles:

Brill, for Kiril Petkov, *The Voices of Medieval Bulgaria, Seventh-Fifteenth Century: The Records of a Bygone Culture* (2008); István Zimonyi, *Muslim Sources on the Magyars in the Second Half of the Ninth Century: The Magyar Chapter of the Jayhānī Tradition* (2016); *John Kaminiates: The Capture of Thessaloniki*, translated by David Frendo and Athanasios Fotiou (2017); Vasilka Tăpkova-Zaimova, *Bulgarians by Birth: The Comitopuls, Emperor Samuel and Their Successors According to Historical Sources and the Historiographic Tradition* (2017); Jos Schaeken, *Voices on Birchbark: Everyday Communication in Medieval Russia* (2018).

Cambridge University Press, for John Skylitzes, *A Synopsis of Byzantine History, 811–1057* (2010).

Center for the Study of Cultural Heritage of Cyril and Methodius for *Cyrillomethodianum* 17–18 (1993–94), 15–39.

Dumbarton Oaks Research Library and Collection, for Constantine VII Porphyrogenitus, *De Administrando imperio*, translated by Romilly J.H. Jenkins, edited by Gyula Moravcsik (1967). © 2016 Dumbarton Oaks Research Library and Collection, Trustees for Harvard University; *Byzantine Monastic Foundation Documents: A Complete Translation of the Surviving Founders'* Typika *and Testaments,* edited by John Philip Thomas and Angela Constantinides Hero. © 2000 Dumbarton Oaks Research Library and Collection, Trustees for Harvard University.

Francis Cairns, for *The History of Menander the Guardsman*, translated by R.C. Blockley (1985).

Walter de Gruyter, for *Chronographiae quae Theophanis Continuati nomine fertur liber quo Vita Basilii imperatoris amplectitur*, edited and translated by Ihor Ševčenko (2011).

Hackett, for Procopius, *The Wars of Justinian*, with an English translation by H.B. Dewing, revised and modernized by Anthony Kaldellis, 2014.

David Higham Associates, for *The Mission of Friar William of Rubruck: His Journey to the Court of the Great Khan Möngke 1253–1255*, translated by Peter Jackson (Hakluyt Society/Hackett, 2009).

Northwestern University Press, for *The Origins of Christianity in Bohemia: Sources and Commentary*, translated by Marvin Kantor (1990). Copyright © 1990 by Marvin Cantor. All rights reserved.

Regnery Publishing, for *Letters of St. Bernard of Clairvaux*, translated by Bruno Scott James (1953).

University of Wisconsin Press, for *The Chronicle of Henry of Livonia*, translated by James A. Brundage (1961).

Special thanks are due to the following authors, as copyright holders, for permission to reproduce text extracts from their books:

Ivan Biliarsky and Anna-Mariia Totomanova, for *Borilov sinodik: Izdanie i prevod* (Sofia: OOD, 2010).

Cristian Gaşpar and Marina Miladinov-Schumann, for *Saints of the Christianization Age of Central Europe (Tenth-Eleventh Century)* (Budapest: Central European University Press, 2013).

Damir Karbić and Mirjana Matijević-Sokol, for *History of the Bishops of Salona and Split* (Budapest: Central European University Press, 2006).

Paul W. Knoll and Frank Schaer, for *Gesta Principum Polonorum: The Deeds of the Princes of the Poles* (Budapest: Central European University Press, 2003).

Petra Mutlová and Martyn Rady, for *Cosmas of Prague: The Chronicle of the Czechs* (Budapest: Central European University Press, 2019).

Martyn Rady and László Veszprémy, for *Anonymus and Master Roger* (Budapest: Central European University Press, 2010).

Mary and Michael Whitby, for *The History of Theophylact Simocatta: An English Translation with Introduction and Notes* (Oxford: Clarendon Press, 1986).

Many thanks also to the following translators for permission to reproduce their translations made on the occasion of this volume: Natalia Aleksiun (University of Florida), Gregory Leighton (Nicolaus Copernicus University, Toruń), Timothy May (University of North Georgia), and István Zimonyi (University of Szeged).

CHRONOLOGY

545 first Slavic raid on the northern Balkans
568 the beginning of the Avar conquest
626 Avars besiege Constantinople
c. 660 Asparukh leads the Bulgar migration to the Oglos, north of the Danube
680 Sermesians under Kuver move out of the Avar khaganate and into the environs of Thessalonica
681 the establishment of the Bulgars in the northeastern Balkans
737 Arab troops under Marwan invade Khazaria and force the khagan to convert to Islam
740 Duke Boruth rules over Carantania
763 Emperor Constantine V invades Bulgaria by land and sea
783 Byzantine troops under Staurakios campaign successfully in the Peloponnese
788 Carantania now within the Frankish kingdom
796 last Frankish campaign against the Avars; the end of the Avar khaganate
804 *placitum* [diet] of Rižana
811 the Bulgar ruler Krum defeats the Byzantine army led by Emperor Nicephorus I
816 peace for thirty years established between Bulgaria and Byzantium
826 birth of Constantine-Cyril
c. 830 Mojmir becomes ruler of Moravia
831 Omurtag dies
852 first charter mention of Trpimir, duke of the Croats; Boris becomes ruler of Bulgaria
860 Constantine-Cyril and Methodius sent as Byzantine envoys to the Khazar court in Itil; the Rus' attack Constantinople by sea
863 Constantine-Cyril and Methodius's mission to Moravia
864 Boris accepts baptism with Emperor Michael III as his sponsor
865 Bishop Formosus of Porto arrives in Bulgaria
865/66 rebellion of the Bulgar aristocrats against Boris's conversion to Christianity
869 Constantine-Cyril dies in Rome
870 first archbishop of Bulgaria appointed by the patriarch of Constantinople
c. 875 construction of the Great Basilica in Pliska completed
879 Branimir becomes duke of the Croats
880 birth of Saint John of Rila
885 expulsion of Methodius's disciples from Moravia following his death; Clement, Naum, and Angelarius arrive in Bulgaria

893 Symeon, Boris's son, becomes ruler; Clement of Ohrid appointed bishop of Velika

896 Symeon defeats the Byzantines at the battle of Bulgarophygon; beaten by the Pechenegs, the Magyars move out of the steppe lands and into east central Europe

c. 900 Khrabr composes *On the Letters*

904 Arab pirates sack Demetrias

905 Naum, bishop of Ohrid, dies

907 battle of Bratislava; end of Moravia

c. 910 Tomislav becomes king of the Croats

911 Byzantine-Rus' treaty regulates trade

913 Symeon receives crown from Patriarch Nicholas of Constantinople

915 first Pecheneg raid on Kiev; Vratislav becomes duke of the Czechs

916 Clement of Ohrid dies

921 assassination of Ludmila

922 Almysh, the ruler of the Volga Bulghars, sends envoys to Baghdad to ask for assistance

925 Wenceslas becomes duke of the Czechs

927 archbishop of Bulgaria elevated to the status of patriarch; Symeon dies; Peter becomes emperor of the Bulgarians

930/31 foundation of the monastery of Rila

935 assassination of Wenceslas

c. 940 Emperor Peter of Bulgaria writes to Patriarch Theophylact of Constantinople asking for advice about the outbreak of heresy in Bulgaria

945 new Rus'-Byzantine treaty in favor of Igor

946 John of Rila dies

955 the Magyars are defeated by Otto I in the battle of the Lechfeld

957 Princess Olga of Kiev receives baptism in Constantinople

958 Athanasios, the founder of the Great Lavra, arrives on Mount Athos

965 Prince Sviatoslav of Kiev attacks and sacks Itil, the capital of Khazaria; the end of the Khazar khaganate

966 Emperor Nicephorus II attacks Bulgaria; Mieszko converts to Christianity

968 Rus' troops of Prince Sviatoslav invade Bulgaria

969 Emperor Peter dies; Boris II becomes emperor of the Bulgarians

c. 970 Saint Nikon Metanoiete arrives in Sparta; privilege of Emperor John Tzimiskes for the monastic communities on Mount Athos

972 Sviatoslav killed by the Pechenegs

973 bishopric of Bohemia established in Prague

976 revolt of the Kometopouloi in Macedonia

980 Vladimir in power in Kiev

985 Samuel sacks Larissa

988 Vladimir converts to Christianity together with his subjects
990 Patriarch of Bulgaria moves to Ohrid
992 Mieszko offers his state to the pope as a fief
997 Samuel proclaimed emperor of the Bulgarians; Duke Géza's son, Vajk, baptized at Stephen
1000 Stephen crowned king of Hungary; Emperor Otto III visits Gniezno and meets with Bolesław Chrobry
1003 Samuel defeated by the Byzantines near Skopje
1014 battle of Kleidion; Samuel dies; Romanus Symeon proclaimed emperor of the Bulgarians
1015 assassination of Boris and Gleb in the struggle for succession after Vladimir's death
1018 beginning of the Byzantine occupation of Bulgaria
1025 Bolesław Chrobry proclaimed king of Poland
1034 Břetislav I becomes duke of the Czechs; Mieszko II assassinated; widespread pagan rebellion combined with a devastating Czech invasion of Poland
1036 Yaroslav the Wise crushes the Pechenegs; building of the cathedral St-Sophia in Kiev
1048 Pecheneg invasion of the Balkans
1051 foundation of the monastery of the Caves
1061 first Cuman raid of Rus'
1063 Pope Alexander II declares the use of Old Church Slavonic in the liturgy to be a heresy
1064 the Oghuz invade the Balkan provinces of the Byzantine empire
1069 King Peter Krešimir IV of Croatia becomes the imperial representative in the Dalmatian theme
1075 Zvonimir crowned king of Croatia by papal legate
1076 Bolesław II crowned king of Poland
1079 assassination of Stanisław, bishop of Cracow
1081 battle of Dyrrachion
1083 canonization of Saint Stephen of Hungary
1086 Vratislav II proclaimed king of Bohemia
1091 Emperor Alexios I Komnenos and his Cuman allies defeat the Pechenegs at Levunion
1097 passage through Hungary and the Balkans of the crusading army led by Godfrey of Bouillon
1102 Coloman crowned king of Croatia
1108 foundation of Vladimir-on-Kliazma
1111 coalition of Rus' princes defeats the Cumans in the battle of Salnica
1138 division of Poland into duchies ruled by members of the Piast dynasty

1142 foundation of the Cistercian monastery of Cikadór
1158 Vladislav II proclaimed king of Bohemia
1163 Emperor Manuel I imposes Stephen III as king of Hungary
1172 Stephen Nemanja surrenders to Emperor Manuel I
1180 Hungarian invasion of Dalmatia
1185 Normans sack Thessaloniki; the revolt of the Vlach brothers Peter and Asen
1190 the archbishopric of Bulgaria established in Tărnovo
1196 Stephen Nemanja abdicates in favor of his son
1197 Johannitsa Kaloyan becomes ruler of Bulgaria
1198 Přemysl I Otakar proclaimed king of Bohemia
1202 foundation of Riga
1203 participants in the Fourth Crusade storm and sack Zara
1205 Johannitsa Kaloyan defeats the crusaders in the battle of Adrianopole
1206 Danish troops conquer the island of Saaremaa in Estonia
1207 Vincent Kadłubek elected bishop of Cracow
1211 synod of Tărnovo condemns Bogomilism
1212 Andrew II calls the Teutonic Knights to Hungary
1216 bishopric of Prussia established in Kulm
1217 Stephen Prvovenčani crowned king of Serbia; King Andrew II of Hungary departs on the Fifth Crusade
1218 John II Asen becomes emperor of Bulgaria
1221 Sava, archbishop of Serbia, summons a council at Žiča to deal with heretics
1222 King Andrew II grants the Golden Bull
1223 battle at Kalka
1224 privilege of King Andrew II of Hungary in favor of the Saxon "guests" of Transylvania
1226 Duke Conrad of Mazovia offers Kulm to the Teutonic Knights; the beginning of the conquest of Prussia by the Teutonic Knights
1230 battle at Klokotnica
1236 Mongol invasion of Volga Bulgharia and Rus'; foundation of the town of Elbing in Prussia
1238 Pope Gregory IX calls on the king of Hungary to proclaim a crusade against Bulgaria
1241 battle at Muhi
1242 Battle on the Ice
1247 John of Plano Carpini appointed archbishop of Bar
1249 Frankish conquest of the Peloponnese completed

SELECT BIBLIOGRAPHY

Bollók, Ádám. *A Century of Gold: The Rise and Glory of the Avar Khaganate in the Carpathian Basin.* Budapest: Archaeolingua Alapítvány, 2021.

Csukovits, Enikő. *Hungary and the Hungarians: Western Europe's View in the Middle Ages.* Viella Historical Research 11. Rome: Viella, 2018.

Curta, Florin. *Eastern Europe in the Middle Ages (500–1300).* Brill's Companions to European History 19. 2 vols. Leiden: Brill, 2019.

—, ed. *The Routledge Handbook of East Central and Eastern Europe in the Middle Ages, 500–1300.* New York: Routledge, 2022.

Dautović, Dženan, Emir O. Filipović, and Neven Isailović, eds. *Medieval Bosnia and South-East European Relations: Political, Religious, and Cultural Life at the Adriatic Crossroads.* Leeds: Arc Humanities Press, 2019.

Džino, Danijel. *From Justinian to Branimir: The Making of the Middle Ages in Dalmatia.* New York: Routledge, 2020.

Feldman, Alex M. *The Monotheisation of Pontic-Caspian Eurasia: From the Eighth to the Thirteenth Century.* Edinburgh: Edinburgh University Press, 2022.

Güttner-Sporzyński, Darius von, ed. *Writing History in Medieval Poland: Bishop Vincentius of Cracow and the* Chronica Polonorum. Turnhout: Brepols, 2017.

Hupchick, Dennis P. *The Bulgarian-Byzantine Wars for Early Medieval Balkan Hegemony: Silver-Lined Skulls and Blinded Armies.* Cham: Palgrave Macmillan, 2017.

Hurbanič, Martin. *The Avar Siege of Constantinople in 626: History and Legend.* Cham: Palgrave Macmillan, 2019.

Kąkolewski, Igor, Christian Lübke, and Przemysław Urbańczyk, eds. *The Dawning of Christianity in Poland and across Central and Eastern Europe: History and the Politics of Memory.* Polish Studies, Transdisciplinary Perspectives 26. Berlin: Peter Lang, 2020.

Kaldellis, Anthony, and Ioannis Polemēs, eds. and trans. *Saints of Ninth- and Tenth-Century Greece.* Cambridge, MA: Harvard University Press, 2019.

Kardaras, Geōrgios. *Byzantium and the Avars, 6th–9th Century AD: Political, Diplomatic and Cultural Relations.* East Central and Eastern Europe in the Middle Ages, 450–1450 51. Leiden: Brill, 2018.

Kotecki, Radosław, Carsten Selch Jensen, and Stephen Bennett, eds. *Christianity and War in Medieval East Central Europe and Scandinavia.* Leeds: Arc Humanities Press, 2021.

Leszka, Mirosław Jerzy, and Kirił Marinow, eds. *The Bulgarian State in 927–969: The Epoch of Tsar Peter I.* Byzantina Lodziensia 34. Łódź: Wydawnictwo Uniwersytetu Łódzkiego, 2018.

Madgearu, Alexandru. *The Asanids: The Political and Military History of the Second Bulgarian Empire (1185–1280).* East Central and Eastern Europe in the Middle Ages, 450–1450 41. Leiden: Brill, 2016.

Mägi, Marika. *In Austrvegr: The Role of the Eastern Baltic in Viking Age Communication across the Baltic Sea.* The Northern World 84. Leiden: Brill, 2018.

Paroń, Aleksander. *The Pechenegs: Nomads in the Political and Cultural Landscape of Medieval Europe.* East Central and Eastern Europe in the Middle Ages, 450–1450 74. Leiden: Brill, 2021.

Petráček, Tomáš. *Power and Exploitation in the Czech Lands in the 10th–12th Centuries.* East Central and Eastern Europe in the Middle Ages, 450–1450 40. Leiden: Brill, 2017.

Pluskowski, Aleksander, ed. *Environment, Colonization, and the Baltic Crusader States: Terra Sacra I.* Environmental Histories of the North Atlantic World 2. Turnhout: Brepols, 2019.

Pohl, Walter. *The Avars: A Steppe Empire in Central Europe, 567–822.* Ithaca: Cornell University Press, 2018.

Popović, Marko, Smilja Marjanović-Dušanić, and Danica Popović. *Daily Life in Medieval Serbia.* Belgrade: Clio, 2016.

Raffensperger, Christian. *The Kingdom of Rus'.* Kalamazoo: Arc Humanities Press, 2017.

Rosik, Stanisław, ed. *Europe Reaches the Baltic: Poland and Pomerania in the Shaping of European Civilization (10th–12th Centuries).* Wrocław: Uniwersytet Wrocławski, 2020.

Sarantis, Alexander Constantine. *Justinian's Balkan Wars: Campaigning, Diplomacy and Development in Illyricum, Thrace, and the Northern World A.D. 527–65.* Prenton: Francis Cairns, 2016.

Selart, Anti. *Livonia, Rus' and the Baltic Crusades in the Thirteenth Century.* East Central and Eastern Europe in the Middle Ages, 450–1450 29. Leiden: Brill, 2015.

Stepanenko, Stepan, ed. *A Viking Century: Chernihiv Area from 900 to 1000 AD.* Hlib Ivakin Memorial Series 6. Paris: ACHCByz, 2022.

Vercamer, Grischa, and Dušan Zupka. *Rulership in Medieval East Central Europe: Power, Rituals and Legitimacy in Bohemia, Hungary and Poland.* East Central and Eastern Europe in the Middle Ages, 450–1450 78. Leiden: Brill, 2022.

Wihoda, Martin. *Vladislaus Henry: The Formation of Moravian Identity.* East Central and Eastern Europe in the Middle Ages, 450–1450 33. Leiden: Brill, 2015.

Zhivkov, Boris. *Khazaria in the Ninth and Tenth Centuries.* East Central and Eastern Europe in the Middle Ages, 450–1450 30. Leiden: Brill, 2015.

Zsoldos, Attila. *The Árpáds and Their People: An Introduction to the History of Hungary from ca. 900 to 1301.* Budapest: Research Centre for the Humanities, 2020.

SOURCES

Ademar of Chabannes. *Historia*, in *Monumenta Germaniae Historica, Scriptores* 4. Ed. Georg Waitz. Trans. Florin Curta. Hanover: Hahn, 1841. Latin.

Marcus Nathan Adler, trans. *The Itinerary of Benjamin of Tudela.* New York: Philipp Feldheim, 1907.

Lucien Auvray, ed. *Les registres de Grégoire IX*, vol. 2. Trans. Florin Curta. Paris: Albert Fontemoing, 1907. Latin.

János M. Bak, György Bónis, and James Ross Sweeney. *The Laws of the Medieval Kingdom of Hungary, 1000–1301.* Bakersfield, CA: Charles Schlacks, 1989. Reprinted under CC BY 4.0 International Public License.

Janet Bately, trans. "Wulfstan's Voyage and His Description of Estland," in *Wulfstan's Voyage: The Baltic Sea Region in the Early Viking Age as Seen from Shipboard.* Ed. Anton Englert and Athena Trakadas. Roskilde: Viking Ship Museum, 2009. Reproduced by permission of the publisher.

R.C. Blockley. *The History of Menander the Guardsman: Introductory Essay, Text, Translation and Historiographical Notes.* ARCA Classical and Medieval Texts, Papers, and Monographs 17. Liverpool: Francis Cairns, 1985; rpt. 2006. Reproduced by permission of the publisher.

Ivan Bozhilov, Anna-Mariia Totomanova, and Ivan Biliarski. *Borilov sinodik: Izdanie i prevod.* Trans. M. Paneva. Sofia: OOD, 2010. Reproduced by permission of the authors.

Josip Bratulić, ed. *Vinodolski Zakon, 1288.* Trans. Florin Curta. Zagreb: Globus, 1988. Slavonic.

James A. Brundage. *The Chronicle of Henry of Livonia.* Madison: University of Wisconsin Press, 1961. Reproduced by permission of the publisher.

Thomas Butler, trans. "Saint Constantine-Cyril's 'Sermon on the Translation of the Relics of Saint Clement of Rome.'" *Cyrillomethodianum* 17–18 (1993–94). Reproduced by permission of the publisher.

L.V. Cherepnin and S.V. Iushkov, ed. *Pamiatniki russkogo prava*, vol. 1. Trans. Florin Curta. Moscow: Gosudartsvennoe izdatel'stvo iuridicheskogo literatury, 1952. Slavonic.

O.I. Chistiakov, ed. *Rossiiskoe zakonodatel'stvo X–XX vv.*, vol. 1. Trans. Florin Curta. Moscow: Iuridicheskaia literatura, 1984. Slavonic.

Anton Chroust, ed. *Quellen zur Geschichte des Kreuzzuges Kaiser Friedrichs I*, in *Monumenta Germaniae Historica, Scriptores rerum Germanicarum*, n.s. 5. Trans. Florin Curta. Berlin: Weidmann, 1928. Latin.

Carolyn L. Connor and W. Robert Connor, trans. *The Life and Miracles of Saint Luke of Steiris: Text, Translation and Commentary.* Brookline, MA: Hellenic College Press, 1994. Reproduced by permission of the publisher.

Constantine VII Porphyrogenitus. *De Administrando imperio.* Trans. Romilly J.H. Jenkins. Washington, DC: Dumbarton Oaks Center for Byzantine Studies, 2016. Reproduced by permission of the publisher.

Samuel Hazzard Cross and Olgerd P. Sherbowitz-Wetzor. *The Russian Primary Chronicle: Laurentian Text* (Cambridge, MA: Medieval Academy of America, 1953). www.mgh-bibliothek.de/dokumente/a/a011458.pdf.

George Dennis, trans. "Rule of Athanasios the Athonite for the Lavra Monastery," in *Byzantine Monastic Foundation Documents: A Complete Translation of the Surviving Founders'* Typika *and Testaments*, vol. 1. Ed. John Philip Thomas and Angela Constantinides Hero. Washington, DC: Dumbarton Oaks Research Library and Collection, 2000. Reproduced by permission of the publisher.

L.A. Dmitrieva and D.S. Likhacheva, ed. *Pamiatniki literatury Drevnei Rusi, XII vek.* Trans. Florin Curta. Moscow: Khudozhestvennaia literatura, 1980. Slavonic.

César E. Dubler. *Abū Ḥāmid el Granadino y su relación de viaje por tierras eurasiáticas.* Trans. István Zimonyi. Madrid: Imprenta y Editorial Maestre, 1953. Reproduced by permission of the translator.

Ivan Duĭchev, ed. *Cronaca di Monemvasia.* Trans. Florin Curta. Palermo: Istituto siciliano di studi bizantini e neoellenici, 1976. Greek.

Susan B. Edgington, ed. and trans. *Albert of Aachen: Historia Ierosolimitana, History of the Journey to Jerusalem.* Oxford: Clarendon Press, 2007. Reproduced by permission of the author.

David Frendo and Athanasios Fotiou, trans. *John Kaminiates: The Capture of Thessaloniki.* Leiden: Brill, 2017. Reproduced by permission of the publisher.

G. Friedrich, ed. *Codex diplomaticus et epistolarius regni Bohemiae*, vol. 2. Trans. Florin Curta. Prague: Wiesner, 1912. Latin.

Cristian Gaşpar, trans. "Life of Saint Adalbert Bishop of Prague and Martyr," in *Saints of the Christianization Age of Central Europe (Tenth-Eleventh Century).* Ed. Gábor Klaniczay. Budapest: Central European University Press, 2013. Reproduced by permission of the translator.

Paul Gautier, ed. Théophylacte d'Achrida. *Lettres.* Corpus fontium historiae byzantinae 16.2. Trans. Florin Curta. Thessaloniki: Association de Recherches Byzantines, 1986. Greek.

Roman Grodecki, ed. *Księga Henrykowska.* Trans. Florin Curta. Poznań: Instytut Zachodni, 1949. Latin.

Hans F. Haefele, ed. Notker Balbulus, *Gesta Karoli Magni imperatoris*, in *Monumenta Germaniae Historica, Scriptores rerum Germanicarum*, n.s. 12. Trans. Florin Curta. Berlin: Weidmann, 1959. Latin.

Henry of Livonia. *Chronicon Livoniae.* Ed. Leonid Arbusow and Albert Bauer. Trans. Florin Curta. Darmstadt: Wissenschaftliche Buchgesellschaft, 1959. Latin.

Theodor Hirsch, ed. *Scriptores rerum Prussicarum*, vol. 5. Trans. Gregory Leighton. Leipzig: S. Hirzel, 1876. Reproduced by permission of the translator.

Hartwig Hirschfeld, trans. *Judah Hallevi's Kitab al Khazari.* London: M.L. Cailingold, 1931. Reproduced by permission of the publisher.

Robert Holtzmann and Werner Trillmich, ed. Thietmar of Merseburg, *Chronicon.* Ausgewählte Quellen zur deutschen Geschichte des Mittelalters 9. Trans. Florin Curta. Darmstadt: Wissenschaftliche Buchgesellschaft, 1985. Latin.

Aleksandr Ivanov and Anatolii M. Kuznecov. *Smoļenskas-Rīgas aktis 13. gs.–14. gs. pirmā puse: Kompleksa Moscowitica-Ruthenica dokumenti par Smoļenskas un Rīgas attiecībām*. Vestures avoti 6. Trans. Florin Curta. Riga: Latvijas Valsts vēstures arhīvs, 2009. Slavonic.

Peter Jackson, trans. *The Mission of Friar William of Rubruck: His Journey to the Court of the Great Khan Möngke 1253–1255*. Indianapolis: Hackett, 2009. Reproduced by permission of the publisher.

Bruno Scott James, trans. *Letters of St. Bernard of Clairvaux*. Chicago: Regnery, 1953. Reproduced by permission of the publisher.

Robert Jordan, trans. "*Typikon* of Gregory Pakourianos for the Monastery of the Mother of God Petritzonitissa in Bačkovo," in *Byzantine Monastic Foundation Documents: A Complete Translation of the Surviving Founders' Typika and Testaments*, vol. 2. Ed. John Philip Thomas and Angela Constantinides Hero. Washington, DC: Dumbarton Oaks Research Library and Collection, 2000. Reproduced by permission of the publisher.

Ljiljana Juhas-Georgievska. *Stefan Prvovenčani, Domentijan, Teodosije*. Trans. Florin Curta. Novi Sad: Izdavački centar Matice srpske, 2012. Slavonic.

Ala' al-Dīn Aṭa Malik ibn Muḥammad Juvaynī. *Ta'rīkh-i-Jahān-Gusha*. Ed. Mīrzā Muḥammad Qazvīnī. Trans. Timothy May. 2 vols. Leiden: Brill, 1912–16. Reproduced by permission of the translator.

Marvin Kantor, trans. *Medieval Slavic Lives of Saints and Princes*. Ann Arbor: University of Michigan, Department of Slavic Languages and Literatures, 1983. Reproduced by permission of the publisher.

—, trans. *The Origins of Christianity in Bohemia: Sources and Commentary*. Evanston, IL: Northwestern University Press, 1990.

Béla Karácsonyi, ed. "Chronica Hungaro-Polonica: Pars I," in *Acta Historica*, vol. 26. Trans. Florin Curta. Szeged: Acta Universitatis Szegediensis de Attila József nominatae, 1969. Latin.

Kekaumenos. *Raccomandazioni e consigli di un galantuomo: Stratēgikon*. Ed. Maria Dora Spadaro. Trans. Florin Curta. Alessandria: Edizioni dell'Orso, 1998. Greek.

W. Kętrzyński, ed. "Vita Sancti Stanislai Cracoviensis episcopi (Vita minor)," in *Monumenta Poloniae Historica*, vol. 4. Trans. Florin Curta. Lwów: Akademii Umiejętności w Krakowie, 1884. Latin.

Paul W. Knoll and Frank Schaer, trans. *Gesta Principum Polonorum: The Deeds of the Princes of the Poles*. Budapest: Central European University Press, 2003. Reproduced by permission of the translators.

Josip Kolanović and Mate Křižman, ed. *Zadarski statut sa svim reformacijama odnosno novim uredbama donesenima do godine 1563*. Trans. Florin Curta. Zagreb: Ogranak Matice hrvatske, 1997. Latin.

Anna Komnena. *Alexiade*, vol. 1. Ed. Bernard Leib. Trans. Florin Curta. Paris: Les Belles Lettres, 1967. Greek.

Marko Kostrenčić, ed. *Diplomatički zbornik kraljevine Hrvatske, Dalmacije i Slavonije*, vol. 1. Trans. Florin Curta. Zagreb: Tiskara izdavačkog Zavoda Jugoslavenske Adakemije Znanosti i Umjetnosti, 1967. Latin.

Efraim F. Kupfer and Tadeusz Lewicki, ed. *Źródła hebrajskie do dziejów Słowian i niektórych innych ludów środkowej i wschodniej Europy. Wyjątki z pism religijnych i prawniczych XI–XIII w.* Trans. Natalia Aleksiun. Wrocław: Zakład im. Ossolińskich, 1956. Reproduced by permission of the translator.

Friedrich Kurze, ed. *Annales Fuldenses*, in *Monumenta Germaniae Historica, Scriptores rerum Germanicarum in usum scholarum* 7. Trans. Florin Curta. Hanover: Hahn, 1891. Latin.

Paul Lemerle, ed. *Les plus anciens recueils des miracles de Saint Démétrius et la pénétration des Slaves dans les Balkans,* vol. 1. Trans. Florin Curta. Paris: Éditions du Centre national de la recherche scientifique, 1979. Greek.

Fritz Lošek, ed. *Die "Conversio Bagoariorum et Carantanorum" und der Brief des Erzbischofs Theotmar von Salzburg.* Trans. Florin Curta. Hanover: Hahnsche Buchhandlung, 1997. Latin.

Ruth J. Macrides, trans. *George Akropolites: The History.* Oxford: Oxford University Press, 2007. Reproduced by permission of the publisher.

Harry J. Magoulias, trans. *O City of Byzantium: Annals of Niketas Choniates.* Detroit: Wayne State University Press, 1984. Reproduced by permission of the publisher.

Juraj Marušić. *Sumpetarski kartular i Poljička seljačka republika.* Trans. Florin Curta. Split: Knijževni krug, 1992. Latin.

Mirjana Matijević-Sokol, James Ross Sweeney, and Damir Karbić, eds. and trans. *History of the Bishops of Salona and Split.* Budapest: Central European University Press, 2006. Reproduced by permission of the translators.

Robert Michell and Nevill Forbes, trans. *The Chronicle of Novgorod, 1016–1471.* London: Offices of the Society, 1914.

J.-P. Migne, ed. *Joannis Cinnami historiarum libri VII*, cols. 662–63. Trans. Florin Curta. Paris: J.-P. Migne, 1864. Greek.

Marina Miladinov, trans. "Lives of the Holy Hermits Zoerard the Confessor and Benedict the Martyr by Blessed Maurus, Bishop of Pécs," in *Saints of the Christianization Age of Central Europe (Tenth-Eleventh Century)*. Ed. Gábor Klaniczay. Budapest: Central European University Press, 2013. Reproduced by permission of the translator.

V.V. Milkov and R.A. Simonov, eds. *Kirik Novgorodec: uchenyi i myslitel'*. Trans. Florin Curta. Moscow: Krug', 2011. Slavonic.

Eduard Mühle, ed. *Die Chronik der Polen des Magisters Vincentius.* Ausgewählte Quellen zur Geschichte des Mittelalters 48. Trans. Florin Curta. Darmstadt: Wissenschaftliche Buchgesellschaft, 2014. Latin.

Petra Mutlová and Martyn Rady, trans. *Cosmas of Prague: The Chronicle of the Czechs.* Ed. János M. Bak. Budapest: Central European University Press, 2019. Reproduced by permission of the translators.

Leonora Alice Neville. "Local Provincial Elites in Eleventh-Century Hellas and Peloponnese." PhD diss. Princeton University, 1998. Reproduced by permission of the author.

Otto of Freising and Rahewin. *Gesta Frederici seu rectius Cronica*. Ed. Franzosef Schmale. Trans. Florin Curta. Darmstadt: Wissenschaftliche Buchgesellschaft, 1965. Latin.

Kiril Petkov, trans. *The Voices of Medieval Bulgaria, Seventh-Fifteenth Century: The Records of a Bygone Culture*. Leiden: Brill, 2008. Reproduced by permission of the publisher.

Anamari Petranović and Annelise Margetić. "Il Placito del Risano," in *Atti del Centro di ricerche storiche Rovigno* 14. Trans. Florin Curta. 1983. Latin.

Procopius. *The Wars of Justinian*. Ed. and trans. H.B. Dewing and Anthony Kaldellis. Indianapolis: Hackett, 2014. Reproduced by permission of the publisher.

Martyn Rady and László Veszprémy, trans. *Anonymus and Master Roger*. Central European Medieval Texts 5. Budapest: Central European University Press, 2010. Reproduced by permission of the translators.

Robert de Clari. *The Conquest of Constantinople*. Trans. Edgar Holmes McNeal. New York: Columbia University Press, 1936.

William Woodville Rockhill, trans. *The Journey of William Rubruck to the Eastern Parts of the World, 1253–1255, as Narrated by Himself, with Two Accounts of the Earlier Journey of John of Pian de Carpine*. London: Hakluyt Society, 1900.

Itala Pia Sbriziolo, ed. *Il sermone di Ilarion "Sulla legge e sulla grazia."* Trans. Florin Curta. Naples: Istituto universitario orientale, 1988. Slavonic.

Jos Schaeken. *Voices on Birchbark: Everyday Communication in Medieval Russia*. Leiden: Brill, 2018. Reproduced by permission of the publisher.

Stephen Neil Scott. "The Collapse of the Moravian Mission of Saints Cyril and Methodius, the Fate of Their Disciples, and the Christianization of the Southern Slavs: Translations of Five Historical Texts with Notes and Commentary." PhD diss., University of California at Berkeley, 1989. Reproduced by permission of the author.

Ihor Ševčenko, ed. *Chronographiae quae Theophanis Continuati nomine fertur liber quo Vita Basilii imperatoris amplectitur*. Trans. Ihor Ševčenko. Berlin: Walter de Gruyter, 2011. Reproduced by permission of the publisher.

Nancy Patterson Ševčenko, trans. "*Typikon* of the Sebastokrator Isaac Komnenos for the Monastery of the Mother of God *Kosmosoteira* near Bera," in *Byzantine Monastic Foundation Documents: A Complete Translation of the Surviving Founders'* Typika *and Testaments*, vol. 2. Ed. John Philip Thomas and Angela Constantinides Hero. Washington, DC: Dumbarton Oaks Research Library and Collection, 2000. Reproduced by permission of the publisher.

Simon of Kéza. *The Deeds of the Hungarians*. Trans Frank Schaer. Budapest: Central European University, 1999. Reproduced by permission of the translator.

John Skylitzes. *A Synopsis of Byzantine History, 811–1057*. Trans. John Wortley. Cambridge: Cambridge University Press, 2010.

Aleksandar V. Solovjev. *Odabrani spomenici srpskog prava: od XII do kraja XV veka*. Trans. Florin Curta. Belgrade: G. Kon, 1926. Slavonic.

Denis F. Sullivan. *The Life of Saint Nikon.* Brookline, MA: Hellenic College Press, 1987. Reproduced by permission of the publisher.

Imre Szentpétery, ed. *Scriptores rerum Hungaricarum tempore ducum regumque stirpis Arpadianae gestarum*, vol. 2. Trans. Florin Curta. Budapest: Academia litter. hungarica atque Societate histor. hungarica, 1938. Latin.

Vasilka Tăpkova-Zaimova. *Bulgarians by Birth: The Comitopuls, Emperor Samuel and Their Successors According to Historical Sources and the Historiographic Tradition.* Trans. Pavel Murdzhev. Leiden: Brill, 2017. Reproduced by permission of the publisher.

A. Zeki Velidi Togan. *Ibn Faḍlān's Reisebericht.* Trans. Florin Curta. Leipzig: Deutsche Morgenländische Gesellschaft, 1939. Reproduced by permission of the publisher. German.

Harry Turtledove, trans. *The Chronicle of Theophanes. An English Translation of Anni Mundi 6095–6305 (A.D. 602–813).* Philadelphia: University of Pennsylvania Press, 1982. Reproduced by permission of the publisher.

Henri de Valenciennes. *Histoire de l'empereur Henri de Constantinople.* Ed. J. Longnon. Trans. Florin Curta. Paris: P. Geuthner, 1948. French.

Elmér Varjú, ed. *Legendae sancti regis Stephani.* Trans. Florin Curta. Budapest: Singer & Wolfner, 1928. Latin.

Geoffroy de Villehardouin. *La conquête de Constantinople.* Ed. J. Dufournet. Trans. Florin Curta. Paris: Flammarion, 2004. Old French.

W. Wattenbach, ed. Vincent of Prague. *Annals*, in *Monumenta Germaniae Historica, Scriptores rerum Germanicarum in usum scholarum* 17. Trans. Florin Curta. Hanover: Hahn, 1861. Latin.

Mary and Michael Whitby. *The History of Theophylact Simocatta: An English Translation with Introduction and Notes.* Oxford: Clarendon Press, 1986. Reproduced by permission of the translators.

Herwig Wolfram, Andreas Kusternig, and Herbert Haupt, ed. *Quellen zur Geschichte des 7. und 8. Jahrhunders. Die vier Bücher der Chroniken des sogenannten Fredegar.* Trans. Florin Curta. Darmstadt: Wissenschaftliche Buchgesellschaft, 1982. Latin.

Victor Wolf von Glanvell, ed. *Die Kanonessammlung des Kardinals Deusdedit*, vol. 1. Trans. Florin Curta. Paderborn: F. Schöningh, 1905. Latin.

Harald Zimmermann. *Der Deutsche Orden in Siebenbürgen. Eine diplomatische Untersuchung.* Trans. Florin Curta. Cologne: Böhlau, 2011. Latin.

István Zimonyi. *Muslim Sources on the Magyars in the Second Half of the Ninth Century: The Magyar Chapter of the Jayhānī Tradition.* Leiden: Brill, 2016. Reproduced by permission of the publisher.

FIGURES

Figure 1.1: Triumphant Avar Warrior on Horseback. József Hampel, *Der Goldfund von Nagy-Szent-Miklós, sogenannter "Schatz des Attila." Ein Beitrag* *zur Kunstgeschichte der Völkerwanderungsepoche*. Budapest: F. Kilian, 1886, p. 115, fig. 56a; eighth century.

Figure 2.1: Saints Cyril and Methodius. Franc Grivec, *Die heiligen Slavenapostel Cyrillus und Methodius*. Olmütz: Academia Velehradensis, 1928, p. 152.

Figure 3.1: Pechenegs Ambush and Kill Prince Sviatoslav of Kiev (971). John Skylitzes, *Madrid Skylitzes*. Madrid: National Library of Spain. Wikimedia Commons; twelfth century.

Figure 4.1: Saint John of Rila. *L'église-monument de Saint-Alexandre Nevsky*. Sofia, Bulgaria: Utro, 1900.

Figure 5.1: Inscription of Süleyman Köy. Sofia, Bulgaria: National Archaeological Museum. Photo by editor; ninth century.

Figure 6.1: Assassination of Duke Wenceslas of Bohemia. Gumpold Codex. Wolfenbüttel, Germany: Herzog August Library. Wikimedia Commons; eleventh century.

Figure 7.1: Saint Adalbert Pleads with Boleslav II, Duke of Bohemia. Cathedral of Gniezno, c. 1170. Photo by Maciej Szczepańczyk. CC BY 4.0 International Public License.

Figure 8.1: Angel. Church of St. George, Kurbinovo, North Macedonia. Photo by Mitko Panov; twelfth century. Reproduced by permission of the photographer.

Figure 9.1: Hermann of Salza. Christoph Hartknoch, *Alt- und neues Preussen*. Frankfurt, Germany: Hallervorden, 1684. Wikimedia Commons.

Figure 10.1: Law Code of Vinodol. Zagreb, Croatia: National and University Library. Wikimedia Commons; sixteenth century.

Figure 11.1: Funeral Sermon and Prayer. Pray Codex. Budapest, Hungary: National Széchényi Library. Wikimedia Commons; late twelfth or early thirteenth century.

Figure 12.1: Seal of Grand *Župan* Stephen Nemanja (1198). Belgrade, Serbia: National Museum. Wikimedia Commons; twelfth century.

Figure 13.1: The Battle of Legnica (1241). Los Angeles: J. Paul Getty Museum. Wikimedia Commons; fourteenth century.

INDEX OF TOPICS

Topics are listed by document number. The index is intended to be used in tandem with the table of contents.

READINGS IN MEDIEVAL CIVILIZATIONS AND CULTURES

Series Editor: Paul Edward Dutton

"Readings in Medieval Civilizations and Cultures is in my opinion the most useful series being published today."

—William C. Jordan, Princeton University

I—Carolingian Civilization: A Reader, Second Edition
edited by Paul Edward Dutton

II—Medieval Popular Religion, 1000–1500: A Reader, Second Edition
edited by John Shinners

III—Charlemagne's Courtier: The Complete Einhard
translated & edited by Paul Edward Dutton

IV—Medieval Saints: A Reader
edited by Mary-Ann Stouck

V—From Roman to Merovingian Gaul: A Reader
translated & edited by Alexander Callander Murray

VI—Medieval England, 500–1500: A Reader, Second Edition
edited by Emilie Amt & Katherine Allen Smith

VII—Love, Marriage, and Family in the Middle Ages: A Reader
edited by Jacqueline Murray

VIII—The Crusades: A Reader, Second Edition
edited by S.J. Allen & Emilie Amt

IX—The Annals of Flodoard of Reims, 919–966
translated & edited by Bernard S. Bachrach & Steven Fanning

X—Gregory of Tours: The Merovingians
translated & edited by Alexander Callander Murray

XI—Medieval Towns: A Reader
edited by Maryanne Kowaleski

XII—A Short Reader of Medieval Saints
edited by Mary-Ann Stouck

XIII—Vengeance in Medieval Europe: A Reader
edited by Daniel Lord Smail & Kelly Gibson

XIV—The Viking Age: A Reader, Third Edition
edited by Angus A. Somerville & R. Andrew McDonald

XV—Medieval Medicine: A Reader
edited by Faith Wallis

XVI—Pilgrimage in the Middle Ages: A Reader
edited by Brett Edward Whalen

XVII—Prologues to Ancient and Medieval History: A Reader
edited by Justin Lake

XVIII—Muslim and Christian Contact in the Middle Ages: A Reader
edited by Jarbel Rodriguez

XIX—The Twelfth-Century Renaissance: A Reader
edited by Alex J. Novikoff

XX—European Magic and Witchcraft: A Reader
edited by Martha Rampton

XXI—Medieval Warfare: A Reader
edited by Kelly DeVries & Michael Livingston

XXII—Medieval Travel and Travelers: A Reader
edited by John F. Romano

XXIII—The Intolerant Middle Ages: A Reader
edited by Eugene Smelyansky

XXIV—The Medieval Devil: A Reader
edited by David Winter and Richard Raiswell

XXV—Medieval Eastern Europe (500–1300): A Reader
edited by Florin Curta

www.ingramcontent.com/pod-product-compliance
Lightning Source LLC
LaVergne TN
LVHW010347080826
844660LV00003B/214
* 9 7 8 1 4 8 7 5 4 4 8 7 4 *